Imperial Berlin

Imperial Berlin

GERHARD MASUR

DORSET PRESS

New York

TO MY FRIENDS
AT THE FREE UNIVERSITY
OF BERLIN

This edition published by Dorset Press
a division of Marboro Books Corporation,
by arrangement with Basic Books, Inc.
1989 Dorset Press

ISBN 0-88029-407-8
Printed in the United States of America
M 9 8 7 6 5 4 3 2 1

CONTENTS

Introduction   1

1   To the Brandenburg Gate   11

2   From Kingdom to Empire   29

3   The Boom Years   57

4   Berlin Society   83

5   "World City? Perhaps"   123

6   Writers, Journalists, and Scholars   151

7   Berlin and the Arts   203

8   War and Revolution   255

Epilogue   297

Notes   303

Bibliographical Note   331

Index   339

ACKNOWLEDGMENTS

I HAVE had the assistance of numerous individuals in the writing of this book. Its subject was first suggested to me by Professor Norman Cantor. In 1965–1966, while I was Visiting Professor at the Free University of Berlin, a light teaching schedule enabled me to do the spade work, a task which was considerably lightened by the help of my assistant, Herr Hans-Jürgen Krüger. During this year I held a seminar dealing with the problems of the imperial city, and in the following year conducted a similar seminar at Berkeley, reaping a great deal of benefit from the weekly discussions.

In 1969, the Historische Kommission of the Free University of Berlin, through its president, Professor Hans Herzfeld, invited me to complete my research in Berlin. The Historische Kommission also arranged a symposium at which the main topics of the book were discussed. Scholars from the United States, Great Britain, and France, together with others from the German universities, participated in the talks. This exchange of ideas helped me to check my own theories, though I have not been able to incorporate all the opinions that were advanced during these sessions. Professor Hans Herzfeld and Professor Wolfram Fischer, as well as members of the Historische Kommission, read specified chapters and pointed out certain discrepancies and contradictions, and these have been eliminated. It is understood, however, that the responsibility for any remaining factual errors is entirely mine.

My wife, Helen Masur, has not only edited this book, as she has done for all my previous books appearing in English, but has also endured the rigors of two Berlin winters with fortitude.

Introduction

EMBARKED on this study of imperial Berlin with a certain amount of confidence. Considering my own background, I believed I could expect clear sailing. I was born in the imperial city in the first year of the new century, and into a family of lawyers and physicians, many of whom had served their government faithfully and well. I attended the Kaiser Wilhelm Real Gymnasium, and spent my free hours roaming through the numerous parks that crisscrossed the city—the Tiergarten, the Charlottenburg gardens, the Bellevuepark. Occasionally I saw the Kaiser in his heavy greatcoat walking along the leafy paths of these parks, or riding at the head of the guards when parades filed down the length of Unter den Linden. Early in life I was taken to the museums and concert halls, the theatres and opera houses that made Berlin a prime example of a gilded age. In due time I became a student at the University of Berlin, and eventually began my teaching career in the classrooms of my alma mater. Fortified by such memories, I advanced upon my assignment with some assurance.

But when, after many years of exile, I returned to the city of my birth to engage in the actual research for this book, I soon realized that I had become the victim of illusions. The city of my boyhood no longer existed. It had been first destroyed by the wanton changes inflicted upon it by the megalomania of Adolf Hitler; later the Allied bombs had ravaged it, and finally the Russian artillery had completed the devastation. What is now called Berlin bears no resemblance to the old imperial city. Entire sections have been wiped out; streets and squares have been renamed and monuments have been shifted. The new buildings could fit very naturally into the landscape of Chicago or Iowa City. It came

3

over me then that I had entered upon a study in archeology. The dust and ashes of the last war had covered both the dross and the glitter, the beauty and the ugliness, the proud and the humble. Probing the layers of destruction and reconstruction, I encountered a vanished world which could be brought to life only by rescuing those vestiges which had escaped the flames of total warfare— diaries, autobiographies, letters, works of fiction, official documents, and the dehydrated realities preserved under the name of statistics.

I lived in the divided city for a year, and found it as different from the town I had known as the Mexico City of today is different from the Tenochtitlan of Cortéz. After some weeks, however, I began to sense a throb of continuity. On frequent occasions I encountered that seemingly indestructible entity called Der Berliner, to whom John F. Kennedy paid homage. There was a thread of continuity in speech and human behavior, and there was still the attitude, at the same time courageous, defiant, and skeptical, for which Berlin had been known throughout its history, and which now gave this new Berlin the strength and the vitality to bear the burden which the myopia of politicians and generals had placed upon its shoulders.

Other cities have been reduced to rubble and ashes and have risen anew, but only Berlin has the doubtful distinction of having been resuscitated for the purpose of becoming one of the storm centers of international conflict, a place of ferment where East and West face each other across a no-man's land of barbed wire, roadblocks, and machine guns held at the ready. That Berlin was singled out to suffer the weight of the unresolved tensions which split our world is a matter of diplomatic record. Why this was done can be understood only through a knowledge of Berlin's Daedalian history. Prior to 1871, the great powers of the world would not have considered the city worth the price of a bitter international struggle. It was the parochial residence of the Hohenzollern, and its attractions were limited. But almost overnight the city of the Prussian kings became a bustling metropolis, capital of the second German empire, a nerve center of international politics, and at the same time, an expanding area of financial and industrial concentration with extraordinary powers. It could boast of one of the finest universities in Europe; Max Planck and Albert

4

Introduction

Einstein taught side by side with Wilamowitz–Möllendorff and Friedrich Meinecke. It was also the theatrical capital of the world where Max Reinhardt revolutionized show business and Richard Strauss conducted the Royal Opera. This was imperial Berlin, but the picture is not complete. There was much else, good and bad, which must be laid on the canvas if the portrait of this bewildering city is to be a veracious one. The transformation of the residential and garrisoned town of the mid-nineteenth century into one of the great urban centers of the West constitutes the core of this book.

The historian who ventures to write the history of a city faces a special predicament. Is it possible to consider a city as a historical unity which will lend itself to analysis and description, or merely as a frame of reference, a name for events that took place within its geographical confines? There are, of course, admirable histories of Rome, of Florence, Venice, Nuremberg, and other great cities, but whether these may serve as models for a history of Berlin is a matter of considerable doubt. Heinrich Heine expressed something of this attitude when he wrote, "Berlin is not really a city; Berlin only offers the locality where a group of people, and among them people of fine minds, congregate. They are quite indifferent to the locality, but they are the people who constitute the spiritual Berlin."[1] These are, however, the doubts of a poet, or, let us say, of an intellectual given to overrating the lucubrations of other intellectuals.

A great city and its history encompass much more than Heine indicates. Beyond the group of thinkers whom he mentions are others—the people who work, who produce and consume, who exchange goods and services; there are the administrators, and the reflection of their doings in literature, the arts, the sphere of entertainment, and so forth. Last, but not least, is the story of a city's individual manner of expression, its human reactions, the kind of thing that differentiates a Londoner from a New Yorker in behavior and verbal communication. If, in addition, a city has been the seat of important political decisions that have affected the histories of other nations, it will demand attention as a focal point in the history of the world. Imperial Berlin can lay claim to most of these attributes, and a study such as the present one may justify itself only if it is able to fill the bill of particulars.

5

But here lies the rub. The reader would benefit little from perusing a block of statistics or from reading a catalogue of names that evoke no image in his mind. .The Berlin of today, though covering the same area as nineteenth-century Berlin, is at a far remove from the City of the Kaisers, and the historian will be obliged to use techniques and methods which differ in large measure from those applicable in other circumstances. If, perchance, some aged inhabitant, long familiar with the imperial city, should find mirrored in these pages some semblance of the city of his youth, this writer would then, and only then, feel satisfied with his work of reconstruction.

Berlin came into greatness much later than any of the other important capitals of Europe. Paris and London were well established as centers of their realms early in the Middle Ages. No one questioned Rome as the heart of Italy even in the days when she was surpassed by Florence and Venice in splendor and genius. Madrid became the capital of Spain in 1561. Moscow had been the Holy City of Russia since the fall of Constantinople, and her position of eminence was confirmed during the "Time of Troubles." Brussels and Amsterdam, Stockholm and Copenhagen had all emerged as centers of political power by 1600. Germany offers a different picture.

Prior to 1871, Germany had never had a capital. It is one of the many paradoxes of German history that the country lacked a focal point of organization for more than a thousand years. Even during the medieval period, when her influence spanned Europe from the Baltic to the Mediterranean, Germany did not possess a governmental stronghold.[2] She had many beautiful cities —Mainz, Cologne, Frankfurt, Bamberg, Lübeck, Danzig. They were the residences of ecclesiastical and worldly princes, emporia of trade and crafts, which had sprung up along the river valleys or on the roads which controlled medieval commerce. Some were free imperial cities, proud of their charters and their liberties, able to form alliances and leagues in keeping with the great wealth they commanded. Yet the country as a whole had nothing that constituted a capital. The reason for this atypical development goes back to the time when the very foundations of her nationhood were laid.

To avoid losing our way in the mists of early Germany history,

6

Introduction

a few signposts may help to guide the traveler. Only a small part of Germany had been conquered and subjugated by the Romans. As a result, by far the greater portion of territory that today we designate as Germany never experienced the unifying force of Roman law. The power of tribal organization subsisted for many centuries and survived even Charlemagne's revival of the Roman empire in 800 A.D. Tribal duchies emerged, solidly rooted in the soil, in local traditions and mores, in legal associations, and in personal attainments. The survival of the empire depended on the cooperation and acquiescence of these duchies; hence the forces of regionalism and sectionalism became deeply embedded in German history. The imperial authority was a superstructure imposed upon tribal duchies whose voice could never be ignored with impunity.

Another component must be added to these original forces of decentralization, that is, feudalism. Feudalism transformed the imperial authority into a personal relationship of liege and vassal, based on the concept that military and political services were to be compensated by grants of land, thereby developing yet another obstacle to centralized power. Although feudalism is not an exclusively German phenomenon, it did in this case contribute to prolonging the fragmentation of the German empire. Finally, there never was a territorial nucleus in Germany, as there was in France, around which the German emperors might have consolidated their power. The French kings, when hard pressed, could always retreat to the domain of the Ile de France whose center was Paris. The German emperors, on the other hand, possessed no comparable sanctuary.

The great enterprises of the medieval emperors involved them in the affairs of the church and drew them inevitably toward Italy and the Mediterranean area. Of necessity, they became travelers, wandering warriors, moving from country to country and from town to town, carrying with them their courts and their offices, such as they were. The German expansion southward and later eastward further strengthened the centrifugal tendencies already at work in the history of the German people.[3] When Frederick II, of the house of Hohenstaufen, the greatest of German emperors, attempted to secure a solid base of power in the kingdom of Sicily, the trend had become patent. From Palermo, he might have been able to control Italy and the papacy, but he could never have succeeded in extending his authority to his distant German domain. Obliged to grant far-reaching concessions to his German vassals, both secular and ecclesiastical, he further increased the forces of regionalism.

With the termination of the Hohenstaufen dynasty (1268), the imperial dream seemed to have run its course. The new Habsburg dynasty transferred the center of its operations to the southeast, with Austria as the rallying point for the formation of a solid territorial base. Vienna emerged as an urban center of tremendous economic, political, and cultural potential for the entire Danube basin. But it was too late to reverse the forces of regionalism. The empire continued to exist, and the emperors were elected from various families until the Habsburg dynasty gained firm control of the title in 1438. But empire and emperor still constituted two different forces gravitating in opposite directions.

The empire was an elective monarchy whose existence was guaranteed by an imperial law called the Golden Bull. Seven electors chose the emperor. Since he was to be elected in Frankfurt am Main and crowned in Aachen, either city might have been chosen as the capital of the German empire, though Frankfurt's position at the confluence of the Rhine and the Main would seem the ideal location. Neither Frankfurt nor Aachen, however, was destined to become Germany's capital.

When eventually Germany developed some form of political representation by means of its Reichstag, no city was designated to house it permanently. It convened if political or financial problems made its meetings imperative, and it gathered at Worms, or Speyer, or Nuremberg, as the case might be. Only after the Thirty Years' War did the Reichstag find a permanent home in Ratisbon.

Shortly before the Reformation, there were several attempts to make the empire "a functioning state or a viable confederation,"[4] but all came to grief through the clash of opposing forces. Their meager results included the establishment of two high courts of appeal: the Reichskammergericht and the Reichshofrat (the High Imperial Chamber and the Imperial Court Council). But, characteristically, the former had its seat near the Rhine, and the

8

latter in Vienna, thus confirming once more the ingrained dualism of all political institutions in the Holy Roman Empire.

It was Germany's tragedy that too many of its towns might have served as nuclei for a capital and that none did so. And the Germans were quite accustomed to a country lacking a metropolis possessing the magnetic attraction that London, Paris, Madrid, Moscow exercised over their respective nations. The empire remained rooted in its traditional habits and in its semifeudal structure.[5]

To the extent that new political forms developed within the old and empty shell, the existence of the empire became ever more precarious. The territorial state of the sixteenth and seventeenth centuries represents the German answer to the demands of early modern history. While the West formed "the new monarchies," Germany continued to have thirty secular princes, fifty church lords, three thousand towns and cities, and numberless members of the lesser nobility. Among the more powerful or affluent, a new form of urban living developed around the residence of the prince, where the court found a permanent home, and where the administrative offices and high courts were located. Occasionally universities were established in these centers. The more enlightened of the princes attracted writers, artists, and musicians to their courts, thus creating a cultural pattern which etched its mark on the spiritual face of Germany. Instead of one capital, the Germans boasted of thirty or more. The result was a decentralization of the national strength which, though having its disadvantages, provided for a greater distribution of forces. Whether the system forced upon them by history operated to their interest was a question that found little agreement among the Germans. Goethe, for one, thought it a blessing, and considered it a mistake to believe that the great empire should have but *one* residence. What, he asked, has made Germany great but the admirable popular culture (*Volkskultur*) which has penetrated all parts of the empire equally? "Suppose that for centuries there had been in Germany only the two residential cities of Vienna and Berlin, or even one only? What then, I would like to know, would have become of German culture?"[6]

A similar feeling was expressed by Schiller: "No capital and no

9

court exercise their tyranny over German [literary] taste." Herder, on the other hand, regretted the atomization of Germany, where there was no voice that represented the general sentiment of the fatherland, no concourse where all eminent minds could be heard and listened to. Everything in Germany, he said, is dispersed. However, he continued, what prevents us from becoming co-workers at the edifice of humanity and from helping each other? It is significant that Herder terminates his argument with this observation: "That we lack a capital does not weaken our cause . . . intelligence, quiet reflections, active experiments, emotions and expressions of that which, individually and generally, may contribute to our peace . . . they reject the walls of a capital and search for free land." There were others, to be sure, who found no comfort in these words, and who continued to yearn for the unifying energy which radiates from a capital, but they were few and far between.

If we ask when and why Berlin became the capital, we must turn once more to history for the answer, and we learn that Berlin became the capital because Berlin was the capital of Prussia, and Prussia imposed her will on the rest of Germany. At first thought Prussia's choice of a capital appears contrary to reason. Situated in the northeast of Germany, at some distance from the sea, there seemed little to recommend her position. But she became the residence of Germany's most ambitious princes, the Hohenzollern, and as such, a city of destiny. Heinrich von Treitschke stated the case quite clearly when he wrote, "We Germans are the only civilized nation (*Kulturvolk*) who have achieved the position of a great power without having had a metropolis."[7]

[1]

To the Brandenburg Gate

$\mathfrak{L}$ITTLE in Berlin's early history predisposed it to future greatness. It was not, like the old cities of Cologne or Mainz, erected on Roman foundations, but a young settlement built on colonial soil in East Elbia. Other German cities had sprung up along the courses of great rivers, the Rhine, the Elbe, the Danube, the Oder, but Berlin was founded on the banks of an unimportant stream that ranked well behind the mightier rivers where commerce and communication could be maintained on a large scale. The Spree was an insignificant artery in medieval times, yet between it and the Havel there was established in the mid-thirteenth century the twin city of Berlin-Coelln.[1] It lay in the Mark Brandenburg, a territory that had once been occupied by Slavic tribes who had gradually been thrown back and overpowered by German settlers.

The clash between Germanic and Slavic people extends over centuries and culminated in 1147 in a crusade, sparked by Bernhard de Clairvaux, under the slogan, "baptism or death." The religious terror which ensued resulted in the christianization and subjugation by German overlords of large sections of land between the Elbe and Oder rivers. The center of these advanced domains of German rule was the city of Brandenburg, a combination of fortress and bishopric under the domination of a Markgraf. The land gained through conquest and conversion was soon populated by German peasants, who worked the virgin soil and made the land arable by rooting out the forests. Soon afterward, the rise of towns which was sweeping all of Europe reached this region. The founding of cities had become the vogue.

The establishment of Berlin–Coelln followed a widespread pattern laid down by the monastic orders. Adjacent to Berlin–Coelln there was already in existence a settlement of the Knights Templars. (Today's visitor to Berlin steps from his plane at Tempelhof Aerdrome onto ground that was first broken by medieval monks.) The twin city's rise was rapid. It became a market place, providing traveling merchants with facilities for buying and selling and, we may assume, adequate quarters for food and rest. Eventually it became involved in distant trade with Hamburg and even with Flanders, and joined the Hanseatic League. In the main, Berlin exported rye and timber and imported Flemish cloth.[2]

The merchants who profited well in their trade soon formed a patrician upper class which ruled the city during the fourteenth century. It was a period of unrest and chaos; several princely houses contended for possession of the Mark Brandenburg and their rivalry resulted in anarchy and lawlessness. The merchants were the favorite targets of the famous robber barons who appeared at this time, and who seized their victims and held them for ransom. The city was left to fend for itself, but a colonial town was not strong enough to hold its own and was obliged to yield to the greater force of a new dynasty which entered the territory at the beginning of the fifteenth century.

In 1415, Friedrich von Hohenzollern received the Mark Brandenburg as an imperial fief. The Hohenzollern family had its roots in Suabia in southwest Germany, and had held the title and office of Burggraf of Nuremberg since 1192. There were two branches, the older one retaining its estates in Franconia, and the younger one setting forth on a remarkable career in Brandenburg.[3]

At a time when royalty has entered the realm of legend, the historian must exert himself to give dynasties their due, but a recognition and an appreciation of the great families who have shaped the destinies of all European states are essential to any true picture of Europe's past. The Tudors and Stuarts, the Habsburgs, the Valois and Bourbons, the Vasas and Oranges, the Hohenzollern and Romanovs, were pivotal figures in early modern history. It has been said that Russia could think of an emperor without an empire rather than of an empire without an emperor, and this holds for the entire Christian commonwealth that was Europe. A future historian will one day write a comparative study of the family traits and traditions which ran through these species and made them distinct from one another, and yet akin in their outlook on life, their sense of power, their stubborn belief in the magic quality inherent in princely blood and in a privileged position granted them by Providence.

Dynastic ambition was already motivating the first Hohenzollern to enter the Mark Brandenburg. As early as 1438, their eyes were set on the imperial crown, but their aspirations were not to be realized at that time. As yet, their position in the German northeast was too unstable and too much in need of consolidation. The twin city of Berlin–Coelln was the first to feel the strong hand of princely authority. A conflict between the patrician families and the craft guilds provided the ruling Hohenzollern with an excuse to break the independence of the town and to bend the patricians to his will.

The prince forced the city to relinquish her ties with the Hanseatic League, assumed the prerogative of judiciary power, and suppressed the privileges of the old patrician families. The people remonstrated, but to no avail. Their opposition was recorded by the chroniclers of the time as the "Berliner Unwille" and would seem a prelude to the attitude of resistance to authority that marks Berlin's entire history, whether the commands came from Frederick the Great, Bismarck, Hitler, or Walter Ulbricht.[4] The anger of the populace did not, however, obstruct the plans of the new rulers. A castle, symbol of the new order, was erected in Berlin, and the town became incorporated in the state of Brandenburg in 1448. A few years later it was chosen as the permanent residence of the Hohenzollern. The importance of the Mark Brandenburg for the whole of Germany was still minimal, and in reality limited to its ruler's position as one of the seven electors who chose the emperor.[5]

The presence of the princes brought about a considerable change in the town itself. A large part of the inner section had been appropriated by the new ruler for the construction of the castle, which for centuries was the nucleus of the city's architectural planning and building. Adjacent to the castle there later arose the *Zeughaus* (arsenal), the cathedral, and much later, the complex of the Berlin museums, and the residences of the members of the dynasty.

Our knowledge of Berlin at the time of Renaissance and Reformation holds scant interest for the contemporary reader. The records tell of festivities, fairs and markets, buildings and streets, and even of a small Jewish community housed in huts and held in contempt. The prince-elector was barely touched by the humanistic currents of the times, and seems to have been primarily occupied by a love affair with a certain Katharina Blankenfelde, wife of a local patrician.[6] The force and energy of the Renaissance failed to leave its mark on the city.

The impact of the Reformation was more significant. Luther's town of Wittenberg was close to the Mark Brandenburg and was part of the diocese of Brandenburg. Luther's writings found their way quickly into Berlin, and though the prince-elector opposed the new religious wave for both dynastic and financial reasons, he was unable to prevent the spread of the new gospel. The nobility and the urban middle class leaned toward the Lutheran teaching, and the ruler was obliged to look the other way. But Berlin never became a religious town. Luther's cult and his dogma prevailed but were subordinated to the city's deeper interests. The churches and monasteries that survived the Middle Ages are neither large nor beautiful, and in the acceptance of the Reformation, worldly considerations played an important role. Church property was appropriated or confiscated; monasteries were converted into secular schools, such as the famous Graue Kloster where, centuries later, Bismarck received his high school diploma. These practices were in keeping with the overall development of princely states in north Germany and were parochial in character.

In his *Memoirs*, Frederick the Great observed that the history of the House of Brandenburg became interesting only at the beginning of the seventeenth century. Then it was that the Hohenzollern laid claim to two inheritances, one in the east and the other in the west of Germany. The elector accepted the Duchy of Prussia, formerly the territory of the Teutonic Knights, as a fief from the Polish crown. In the west he aspired to the dukedom of Jülich and Cleve, on the lower Rhine. Jülich and Cleve were part of the strategic route which connected the Spanish Netherlands and the Upper Rhine. By way of the Swiss Alps, the route continued to Italy. The possession of this artery was of crucial importance to Catholics and Protestants alike on the eve of the Thirty Years' War. In order to secure their claims, the

Hohenzollern allied themselves with the young Dutch republic, becoming Calvinists in the process.

The small state was thus precipitately drawn in two directions, each heavily charged with political tensions. The Prussian inheritance, which eventually gave the state its name, connected Brandenburg with the Baltic and the northeastern corner of Germany and carried with it relations to Poland, Sweden, Russia, and the Baltic Sea. Jülich–Cleve drew Brandenburg into the religious conflicts that were soon to convulse Western Europe. The Dutch republic was then at the height of its power, and the Hohenzollern looked toward its administrative and commercial practices as inspiration for many of the innovations they wished to introduce in their more backward domains. Their alliance was further strengthened by dynastic marriage when Frederick William, the Great Elector, married a princess of the House of Orange.

Frederick William's second wife, Dorothea, remembering the beautiful lanes of Holland, planted Unter den Linden. This avenue extended the city westward from the castle, and it soon became the principal thoroughfare. Its line of growth was thus east-west, rather than north-south, and this was characteristic of Brandenburg's future expansion. Dutch architecture was also featured in Berlin, especially in the houses of the middle class, with their small frontages and brick gables.

The Great Elector had broken with the German custom that made the religion of the prince compulsory for his subjects, and his residence now included both Lutherans and Calvinists. As in Holland, a climate of toleration began to prevail within the confines of the city and was greatly enhanced when the Great Elector issued the Edict of Potsdam in 1685, in which the Huguenots, who had been expelled from France by order of Louis XIV, were invited to make Brandenburg their home. The influx of some 6,000 Frenchmen changed the life of the city in many ways. Not only were the Huguenots good Calvinists, sober, devout, given to work and thrift, but they also brought with them many arts and crafts which were new to the Berliners. The manufacture of jewelry, the production of silk and fine cloth, the making of felt for hats remained in their hands for decades. Tax exemptions and state subsidies were granted them, and they soon became an indispensable element of the economy. More elegant customs in regard to deportment, dress, and food were also introduced, and to these the Berliners accustomed themselves with ease. French white bread, cauliflower, asparagus, and artichokes became popular foods.[7] The Huguenots maintained their own churches and schools, and instruction was imparted in French. This minority group soon formed the nucleus of an upper class of merchants, bureaucrats, and officers who amalgamated with the nobility of Prussian origin, giving it some of their esprit, grace of expression, and toleration.

The rule of the Great Elector, 1640–1688, gives evidence for the first time that the driving force in Prussian politics was dynastic ambition. Frederick William's territory, as we have noted, was scattered across the map of Germany from the Rhine to the Baltic coast. The prince was a vassal of the Holy Roman Emperor and of the king of Poland at the same time. During the protracted negotiations which ended the Thirty Years' War he had reached the conclusion that the role in international politics which he aspired to play demanded a power base. His first concern was the establishment of a standing army and the fiscal revenues to support it. The landed nobility, however, would give their consent to a standing army only upon receiving the right to perpetuate the longstanding servitude of the rural labor force. In this manner the Junker class came to be recognized as a pillar of Brandenburg Prussia. Although the attempts of the Great Elector to elevate his state to the rank of an influential power were without success, he did lay the foundations on which his successors were able to build, though his own son looked for status rather than power.

The desire to reach a higher footing among the countries of Europe fascinated many a German prince of the period. The Hanoverians were in line for the English throne and the Elector of Saxony had become the king of Poland. Frederick I of Brandenburg–Prussia made use of the intrigues preceding the War of the Spanish Succession to obtain the title of king in Prussia (1701). This restrictive title—king *in*, but not *of*, Prussia—was designed to curb the ambition of the prince and to remind him that he was still subordinate to the emperor. But he had bagged the royal designation, and prestige was an important item in the world of the ancien régime. Frederick I was quite conscious of the obligations imposed upon him through his new dignity. He began the transformation of Berlin into a royal residence. The greatest architect-sculptor of Germany was summoned and charged with the assignment of changing the face of the capital. Andreas Schlüter was a master of the baroque and had studied French and Italian models, but his work bears the stamp of his own genius. The ancient castle was given an impressive façade, where old and new were fused in an imposing whole, and a short distance away he built the *Zeughaus* with its unforgettable sculptures of dying warriors.

Schlüter was the first genius to make his home in Berlin, but other illustrious men followed him. From Hanover, Queen Charlotte summoned the most renowned figure that Germany had produced since the Thirty Years' War, Gottfried Wilhelm Leibniz. In 1700 he founded the Academy of Science in Berlin. The academy was inspired, as its founder had been, by the idea of advancing the theory that harmony exists between the traditional theological philosophy and the modern physical-mechanical forms of thought. It was the first time that science and philosophy entered the sober and prosaic setting of the Prussian realm; there seemed to be a promise of greater things to come.[8]

These fair auguries were for the distant future, however; the first tender sprouts of a nascent appreciation of science and philosophy were soon trampled underfoot. The shift took place with the advent of King Frederick William I in 1713. He has been called the sergeant king, the soldier king, and even the Führer of Potsdam. Despising the ostentatious attitude of his father and scorning the philosophical interest of his mother, he set out to make Prussia a garrison state. He reorganized the administrative apparatus of the kingdom and established his own sovereignty as a "rocher de bronze." The army became the backbone of the state.

The city of Berlin now numbered some 80,000, and 8,000 were soldiers. Soldiering became, not only the pastime of the king, but a dominating factor in the life of the town and its people. The king ordered the construction of a wall to enclose the different sections of the city, and at the fourteen gates which punctuated it, tolls and taxes were collected. Both inside and outside the walls were drill grounds. Textile manufacturing was encouraged mainly because the soldiers had to be outfitted. Frederick William was a hard taskmaster, ordering his subjects about, supervising their habits of production and consumption, as though the state were his private domain.

Wide streets were laid out to connect the southernmost section of the city with the north and the center. The king saw to it that they were carefully paved since parades moved more easily on paved roads, and the soles of the soldiers' boots were made to last longer. The Friedrichstrasse and the Wilhelmstrasse were two of these thoroughfares, the latter destined to become the headquarters of the Prussian bureaucracy. High officials and wealthy noblemen were "invited" by the king to build their town houses along the Wilhelmstrasse and were given a piece of ground and 10 percent of the building costs. Those who were foolish enough to ignore the royal request found it necessary to flee from the city to escape the king's fury.[9]

Given the autocratic character of the regime, it was only to be expected that the city itself would fall under the control of royal officials, and that the meager remnants of self-government should disappear altogether. Army officers and tax collectors intervened in many aspects of the city's life, such as the sparse beginnings of industrial production, the supervision of guilds and their products, and so forth. Clearly the city was the subject of mercantile control in its most rigid form. These innovations left their mark on Berlin. What had once been an agricultural and commercial center acquired some of the characteristics of an industrial city.

At the time of Frederick William's death in 1740, Berlin was still an average, somewhat mediocre German town; fifty years later she was on a par with other important European centers where great politics were fashioned. Her transformation came about during the reign of Frederick the Great. Once again the personality of the ruler was the decisive factor in the development of the city. The political ambition and the military prowess of Frederick the Great are well known. At the expense of Austria, he enlarged the Prussian territory in three wars and was able to maintain his conquests against the determined opposition of the other continental states. He made Prussia into a great power and changed the political balance of Europe immeasurably. Although

Frederick built his charming retreat, Sans Souci, at Potsdam and preferred it to Berlin, the capital was not neglected.

Frederick continued the architectural plans begun by his grandfather and Andreas Schlüter. As we have said, the castle had been completed and the arsenal had spread toward Unter den Linden. Now the king and his favorite architect, Knobelsdorff, envisaged a grandiose scheme; the erection of the Forum Fredericianum. A few hundred yards westward from the arsenal an immense square was laid out. Along one side, the opera house was built, flanked by a baroque palace (called the commode by the Berliners because of its elegantly curved façade). On the other side of the square, facing the opera house, rose the palace of the king's brother, Prince Henry, also bearing the mark of the baroque, though in a less flamboyant manner. Prince Henry's palace was destined to house the University of Berlin. Other princely residences connected the forum with the royal castle. Adjacent to the opera house rose the Hedwigskirche with its low cupola, the first Catholic church in Protestant Berlin. The Forum Fredericianum was a project worthy of the monarch who fathered it, and it remained the glory of Berlin until the downfall of the city in 1945.

The wide reaches of the Tiergarten were replanted with trees and flowering shrubs and became one of the famous parks of Europe. Some of the old city gates were torn down and replaced with elegant colonnades. Although the architecture of the period is late baroque or early rococo, it is more muted than that of Vienna, Dresden, or Munich, and gives evidence of the Spartan character of the king and his state. There is a classic note in Frederick's buildings, a somber sense of artistic restraint, blending easily with the classic style which developed at a later period.

"The Prussian style" is a phrase coined by Moeller van den Bruck, who dedicated an interesting book to its description.[10] The Prussian style was not limited to Berlin, of course, but it is in Berlin that it found its most representative manifestation. Side by side with the royal palaces and the official buildings, there were, in ever increasing number, the town houses of the wealthy nobility, the merchants, and the Jewish financiers. The stately residence of the banker Ephraim was an example of the latter. Like most kings, the Prussian kings encouraged building since it gave substance to the appearance of symbolic opulence. Furthermore, the increase in population provided a reasonable basis for their frantic building activities. The population of Berlin rose from 90,000 in 1740 to 147,000 in 1786. Nearly one-fourth of the latter, however, were soldiers for whom Frederick the Great erected barracks to avoid billeting them in private homes. Eight such barracks were built during Frederick's reign and they were a significant part of the Berlin landscape until the downfall of the Hohenzollern in 1918. In them were housed the guard regiments for whom the Berliners had mixed emotions, half affection, half mockery.

The industrial development of the capital accelerated at a rapid pace, encouraged and controlled by the all-powerful bureaucratic machinery of the state. The manufacture of cloth now had a steady market in the constantly expanding army. Metal work was introduced. More important still was the manufacture of silk and velvet, which, for a time, enjoyed a great prosperity, since it was the king's special interest. To further Berlin's independence from other cities, such as Hamburg, the king set up his own banks. With porcelain becoming the vogue, Frederick built his own factory, which took the royal sceptre as its trademark. The royal Berlin porcelain differed from Meissen or Sèvres; in keeping with the sober Prussian style, it specialized in white. To increase the sales of Royal Berlin porcelain, all Jewish brides were obliged to buy their dinnerware at the royal factory.

The importation of foreign labor and foreign know-how was a necessary adjunct of all this hectic activity. Workers came in from France, from Bohemia, from Flanders, from Switzerland, swelling the numbers of those Germans who came from Saxony, Silesia, and Thuringia. The easy fusion of these newcomers with the native inhabitants produced a new human type, the Berliner, and is one of the notable characteristics of the period. When visiting Berlin in 1778, Goethe noticed a special breed which he called "ein verwegener Menschenschlag" (an audacious type of human being). Another visitor noted the gay mood of the Berliner and explained it as "the result of reflection, manly activity, considerable freedom, good civic security, and some frivolity." And he added, "There is a surprising number of intelligent people among the bourgeois, the craftsmen and soldiers, who think sharply and accurately, and who know how to express themselves."[11]

To the Brandenburg Gate

"Der Berliner" was a peculiar amalgam of the native population from the Mark Brandenburg and the many other elements which had come into the city from other places. Fontane thought that the Berliner was sober, full of character, and gifted in many ways, but lacking in enthusiasm and genius.[12] And it is true that few great men were born in Berlin. The influx of foreign components, however, helped to minimize these inadequacies. The Berliner who emerged from this admixture represents a combination of traits from the hardworking middle and lower classes plus the stoicism and endurance of the veterans and pensioned soldiers who made their homes in Berlin. The language spoken was also a special patois of Low and Middle German, the native language of the Mark Brandenburg, and whatever French and Yiddish words could be incorporated for everyday use. It was a language which suited the humor of these people, who were able to adjust themselves to any situation provided they were permitted to express their reactions with an ironic remark or a quick retort.

It was not by accident that this new type of *genus homo* made its appearance during the reign of the great king. The population identified itself with his adventurous and heroic policy and basked in his glory. They were quite willing to endure hardship if hardship were to be their lot, as, for instance, in 1760 when the capital was ransacked by the Russians. In his later days Frederick became "der alte Fritz," whose stoicism and sense of duty they admired, even though they grumbled about the police-state methods he sometimes employed.

Much of the harmonious relationship between king and people was a result of the freedom of expression and the religious toleration allowed and practiced by the king. Since everyone could seek his salvation in his own manner in Frederick's realm, Lutherans, Calvinists, and Catholics entered a new type of coexistence under the protection of enlightened despotism.

There is no doubt about the king's wholehearted belief in the tenets of the Enlightenment. It was, in fact, the one element of his complex genius that had taken shape before all others. A deeply rooted love for music, for beauty, and for the contemplative pleasures of the human mind had attracted him while he was still a boy throwing him into a tragic conflict with his narrow-minded militaristic father. He emerged from the encounter more than ever convinced that the philosophical movement which was sweeping the century held the clue to human happiness. He drank deeply from the springs of the French Enlightenment and took Voltaire as his teacher and confidant. Frederick invited the French sage to his court and entrusted him with his own philosophical and historical writings, which he asked him to edit. The Academy of Arts and Sciences was resuscitated in 1744, and many distinguished French scholars were appointed to its faculty. The king corresponded with the leaders of the French Enlightenment, and he shared their belief that the passions and the prejudices which had controlled man up to the present could be overcome by reason, and that a golden age would soon dawn on the world.

One of the many paradoxes of Frederick's nature was that he tried to combine his yearning for a contemplative life with a thirst for military glory. He felt he must think as a philosopher but act as a king. Not since Marcus Aurelius had there been a similar psychological conflict. As a philosopher Frederick shared the optimism of the age; as a statesman he was deeply pessimistic and lavished a flood of insult on mankind in general. Perhaps the greatest among the many contradictions which ravaged his life was his blindness to the diffusion of the Enlightenment among his own subjects.

And yet the mood of the Enlightenment was one of the most important links between Frederick and his subjects. He was unaware that during his reign Königsberg had become one of the philosophical centers of Europe. It was in Königsberg that Kant defined the Enlightenment as man's exit from his self-inflicted tutelage. "Sapere aude" (have the courage to use your reason) became the motto of eighteenth-century Germany. Nowhere was the atmosphere of enlightened thinking stronger than in Berlin. Here Lessing represented the new spirit in two of his works, *Minna von Barnhelm* and *Nathan the Wise*. *Minna von Barnhelm* is the first German comedy, and it sparkles with the spirit of an enlightened serenity which rises above the prejudice of status and preconceived military notions of honor. *Nathan the Wise*, we recollect, was written as a plea for religious toleration. From the encounter of the three great monotheistic religions, Judaism, Islamism, and Christianity, the only viable solution to emerge is tolerance.

It has been asserted that Lessing's model for Nathan was the philosopher, Moses Mendelssohn. Mendelssohn had entered Berlin under the degrading regulations imposed by the absolute state on the Jewish people, but he had risen to recognition both as a manufacturer of silk and as a speculator in the field of philosophy. He was not an original thinker, adhering to the platonic tradition of the Good, the True, and the Beautiful, which he combined in an eclectic manner with his own belief in God and immortality. Associated with him was a popularizer and disseminator of the Enlightenment, Nicolai, a determined fighter against superstition and the unreasonable, but in his ideas dogmatic, pedestrian, and pedantic.

A new climate of opinion became discernible as the result of this publicity so that the Jewish population was acknowledged as part of the Berlin society before it became legally emancipated.[13] Before long the Mendelssohns became one of the distinguished families of the town, and their house a social meeting place. Berlin translated Frederick's philosophy into its own idiom and made it into a living condition. The city never had a ghetto, and the more affluent and the more civilized Jews easily found acceptance among the Berliners.

At the close of Frederick's rule, Berlin had already become a large urban center, at least by German standards. She rivaled Vienna for first place among German cities. Berlin was the more aggressive, the more dynamic, and she outdistanced Vienna in military acumen and technology. On the other hand, Vienna was older, more aristocratic, more elegant. She was still the home of the Holy Roman Emperor; her architectural history reached from High Gothic to the baroque; she was the musical capital of Europe, and she far surpassed Berlin in splendor. Oriented toward the south and the southeast, Vienna was the magnet for the Catholic, tradition-minded forces of Germany. Berlin's attraction was limited to the energies of North and East Germany; she was predominantly protestant, philosophical, and scientific. And every phase of the city bore the mark of the army. For one hundred and twenty-six years, the Austro-Prussian dualism established by Frederick remained the prevailing feature of German politics. Germany had become an ellipse whose foci were Vienna and Berlin.

The twenty years from Frederick's death in 1786 to the Battle of Jena in 1806 constitute a strange interlude in the history of Berlin. The royal coilspring once removed, state and society fell into lethargy and complaisance. The new king, Frederick William II, was an indolent and pleasure loving man; his son, who succeeded him, Frederick William III, an indecisive and hesitant ruler of scant talents.

While Europe became engulfed in a titanic struggle with France and the ideas of the great revolution, Prussia appeared content to live by the maxims of an enlightened despotism. In the words of Queen Louise, Prussia had gone to sleep on the laurels of Frederick the Great. Yet during these tranquil but fateful twenty years, a new center had appeared in Germany. The small, provincial town of Weimar, with some 6,000 inhabitants, became the spiritual capital of the nation. Here Goethe, Schiller, Herder, and Wieland formed the nucleus of a civilization that was at once cosmopolitan and national. Soon the nearby university of Jena was a gathering place for the most adventurous minds of the period—Fichte, the Schlegels, Schelling, and Hegel. Weimar was the capital of a small German principality, the Dukedom of Saxe-Weimar, but for fifty years it was as important in the life of the nation as Berlin or Vienna. Weimar came to represent the most spiritual and the most elevated energies then pulsating through Germany, while Berlin was the nerve center of a powerful state dominated by a hierarchic society rooted in the prejudices of the ancien régime. Yet the antagonism between "Macht und Geist," explicit in Berlin and Weimar respectively, became more marked in the latter part of the nineteenth century.[14] In the late eighteenth century Berlin reached out to absorb the finest manifestations of the Weimar spirit. Wilhelm and Alexander von Humboldt were both friends and admirers of Goethe and Schiller, and along with such romanticists as the Schlegels and others who moved from Weimar to Berlin, began to spread the new gospel according to Johann Wolfgang Goethe. The dramas of Schiller were performed in the Berlin theatre, now called the German National Theatre, and were given a rousing reception. The operas of Mozart and Gluck were played before crowds of appreciative music lovers, and Beethoven gave a royal court recital.[15]

The mellowing influence of a higher culture seemed to be changing the harsh profile of the Prussian capital. In these years Berlin's architecture received its classical form. In 1793 Langhans began the construction of the Brandenburger Gate. Its majestic outline, its sober Doric columns, crowned by the chariot of victory, became the city's symbol. Situated at the end of Unter den Linden, it connected the old center of the town with the Tiergarten and the outlying districts of the west, especially the growing suburb of Charlottenburg. The gate was the entrance to Berlin's via triumphalis.

The style chosen by its architect for the monument was more Spartan than Athenian in character; nothing could have suited the spirit of the city better than the restrained dignity of this gate. It remains the epitome of the "Prussian style." At the time, there was in Berlin a whole galaxy of young artists who aspired to bring to the city the inspiration of classic antiquity, with the aim of making Berlin into a synthesis of Greece and Rome. Wilhelm Schadow, David and Friedrich Gilly vied with each other to transform the city into a home for the ideals and values of that humanism then being expressed by Goethe, Schiller, and Hölderlin in their poetry. The most influential of these artists was Carl Friedrich Schinkel.

According to Schinkel, the architect ennobles all human relations and he must, therefore, encompass all the arts in his activities. The artist, he said, merges sculpture, painting, and the art of spatial proportions, according to the moral and rational conditions of human life, into one whole.[16] It was a program as ambitious as Richard Wagner's *Gesamtkunstwerk*. Schinkel gave Berlin its most impressive classic buildings. Some have survived the war's destruction, and some have been restored from the ruins, as for instance the Old Museum with its beautiful Ionic columns, or Die Neue Wache, which housed the guards and which is today a memorial for the victims of fascism. But Schinkel's activity was not restrained to the erection of official buildings; it included residences of the nobility and the upper bourgeoisie. In these years Berlin became the home of a cultural elite allied with the best that Germany produced, as well as the center of a powerful state. These attributes it retained until 1871. It cannot be said that Schinkel's art was entirely original; he copied ancient and medieval art forms, and their application in this progressive city was not always successful. Medieval designs especially remained alien to the spirit of a modern capital. To the observer they resemble an attempt to impose the shackles of an artificial German renaissance. Yet, withal, his was a noble talent and played its part in molding the lineaments of Berlin.

A visitor to the city during these years would have encountered many contradictions. Side by side with representative monuments might be seen the remnants of primitive settlements still given over to agriculture or dairy farming. When Frederick the Great asked a Frenchman whether Berlin could not hold its own in comparison with Paris, he received the sardonic reply: "In truth, your Majesty, except that in Paris we neither sow nor reap."

In the years before 1806 Berlin could boast of many ingratiating traits.[17] The barriers between the classes had grown less rigid. The salons of spirited Jewesses, like Henrietta Herz and Rachel Levin, attracted the court aristocracy fully as much as the receptions given by the high bureaucracy and the intellectual elite. Mixed marriages were taken as a matter of course. In general, it seemed as though the crusty shell of the Prussian state was gradually softening under the gentle persuasion of values and ideals other than those of military discipline and honor. Yet, as was the case so often in German history, appearances were deceiving. The perceptive Madame de Staël was not taken in by the superficial cordiality between power and genius, status and intellect. "The two classes of society—the scholars and the courtiers—are completely divorced from each other," she complained when visiting Berlin on one of her restless journeys across Europe. And she continued, "The thinkers are soaring in the empyrean, and on the earth you encounter only grenadiers."[18] And not the best of grenadiers at that! The day was not far off when their talents would fail the test and the laurels would crown Napoleon's legionnaires instead of the blond heads from Berlin.

[2]

From Kingdom to Empire

$\mathfrak{T}$HE enlightened despotism of Frederick the Great came to an end on the battlefields of Jena and Auerstädt. The politics of the Prussian state during the years preceding the debacle had been those of vacillation and confusion. Prussia had entered the war against revolutionary France side by side with Austria, yet after three years of inglorious fighting, she signed the peace of Basel (1795) and retreated into a policy of neutrality and an attitude of apathy. England, Russia, and Austria were left to continue the struggle, and Prussia contented herself with being the dominating power in Germany north of the Main River.

The years from 1795 to 1805 constituted a period of great intellectual flowering in North Germany, and the tremendous outburst of philosophical and poetical productivity has frequently been advanced as an extenuating circumstance for Prussia's neutral position. But it also gave rise to a feeling of euphoria which expired abruptly when Napoleon turned on Prussia after the battle of Austerlitz. She was then completely isolated, lacking powerful allies from without and popular support within. Forty-three years had passed since the conclusion of the Seven Years' War; the leadership of the monarchy had become rusty and impotent in an atmosphere of untested complacency. The commanding officers of the army were fossils of a bygone period who proved to be the inferiors of their French opponents in every respect.

In a single day, on October 14, 1806, Napoleon defeated the Prussian forces. When news of the disaster reached Berlin, the governor, von Schulenburg, issued the following proclamation: "The king has lost a battle. To remain calm is the first duty of the citizen."[1] His words expressed a sentiment typical of the

31

ancien régime, but under the circumstances the minister's instructions were somewhat difficult to follow. On October 27, Napoleon rode through the Brandenburg Gate at the head of his victorious army. His entrance marked the beginning of an era which became deeply etched in the memory of the people, the time of French domination, *die Franzosenzeit*, as the Berliners called it. Napoleon took up quarters in the royal castle, while his armies conquered the remainder of northern Germany. What resistance they encountered was sporadic and ineffective.

The humiliation of the once proud state was complete. Napoleon imposed a heavy indemnity on the prostrate country, amputated large sections of its territory, and forced it to adhere to his system of imperial domination, the continental blockade. Prussia had lost her status as a great power; even the capital was for a time transferred from Berlin to East Prussia.

It was here that the king received a group of professors who urged him to found a new university in Berlin to compensate for the loss of academic institutions which had been surrendered to the invader. In this moment the uninspired king found the inspired words that were to guide Prussia toward her moral and political rejuvenation. "The State," he said, "must replace through spiritual forces what it has lost in physical power."[2] His statement might be taken as a motto for the entire movement that goes under the name of the Prussian Reform.

A new generation now appeared on the political scene and fresh life was breathed into the humbled and crippled state. Their spokesmen came from different parts of Germany: the Baron vom Stein, Hardenberg, Scharnhorst, von Boyen, Gneisenau, von Schoen, and Wilhelm von Humboldt. They were united in the conviction expressed by Fichte, who said, "The military struggle is over; there begins . . . a new struggle, the fight for principles, for ethics, for character."[3] Though most of these men were born to rank and privilege, they had experienced in varying degrees the liberating currents then floating through Europe, and they were determined to rebuild Prussia into a body-politic where power and spirit would be combined. Only in this manner, they felt, could a modernization of the absolute state be brought about. The road to revolution was not open to the German people and was, in any case, alien to its habits; only the slow advancement through evolution and reform could accomplish its aims.

The transition from the absolute monarchy of the ancien régime to a modern state was achieved through the labors of a new group, the enlightened bureaucracy. It was lodged between the king and his subjects and assumed an almost dictatorial power.[4] Its prerogatives were justified by the need for rational progress imposed from above. This rule by an enlightened bureaucracy remained one of the characteristics of Germany until the fall of the second empire. Its natural center was Berlin, and this fact had a great influence on the city. Entire sections were occupied by their offices, for the most part along Unter den Linden and the Wilhelmstrasse, and the region near the Tiergarten became their favorite habitat.

The transformation of the political structure was not undertaken according to a preconceived blueprint, but though it was carried out piecemeal, there were certain projects that loomed larger than others. First and foremost came the liberation of the serfs; next was the reform of the army from a body of mercenaries to a popular force based on military conscription after the French example; municipal self-government was established, designed to lead the country toward national representation; economic activities were freed from outworn restrictions and prohibitions; and last, but by no means least, came the reform of the educational institutions. The capital was especially influenced by the municipal reforms and the educational innovations.

Napoleon himself had ordered that Berlin should receive a constitution drawn up after the French model.[5] This was, however, an emergency measure destined to be superseded by the introduction of the *Städteordnung* (municipal ordinance) of 1808. According to the new law the citizens could elect their own government consisting of a city council, a magistrate, and a mayor (*Oberbürgermeister*). Not all the inhabitants were considered citizens, however, and in Berlin, out of a population of 160,000, only 8 percent had the privilege of voting. Furthermore, the heads of the administration could be nominated only by the city council and were appointed by the Minister of the Interior or the king himself. The police force and the courts remained in the hands of the state.[6] The head of the police (*Polizeipräsident*) held a powerful position, playing an important role in the life of the capital. Under one pretext or another, he intervened in many aspects of the activities of the citizenry, from the political to the artistic. All in all, it was a modest effort to bring self-government to the people of Berlin.

The educational reform, on the other hand, was a significant achievement. At the beginning of the nineteenth century the necessity for such a reform was widely recognized in Germany. Three eminent thinkers had tried to define the essence of the university: Schelling, Fichte, and Schleiermacher.[7] They looked to philosophy as the one discipline that imparts unity to knowledge and gives sanction to a true *universitas*. Schleiermacher's *Occasional Remarks about Universities in a German Sense* is the most lucid exposition of the question. For him, the university does not primarily impart or produce knowledge; its true meaning is "the learning of learning," the awakening of the idea of knowledge in the minds of the students.[8]

The realization of these lofty ideals fell to Wilhelm von Humboldt. He was himself a Berliner; the family estate was located close to the capital in Tegel. He was a convinced individualist and had voiced his dissent from the all-embracing activities of the absolute state. He had given over his life to the study of ancient culture and those manifestations of German poetry which he felt to be germane to the sensibility of Greece, namely the poetry of Goethe and Schiller, both of whom became his close friends. Fate had allowed him to cultivate his personal tastes as Prussian envoy to the Holy See. From Rome he was called back to organize the educational reform in 1809. Although he accepted the appointment with reluctance, he was, nevertheless, able to launch the new University of Berlin after only one year in office.

The philosophy on which the university was built is expressed in one of Humboldt's memoranda: "Only that knowledge which stems from the most intrinsic, and is planted in the most intrinsic, forms character. Neither the state nor humanity is interested in knowledge or rhetoric (Wissen und Reden), but in character and action." It was the program of the German neo-humanism in its most concise form.[9] The university was given a splendid home in the palace of Prince Henry of Prussia, opposite the Opera House.

As the offspring of the state, the fate of the university became tied inextricably to German destiny.

Fichte was the first dean of the Faculty of Philosophy. In 1807–1808 he had delivered in Berlin his famous *Addresses to the German Nation* in which he expressed a messianic nationalism, praising Germany as the home of the primordial people (*Urvolk*), and the German language as the one language in which the mind appeared with unbroken force and clarity. Taking up his position at the university, Fichte continued his work in conjunction with such men as Schleiermacher, Schmalz, Savigny, Thaer, Hufeland, and others. Already existent institutions, such as the Academy of Science and the medical establishments were fused with or attached to the newly founded body, which was built on three maxims: freedom of the individual, freedom of research, and freedom of the nation. The university enjoyed the privilege of autonomy and elected its chancellor (*Rektor*) and its deans. A tradition of its own was soon established, and a Founder's Day gave occasion for many eloquent addresses in which the professors acquainted the world with some of the transcendent problems they had encountered.

The people of Berlin were proud of this new center of learning. They enjoyed reciting the names of its famous teachers, indulging themselves in some sort of vicarious intellectual glory, a propensity which contributed in some measure to the proverbial arrogance of the Berliner who knew more and better than the rest of the world.[10]

Under the principles that we have stated, the university became a haven for the German spirit suffering under foreign domination. Yet the nation so addressed and so formed in this process was Prussia rather than Germany. Prussia had always been more of a political than an organic creation, and this she continued to be under the leadership of the enlightened bureaucracy and the dedicated professors who came to Berlin. She was a political nation (*Staatsnation*), not a cultural entity (*Kulturnation*), as Friedrich Meinecke observed. It was already apparent that Prussia might lead Germany and even unify her, but that she would unite her was clearly beyond her immediate power.[11]

In the year following the founding of the university, another group made its appearance in Berlin, the Christian Germanic Association. This was a loose assembly, something like a club, made up of poets, literati, noblemen, and officers, who were united in their hatred of the French. They were antirevolutionary, anti-liberal, and anti-Semitic. They were opposed not only to the foreign oppressor, but also to the reforms which they thought tended to convert Prussia into a "newfangled Jew-state." Among the members of the Christian Germanic Association were Achim von Arnim, Heinrich von Kleist, Adam Müller, Clemens Brentano, and von der Marwitz. They expressed some of their ideas in a short-lived publication called *Die Berliner Abendblätter* (*The Berlin Evening Pages*).

Die Berliner Abendblätter was representative of the turn that the German romantic movement was taking in this decade. The emotional subjectivism of the romantic movement now somersaulted and embraced the collective order on which the Middle Ages had built the church, the nobility, and the monarchy. It was called "the organic theory of the state" in contradistinction to the atomistic ideology of the Enlightenment and the French Revolution. The defenders of the organic state were the apologists of an aristocratic society with its caste character and its class privileges. A new type of nationalism came into being, romantic nationalism, and Berlin became one of its strongholds.

The tragic figure of Heinrich von Kleist reflects the movement in all its complexity. Born into one of the oldest Junker families, he chose to live the life of a free-lance poet, but he had encountered disappointment all along the way. The conquest of Germany by Napoleon was responsible for his turn to radical nationalism, and he set out to use the theatre as a soundingboard for his inflamed patriotism. His last and finest drama, *The Prince of Homburg*, ends with the battle-cry: "Death to all enemies of Brandenburg." Of the French invader, he wrote, "Schlagt ihn tot! Das Weltgericht fragt euch nach den Gründen nicht!" (Kill him! History will not ask you for the reason). Kleist ended his life by suicide in 1811 on the shores of the Wannsee, a few miles from Berlin. It is difficult to say whether disillusioned patriotism or disillusioned individualism prompted his act.

The Prussian rulers looked with misgiving at the romantic hotheads and threw the most vociferous of them into prison. The government was not willing to gamble the existence of the state in a premature challenge of Napoleon's power. From 1807 to 1812, Prussia submitted reluctantly to all demands of the Corsican conqueror and even went so far as to participate in his campaign against Russia. Only after Napoleon's retreat from Moscow, did the government join the forces which were determined to end the French domination of Europe.

A great many Berliners had been waiting for this moment, particularly the youth of the upper-middle class. They had been attracted by the ideas of two men who had given the romantic nationalism a practical application: Ernst Moritz Arndt and Friedrich Ludwig Jahn. Both are among the godfathers of the "völkische" ideology, the German glorification of racial purity and strength. Jahn had formed a gymnastic association in Berlin, the *Turnverein*, in which the youths were instructed in physical fitness, making sport the first step to military drill.[12] The boys who had been exposed to the teaching and practice of Jahn, who believed that drinking, smoking, and the consumption of sweets were ungermanic, responded to the call to arms. When the king issued his proclamation, *To My People*, in March 1813, students of the universities and gymnasia flocked to the colors. At the Graue Kloster, the entire senior class volunteered.[13] The war of liberation had begun.

Berlin was very close to the center of military operations, and more than once was threatened with a Napoleonic victory. When the final decision came at the Battle of Leipzig, the city was swept by a wave of patriotic intoxication. On August 7, 1814, the victorious army returned to Berlin through the Brandenburg Gate, bearing with them the chariot of victory that Napoleon had taken to Paris. Once more, Unter den Linden was the via triumphalis, and soon the streets and squares of the city were renamed in honor of the generals and their battles.

There were a few who remained calm and detached in the midst of the turmoil engendered by the national liberation, and Goethe was one of these. He was not, he assured a friend, indifferent to the great ideas of freedom, fatherland, and people. But he questioned whether the German people had really been awakened to their destiny.[14] And well he might. The Germans called their war against Napoleon a war of liberation, but was there any guarantee that the new order which the victorious powers agreed upon would give the German people the freedom they had fought for, and were the German people ready and determined to assert themselves if their aspirations were ignored?

Prussia emerged from the Congress of Vienna once more a great power. Her territory was vastly enlarged and now included the Rhineland from Coblenz to Cologne, together with a substantial part of the kingdom of Saxony. But the Prussian patriots were soon faced with the realization that their capital was not to become the center of German politics. A shift to the southeast, to the Austrian empire, had taken place.

The loose confederation which replaced the Holy Roman Empire, the *Deutsche Bund*, consisted of thirty-nine states, which sent delegates to an assembly. A common organization of the military and domestic forces of Germany was planned but never effected.[15] The charter of the confederation contained a conglomeration of promises, such as the introduction of constitutions in all German states (Article 13), religious toleration, freedom of the press, and a status of civic equality for the Jewish population, but they remained lifeless words on a page of history. On November 5, 1816, at Frankfurt am Main, the assembly of the confederation met for the first time, Austria holding the presidency in perpetuity. Once more, Vienna had outdistanced Berlin, since the agreements reached in Frankfurt were the resolutions already made by Metternich in Vienna.

The period between 1815 and 1848 has been called a period of oppression by some and a period of restoration by others. The freedom-fighters who had set their minds on constitutional guarantees became disillusioned and rebellious, but those who longed for peace and tranquillity after twenty-three years of revolution and warfare gloried in the advent of the "halcyon days." For Berlin, it was a time of reconstruction, a breathing spell in which to repair the ravages that war had brought upon her. It was the age of Biedermeier, with its dainty furniture, its fragrance of lavender and cherrywood. It was the age of late romanticism, of late idealism, of late individualism, a peculiar blend of lofty thought and philistine subservience to the powers that were. The architecture that had dominated the capital during the period of classicism continued to determine the profile of the city. Schinkel was still the master, and proved his excellence in the construction of theatres, public monuments, and private residences.

Hegel occupied the chair of philosophy at the university in 1817 and exercised an unparalleled influence over the academic youth. His was a system of objective idealism, in which the universe is seen as a cosmos, the essence of which is reason, or, as Hegel preferred to call it, spirit, or mind. But to this platonic belief, Hegel added a variant pregnant with revolutionary consequences. He saw reason in motion, advancing in an endless dialectic process from thesis to antithesis to synthesis, ad infinitum. In Berlin, he applied this premise to the world of history. The one thought, he told his audiences, with which philosophy approaches history is the simple thought of reason: that reason rules the world, and that there is rational progress in the history of the world.[16] Hegel defined the goal of this process as "the progress in the consciousness of liberty." An important role was assigned to the state in the general advance toward the realization of reason. The state was declared "the divine idea on earth," and the great men in history were the agents and executors of the world spirit. These words have often been interpreted as an unqualified deification of the state. But this was not at all Hegel's intent. He did not believe the state to be the highest manifestation of the spirit; this was reserved to philosophy, religion, and the arts. The state belonged to the "finite world"; it was God on earth, but on earth only, and there subject to the verdict of history.

Hegel's was an imperial view, and it is not difficult to understand why it attracted the best minds of the epoch. He had stated "the university is our church," and his philosophy became for many a substitute for a declining Protestantism. Hegel was not an absolutist, least of all a worshipper of the ancien régime and "the good old days." His ideas were best suited to the enlightened bureaucracy, which could see itself mirrored in the proud march of the world spirit.

The rule of the master lasted until his death in 1831, but then the left wing of the Hegelian school raised its head, and, as Karl Marx put it, "the putrefaction of the absolute mind" began. Marx himself was, if not the heir, at least the pretender to the Hegelian heritage. By rights, Berlin should have become the headquarters of the world revolution. But, as everyone knows, *Das Kapital* was assembled in London and invested in Moscow.

Prussia between 1815 and 1848 offers the observer a contradictory picture; it was a state with two souls. The reform movement had ground to a halt in 1819 when the king dismissed Wilhelm von Humboldt and Boyen, the two ministers who had urged the granting of the promised constitution. Instead, the Prussian government accepted all the reactionary measures proposed by Metternich in the Carlsbad Decrees aiming at repression of the liberal spirit in the universities and the press. The censorship extended even to the correspondence of high ranking officials whose letters were opened and perused in the so-called black cabinet in Berlin.[17] Prussia, it appeared, had abdicated her role of moral leadership in Germany.

But this was not the whole truth. The enlightened bureaucracy did not resign itself to a policy of stagnation; although it could not advance the cause of liberalism against the opposition of the king and the Junker-aristocracy in the realm of representative government, it was able to accomplish a great deal in other fields. As Niebuhr asserted, "Liberty is based more on administration than on constitution," and this opinion was frequently echoed.[18] The enlightened bureaucracy was in great part responsible for converting Prussia into a homogeneous state. The Rhineland was allowed to preserve its own legal and administrative structure and submitted peacefully to the authority of Berlin.[19] Even more important were the steps taken to introduce a measure of freedom in the commerce between the German states.

The years between 1815 and 1848 are notable as the period of incipient industrialization in Germany. "Railways, express mails, steamboats, and all possible means of communication are what the educated world seeks," wrote Goethe in 1826, with a nostalgic sigh. But the attitude of the merchants and manufacturers was not so regretful. They felt that the people's welfare was curbed by the restrictions still imposed on production and the exchange of material goods. "Only when they establish among themselves a general, free, and unrestricted commerce will the nations of the earth reach the highest level of physical well-being."[20]

It was this belief that inspired the Prussian statesmen, Friedrich von Motz and Karl Maassen, to work for the creation of a German customs union, the Zollverein. Political and economic motives were entwined in this project. An identity of economic interest between the German states would inevitably lead to an identity of political interest, thus clearing the way toward political unity. The new economic policy which went into effect in 1818 brought about the economic integration of Prussia. The tariffs which still existed between the various parts of the monarchy were abolished and a market with freedom of communication was established.[21]

Berlin was one of the few cities in Prussia having the potential of an industrial center. A new phase in the growth of the town now began, and it gradually became the nucleus of a manufacturing and commercial expansion. The economic upswing of Berlin, however, was not a copy of other industrial centers, say Manchester or Birmingham, since it was not alone the result of the dynamics of economic forces. The powerful hand of the state, guiding and directing, gave to Prussian commerce its individual cast.

It became necessary to concentrate the affairs of industry and commerce in a department which would be independent from the older branches of the administration. The Prussian Ministry of Commerce, first established in 1817, was definitely consolidated in 1848.[22] It fell to this office, under the leadership of Christian Peter Wilhelm Beuth, to grapple with the problems posed by the transition from a mercantile to a liberal economic policy.

The change to a laisser faire, laisser aller policy found Prussia at a disadvantage. In Western Europe, especially in England, France, Belgium, and the Netherlands, the industrial revolution had advanced rapidly in response to the adoption of two innovations: the use of machines and the adherence to the factory system. In Berlin, "the domestic system" existed side by side with centralized production in factories, geared to division of labor and mass production. Systematic encouragement and implementation of machine output were essential. In due time this would lead to the obsolescence of the "domestic system" and the work of the home-based craftsman.

The state undertook the promotion of mechanization and motorization, which in that day meant the introduction of steam engines. These were installed in Berlin with the help of English manufacturers and were soon copied by other industrialists in the area.[23] Besides outright donations and subsidies from the state, prizes were awarded for the best products. Industrial exhibitions were set up in 1822 and 1827, expanding to remarkable proportions by 1844 when the entire German Customs Union displayed the results of the growing industrialization in Berlin.

The systematic encouragement of the state began to pay dividends. A new type of Berliner, the entrepreneur, appeared, emerging generally from the lower bourgeoisie, who combined the skill of the craftsman with the drive and ability of the manager.[24] The most outstanding example of this type was August Borsig. Trained as a carpenter, he switched to machine production and set up his own factory outside the city gates. It was the kernel of the famous *Borsig Werke*, which for many years specialized in locomotives. When Borsig died in 1854 at the age of fifty, his factory had built five hundred locomotives. A similar expansion can be noted in commerce where the old merchant guilds merged into one corporation. Yet it would be unwise to exaggerate the technological advancement of the city. A great deal of it was based on foreign, especially English, know-how. It was an English firm that introduced gaslight to Berlin in the 1820's, and it was an English company which set up Berlin's potable water supply.

The process of industrialization, however, proved to be inevitable and irreversible. The population of the capital grew rapidly between 1815 and 1848, doubling to a count of 400,000. There was an industrial reserve army in Berlin, as Marx would have said, and on this the entrepreneurs could depend for their labor supply. Many of those who were responsible for the increase in population lived outside the city gates in makeshift huts or in barns from which the district received its name, Scheunenviertel, a locality where people were huddled together in wretched circumstances and where crime and prostitution were rife.

Although Prussia was the first state in continental Europe to pass factory legislation forbidding the employment of children under nine and limiting the workday to sixteen hours, the situation cried out for help.[25] Characteristically, it was one of the late romanticists who raised her voice to call attention to the scandalous living conditions of the workers. In 1843, Bettina Brentano, wife of the poet, Achim von Arnim, published *This Book Belongs to the King*, in which she described the poverty, disease, hunger, and misery borne by the workers, and as her title indicates, called upon the government to alleviate their hardships.[26] But there was no immediate reaction to her protest, and the working class districts continued to be an eyesore and a disgrace to the city.

Many of the workers found employment in the building of railways, which began in 1838, first with the construction of short lines linking Berlin with Potsdam, Frankfurt an der Oder, Stettin, etc. This effort was paralleled by the enlargement of the waterways that crisscrossed the city. Some of these, such as the Landwehrcanal with its rows of chestnut and willow trees, became landmarks of great beauty. They combined to make Berlin one of the busiest inland ports in Germany.

The industrialization of Prussia in general and Berlin in particular proceeded, as we have noted, under the watchful eyes of the administration which encouraged it with tax exemptions, subsidies, and technical guidance. But inevitably the peaceful coexistence of absolute monarchy and industrial society came to a violent end. The placid idyll of the Biedermeier vanished in the revolution of 1848.

Frederick William IV had become king of Prussia in 1840. He was a gifted dilettante who combined personal charm and a lively wit with a pathological aversion to making decisions. He had grown up during the Napoleonic period and wholeheartedly embraced the Christian-Germanic ideology. He believed in the divine right of kings, the aristocracy, the established church, and the whole paraphernalia of a gothic revival in the midst of a century committed to technical advancement and democratic expansion. But, true romanticist that he was, he also wished to be the well-beloved monarch, popular with the people, whom he still considered His Majesty's subjects.

A few promising signs marked the beginning of his reign. He called some of the liberals (*die Göttinger Sieben*) who had been persecuted in Hanover to Prussia and appointed them to prominent positions. But the honeymoon was brief. Although he continued to assure everyone that he welcomed opposition, he soon recanted. Censorship remained a tool of the state, and the poet Hoffmann von Fallersleben, author of the German national anthem, was dismissed from his chair at the University of Breslau after twenty years of service and placed under police surveillance.[27] These repressive measures, however, served to increase the mounting chorus of dissent. "Young Germany" demanded to be heard. The opposition included poets, philosophers, and thinkers: Heinrich Heine, Ludwig Börne, Georg Herwegh, and the left-wing Hegelians, Arnold Ruge, the brothers Bauer, Karl Marx, and Friedrich Engels. In 1826 Börne had written, "We think well, and speak badly; we talk much, and act little; we do something, and accomplish nothing." Many of these irreconciled young men had been driven into exile by the constant pressure from the police, the censorship, and the general feeling of frustration. They lived in France, in England, in Switzerland. But their writings found their way into Germany, and they encountered an avid reading public in Berlin.

At the time, Berlin had an institution which catered to the as yet unorganized political factions in the capital. This was the Konditorei, a combination of coffee house and sweet shop that had been introduced by a few enterprising Swiss: Josty, Spargnapani, Stehely, and others. Some were frequented by the bureaucracy, some by the officers of the guards, and some by the enemies of the regime, who read the Rheinische Zeitung for which Karl Marx was writing.[28] Besides the privilege of reading German and foreign newspapers, the visitor to these establishments could indulge in smoking his pipe or cigar, a pleasure which, by royal order, was denied him on the streets. But the coffee houses were only an ersatz, a poor echo chamber, for a real public opinion. This was afforded the Berliners on March 18, 1848.

We will not enter the debate as to whether the events of 1848 constituted a true revolution or only a revolt, nor will we discuss Mr. Trevelyan's aphorism that 1848 was the turning point at which history failed to turn. For Germany, for Prussia, and for Berlin, the consequences of the March uprising were deep and far reaching.

The revolution reopened the question of German hegemony which had been in abeyance since the Congress of Vienna. The codominion of Austria and Prussia in German affairs was dissolved; the Austrian empire, deeply engulfed in revolutionary upheavals, was unable to prevent the attempts by the German people to secure freedom and unity in a national state. Thus there appeared for a short time a new German center, Frankfurt am Main, where the first German parliament gathered to create national unity in free deliberation and self-determination.

In Berlin, the revolution produced the first violent clash between the authorities and the people. The king and the heir apparent, his brother, the Prince of Prussia, had hoped to stem the tide with halfway measures.

But the promises of participation in a German reform program —constitutionalism in Prussia, and a change of the cabinet—failed to convince the people, and on March 18, fighting broke out on the streets of Berlin.[29] Barricades were set up, defended by men from the middle class, students, craftsmen, and workers, who closed ranks against the common enemy, the state and its army. It is difficult to decide who scored a success in the actual fighting; partisanship and hindsight color the reports. But it is certain that Frederick William IV lost his nerve, and confessed: "We all lay flat on our bellies." When a proclamation, "To my dear Berliners," fell on deaf ears, he gave orders to withdraw the army from the capital. Nor did this complete his humiliation; the victims of the fighting were carried into the inner courtyard of the royal castle, and the king was obliged to pay homage to them. An amnesty for all political crimes was declared on March 21, and the king rode through the streets of Berlin displaying the new national colors, black, red, and gold, and solemnly promised: "Henceforth Prussia will merge with Germany."

Without doubt, the promise was given under duress, and if the king intended to honor his word, it would have to be in his own fashion. For at least six months, the revolutionary crescent rose, and a citizens' guard was formed to secure the initial gains of the uprising. On March 22, those who had died on the barricades were accorded an impressive burial, the funeral cortege being led by Alexander von Humboldt and the professors of the university. The majority of the victims came from the middle and working classes. Rudolf Virchow, later one of Berlin's most famous physicians, wrote to his brother: "It was essentially the workers who decided the revolution . . . this revolution is not simply political, but fundamentally social."[30] Virchow was quite correct in his assessment, yet the combination of political and social revolution was precisely the crux of the matter, and ultimately brought about the failure of the revolution, since the political problems in themselves were of such magnitude that they would have demanded a mature and hardy generation to solve them. The generation of 1848 did not meet the test.

The German revolution of 1848 was faced at once with the task of introducing a measure of freedom to those states which were still deprived of constitutional guarantees, especially Prussia. In the second place, they were confronted by a thorny question: what form should the political unity of Germany assume, that of federation (*Bundesstaat*) or confederation (*Staatenbund*)? Woven inextricably into this issue was the third and most difficult question: which parts should be included, and which excluded, from the new Germany? The last problem especially affected the Austrian empire, composed as it was of large numbers of Magyars, Czechs, Slovaks, Croatians, and Italians, but ruled by a German-speaking minority. Thus the revolution split on a question for which there was no solution: a great Germany versus a little Germany.

In May of 1848, Prussia had acquired its own national assembly elected on a democratic basis. The deliberations of the assembly in Berlin were stormy, and they evidenced a shift toward the radical left. The situation was further complicated by the rapidly growing unemployment in the capital. Commerce suffered heavily from the political uncertainty, bankruptcy petitions rose in number, and the state was forced to intervene with an emergency program for public works. The fear of a socialist uprising seemed to be supported when a mob invaded the arsenal on June 14 and seized the weapons. In August the first general German Workers' Congress met in Berlin.[31]

There was, however, more smoke than fire in these manifestations of the working class, and, if anything, their riotous demands hastened the doom of the revolution. The bourgeoisie became frightened by the "spectre of communism" that, according to Marx and Engels, was haunting Europe. The revolutionary front that had overpowered the old authorities in March of 1848 fell apart and facilitated the counterrevolution.[32]

In truth, the forces of the old order, the landed aristocracy, the army, and the bureaucracy, had been stunned rather than defeated by the revolution. They were quick to perceive the split in the revolutionary movement and to turn it to their advantage. The Junker class organized its own newspaper, *Die Neue Preussische Kreuz-Zeitung*, taking the Iron Cross as its emblem, and as its motto, "Forward with God and King and Fatherland." The Junkers also formed their own association for the protection of property and played the depressed class of artisans and craftsmen against the wealthy bankers, entrepreneurs, and merchants. But their most powerful weapon was the formation of the camarilla, a shadow government behind and above the constitutional government dominated by Leopold and Ludwig von Gerlach. The camarilla advised the neurotic king to break with the Prussian Assembly and to adjourn it to Brandenburg. In November 1848, Berlin was put under marshal law, and once more the army was given the reins. A new government under the leadership of Count Brandenburg, the uncle of the king, was set up and granted a constitution on December 5. Prussia had become a constitutional monarchy, not by the will of the people, but by royal concession. Again, the principle of monarchic sovereignty asserted itself. The leader of the Prussian conservatives, Stahl, put forth the slogan: "Authority not majority."

The failure of the revolution was accepted by the people of Berlin, if not with indifference, at least with resignation. The middle class heaved a sigh of relief that the danger of "communism" had been averted. After all, to remain calm was the first duty of a citizen. Men like Bakunin felt nothing but scorn for the philistine acquiescence of the Berlin populace, and he quoted the inscription accompanying the display of the Prussian eagle above a tailor's shop:

> Under your wings
> Quietly I can do my ironing.[33]

A period of reaction followed the revolution. Prussia remained a constitutional monarchy with the accent on monarchy. The electoral law was revised to favor the property-owning classes, introducing the three-class electoral system which remained on the books until the end of the second German empire. The upper house was transformed into a House of Lords (Herrenhaus) to fill one of the romantic whims of the king. The Minister of the Interior, Ferdinand von Westphalen (the brother-in-law of Karl

Marx), brought censorship and political surveillance back into practice. Religion was considered the panacea for the corroding influences of science and philosophy, and the bigots had a heyday.[34] "Science must reverse itself," was the motto proclaimed by Friedrich Julius Stahl. However obnoxious the activities of the reaction were, they were not successful in suppressing the energies of the two classes who had fought in the revolution of 1848—the bourgeoisie and the working class.

The events of 1848 had failed to unite Germany. The Prussian king had refused to receive the imperial crown from the hands of the people's representatives, but when he aspired to unite Germany on terms more acceptable to himself and his peers, he found himself blocked by Austria and Russia. The Treaty of Olmütz (1850) halted the movement for German unification and reestablished the *Bund* as it had existed from 1815 to 1848. But the attempt to turn back the hands of the clock was no more successful this time than before.

The German dream of unification was followed by a rude awakening in which the bourgeoisie came to realize the causes of its failure. It was the lack of power, political, military, and economic power, which had precipitated its defeat. The bourgeoisie relinquished its cherished hope that democratic ideals could be called into existence by a mere fiat. Realism became the vogue in politics, literature, the arts, and music. Schopenhauer became the fashionable philosopher of the day; the music of Wagner replaced the romanticists, and the empirical sciences progressed by leaps and bounds. The word *realpolitik* was coined in 1853.[35]

It seems providential that the period of political oppression coincided with an upswing of economic activity, bringing a prolonged wave of prosperity to Germany. The boom lasted for more than twenty years. It is the "take-off" period of German industrialization which compensated for the vanished dreams of German unity. In it, the German bourgeoisie found an outlet for energies which had been frustrated in the field of politics.[36] The new prosperity was in some measure a result of the revolution, which had removed the last vestiges of serfdom in Germany. When the revolutionary movement had run its course, the Prussian government wooed the masses, both urban and rural, by an extensive program of social welfare, which indicated a recognition of the problems besetting a society in transition from agrarianism to industrial capitalism.[37] The production figures of the Zollverein in these years speak an eloquent language. Capital and consumer goods more than doubled, foreign trade increased, and the standard of living rose.

These circumstances had their effect on Berlin. The city grew from 529,000 to 658,000 inhabitants by 1865. A certain liberalization even took place in the laws governing the city. Everyone over twenty-four years of age, who paid his taxes and exercised a profession, was now deemed a citizen. Nevertheless, the pressure of the conservative reaction weighed heavily on the administration, and it is not surprising that many of the tasks of growing urbanization were solved not by the organs of municipal government, but by the head of the police. Carl Ludwig von Hinkeldey held this position and for many years was considered the prime example of willful police interference. In retrospect, one recognizes that he may be credited with a number of measures that modernized the aspect of Berlin. He reorganized the city's police force, giving it once again the character of a paramilitary body. Without the consent of the city fathers, he initiated a professional fire department, which, for good measure, was also responsible for street cleaning and the removal of refuse. He organized public baths and contracted for the erection of the famous "Littfass column," on which were posted public advertisements and notices, and which may still be seen in Berlin today. Against the will of the shortsighted citizenry, he engaged an English company to construct waterworks on the Upper Spree, outside the city gates. He died in a duel with one of the arrogant members of the Junker class whose gambling habits he had failed to condone.

It was also the police who decreed new ordinances for the building of apartments badly needed to accommodate the growing number of people who poured into Berlin in search of jobs. However, the regulations demanding a minimum area for each apartment and a minimum height between each floor neglected to specify the height and the depth of the buildings. Thus the floodgates were open for the construction of rental barracks or *Mietskasernen*, as the Berliners called them. The full depth of the lot was used, and the height rose to four or five stories. The lower apartments opening on the various courtyards were, therefore, entirely without sun. Fifty-three people were housed in each building, which occupied a space of ground the size of a London duplex for eight persons. A kind of "rental feudalism" came into existence which exploited most those who could least afford it.[38] The situation was not greatly ameliorated by the *Generalbebauungsplan*, an overall architectural plan adopted in 1863. Berlin owes to it a network of wide streets lined with trees—linden, birch, or oak—but on each side the houses maintained the sober, depressing character of a barrack town. This was especially true of the industrial sectors in the north, east, and southeast, where the factories were located. Here the population had doubled in twelve years.[39] Railroads had assisted their growth, allowing the workers to reach their jobs by means of cheap transportation. Administratively speaking, these suburbs did not belong to the capital, but few of the local dwellers were aware of the fact, and it affected their lives not at all.

The building of railways had dragged Berlin out of its economic stagnation, as Treitschke noted, and was particularly favorable to the development of machine industries. In addition to the industries occupied with the development of the railways, there appeared the electro-industry, in which Siemens and Halske took the lead. Chemical and pharmaceutical industries followed. Their names were household words in Berlin—Spindler for dyes, Schering for medicines.[40]

Berlin also began to make a name for herself as a commercial center in the distribution of iron, grain, and wool. In 1850, a Chamber of Industry and Commerce was founded which could rightfully boast that Berlin was well on its way toward entering the marts of world trade. There were, however, few joint stock companies in the Prussian capital, since the government was averse to encouraging speculation, and banks of importance were scarce. The financial centers of Germany were still in the West, in Frankfurt or Cologne. It was not until 1856 that David Hanseman founded the Diskonto Bank, soon to be followed by the Berliner Handelsgesellschaft, the Berliner Bankverein, and others. These were credit institutions for the budding industrial establishments. The industrialists and wholesale dealers of Berlin favored a unification of Germany believing that it would bring about the standardization of weights, measures, and currency, thus removing the obstacles which still hindered German commerce.

The unification of Germany received a fresh impulse when Italy embarked on its great national venture in 1859. A national association was founded which turned again to Prussia to take the lead.[41] In Prussia, Frederick William IV had succumbed to a mental disorder, obliging his brother William to take over the regency, and in 1861, the throne. The latter made an attempt to reconcile the liberals who had been in opposition since 1849 by proclaiming a change in policy which was endorsed by the electorate with great enthusiasm. A moderate liberal party won the majority in the Prussian parliament, and the road to unification seemed open. Open, but not paved. In fact, it was full of pitfalls. The liberal majority of the Prussian parliament fell out with the king on the subject of the army reform and this conflict soon took on the grave coloring of a constitutional struggle.

This is not the place to recount the details of the fight. There can be little doubt that the government's demand for an army reform was justified; there had been no overhaul of the army since 1814. While the population had doubled in size, the army lists had remained the same. The liberals were fully aware that it would take a strong Prussia to advance the cause of unification, and a strong Prussia meant the numerical expansion of the army. Nevertheless, there were certain features of the government's reform bill to which they objected, especially the extension of the period of service from two to three years, and the reorganization of the reserve, which would have weakened one of the institutions most dear to the liberals, namely, the *Landwehr*.[42]

The liberals were justified in their distrust of an army which had been instrumental in quelling the revolution of 1848 and ushering in the era of reaction. It is possible that the officers who argued the necessity of a three-year service period were without political motivation. Certainly the Minister of War, von Roon, was a technician rather than a man of political ambitions. But even von Roon had strong conservative leanings, and other officers, like von Manteuffel, had every expectation that the army reform would rid them once and for all of the whole "constitutional swindle." The liberals had good reason to doubt the king and his ministers in view of the situation. The conflict went from bad to worse; the king clung stubbornly to his program; the liberal majority, equally determined, refused to approve the budget, without which the state could not function. Under the circumstances, a liberal triumph might have been the result; the king was old, not likely to provoke a civil war, and would have abdicated rather than surrender to ideas he deemed pernicious. On the other hand, his son and heir entertained strong liberal convictions, and these were strengthened by his wife, the British princess, Victoria. The couple made no secret of their sympathy for the liberal cause, and the party would have welcomed their reign with open arms. But the rise of Otto von Bismarck blocked the way.

At the very height of the crisis, when the king had already drafted his abdication, Bismarck was called to assume the office of Prussian prime minister. It was his voice that persuaded the king to hold his ground until victory for the principle of monarchic sovereignty was assured. Over eight years of tactical maneuvers, skillful diplomacy, and warfare followed, crowned by Bismarck's triumph over the forces that had struggled for a liberal Germany. He brought about the unification of Germany, placed the Hohenzollern on the throne of the emperor, and made Berlin the capital of the Second Reich. The issue of the army reform must, therefore, be considered one of the decisive conflicts of German history. As in 1819 and 1848, the country stood at the crossroads, and chose militarism over liberalism, authoritarianism over parliamentarianism, and nationalism over the respect for human rights.

Berlin was understandably the storm center of the struggle. It was the residence of the king and his minister as well as of the Prussian parliament. In moments of despondency the king predicted his execution on the Forum Fredericianum, after the manner of Charles I, of England. But Berlin was not London and the Prussian parliament was not the House of Commons. No Pym, no Hampden, no Sydney came forward to challenge the crown. The liberal deputies opposed Bismarck with words rather than deeds, and Bismarck's irony was only too pertinent when he told them that the great questions of history were solved not by parliamentary debate, but by "blood and iron."

The capital voted consistently for the liberal opposition. Addresses to support the deputies in their fight with Bismarck were drafted and were signed by as many as 40,000 citizens. Demonstrations against the prime minister occurred in the streets, and the city fathers resolved henceforth to ignore all events that concerned the royal family. Berlin, in short, was progressive and liberal. Nevertheless, the appeal to block the government's policy by means of a tax boycott was disregarded. Neither the Berliners nor the rest of Prussia dared to take the one step that might have halted Bismarck. The violation of the constitution, though denounced, did not move the people from legal dissent to active resistance. In retrospect, it would seem that the continued prosperity overshadowed the constitutional issue, and that the passions aroused by Bismarck's policy were not deeply rooted. Germany was again in the process of proving that revolution was alien to its habits of political behavior.[48]

When in 1864 Bismarck turned to the field of foreign policy and obtained in a short war the duchies of Schleswig and Holstein from Denmark, the mood of the population changed from passive resistance to open approval and acclamation. Two years later Bismarck provoked a military showdown between Austria and Prussia designed to solve the question of German leadership. The Austro-Prussian dualism ended on the battlefield of Königgrätz in July 1866 with the resounding victory of the Prussian army. This tended to confirm the wisdom of the government in its insistence on army reform.

The outcome of the so-called Seven Weeks' War caused many Germans to feel that their world was falling in pieces. This was especially true in Bavaria, Würtemberg, and Saxony, which had fought on Austria's side. Bismarck demanded no territorial concession from these three, but in the case of Hanover, the defeat was accepted with bitter resentment when Bismarck took the little state over as a Prussian province. For many years Germany had pondered the answer to the question of unification. Should it be the Little or the Great German solution? Now, and overnight, she had the answer: the fait accompli of the Great Prussian solution. All along, this had been the core of Bismarck's design, and he now strengthened his position by the incorporation into the Prussian realm, not alone of Hanover, but also of Schleswig-Holstein, a portion of Hesse, and the city of Frankfurt.

For the time being he was obliged to content himself with unifying the states north of the Main river, in order to avoid the intervention of Napoleon III. However, the North German Federation of 1867 was so constituted that other states could join the federation without difficulty. Furthermore, nonmembers were persuaded to enter a military alliance with the federation, thus sowing the seeds of a more perfect union.

It goes without saying that Berlin was not counted among those cities that mourned the defeat of the Austrian monarchy. The capital continued to vote the liberal ticket. Elections to the Prussian parliament were held on the day of Königgrätz, July 3. The liberal party throughout Prussia lost half its strength to the parties of the right; in Berlin, however, the progressives managed to keep the seats they had held before 1866.

But despite Berlin's adherence to its liberal convictions, the city could not escape the changing mood of the country as a whole. In Prussia as well as in Germany, liberalism had suffered a defeat. Although Bismarck extended the hand of reconciliation to the opposition when he asked for a retroactive approval of the illegal expenditures of 1862–1866, the bitter sting of failure continued to prick the liberal conscience. The party split over Bismarck's "indemnity law"; the progressives persisted in condemning the arbitrary rule of the great statesman, while the more national-minded formed a new party, the National-Liberals, who were willing to allow bygones to be bygones and to bow to the genius of the Iron Chancellor.[44] The indemnity bill was passed by 230 votes with an opposing vote of seventy-five. The constitutional conflict had run its course.

Berlin was now not only the capital of Prussia; it was also the capital of the North German Federation, the parliament of which convened in Berlin. This new assembly was to be elected on the basis of universal manhood suffrage, a revolutionary innovation for Germany and especially for Berlin. The election of February 12, 1867, characterized the mood of the city in continuing to vote the liberal ticket. The conservatives had expected to overwhelm the city by the resounding names of Bismarck, Moltke, and Roon, but none of the three was elected to the Reichstag in Berlin.

Bismarck's leadership and the advance of German unification were not to be halted by Berlin's protest vote, however. Between 1867 and 1871 the city witnessed the acceptance of a new constitution by the Reichstag which would eventually encompass all of Germany.

During the next year another kind of parliament made up of the representatives of the German Customs Union met in Berlin. Whereas the political unification of Germany was obliged to wait for an auspicious turn of events, the economic unification advanced with speed. Without doubt, the historian will interpret this fact as symptomatic of the dynamics of economic forces which more than any other factor account for the triumph of the German national movement. During the three years of its existence, the parliament passed a general tariff law for all of Germany and opened many doors to German trade in Central Europe and across the seas.[45] It might have been better for Germany and the world in general if the peaceful economic development had restricted itself to the nation and the consolidation of its gains. But history was writing another story, fulfilling Bismarck's words of February 23, 1868: "To attain with one blow a homogeneous structure for Germany is only possible in the event of war."[46] Although he refused to predict or to precipitate the event, he was quick to seize the opportunity presented to him in 1870, and provoked a war with France.

For the third time in eight years, the Prussian army proved its superiority in leadership, manpower, and equipment. It was a popular war, both in Paris and in Berlin. There is a fascinating painting from the brush of Adolf Menzel depicting King William I's departure for the front. It shows the old gentleman driving in an open carriage along Unter den Linden; the populace bows and cheers as he passes along the flag-lined street in the July heat. On September 1, 1870, Napoleon III surrendered at Sedan after a single month of resistance.

[3]

The Boom Years

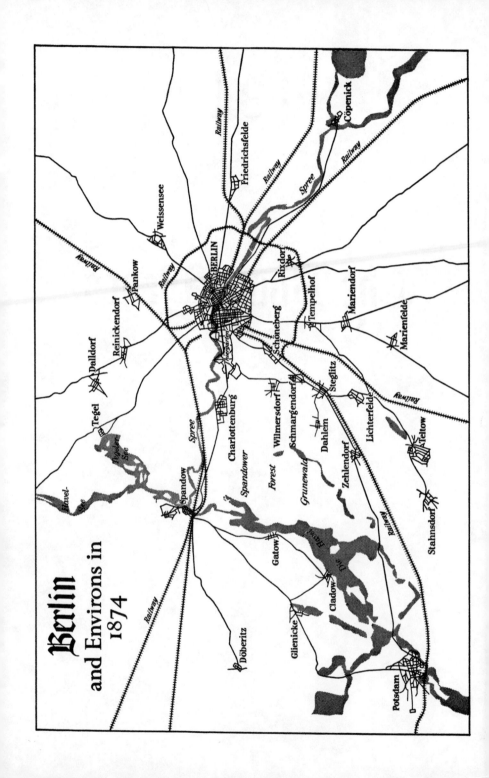

Berlin
and Environs in
1874

𝕿HE second German empire was forged in the heat of war and accompanied by the country's jubilation over triumphs such as Germany had not known for centuries. The Second Reich was a hybrid affair, the result of contradictory and conflicting forces. Although the empire was an answer to the ardent nationalism that had moved the German middle class since 1815, it was nevertheless the product of Bismarck's diplomatic genius and Moltke's strategic planning, and owed little to the people or their representatives.

The empire was officially proclaimed at the Royal Palace in Versailles on January 18, 1871, and the place chosen for the ceremony bespeaks the intoxication with victory which had seized Germany's leaders. That the new state was called into existence in the Gallery of Mirrors rather than at a constituent assembly in Berlin was to have tragic consequences. Its constitutional structure was, at best, a compromise between princely and popular sovereignty, an "insurance against democracy," as the social democrat, Liebknecht, called it. The German princes were to be represented in an upper house called the Bundesrat, in which Prussia had, if not the majority, at least the veto power. It was a replica of the old Bundestag, albeit transformed in a manner designed to correspond to the hegemony of Prussia in the new Reich. The Reichstag, elected on the basis of universal manhood suffrage, was to proclaim the will of the people, and its power rested on its right to debate and approve the annual budget. However, extraordinary provisions for military expenditures weakened the power of parliament from the start.[1] No ministerial responsibility was written into the constitution; in fact, only secretaries of state, subordinate to the chancellor, were designated.

59

This office was tailored to Bismarck's own ambitions and expectations; it was the "fulcrum of power," since the chancellor of the new Germany was usually the foreign minister and the prime minister of Prussia.[2] Only a man of Bismarck's ability would have been capable of shouldering this threefold responsibility with any degree of success, and even he became the victim of his own invention. The Reichstag could not vote the chancellor out of office, much less impeach him, but the emperor could dismiss him at pleasure, and this became William the Second's pleasure when he booted Bismarck out in 1890.

The head of the state was called the emperor, a title chosen by Bismarck for a variety of reasons. It appealed to the imagination of the people, who saw in this restoration of medieval splendor a promise of future greatness. The princes found it easier to acknowledge the leadership of a German emperor than that of the king of Prussia, though in reality, the bearer of the crown was both at the same time. But even here the constitution showed the stigma of compromise. The official title was not emperor of Germany, nor of the Germans, but simply German emperor. That the Hohenzollern would be called upon to wear the crown had been a foregone conclusion since 1866.

Thus the structure erected by Bismarck in 1871 combined some of the features of the Confederation of 1815 with the ideas of the Frankfurt constitution of 1849. It gratified and satisfied almost everyone who had believed such a synthesis to be well-nigh impossible. In the eyes of the Germans, Bismarck had accomplished nothing less than the squaring of the circle. There were few who realized, as did Ferdinand Tönnies, that the compromise between princely and popular sovereignty could not last, that the carefully worked out balance would have to yield in proportion to the amount of influence gained by the masses in an industrial society.

There were other aspects of German constitutional life where the unification solved some problems while creating a host of new ones. Bismarck had limited the power of the imperial government to bare essentials in order to avoid any infringement on the susceptibilities of the individual states. But the dynamic of social forces would, before long, call for more centralized power. In certain states, especially Prussia, the electoral system was at variance with the democratic method by which the German parliament was to be chosen. Bismarck saw these contradictions between German and Prussian voting laws very clearly, but he retained them because they suited his penchant for playing one element of power against another.[3]

In retrospect, the most glaring flaw of the German constitution of 1871 would seem to be the absence of a bill of rights. In the constitution of 1849 the bill of rights had figured prominently, but in the second empire the Germans as Germans had no "inaliena-ble human rights." German liberalism had been defeated by Bismarck in 1866 and was too weak to demand the incorporation of a bill of rights in the imperial constitution. The liberals were obliged to console themselves with some degree of unification in such matters as currency, weights and measures, consular representation, and civil law. In other words, liberalism was restricted to the economic activities of the new state.

German liberalism had sold its birthright for a mess of pottage; however, the reasons are not solely to be found in its own weakness, but rather in the strength of its opponents, namely the conservative forces. In the words of Otto Pflanze, Bismarck had amputated liberalism from nationalism and had compounded a new synthesis between "German nationalism, Prussian militarism, and Hohenzollern authoritarianism."[4]

Naturally, the classes and groups which embraced nationalism, militarism and authoritarianism were those who wished to reap the harvest of Bismarck's "revolution from above." The architects of German unification were all members of the aristocratic power structure—the king himself, Bismarck, von Roon, von Moltke, and so forth. As a result, the dynastic principle was given a new lease on life, and the Junker class, whose sons held the lead in diplomacy and the army, enjoyed a prestige far beyond its social usefulness in a time of growing industrialization. Germany's political system became that of a pseudoconstitutionalism (Max Weber); her social system became that of a class-society based on aristocratic privileges and caste prejudices.[5] Both the political formation and the social configuration might yield to the productive energies then pulsating in the German people or harden into an archaic neofeudalism. That Germany chose the latter alternative spelled her misfortune for which she and the world were to pay a heavy price.

The road Germany was to travel became apparent during the peace negotiations with France. The military arguments for the annexation of Alsace and Lorraine far outweighed any other consideration, and the annexation was made the condition sine qua non for peace. Bismarck was not greatly concerned over the fact that the people of Alsace and still more those of Lorraine were unwilling to become a part of the new Germany, and his attitude was heartily supported by such propagandists as Treitschke, who maintained that these people should be forced to admit the values of Germany's cultural superiority.[6]

The indemnity imposed on France is another case in point. The amount of five billion francs was perhaps no more than France was able to pay, but the manner in which this sum was distributed reflects once more the priority given to rank and class. Bismarck and the victorious generals received generous "donations," while the amounts earmarked for the pension funds of invalids, war widows, and orphans was limited.[7] However, it is not to be denied that it was the French indemnity, the "bliss of the billions," that transformed Berlin from a second-rate residential town into an industrial metropolis. Berlin lost no part of her image as the center of a victorious monarchy by this transformation; on the contrary, it retained all the bellicose trappings of uniforms, parades, and official glitter. But the officialdom of the second empire gradually superimposed itself on the older and more sober structure of the Prussian capital. Eventually the "Prussian style" disappeared under the onslaught of the new energies unleashed by imperial Germany. There were many who regretted the changes wrought on the face of Berlin by this transformation and who clamored for a return to the old days when life had been simple and its pleasures to be enjoyed at little cost. But their voices were raised to no avail.

The influx of five billion francs stimulated the economy to a fever pitch. Of course, the entire amount of the French indemnity did not reach Berlin nor did all of the money which came to Berlin remain there, but the greater part of it passed through the city and created in its path a hectic growth. The population continued its rapid increase, swelling from 657,690 in 1865 to 964,-240 in 1875. Whether such growth was the result of economic factors or of the magnetic attraction exercised by the imperial capital over the provinces is difficult to say. Whatever its cause, it produced a steady demand for goods and housing, and since money was plentiful, speculation flourished.

The channeling of the French money into the German economy has not yet been fully explored. Its arrival coincided with the end-phase of the great wave of prosperity that had swept Europe since 1850. It also coincided with the spread of economic liberalism to which the German empire adhered until 1879. By 1870 the government had abandoned its opposition to the establishment of joint stock companies. Special licenses were no longer required, and new companies came speedily into existence, among them the famous Deutsche Bank, founded in 1870 by a member of the enterprising Siemens family. From 1870 to 1872, 780 corporations were formed in Prussia alone, some of them being old enterprises transformed from privately owned companies into joint stock concerns. Where did the money come from to finance this rapid expansion?

The Franco-German war had been financed by Prussia and the south German states by means of war loans offered to the public, and the loans had been quickly oversubscribed. When the war ended and the French reparations began to come in, the governments hastened to repay the loans, assuming the attitude of the penurious paterfamilias who does not wish to burden his budget with debts. The general public had purchased their war loans with money drawn from their savings accounts, but after the war this type of safe investment was largely abandoned. The Germans, and especially the Berliners, were caught up in a speculative fever. Everyone figured he had been born with a silver spoon in his mouth which his mother had failed somehow to mention and which he now hastened to retrieve.[8] There was a general belief that the military victory would be followed by an economic victory on the home front which would make everyone rich overnight. Money in circulation increased rapidly, and the interest rate fell from 5 to 3 percent. Under such circumstances the psychological mood of the famous Gründerjahre was born, eventually giving the name to the entire period following the foundation of the German empire. The appellation stood for wild speculation, ostentatious behavior of the upper classes, and materialistic thinking and acting by almost everyone—attitudes which appalled the

finer grained minds such as Friedrich Nietzsche and Jacob Burckhardt.

The stock exchange was the natural and principal vehicle in
this drive to acquire wealth in a hurry. Berlin had been a poor
city with ingrained habits of thrift and modesty; now it gloried
in its new affluence. Large and small investors alike rushed to lay
out their funds in real estate, railways, construction firms, banks
and insurance companies, metal works, and breweries.

The participation of banks in launching and liquidating the
war loans, the increase in trading at the stock exchange, and the
financing of new corporations made Berlin the financial capital
of Germany, replacing Frankfurt am Main, which had been the
predominant money market until 1866. Financial power followed
the drift of political power, thus increasing the trend toward centralization and causing a chain reaction. Financial power logically
attracted industrial enterprises, some of which transferred their
headquarters to Berlin, and others set up new forms of manufacturing whose seat would be in Berlin. The speculative fever
that gripped Berlin was accompanied by an amazing increase in
industrial productivity which some writers believe to have been
as high as 15 percent annually during the first years of the empire.
One might say that the Gründerjahre were akin to a children's
disease, a malady which most capitalistic countries have suffered
during their years of growth. The Mississippi Bubble and the
South Sea Bubble give evidence of this in France and England.
Obviously, the workers did not and could not partake in the speculative boom, since their savings, if any, were small, but all other
classes, from the aristocracy down to the lower-middle class,
jumped on the bandwagon.

Entrepreneurial talents were, as yet, scarce among the Germans,
and it was only natural that promoters played a large role in this
precipitous growth of the German economy. Among them could
be counted a fair number of Jews. One man especially has been
singled out as the culprit in promoting and peddling fraudulent
companies: Henry Bethel Strousberg.[9] Son of a Jewish merchant
from East Prussia, he had specialized in the financing of railroads
in Prussia, Russia, and Rumania. Along the way, he assembled a
huge fortune consisting of country estates, factories, mines, and
a town house at the Wilhelmstrasse in Berlin sufficiently elegant

to accommodate the British Embassy some years later. In 1873 Strousberg's empire collapsed, and his downfall brought the post-war prosperity to an end. The Germans were only too eager to make him the scapegoat for the crash which followed and which ruined many investors. He defended himself in an autobiography, maintaining that promotion on a grand scale was not only beneficial but necessary.[10] He might have added that the crash was inevitable in any case, since the business cycle had run its course, not alone in Berlin, but in London, Vienna, and St. Petersburg as well.

The Strousberg debacle produced the first wave of anti-Semitism in the new Germany. Ironically enough, Strousberg was made the principal culprit not only by professional Jew-baiters, but also by some of the Jewish liberals, Eduard Lasker for one, who accused him of being the prime instigator of the short-lived boom. In a long speech in the Prussian parliament, Lasker attacked Strousberg and also denounced high-ranking aristocrats and bureaucrats who had hoped to gain from the speculation in railway stocks.[11] Among them was a certain Prince Putbus who henceforth was dubbed Prince Capútbus by the Berliners. Bismarck was seriously concerned about the involvement of the Prussian nobility in the railway speculation and commissioned his private banker, Gerson von Bleichröder, to disentangle the Strousberg affair. In his speech, Lasker had condemned not so much Strousberg and his associates as the system which, in his words, led to fraudulent manipulations of stocks, tax evasion, and the cheating of small investors who were unfamiliar with the fine points of playing the market.[12] Much of his criticism was justified and led to a reform of the corporation law.

As far as the city of Berlin was concerned, the most striking aspect of the speculative furor was the rise in the price of real estate. There seemed to be an inexhaustible market for houses with high rents yielding annual incomes well above those of industrial dividends. In consequence, realtors, mortgage banks, and building contractors had a heyday. The small investor was easily lured into laying out his money on enterprises which looked solid enough on paper, but soon crumbled when money became scarce or when overproduction led to a drop in rents. In spite of the loss of such investments, however, the more affluent and experienced investor, realizing that setbacks may be seasonal or transitory, weathered the moment and set his eyes on the continued prospects for a steep rise in real estate and building activities.

The particular situation of Berlin and its relation to the surrounding countryside was responsible for the prolongation of profitable investment in real estate. In 1871 the German capital was still restricted to a rather small area; the city limits had been marked by a wall some six yards high and by gates where revenue officials collected duties on meat and flour.[13] This relic of the absolute state lasted into the 1860's, when the wall was finally removed and the tax abolished. In the meantime, the outlying districts, Schöneberg, Friedenau, Wilmersdorf, Charlottenburg, and Westend, had preserved much of their rural character. They were still villages, given over to dairy farming, or they were country estates, a curious circumstance considering their proximity to the German capital. It was on these regions that the speculators concentrated.

Thus Berlin grew not according to judicious urban planning, but indiscriminately, in a helter-skelter manner, and showed it only too clearly. There were a few, like the English-trained merchant, J. A. W. Carsten, who had experimented with one-family developments in Hamburg and who hoped to accomplish something similar for Berlin. He bought the estate of Lichterfelde, still officially listed as *Rittergut*, and proceeded to develop it into a colony of "villas," as they were called by the Berliners. Carsten had interested von Roon and Bismarck in his projects and had even gained the ear of the old emperor. "Your Majesty," he said, "after the achievements of 1866, Berlin is called upon to become the first city of the continent. Berlin and Potsdam must grow to form one great city connected through one great park, the Grunewald."[14] Such planning involved, of course, much more than the construction of buildings. There were streets to be laid out and paved, trees to be planted, water and gaslight to be brought into the districts, and communication by rail or horse-drawn cars to be secured. Small wonder that Carsten overextended himself and incurred stiff opposition from the narrow-minded Prussian bureaucracy, who sabotaged his plans at every step.

But Carsten's conception of Berlin as the first city of the continent impressed even so sober a man as Bismarck, who also dreamed that Berlin would one day surpass, or at least, equal the French capital. He gave expression to his hopes in a memorandum in which he stated that Berlin should have an avenue like the Champs Elysées connecting the Tiergarten with the Grunewald, in the same way that the center of Paris was linked with the Bois de Boulogne.[15] This would have to be the Kurfürstendamm, a carter's road that connected Halensee with the most western portions of old Berlin. But, as is well known, the Kurfürstendamm never quite made it. When it was finally completed and paved, it was only half as wide as its Parisian model and had no such glorious perspectives as the Place de la Concorde or the Place d'Étoile. Instead, at one end stood a railway station, and at the other a romanesque church, built by the Kaiser, the Kaiser Wilhelm Gedächtnis Kirche, one of the few buildings to be improved by the fall of bombs and the ravage of fire.

Berlin's expansion did not follow an architect's blueprint; it was rather the result of capitalistic foresight and cunning. Promoters, mortgage banks, and private entrepreneurs bought up large sections of Schöneberg, Wilmersdorf, and Grunewald, and developed them when the time seemed to be right. The profits from such speculations were nothing less than fantastic; in some instances prices rose to 600 percent above the amount of purchase.[16] A new type of the nouveau riche came into existence, the peasant millionaire, who became a popular figure in novels and musicals. Many of these farm owners continued to live in their old homes, selling only the potato fields and the pasture lands. But their sons became dandies and their daughters set their caps for the young men of the ruling class, an army officer if possible, or, at the very least, a public official.[17] Some feeble attempts to organize building activities on a cooperative basis were made, as for instance, the *Deutscher Zentralbauverein*, which contemplated the building of modest family homes in Westend, but, like many others, was transformed into a joint stock company and became a victim of the crash.

The expectations of the realtors and contractors were as extravagant as their profits; in fact, the one constantly stimulated the other. It was believed that Berlin would one day house a population of nine million people, a dream that fortunately was never realized. Of the fifty odd construction firms that had sprung up during the boom years, a mere seven survived the year 1873.

It would be a mistake, however, to think that the end of the boom jeopardized the steady growth of the capital. In addition to the building of dwellings, the city was faced by a number of other municipal tasks of a pressing nature. The construction of an adequate sewer system was one of them. Even some of the elegant streets, such as the Leipzigerstrasse, were serviced by sewer tanks which were emptied at night by brigades of women, leaving the streets filled with appalling odors.[18] A central market, after the order of the Paris Halles, was urgently needed to replace the primitive open markets scattered about the city. When the central market was finally built, in a location near the Alexanderplatz, great store houses were erected in the vicinity, and this in turn made the expansion of the communication system and its link with the railway system, already in existence, a necessity. Street-cars, drawn by horses, but run on rails, connected the inner city with Westend and Charlottenburg. An "elevated" called the *Ringbahn* which still provides transportation in divided Berlin was begun and completed in 1877.

In keeping with the spirit of economic liberalism, the great wave of speculation left the working-class section untouched, since the workers could not afford the high rents that alone guaranteed high profits. We have already noted that housing conditions among the working class left much to be desired even before the founding of the empire. The steady influx of labor from the provinces into Berlin after 1871 did not improve matters. Most of the workers came from the rural areas of East Elbia and were attracted both by the multitude of jobs and by the relatively high wages paid by industry. Neither the state nor the municipal authorities, however, made any effort to cope with the housing problem that ensued. A room or rooms might be found in the housing barracks already mentioned, but frequently the quarters had to accommodate more than one family. Many were obliged to be content with damp and unhealthy basement rooms. More than 100,000 people lived in these "basement apartments," actually dungeons, which produced sicknesses of all kinds from rheumatism to tuberculosis. Sanitary arrangements were completely inadequate, and the overcrowded rooms allowed for no separation of the sexes, a situation that led to incest, illegitimacy, and venereal disease.[19] In certain cases, whether from motives of greed or compassion, a family would take in some homeless unfortunate and allow him to bed himself down at night in a corner of the room. This custom continued in Berlin for many decades (*Schlafburschen*, or sleep-ins). Many there were who either could not find such accommodations, or could not afford them, and were obliged to live in makeshift huts outside the city limits. One such settlement was located in eastern Berlin and gave refuge to forty-two families. But the police considered these working-class colonies a nuisance and against regulations. When ordered to abandon their habitations, the workers resisted and were then driven out by force of arms.[20] The bloody riots which followed sent a shudder of fear down the spines of the propertied classes; the mutter of the Paris Commune was all too fresh in their ears. Following the riots, the homeless workers took refuge in the city asylums or slept in hallways from which they were routed and often shipped to correction centers.

The eastern and northern sections of Berlin remained for years the home of the working class. It was symbolic that the headquarters of the police (*Das Polizeipräsidium*) were located at the fringe of these sections of the city, at the Alexanderplatz, leading into the great conglomeration of factories and working-class slums. Here were the hideouts of criminals and prostitutes. Jacob Wassermann and Alfred Döblin have tried to capture the weird atmosphere of this region in novel form. Other European capitals were also guilty of capitalistic exploitation, and to the same appalling degree. An industrial economy shifting into high gear has many byproducts, and among them are the segregation and degradation of the working classes.

The appearance of a metropolitan press was another feature of the boom years. Berlin had enjoyed newspapers prior to the founding of the empire, but they were politically oriented and supported by the parties, such as they were. The *Kreuzzeitung* appealed to conservative tastes; the *Volkszeitung* was the people's journal and appealed to liberal voters. The freedom of the press was severely curtailed during the period of reaction, and in consequence liberal papers had hard sledding in their struggle for survival. With the foundation of the empire prospects brightened. A new press law came under discussion as early as 1871 and was enacted in 1874. It exempted the newspapers from the stamp tax (*Stempelsteuer*) which the reactionary governments had used to curb the power of the press. A generation of bright young men sensed the economic potential that dailies would have in a rapidly growing metropolis and ventured to exploit it. They addressed themselves to certain interest groups in society and catered to the taste of various sectors. Technical inventions, such as the telegraph, telephone, and railway, not to mention linotyping and photography, facilitated the appearance of a new type of newspaper. Advertising became the financial backbone of all newspapers except those which had the support of powerful pressure groups. The founders of Berlin's new type of daily were competitors for the advertising market and were all shrewd entrepreneurs, like Rudolf Mosse, Leopold Ullstein, and August Scherl. Their enterprises were run as family concerns, or, as in Scherl's case, as a one-man show.[21]

Rudolf Mosse was the first to capitalize on the economic possibilities Berlin offered. He launched the *Berliner Tageblatt* in 1871, with the following announcement: "At a time when the eyes of the world look toward Berlin, we present to the public the *Berliner Tageblatt*. The capital of Prussia has become the capital of Germany; the royal city of Prussia, the imperial city of Germany. As Paris . . . was France, so Berlin will and must become Germany, a metropolis, a world city. . . . We must be inspired by the thought that he who writes for Berlin, writes for the civilized world."[22] This ambitious program was not without foundation, and the *Berliner Tageblatt* became one of the most respected voices of German liberalism, maintaining its position up to the days of the Third Reich.

In 1878, Leopold Ullstein, a merchant and a member of the Berlin City council, started the *Berliner Zeitung*. A year later the ubiquitous Henry Strousberg tried his hand at journalism with the *Kleine Journal*. There was also the *Germania*, representing the opinion of the Catholic party, the *Tägliche Rundschau*, and scores of others. In 1883, August Scherl surprised the capital with a different type of paper, the *Berliner Lokalanzeiger*. It was a daily that refrained from expressing any particular political ideology but set out with no scruples or inhibitions to woo the masses. A clever publicity stunt initiated its appearance: every inhabitant listed in the Berlin city directory was to receive the issues free for a certain number of days. Advertisers were attracted by lower rates than those charged by Mosse or Ullstein. The paper concentrated on sensational reports of crime and scandal and introduced the installment publication of novels, which were geared to the sentimentality of lower-middle-class women readers, who consumed them faithfully each day. Scherl started a trend which neither Mosse nor Ullstein could ignore. A paper with mass appeal and mass circulation with no apparent political commitments appeared to be the answer to the economic problems of the newspaper business whether in Berlin, London, or elsewhere. Ullstein copied Scherl's model in the *Berliner Morgenpost* and competed for the same type of subscribers.

It became clear that newspapers had become big business. Eventually Ullstein and Scherl agreed not to undercut each other's publications, a course that was in keeping with the German trend toward trusts and cartels. The three great Berlin papers were located in the heart of the city and separated from each other by only a few blocks. The Zeitungsviertel was Berlin's Fleet Street.

It is sociologically revealing that the three enterprises were still quite conscious of their obligations to the educated middle class. The "feuilleton" played a large role in the make-up of all dailies; drama and music criticism appeared prominently and were of high quality. Ullstein and Scherl went so far as to publish prestige papers which were not remunerative and existed on the profits of the dailies. Such a publication was the *Vossische Zeitung*, one of the oldest Berlin papers, bought by Ullstein and maintained till the advent of Hitler. For his part, Scherl put out *Der Tag*, which addressed its editorial comments to the well-informed upper classes. There were also journals for the stockbroker and the banker; there was a noonday paper, the *Berliner Zeitung am Mittag*; there were evening papers and tabloids. Each of the great trusts had its own satirical weekly, and these enjoyed considerable popularity in Berlin. With the advancement of photography, illustrated weeklies began to appear; Scherl published *Die Woche*, Ullstein *Die*

Berliner Illustrierte Zeitung. Between 1867 and 1895, the number of daily, weekly, and monthly publications in Berlin more than tripled.[23]

It should be noted that the working classes did not have a paper of distinction. At first, the social democrats were greatly hampered by the restrictions imposed on them by the so-called socialist law. But even after it was lifted in 1890, the socialist press remained lifeless and dogmatic. Its principal publication was *Der Vorwärts* appearing in 1891 and directed first by Wilhelm Liebknecht and later by the hapless Kurt Eisner. Other distinguished social democrats wrote for it as well: Friedrich Engels, Karl Kautsky, Franz Mehring, and Eduard Bernstein. Although most of the card-carrying social democrats subscribed to *Der Vorwärts,* their women folk preferred the *Morgenpost* or the *Lokalanzeiger,* where they were sure to find the latest court gossip, or the most recent divorce scandal, together with many other juicy tidbits and the tear-jerking novel "to be continued." The socialist leaders were quite aware that *Vorwärts* lacked mass appeal and conceded that it was written by Marxists for Marxists, but they were not able to free themselves from their shackles.[24]

However, it would be a mistake to assume that the social-democratic press was alone in being stifled by pressure from the powers above. William II was not altogether wrong when he wrote to his uncle, Edward VII: "The press is abominable on both sides, but here it has no influence (*hier hat sie nichts zu sagen*), because I am the only master of German politics."[25] Liberal and even conservative papers were severely penalized when they opposed the strong-willed Bismarck, who, in the words of the *Berliner Zeitung,* treated the Germans like "a conquered nation".[26] In 1879 the regiments of the guards were forbidden to read the liberal journals. Frequently entire issues were confiscated. But the most harassing administrative measure was the persecution of the editorial staff of the liberal papers. Under various pretexts and disguises, fines were levied on them, and a number of journalists served jail sentences for nothing more incriminating than voicing the unrest caused by the iron rule of the Prussian government. This was especially true in the 1880's, when the socialist law was in force, and the liberal press took it upon itself to defend the outlawed party against the oppressive practices applied by the government to crush the working class. At this time the press was muzzled, every criticism was considered lèse majesté or a crime against the state and Bismarck was only too willing to construe a political attack as slander or as a personal insult, or both. The public prosecutor (*Staatsanwalt*) for his part tried to outdo the chancellor and initiated proceedings against the editors, threatening them with long prison terms.

Even after the repeal of the socialist law, the press was never as free in Berlin as it was in France or in the Anglo-Saxon countries. This may explain why the German metropolitan press remained somewhat provincial, and why it never had a newspaper that ranked with the *London Times*, or *The New York Times*, or *Figaro*. In spite of their numbers, the Berlin newspapers could not speak with an authoritative voice for all of Germany.

The results of the Gründerjahre for Berlin are not easily summarized. The working-class sections in the north, east, and south expanded as rapidly as the west, where the middle class and the upper bourgeoisie had their dwellings. Great enterprises like Siemens and Halske, and the Borsig Works were obliged to move out of the city proper and build new factories on cheap terrain. Siemens thought it wise to provide housing for its workers and founded Siemensstadt. The old thoroughfares such as Leipzigerstrasse and Friedrichstrasse lost their character as residential streets and became shopping centers for the well-to-do. Other parts of Berlin were swallowed up by the garment industry which became one of the most important branches of manufacturing in Berlin.[27]

Like the second empire which was a finely balanced compromise between the old and the new, the capital itself also showed a dual profile. Its rapid growth was paid for by a lack of unity and style. Only Unter den Linden and the Wilhelmstrasse preserved the sober elegance of the Prussian taste. The sections around the Tiergarten still clung to the slow rhythm in which Berlin had moved before she became an imperial city. Here lived the university professors and the high bureaucracy who enjoyed the half-hour walk to their classrooms or their offices. Both apartment houses and villas were to be found in Der alte Westen, as the section was called, and many of the more conservative millionaires who resisted the lure of the Grunewald had their homes here.

Zoning laws were not unduly strict, and many apartment houses accommodated cobblers, tailors, or grocery stores in their basements or on their ground floors. The Old West preserved some of the charm of the Biedermeier period in its peaceful streets. Many antique dealers had their shops nearby where strollers came in to admire, to touch, and perhaps to buy, and all of this produced an atmosphere of leisure and contentment.[28]

The new west had its center in Schöneberg and Charlottenburg, and the sumptuous Kurfürstendamm was its axis. Houses were the exception here and apartments the rule. Christopher Isherwood remarked that it was a section where one could find "all styles in cheap and expensive ugliness." Architects were brushed aside, and the contractors who put up the apartments reveled in the exercise of their own ideas. "Here is an Assyrian temple beside a patrician mansion from Nuremberg; a bit further on is a glimpse of Versailles, then memories of Broadway, of Italy, of Egypt—terrible abortions of a polytechnical beer-imagination."[29] It was a hodge-podge of all periods and styles and, as one critic said, gave clear evidence of its colonial origin. It had not grown, but had been taken over by newcomers without roots or traditions. Usually the buildings were constructed of brick which was then covered with a veneer of plaster or stucco. From this background, protruded arches, balconies, columns, and any other kind of ornament that the contractor considered elegant or beautiful. Walter Rathenau called it "Chicago on the Spree"; many considered it the most American of all the European cities. It was the nouveau riche capital, and the capital, to be sure, of the nouveau riche. But Rathenau, who was himself an industrialist, could not fail to see that Berlin was also well on its way to becoming one of the greatest manufacturing centers of Europe. The great plants, with their whirring machinery, their smokestacks, their warehouses, docks, branch railway lines, were to be found in Tempelhof, Wedding, Kreuzberg, Treptow, Rixdorf, and made up, as Rathenau said, "the city that nobody knows." Later in this book, we will make its acquaintance.

The architectural decadence of Berlin reflects the inner tension which gripped Germany and its capital. Granting this, one views the Gründerjahre more as a symptom than a cause. The crash of 1873 neither ended nor arrested Germany's industrial expansion. It can only be maintained that it slowed Germany down for a few

years and forced her into a process of restriction and readjustment
from which she emerged with undiminished energies. The period
has been called "the great depression of the Bismarck era," but if
it was a depression, it had some distinctly unique features. Although
prices dropped, wages remained stable and increased in purchasing
power.[30] Both management and labor, though fighting each other
in the political arena, found ways whereby they could adjust and
conform to changed conditions. Once the crash had been absorbed,
the wage earners were no worse off than they had been before.

These years of wild and undisciplined speculation had, never-
theless, a deep-reaching psychological effect on Germany and on
Berlin. We have noted that the small investors suffered more than
others when the bubble burst. These blamed the Jewish promoters
for their losses, and anti-Semitism, always an undercurrent in
German history, again became virulent. In this renewal of anti-
Semitism, even Bismarck was accused of being "owned by the
Jews and the promoters."[31]

Another favorite target of the anti-Semites was the "Jewish
press." A large portion of the liberal press was Jewish-owned,
and many of the writers on the editorial staffs were Jews, but the
influence wielded by these papers was blown out of all proportion
by their opponents. Anti-Semitism must be regarded as one of
the elements of the reaction against liberalism which came to the
fore after 1873. It was a movement in which Catholic and Protestants, conservatives and socialists could and did join. Certain
German intellectuals—Konstantin Frantz, Rudolf Meyer, Paul de
Lagarde—provided the fighting slogans.[32] Liberalism was declared
a conspiracy, the gray international as distinct from the red international; it had neither roots nor fatherland and was "the greatest
danger to any nation."

Political liberalism had been defeated by Bismarck in 1866;
now economic liberalism came under attack. It was held responsible for the losses sustained by the investors, big or small, during
the recession, and it was thought to be nothing more than a
convenient cover for the Jews to gain control of the German
economy. "For the sewer of speculations and the influence of the
stock-exchange, the world has to thank the Jews."[33] Germany
turned her back on the doctrines of laisser aller and laisser faire
and prepared herself for an economy that could prosper behind the

walls of protective tariffs and social legislation. In vain did the liberal journals argue that it was the investor's own greed and not the stock exchange that had brought about their losses. The pot was still calling the kettle black.[34]

The change from a liberal to a conservative economic policy was six years in gestation and came into being in 1879. It presents a complicated picture. The master mariner who charted the course of German events, Bismarck, decided to ride the tide of liberalism with an eye on his own goals. Then he launched a three-pronged attack. Industry and agriculture stood in fear of foreign competition, and Bismarck consented to the introduction of protective tariffs to assuage their apprehensions. Simultaneously, the "socialist law" was passed, its intention being to break the political power of the workers and to make them once more a docile tool of the ruling classes. As a compensation to the workers for the loss of their political aspirations, he brought before the Reichstag comprehensive social legislation guaranteeing the worker old-age pensions as well as invalid and sickness insurance. It was the first state insurance of this kind to be enacted in Europe, and one of the most enlightened acts of the new Germany.

But Bismarck's complex program, understanding though it was, fell short of his expectations. The socialist law failed to destroy the social-democratic party; instead, it drew the different factions together and strengthened their belief in the Marxian principle that class struggle was unavoidable and that it would lead inevitably to the triumph of the proletariat. The law united the working class and energized union power as the economic backbone of labor.

It was soon apparent that neither stick nor carrot would work. The social legislation failed to convince the persecuted workers, who realized that the intention of the government and the ruling classes was to keep them quiet. They looked upon the state as a "Junker-bourgeois conspiracy" designed to keep labor muzzled and subservient by means of paltry hand-outs which were scarcely an answer to their substantial grievances. The policy of protective tariffs alone proved successful, providing German economy with a shield behind which it continued to expand at an amazing rate.[35]

"Neomercantilism" appealed to the deep-rooted habits and traditions of a people who had been accustomed to state authority and who had never adjusted themselves to the interplay of free enterprise and free competition. The drift toward "collective protectionism" propelled the economy forward.[36] In Berlin the crash was soon forgotten in a new wave of prosperity. A few facts and figures will serve to establish our point.

Berlin's industrial expansion was not confined to one or two interests. There was a great diversity in both goods and activities. Ludwig Loewe, who had specialized in arms and ammunitions, opened a factory for machine tools, emulating an American model. In 1873 the first sleeping car was put into service between Berlin and Ostende. Also in 1873, a company for the production of aniline was founded which was later absorbed by the dye trust (I. G. Farben). A year later, the German minister for post and telegraph, Heinrich Stephan, organized the international postal association to which twenty-two countries adhered.[37]

In 1875, Berlin's industrialists began to close ranks. The cloth manufacturers set up an association to watch over their interests, and this was soon followed by an association to watch over the interests of the chemical industry. A central organization of the entire German industrial management seemed essential. When it was drawn up, it was known as Der Zentralverband deutscher Industrieller. In 1879, the merchants and industrialists of Berlin founded their own corporation. In the same year the moving-van and storage companies established their organization. Their growth was a symptom of the rapidly increasing mobility among the Germans and the Berliners in particular. Siemens experimented with electric trains, and electric lighting of the streets was introduced. In 1880, telephones were set up in Berlin for 200 subscribers. It is evident, without further enumeration, that Berlin was well on her way to becoming the industrial center of the continent. Her next step was to catch up with London and Paris in international finance.

Among Berlin banking establishments were certain older credit banks, such as the Disconto Gesellschaft and the Handelsgesellschaft, and these had contributed greatly to the industrial growth. Side by side with these anonymous firms were the smaller banks that were run as family enterprises. During the boom years the house of Bleichröder was outstanding.

The Bleichröder bank had been founded in Berlin in 1803. In 1830, it established connections with the all-powerful Rothschilds. It was one of the Rothschilds who had called Bismarck's attention to the abilities of Gerson Bleichröder, and Bismarck had made him his financial advisor and assistant when he rose to power in Prussia. Bleichröder helped Bismarck to prevail in the financial crisis during the years of the army conflict when the government operated without a parliament-approved budget, and Bleichröder was also instrumental in supplying capital for the war of 1866. Small wonder then that Bismarck entrusted him with the transfer of the French indemnity—and with the investment of his personal fortune. Both men profited from this alliance. Bleichröder was knighted and Bismarck had the satisfaction of knowing that he had at his side a man who understood the intricacies of the international money market and could be relied on to carry out complicated financial transactions with discretion and probity.[38]

There were other talents among the Berlin banking establishments. Carl Fürstenberg learned his trade in Bleichröder's organization prior to becoming the wizard of German industrial financing, as famous for his economic foresight as for his witticisms which were repeated throughout Berlin. Many private banks weathered the storm with unscathed reputations: Mendelssohn, Delbrück-Schickler, and others. But there were an equal number of fly-by-night operations which succumbed in 1873. The crash proved to be a rather healthy weeding out of the weaker and shakier institutions. The growth of Berlin banking firms was thereby not delayed, but, on the contrary, was given new impetus by the replacement of private bankers and brokers with larger and more powerful companies. The origins of these institutions were often revealed in their names—the Darmstaedter Bank, the Dresdener Bank—but they had all gravitated to Berlin as the natural center of activities in the new Germany. Their headquarters were in old Berlin, not far from Unter den Linden. Here too was the newly created Reichsbank, the older Prussian State Bank, and, of course, the Stock Exchange. This banking sector, the Bankenviertel, was fully as important to metropolitan Berlin as the newspaper or garment industry centers. Most of the great banks opened branch offices in the various districts of the sprawling city. These were important in facilitating business activities, but also provided

Berliners with a handy means of depositing their salaries. The banks were considered sound, and the citizens had complete faith in them. Until 1931, no large bank was to fail. The Darmstaedter Bank became the first casualty of the great depression.

It would appear inevitable that sooner or later the leaders of the banking establishments would be drawn into the policy-making circle. As Germany became ever more imperialistic, as she acquired colonies and her overseas investments accumulated, the council of bankers became more influential, and such names as Dernburg, Helfferich, Rathenau, and von Gwinner became important.

To this new element in Berlin, another must be noted to complete the picture. Since the Reichstag met in Berlin, it was only natural that the parties had their headquarters there. At the beginning of the second empire, the German regard for nobility and power was reflected in the parties. Out of 357 Reichstag deputies, no less than 147, or 40 percent, were of noble descent.[39] There had been no adequate building to house the German parliament, and after much delay, a new one was commissioned. It was begun in 1884 and completed in 1894 by Paul Wallot, and was situated at the Königsplatz, the huge square where a column of victory had been erected to celebrate the German triumph over France. Across the Königsplatz from the Reichstag were the headquarters of the German general staff, and the proximity of military might and popular representation seemed symbolic of modern Germany's power structure.

The Reichstag building occupied a large, four-cornered space and was overloaded with baroque decoration including a tower-like construction at each corner.[40] Berlin edifices tended toward the monumental, in keeping with the nationalistic feeling of boastful pride. Over the entrance in letters of gold was the inscription: "To the German People" (*Dem Deutschen Volke*). The German people, however, had no great love for either the building or the activities inside it.

The offices and conference rooms of the parties were located in the Reichstag, and the agents of the new pressure groups in industry and agriculture were often in evidence. The interests of industry and agriculture did not always coincide, but after the turn to collective protectionism, they became closely allied. Bismarck frowned on the parties and their organization; their

79

growing power and their interference in governmental business irritated him and he occasionally toyed with the idea of moving the Reichstag to some small provincial town where it would not be subject to the pressures of party politics. But circumstances gave him no opportunity to carry out his idea.

Most of Germany's legislation was the result of the "Junker-bourgeois" coalition, representing an economic nationalism which soon equalled the military and political nationalism responsible for the unification.[41] The pressure groups produced a new type of politician, the liaison officer, who kept the economic associations informed in regard to the projects of the bureaucracy and the mood of the parties. The Central Association of German Industrialists (Der Zentralverband deutscher Industrieller), the Federation of Agrarians (Der Bund der Landwirte), and the Federation of Farmers (Der deutscher Bauernbund) became powerful lobbies in imperial Germany. Many trained bureaucrats left government service for more lucrative positions, attracted by the higher pay and the greater economic opportunities offered by the booming economy. Actually such individuals were ideally suited for the position of go-between, and no amount of public criticism could halt their activities. On the other hand, there were young politicians who rose from being representatives of pressure groups to being duly accredited members of the Reichstag—Gustav Streseman, for instance, who was a board member of powerful companies, but continued to maintain his seat in the Reichstag.[42]

Suitable quarters were found for these new associations either along Unter den Linden or in the Old West, sections of the city which were also undergoing great changes. As the surrounding countryside was swallowed up by the promoters, just so were large portions of old Berlin altered beyond recognition. A fine eighteenth-century house in patrician style rubbed shoulders with a department store.

It must be admitted that the facilities offered by old Berlin were no longer adequate. The Prussian State Library's reading room accommodated no more than forty readers. Eventually it was replaced by a monumental palace, since the Kaiser cherished such signs of pomp and circumstance, but it disrupted the elegant lines of the Forum Fredericianum. The great economic organizations—banks, associations, etc.—preferred the style of the Italian

Renaissance palace and combined elements of the Palazzo Strozzi with those of the Farnese. The Berliners failed to be impressed and had their own names for these creations.

Certain parts of the city escaped the frenetic energy of the promoters. The cemeteries, embedded in various sectors of the town, remained untouched, and the graves of Hegel, Fichte, Ranke, or Scharnhorst could still be visited by those who had a longing for the past. Most cemeteries were denominational—Lutheran, Catholic, or Jewish—and the Jews called them "the good place," from which they could not be expelled. Here were the resting places of men like Bleichröder or the physician, Wolfgang Strassmann, who had risen to become deputy to the Prussian Landtag and president of the city council of Berlin.[43]

Like most great cities, Berlin had its paradoxes and contradictions. One thing, however, was clear: a new type of society had emerged from the ferment of the Gründerjahre.

"Essential for the state is a capital-city to act as a pivot for its culture," said Heinrich von Treitschke, and he continued, "No great nation can endure for long without a center where its political, intellectual, and material life is concentrated, and its people can feel united."[44] Even though Treitschke admitted that the Berliner was the most insupportable figure in all of Germany, he still insisted that Berlin must increase in population and must draw the national forces into its orbit. Others had argued that Hamburg or Frankfurt am Main were better suited by their location to become the capital of Germany, but Berlin remained the first city of the new empire until its downfall.

We have taken note of some of the material changes wrought by the transition from royal to imperial city. Now let us consider their effect on Berlin society.

[4]

Berlin Society

𝕴 INTRODUCE here the term *society* with a certain amount of trepidation. The word is ambiguous and its connotations vary according to context. It is used to describe local as well as national and supranational communities. It may identify the economic forces determining the structure of a given organization, or the prestige which certain groups command in a community. Its concept finds expression in a multitude of facets in human life from fashion and sports to occupations and professions, from the monotonous occurrences of daily life to the convulsions of revolutionary processes.

If we plan to go beyond the superficial impressions evoked by the word society, we must keep this bewildering variety of meanings in mind. In one way or another all societies are hierarchical, although the criterion establishing and maintaining these hierarchies may differ from age to age and environment to environment. In the case of Berlin, we observe a further complication when we note that the monarchical, aristocratic, and military structure of the city had been invaded by an industrial order geared to capitalistic development. As a result, the society of Berlin evidenced many contradictory features. To be sure, Berlin is not the only example of such a social change during this period, but nowhere do we find the realignment so pronounced. "Upper class good; middle class not very good; lower class very good," such was the judgment of a Czech visitor to Berlin in Fontane's *Stechlin*.[1] Today we may not agree with this evaluation of Berlin's three classes, and ask for a more explicit differentiation. However, it may be as well to use it as a starting point.

The upper class was aristocratic and militaristic and was centered in the dynasty and the court. The Hohenzollern rulers who occupied the throne from 1871 to 1918 represent three generations, but the hapless Frederick III ruled for only ninety-nine days, and we must, therefore, focus our attention on William I and on his grandson, William II.

The older William was a typical product of his Prussian upbringing, an officer and a gentleman. His outlook on life was militaristic and conservative, but he was also an aristocrat who preferred to live by the principle of "noblesse oblige" whenever possible. He was fortunate in having gifted military advisers, such as Moltke and Roon, and in having sufficient common sense to submit to the political resourcefulness of a genius like Bismarck, even though he sometimes sighed that it was not easy to be emperor under this chancellor. Married by convenience rather than by inclination to a strong-willed woman, his union with the princess Augusta of Saxe-Weimar was the pinnacle of the social pyramid. Augusta's interests and predilections lay in the fields of literature and music, and the life of the imperial couple was remarkably free from the ostentation that characterized the German court in later years. The circle of their acquaintance was, nevertheless, limited, by and large, to members of their own group, that is, the dynasties of which there was such a surplus in Germany, and the aristocracy with whom they had been surrounded since childhood.

The German aristocracy still preserved the memory of its standing in the days before the French Revolution had dusted off its shopworn glory, but the finer points of social distinction need not delay us here.[2] Roughly speaking, the aristocracy was composed of two groups: those belonging to the *Schwertadel* (the nobility of the sword) and the *Briefadel* (the service nobility). It was from these two groups that the high ranking officers and diplomats were chosen. They formed the social elite of Berlin, those who were entitled to attend the gala dinners, the court functions, and the charity balls sponsored by the imperial couple. An enumeration of these events would tire the reader. They must have been a source of overpowering ennui to everyone except the uninvited. The latter could read the spirited accounts in the morning papers wherein attendance, menus, and costumes were faithfully recorded.[3]

At all court functions as well as in their daily life the emperor and empress were attended by an entourage which still clung to titles inherited from the days of the Holy Roman Empire, the

Oberstkämmerer (first chamberlain), the *Oberstmarschall* (first marshal), the *Oberstjägermeister* (first master of the hunt), and so on, ad infinitum. These officials were selected from the oldest families, and their duties were ornamental rather than functional. They, in turn, had their assistants, also of necessity members of the aristocracy. In many instances officers from the imperial guard were appointed and were only too happy to fill an office which might very well open the door to more important appointments.

It is hardly surprising to learn that foreign diplomats viewed the Berlin court as a kind of museum where the furniture, the ornaments, the ceremonies had become immobilized.[4] In addition to the imperial family and its entourage, there were members of the other dynasties, high ranking officers, and a few representatives of the Junker class who for one reason or another lived in Berlin. In the main, members of this latter group preferred to live on their estates and came to the capital only on business. Foreign diplomats, ambassadors, and envoys were also found in this upper group of Berlin society, but few ever penetrated to its inner core. Being in but not of the Prussian social hierarchy, they were more able to see the weaknesses and foibles of this society than those who took it for granted. A diplomat who lived in Berlin during the 1880's remarked, "Nowhere is there a greater differentiation between the classes which compose the nation than in Germany, than in Berlin."[5]

The cleavage between the classes was further aggravated by the fact that the nobility represented a very small minority of the population. In 1871, only 7,575 (less than 1 percent) of the inhabitants of Berlin were of noble descent, and the influence they wielded was out of all proportion to their numbers. The victories of the army and of diplomacy during the wars of unification had strengthened their prestige to the point where one can speak of neofeudalism as one of the characteristics of imperial Berlin. It gave to a class which was in reality superannuated a temporary extension of authority and allowed it to dictate in large part the canons of Berlin society.

Certain liberals, such as the novelist, Gustav Freytag, had predicted the inevitability of this situation, but, like many others, he saw no way to stem the tide.[6] The aristocracy completely dominated the regiments of the guards who were stationed in Berlin or in nearby Potsdam, an added factor in estimating their importance. In one regiment alone, there were thirteen princes and ten counts in the officer corps. In the cavalry regiments the proportion of aristocrats was even more startling: not a single bourgeois could be found among the officers, though they could boast of thirty-four princes and fifty-one counts.[7] The influence of this neo-feudalism on the bourgeoisie will be discussed later, but it is clear that the officer dominated the public life of the city as he did nowhere else. And to augment his importance, Berlin was the seat of two of the most powerful military establishments in the empire: the Prussian ministry of war and the office of the General Staff. The military caste was closely linked to the court, especially under William I, who felt himself to be one of them, and to whom it seemed only natural to give it special consideration.

Court society was classified according to fifty categories, and we find that the rectors of the universities and the court chaplains occupied category number forty-seven. A few carefully chosen individuals of bourgeois descent were invited to some of the court functions—historians, such as Ranke; the painter, Menzel, who has left us a brilliant pictorial record of these affairs; even the Jewish banker, von Bleichröder, whose financial genius had been of such importance to the Prussian state. (Though it was character-istic that on one such occasion none of the officers felt impelled to ask Fräulein von Bleichröder to dance until the liberal-minded crown prince gave the order. Even then, the officer apologized to his comrades for being obliged to break the anti-Semitic code of the officer-corps.)

The crown prince, Frederick William and his English-born wife, Victoria, were not in sympathy with the prevailing mood of the court. Victoria was the eldest daughter of the queen of England; her political opinions were naturally colored by those of her home-land, and she exercised a powerful influence over her husband. From the beginning, the couple had opposed Bismarck both in his domestic and in his foreign policy. But they were hardly a match for the wily chancellor, certainly not as long as he could rely on the confidence of the emperor, and this reliance was vouchsafed him for many long years until finally William died at the age of ninety-one. Then, and then only, was the crown prince released from the long torment of waiting for a father to die before he could bring his liberal ideas to fruition. In the mean-time, however, the crown prince and his wife formed a center of social and political contact for those who opposed the Bismarck regime. The members of the liberal opposition in the Reichstag and the Prussian parliament were naturally attracted to this group, but others also came into the circle, such as the novelist, Gustav Freytag, and ambitious officers, like the general, von Stosch, who was said to covet the chancellorship, when and if Frederick William ascended the throne.[8] The cruel fate that awaited the new emperor, however, brought a speedy end to all such aspirations and deprived German liberalism once more of an opportunity to leave its mark on German history. Frederick William died in 1888 after a brief and agonizing reign and was followed by his son, William II.

Known to millions simply as "the Kaiser," William II left his imprint on Germany as a whole as well as on Berlin. We will not indulge in a full length portrait of the man whom his uncle, Edward VII, called "a splendid failure"; but we cannot leave him wholly to conjecture, since he came to be the manifest symbol of the new Germany and all that she stood for in the eyes of an unsympathetic world. His ubiquity, his misguided and boastful eloquence, his med-dling and obstructionist tactics, his infantile vanity—all were qual-ities which his countrymen may have deprecated, but to which the outside world affixed the label, "modern Germany." It is not by accident that this entire period of German history is called the Wilhelminian era. Even though we cannot identify Germany in toto with the military posture and arrogance of the Kaiser, neither can we excuse her toleration of the imperial "clown," as Max Weber called him. At no time did the country evidence any desire to divorce itself from the crowned megalomaniac who ran the gov-ernment "by the grace of God." To the best of my knowledge, no attempt was ever made on his life, nor was any check made to his power by constitutional means.[9]

That he was a neurotic was clear to all who knew him well. Historians and interested amateurs alike have tried to uncover the roots of his deep-seated ailment and have come up with con-tradictory answers. His great uncle, Frederick William IV, had died of a brain illness, and it is tempting to look for an inherited weakness. But the Kaiser was preeminently sane in his everyday life and lived to be eighty-two years of age. Nor can he be considered a romantic throwback to medieval rule and to the belief that he was the Lord's anointed. These were mere poses which he assumed whenever he had singled out a target whom he wished to impress. Much has been made of the medical error that caused him to be born with a left arm which was shorter than his right one. Obviously this was a serious handicap for one who was obliged to be constantly in the public eye as the representative of all his country's virtues. It may well explain his hatred for his mother, many of whose character traits he inherited. Yet any attempt to go deeper than a simple statement of the facts or to apply psychoanalytical clichés has seemed fruitless.[10] As far as we know, the Kaiser did not suffer from any sexual complex that might lead to an explanation of his erratic behavior.

That one of the first acts of his "personal regime" was Bismarck's dismissal gave pause to many observers such as Fontane and Meinecke. Yet had he been able to carry out his avowed purpose—to win the working class over and to woo them into recognizing the new empire—he might have reaped some benefit from this rash measure. But the Kaiser's friendly gesture toward the working class, like most of his initiatives, failed and was soon abandoned. One year after the dismissal of Bismarck, he informed the soldiers that they would be obliged to kill their brothers and parents if they were found to be engaged in socialist agitations.[11] This speech of the Kaiser's was never forgotten by the German workers.

The same inconsistency marked William's choice of successors to the Iron Chancellor. Count Caprivi was chosen because, as an officer, it would be his duty to carry out the emperor's orders without objection or remonstrance. When Caprivi proved to have more character than had been expected, he was replaced by the old Prince Chlodwig zu Hohenlohe Schillingfürst, who was neither conservative nor liberal, neither ultramontane nor progressive, neither clerical nor atheist.[12] At the age of seventy-five, he assumed the burden of office strictly from a sense of duty, and his influence on the imperial policy was, to say the least, negligible. The government lay in the hands of the secretaries of state, or lesser officials, such as Baron von Holstein, who was responsible for the disastrous course that Germany steered in foreign affairs. When Hohenlohe resigned, von Bülow became chancellor, an undisguised representative of the fundamental defects of the ruling class. He was a man of the world, a fluent orator, and an accomplished flatterer, a gift that carried him far with his imperial master.[13] If one were to single out a prime culprit for Germany's growing isolation, for her lack of direction in both domestic and international affairs, Bernhard von Bülow would stand accused. But we will not reach a deeper understanding of the omissions and commissions that carried Germany into the abyss by denouncing any one individual. The men and women who formed the upper crust of society were well aware of the shortcomings of the Kaiser and of his favorite chancellor, von Bülow, but disobedience or rebellion was unthinkable, and it is only too easy to find proof that the spineless German society bowed to the imperial whim without argument. Like the Catholics during the Renaissance, they might have said, "For a bad emperor, there is no remedy but prayer," but the Germans did not appeal to God. They might go so far as to criticize or grumble in letters or diaries, perhaps even in private conversation, but prior to 1908, public opposition was practically unknown.

Fontane, for example, foresaw that the emperor's goal was an impossible one, and that only a miracle could raise Germany to "world power." Popular devotion alone might accomplish this miracle, but instead of courting the people, the emperor played up to the nobility whom Fontane classed as "Germany's misfortune."[14] The Baroness von Spitzemberg confided to her diary her objections to the interminable speeches, the theatrical pose to the world, the bravado that sent a shiver her spine, and she recalled Bismarck's remark that the Kaiser was lacking in "*Augenmass*" (a sense of proportion).[15] An American would have said that the emperor was afflicted with "foot in mouth" disease. He spoke of the glorious future toward which he was leading the German people, of Germany's destiny "lying on the water," of the "mailed fist" that should be raised against any threat, and he went so far as to call his own soldiers Huns when he sent them to China to quell the Boxer rebellion. Small wonder that the world made the most of this reference to Attila's hordes when German aggressiveness lived up to the Kaiser's boast.[16] Many of the high-ranking diplomats on his staff spent much of their time attempting to restrain the restless monarch from committing more blunders, such as the Kruger telegram, or his Jerusalem declaration, in which he assumed the protectorate over three hundred million Moslems without so much as consulting a single one of them, or his claim to a naval station in "Baja California." His impetuous interference seemed endless and was only cut short by the famous *Daily Telegraph* affair of 1908, when in an interview the Kaiser managed to offend not only the public in England but in Germany as well.[17] The interview was condemned by all parties of the Reichstag; von Bülow was obliged to disavow his imperial master and to promise that henceforth the emperor would be restrained from interference, "in the interest of a consistent German policy." The effects of this reaction on William are psychologically revealing. He called in the crown prince and authorized him to act as regent, he confessed his desire to abdicate, and represented himself as the victim of injustice and ingratitude. In time the storm blew over, but the Kaiser had, for one reason or another, forgotten to abdicate.

Aside from such critical situations, there were others of less importance wherein the Kaiser's idiosyncrasies exposed him to ridicule. His perpetual restlessness, his desire to be forever on the go, to travel hither and yon, caused him to be spoken of as the *Reise-Kaiser*, or traveling emperor; his childish love of uniforms, which he changed several times a day, led to such ludicrous incidents as his appearance at a performance of *The Flying Dutchman* decked out in the apparel of a naval officer. Moreover, he was tactless, and his indulgence in practical jokes, often with his fellow rulers as victims, was somehow difficult to reconcile with his pompous claim to rule Germany *Dei gratia*.[18] The list of his foibles seems endless—his attempts to compose music, to direct plays, to act as arbiter in questions of the fine arts, a disastrous business about which we will have more to say later on.

Of course these eccentricities do not mark the whole man. Even his severest critics concede William's fascinating personality, his eagerness to impress all who came in contact with him. Although he was bored by the daily routine of government work and leapt from one subject to the next, he was, nevertheless, able to read a manuscript of twenty pages in a few minutes and to assimilate its essentials. This faculty enabled him to prepare himself for audiences with foreign dignitaries, or the representatives of industry, commerce, banking, or science. These individuals were frequently overwhelmed by his apparent knowledge and intuition and yielded with few objections to the Kaiser's wishes. Even sober men like Ballin, president of the Hamburg-American Line, or such scholars as Adolf von Harnack succumbed to his charm.[19] But unfortunately, these encounters served to increase his insatiable vanity, and the emperor was soon surrounded by courtiers who applauded, or at the very least, acceded to his every whim. "Byzantianism" came to be the accepted procedure for anyone who desired to advance his cause or his fortune. This held even for military matters, where the judgment of the Kaiser prevailed over that of experienced officers; those who presumed to oppose him were threatened with the royal displeasure or early retirement.[20]

Again the question arises: why did the German people tolerate such a regime? Without doubt, the nobility feared that any curtailment of the power of the monarch would lead inevitably to a decrease in their own influence as the ruling class in imperial Germany. On the other hand, if they had been able to count on the support of the bourgeoisie in opposing the Kaiser, they might have taken some positive steps, if only to save their own skins. But such a buttressing of their position was not forthcoming. The German *Bürgertum* tolerated without protest the Kaiser's constant references to "my" army, "my" navy, "my" soldiers, even though these forces were maintained by popular taxation to which the bourgeoisie contributed its fair share. In truth, the "German bourgeoisie" is a misleading term if we are to understand it as designating a single class. Occupying a place between the aristocracy and the proletariat, the so-called bourgeoisie displayed a bewildering variety of interests in many fields—economic, social, political, and cultural. In German parlance they are generally lumped together as the *Mittelstand* (middle class), but a closer study makes the term untenable. The gap in living standards and income had widened to the point where this classification was no more than a fiction.[21]

Statistics of the period divide the population of Berlin in the following manner: aristocracy, 1 percent; bourgeoisie, 42 percent; working class, 57 percent. However, we find the largest number of millionaires among the 42 percent of the bourgeoisie, with the aristocracy trailing far behind. The Kaiser was the richest inhabitant of Berlin with a fortune of over 140 million marks, but the second richest man was a Jewish entrepreneur whose wealth was estimated at forty-seven million. Herr von Friedländer–Fuld had made his money in mining and had built himself a palace at the Pariser Platz, close by the French embassy and the Brandenburg Gate. But there were other industrialists of great wealth: the Siemens, the Borsigs, the Rathenaus, the Loewes, Eduard Arhold, the textile manufacturers James and Eduard Simon, the great newspaper owners such as Mosse, Scherl, and Ullstein. In addition there were the families who controlled the great department stores: Wertheim, Tietz, Rudolf Hertzog, Gerson; the presidents of real-estate developments, such as Haberland; and last but certainly not least, the chairmen of the large number of breweries and distilleries.[22]

The new millionaires, most of whom had acquired their fortunes after 1850, lived in the Tiergarten or near the Wilhelmstrasse, and later, in the Grunewald, which became known as a millionaires' suburb. The discrepancies in the social hierarchy were characterized by many anomalies; for instance, when Chancellor Bülow lived in the Wilhelmstrasse, he voted in the Prussian parliamentary elections as a member of the third class since he was outranked in wealth and taxable property by so many others in the same district.[23]

The foregoing group obviously constituted the upper bourgeoisie and counted among their ranks the presidents of the important banks, which, as we know, exerted a tremendous influence on the German economy. As a rule, the upper bourgeoisie has little sympathy for revolutionary or even hostile gestures against a reigning house. It tends to accommodate itself to prevailing conditions and resorts to peaceful persuasion in obtaining its goals. This tendency was further strengthened in the case of Berlin's haute bourgeoisie by a phenomenon to which we have already referred: the neofeudalization of German society.[24]

The majority of those who have attained riches in a society where money itself is not the prime value soon set out to acquire the patina which age and tradition bestow on wealth. The Berlin bourgeoisie was no exception. Country houses were acquired, preferably old manor houses once inhabited by aristocratic families, or perchance farms belonging to the royal domain which sometimes were up for sale. Horseback riding and hunting parties were popular diversions, and great joy was felt if a member of some dynastic house or aristocratic family should happen to accept an invitation to such an outing. Many members of the bourgeoisie became art collectors and built up some of the finest collections in Europe. The Berlin museums benefited by numerous donations; the famous Nefertiti was a gift from James Simon. Others endowed charitable institutions, some of which are still operating in today's Berlin. Intermarriage between the "landed and the funded" gentry became fashionable, though by no means as widespread or acceptable a practice as in England of the same period. Many a Junker growled about the heiresses, or "queen bees" as they were called, who spared no effort in landing an aristocratic husband to sire their offspring, after which they would, in the manner of "queen bees" kill the husband (in other words, drag him down to their own bourgeois level). "Our boys compete for these girls," said one member of the Prussian aristocracy, "and in the end there will be nothing left of the good Prussian nobility but the name."[25]

However, the most important institution for the feudalization of the bourgeoisie was the Reserve Officer Corps.[26] It had been created as a necessary corollary of universal military training in 1814, but had changed complexion during the nineteenth century. In Germany it became an element in the spread of militarism in a class which by tradition and self-interest was opposed to the militaristic spirit. "Every society," observed Fontane, "every household, has a certain idol. There are only six idols in Prussia, but the principal idol, the Vitzliputzli of the Prussian cult, is the officer of the reserve."[27] The position of an officer of the reserve, preferably in one of the elegant regiments, the guards or the cavalry, or even the guard cavalry, was the key to every social position. Everyone who could boast of the distinction lost no time in having the title engraved on his calling cards. This occasionally led to absurd situations. One of the richest industrialists in West Germany, Baron von Stumm, was also an officer of the reserve. One day, at the time of the debate over the naval bill, the Baron, who was a deputy to the Reichstag, encountered the Kaiser taking his morning stroll in the Tiergarten. William halted, and in a commanding voice, ordered von Stumm to return to the Reichstag and inform the representatives of the German people that he, the emperor, would dissolve parliament and make a coup d'état if the naval bill failed to pass. And the Baron obeyed, not because he was in agreement with the Kaiser, but because, as an officer, he was obliged to carry out the command of his superior.[28]

The sons of Jewish families were, of course, excluded from the rank of reserve officer, at least in Prussia. The South German states, especially Bavaria, were more lenient, but in Prussia, and especially in Berlin, the rule was so hard and fast that a member of the aristocracy admitted privately that the "most reactionary chauvinism" was the practice. No amount of money or economic power could bridge this gulf, and even the Rothschilds and the Rathenaus became second-class citizens when dealing with the officer corps. It should be said, however, that this anti-Semitism was not racial, and that conversion to Christianity was usually an open sesame, even to the gates of the reserve officer corps.

This was not the first effort of the bourgeoisie to emulate the aristocratic manner of life; consider, for instance, Molière's *Bourgeois Gentilhomme*. But times had changed. In the seventeenth century, the nobility was at the height of its influence; by the nineteenth century it had become an anachronism. When the German bourgeoisie began to ape the customs and the attitudes of the military caste, it fostered a negation of its own rights to self-expression and its expectation of occupying a position of leadership in the new Germany. The inherent perils of this neo-feudalism did not escape the writers and cartoonists of the day; the situation was even a target for music-hall satire. Nevertheless, the trend prevailed.

A well-known episode demonstrating the submission of civilianism to militarism centers about the famous escapade of the Captain of Köpenick.[29] Its central figure was a man named Wilhelm Voigt. Born in East Prussia, he became a drifter and a criminal, and had been frequently imprisoned. Having lost his citizenship, a simple police order served to expel him from any German town. By 1906 he had reached Berlin, but as usual, was denied the right of residence. He later maintained that his one wish was to secure a passport in order to emigrate. However that may be, he set forth on a very curious program one fine day in October of the same year. After outfitting himself in the uniform of a captain, he made a visit to the barracks of one of the guard regiments. With all the authority of an officer, he ordered a detachment of some ten

96

soldiers to accompany him by train to a suburb in the eastern sector of Berlin called Köpenick. On their arrival, Voigt told the soldiers to occupy the city hall and to brook no resistance. He then, in short order, arrested the mayor and his clerk, but by some caprice of fate, he was moved to release the inspector of police who pleaded his need of a bath! This was the one official who had the authority to issue the desired passport. Claiming that he was under orders from the civilian authorities who wished to clear up a number of irregularities in the municipal offices, the impostor next seized the available cash, some 4000 marks, overlooking two million marks in negotiable securities, and returned to Berlin. He had failed to obtain a passport, but had replenished his funds. No one had thought of halting him, or questioning him, or resisting his orders. He disappeared into the city, and all might have gone well with him, had he not, during one of his many incarcerations, boasted to a fellow prisoner about his plan to outwit the authorities. Following a tip from this man, the police captured Voigt, and in due time he was convicted, but not before Germany and its capital had become the laughing stock of the world. The country of Goethe and Schiller had become a land of barracks, where the uniform cast a spell, and the sergeant called the roll.

One part of the bourgeoisie still prided itself on continuing to maintain the spirit of an earlier age, the age of Goethe. This group avowed its belief in the humanistic ideals and values that had once inspired German culture. It took the name, *Bildungsbürgertum* (educated bourgeoisie), as distinct from that section of the bourgeoisie who held money to be the main goal, and whom they dubbed the *Besitzbürgertum* (propertied bourgeoisie).[30]

The cleavage between the propertied bourgeoisie and the educated bourgeoisie is one of the salient features of imperial Germany, and Fontane made it the theme of his novel *Frau Jenny Treibel*.[31] The educated bourgeoisie was made up of several layers. In the top layer could be found the ministerial bureaucracy of bourgeois descent and the university professors. The latter enjoyed a much greater prestige than that accorded them in Anglo-Saxon countries. At the beginning of the imperial period, the majority of university professors were, by and large, of a liberal persuasion; conservatives were the exception, and socialists were automatically excluded. The University of Berlin could boast on its faculty some of the most distinguished physicians, historians, jurists, and political scientists of the age. Rudolf Virchow, Theodor Mommsen, Rudolf Gneist, Ernst Curtius are only a few of the names that come to mind. Most of these men were content to commemorate themselves in their work. Few wrote autobiographies or memoirs, and we are not as well informed about them as we are about the lives of the aristocracy. Their social life still preserved some of the simplicity and unpretentiousness that had characterized it in the age of Biedermeier. As we have noted, they lived in the so-called Old West, near the Tiergarten. They subscribed to the concerts of the royal and the philharmonic orchestras and contributed to the sophisticated journals, such as the *Deutsche Rundschau* and the *Preussische Jahrbücher*.

As the empire progressed from success to success, the educated bourgeoisie lost much of its initial idealism and was inclined to make its peace with the ever growing nationalism and materialism of the new Germany. A foreign diplomat of the time found it inconceivable that these men who, in his opinion, were best qualified to bring about the consolidation of the new Germany, made no attempt to scale the barriers which separated them from the aristocracy, an inferior but unassailed group secure and unchallenged behind the walls of their upper-class impenetrability.[32]

Heinrich von Treitschke is the most outstanding example of the capitulation of the educated bourgeoisie before the nationalistic, militaristic spirit of the new Germany. When Ranke retired from his chair at the University of Berlin, the faculty wished to appoint Jakob Burckhardt. But the great Swiss historian refused to be lured away from his retreat in Basel.[33] Eventually Treitschke was appointed, and with him the idols of the new Germany entered the University of Berlin. To reach its potential in world history, said Treitschke, Germany must subordinate everything to the state; the state could arise to full greatness only by means of power, power, and more power.[34] Many students succumbed to the dangerous doctrines to which they were exposed, and it is small wonder that they accepted the ideas of militarism and its institutionalized expression, the officer of the reserve. The scientist, duBois Reymond, did not err when he called the University of

Berlin "His Majesty's intellectual regiment of the guards." Whatever opposition there may have been to the militaristic spirit of the new Germany was held within the limits of academic discussion.

We have no desire to belittle the spirit of those who attempted to approach the problems of the working class with an open mind, or those who protested against the first danger signals of spreading anti-Semitism in Berlin. Men like Schmoller, Adolf Wagner, or the young Max Weber, who labored for an enlightened policy toward the working class, deserve our respect as much as the notables who protested against Treitschke's anti-Semitism.[35] Yet their words were rarely matched by deeds. University professors were, after all, public servants, and lived under the code of subservience to authority which permeated all of Germany. There were, it is true, certain instances in which the University of Berlin refused to bow to the wishes of the Kaiser and held firm in her defense of her corporative autonomy. Among the lecturers in physics was a young Jew, Dr. Arons, who was a member of the social-democratic party. When the Kaiser ordered his dismissal, the faculty refused to be intimidated and upheld its principle of academic freedom.[36]

Beneath the upper crust of professor and bureaucrat, there was a fairly wide stratum of professionals—judges, civil servants, and teachers—who must also be counted among the educated bourgeoisie. If the statistics are reliable, they numbered some 20,000 people. Their standards were set by the elite; they were devotees of militarism, and they asked for nothing better than to become officers of the reserve. The influence of the educated bourgeoisie did not match that of the propertied groups. In the first place, they lacked the funds to make their weight felt in any comparable manner. They did not own newspapers, and they did not form pressure groups. The propertied bourgeoisie maintained the Zentralverband deutscher Industrieller in Berlin, also the Bund deutscher Industrieller, the former representing the interests of heavy industry and the latter representing consumer products.[37] The agrarians had their Bund der Landwirte. The educated bourgeoisie did not favor any organization of its material or social interests for obvious reasons: those who had civil service status could not organize and felt no need to organize, since they were adequately protected by their retirement pensions.[38] As for lawyers, doctors, journalists, and artists, any professional organization with lobbying as its goal ran counter to their creed of individualism. Consequently, the vote of the educated bourgeoisie was never a unanimous party vote and was fragmented by personal interests in the case of important issues. The more vociferous pressure groups of the propertied bourgeoisie did not find it difficult to dupe them in such matters as, for instance, the demand for German colonies or a German navy. Even the problem of reforming the three-class electoral system which so patently curbed their influence did not rouse them to public utterance until the days of World War I. Only then did men like Friedrich Meinecke raise their voices in support of substantial corrections in Prussia's electoral system.[39] We must, therefore, acknowledge that the educated bourgeoisie of Berlin, though occupying the place of the cultural elite, failed to attain any similar position in the field of politics except in the city government.

The analysis of the middle class cannot be based on economics alone. There were certain groups who by income, living standards, and economic insecurity were closer to the working class than to the bourgeoisie, but who clung desperately to their middle-class standing even though this was very likely an illusion. These were the petty bourgeoisie, the *Kleinbürgertum*, a class which, according to Marx, was destined to extinction, being pulverized between the upper and the nether millstone. Although economic events failed to abide by the Marxian pattern, nevertheless, the craftsman, the small shopowner, and the white-collar worker were hard pressed to preserve even a shadow of their former economic independence.

The craftsmen were increasingly threatened by competition from machine- and mass-production which offered goods at lower prices and had no difficulty in underselling the individual artisan. The clothing industry switched from tailor-made to factory-made suits and overcoats. Some tailors found work in factories as foremen, but many were obliged to accept work in sweat shops under degrading conditions. This was particularly true of women who were employed in the industry.[40] Since Berlin was rapidly becoming the center of Germany's clothing trade, this situation became an important factor in the life of one sector of the petty bourgeoisie. The furniture industry met with the same problems, and many an independent carpenter was faced with ruin. Adolf Damaschke, later one of Germany's leading social reformers, has given us a moving description of his carpenter father's hopeless struggle with the mechanized furniture industry which had the advantage of credit and banking facilities not available to the craftsman. "How often, on Fridays and Saturdays, would my mother scurry down to the pawnshop to hock some precious heirloom in order to have money for the week's wages."[41] Eventually the elder Damaschke capitulated to the all-powerful competition and contented himself with working as a repair man.

There were a number of artisans in Berlin who kept to the medieval tradition of arts and crafts and were proud of their handiwork and of the title "master." Because of the general prosperity of the era, they were still able to eke out a meager living and were willing to endure the straitened circumstances resulting from their stubborn traditionalism.[42] One mark of their middle-class consciousness was manifested in their ambition to better their children's fortunes. The young ones were sent to a neighboring high school where a scholarship might be obtained and where they might be prepared for a career in the civil service among the lower echelons of the bureaucracy. In certain districts we find that as many as 56 percent of the pupils belonged to the lower-middle class.[43]

It is more difficult to get a clear picture of conditions among the employees and the white-collar workers. We do know that their number increased constantly. In part this was the result of the expanding bureaucracy at all levels, imperial, state, and municipal, and the need for secretarial assistance in banking and industrial enterprises. In addition there was the demand for salesmen and saleswomen in the great department stores.

Such a development is typical of any industrialized nation and has its counterpart in England and in the United States. It is impossible to say whether all the white-collar workers still aspired to be members of the middle class. Many must have voted the social democratic ticket, to judge by the steady rise of the party's vote in the elections held between 1890 and 1912. Nevertheless, a fairly large section remained faithful to middle-class values and standards and even made some attempts at organization. However, it should be clear that this group occupied a position somewhere between the recognized middle class and the working class. We must now turn our attention to the latter.

During the fifty years of the second empire, the German working class rose to a position of leadership in the international organization of Europe's industrial proletariat. France had held this distinction during the early part of the nineteenth century, but the frenetic outburst of the Paris Commune crippled the political ambitions of the French working class. Germany and Berlin assumed the leadership until 1917 when Russia took over. During the last decades of the nineteenth century, London, where Marx resided, was the headquarters of socialism, but Berlin, with such leaders as Ferdinand Lassalle, Wilhelm Liebknecht, August Bebel, Karl Liebknecht, and Rosa Luxemburg formed the frontline.

The gulf between the petty bourgeoisie and the working class was by no means as wide as a superficial glance at the German social structure might suggest. The petty bourgeoisie not only gave a considerable number of its rank and file to the working class, but, of greater importance, provided it with many of the leaders of the movement.[44]

These men believed that the theories of Karl Marx must prevail over all other socialist ideologies before the future of society could be decided. Only then would the working class become conscious of its own struggle and its own goals, a consciousness which was an indispensable prerequisite for its success. The socialist appeal was directed mainly to the urban masses, and it was from them that any overall change in society was expected to come.[45] The German socialist movement came first under the influence of Ferdinand Lassalle whose leanings were toward some form of state socialism. His early death facilitated a steady swing toward Marxian thought. The Social Democratic Labor party, founded in 1869, represented a compromise between the two figures, Marx and Lassalle. By 1875, the two opposing factions merged, though Marx was far from satisfied with this turn of events.[46] In spite of inner rifts and contradictory tactics, the party continued to thrive, and in the election of 1877, it gained twelve out of 397 seats to the Reichstag. Although this does not appear to be an overpowering victory, it frightened all other classes from the bourgeoisie to the conservative right. It was viewed as the prelude to a social holocaust such as Paris had witnessed during the Commune. The socialists naturally made every effort to strengthen this fear.[47] Everything contributed to the growing isolation which surrounded the initial appearance of the social democratic party. Since the Reichstag offered the best forum for a public advocacy of the aims of a socialist society, it comes as no surprise to find that the labor movement was more vigorous and more articulate in Berlin than in almost any other German city. The cry, *"Berlin gehört uns"* (Berlin belongs to us), was heard long before it became a reality.[48]

We have noted that immigration into Berlin continued to rise after the founding of the empire, the greater number of immigrants coming from the eastern section of Prussia. The largest percentage of these uprooted arrivals was absorbed by Berlin's rapidly expanding industries, though some remained disoriented and ill-adjusted and gradually drifted into the ranks of the lumpenproletariat.[49] By 1895, the workers made up 60 percent of the population of Berlin and were concentrated in the northern and eastern sectors of the capital. The center of Berlin, the so-called city, became more and more the location of business enterprises. The propertied classes were mostly to be found in the southern and western districts.[50] It would be a mistake to assume that the entire labor force of Berlin identified itself with the socialist movement. In the early 1870's, only a fraction expressed its adherence to the socialist aims. But gradually the ideas of Marx and Engels worked their way into the minds of the workers, even in the face of violent opposition from the political authorities, or very possibly were hastened by the repression they encountered.[51]

In 1878 Bismarck attempted to suppress the entire movement, root and branch, by outlawing the party. We have already sketched the draconic measures introduced by the Socialist Law. All associations and organizations aiming at the overthrow of the existing social order were ordered to be dissolved. The police were given the power to confiscate all printed material of the same nature and to exile persons from the towns in which they were living upon suspicion of any activity in the socialist movement. Punitive provisions were set up by means of which Bismarck expected to quell the "enemies of the state."[52] Nowhere was the law applied more vigorously than in Berlin. Bismarck did not hesitate to declare a state of siege in order to rid the capital of sixty-seven of the most notorious leaders of the social-democratic party. Parliamentary immunity alone saved the members of the Reichstag.[53]

This law remained on the books for twelve years, a period which may be called "the heroic years" of German socialism through which it passed with flying colors. Although there was, understandably enough, some confusion among the party leaders about ways and means to cope with the situation, the workers were equal to the occasion. Measures were taken to care for the families whose heads had been exiled; a courier service was initiated to keep the underground movement alive; socialist newspapers, printed in neutral countries, were smuggled in and distributed. Friedrich Engels, who acted as advisor from his residence in England, was well satisfied with the impact of the law on the masses and credited it with "sweeping the movement back into the revolutionary current."[54]

It seems remarkable that the working class was able to hold its own against the army of spies, agents provocateurs, and the organized police force which the Polizei-Präsident of Berlin, von Madai, had at his disposal, but the bark of the police was worse than its bite, and the workers showed extraordinary inventiveness in avoiding the dragnet of the authorities. Meetings were held under the guise of picnics or outings; funerals could be used for the purpose of staging mass demonstrations against which the police were helpless. The large industrial centers lent themselves to this cat and mouse game with more facility than the rural districts. On August 31, 1884, the day on which Lassalle had died twenty years before, the workers of Berlin arranged a demonstration which was on the surface nothing more than a peaceful march to the banks of the river Spree. Eventually the police arrived, but too late to prevent the hoisting of a red flag bearing the inscription, "Liberty, Equality, Fraternity."

One of the results of the Socialist Law was the party's shift from political effort to trade-union activity. The trade unions declared themselves apolitical, and their number in Berlin grew from eighteen to fifty in two years. They carried on the fight for better wages, shorter working hours, and the termination or alleviation of the many grievances that the working class harbored against the existing social order.[55] The growth statistics of the so-called free trade unions (a euphemism for the social democratic trade unions) speak for themselves. As a result of agitation, strikes increased in spite of constant repressive measures from the state authorities. The government vacillated between increased brutality and soothing promises for milder ordinances. All was in vain.

No one was more conscious of the failure of Bismarck's policy than the man charged with suppressing the movement in the capital, Berlin's Chief of Police. In November of 1889, shortly before the law was repealed, he summed up the situation as follows:[56] The antagonism between the classes has sharpened and a gulf separates the workers from the rest of society. The expectation of victory among the socialists has grown. The German socialist party holds first rank in Europe because of its superior organization. It has outstanding leaders, especially Bebel and Liebknecht, and it is united. Clandestine papers continue to appear in spite of all confiscatory measures. The trade-union movement increases steadily, and the party can look forward to considerable gains in the next elections to the Reichstag.[57]

As a result of this report, the Kaiser opposed Bismarck's wish to renew the Socialist Law, but the impressions built up over twelve years of oppression endured in the memories of the workers, and all attempts to erase them were doomed. The social-democratic party remained faithful to the Marxian dogma as formulated by Karl Kautsky and even refused to consider the more realistic appraisal of the revisionist, Eduard Bernstein. Its political attitude hardened in a complete rejection of the monarchic form of government which prevailed in Germany, making any attempt at reconciliation (such as Friedrich Naumann's) well-nigh impossible. These were the theories emphasized in socialist publications and speeches, but the party was, nevertheless, obliged to cooperate with the existing parliamentary institutions in many ways. Thus an element of contradiction and incertitude that has never been resolved marks the politics of the German socialists.[58] It was feared that every great international crisis might produce another antisocialist law, and it is characteristic that the party dispatched its entire treasury to Switzerland in 1914.[59]

However, it would be a mistake to believe that the survival of the social-democratic party was a result of the stupidity of the German police force. Economic conditions also favored the working class and contributed to its continued growth. We have mentioned the legislation introducing a measure of social security in the Second Reich. Although the party belittled these laws as paternalistic and palliative steps, it took advantage of them in many ways. Health and invalid insurance, old-age pensions, small though they were, gave to the working class a minimum of protection against hardship in the class struggle.

Perhaps even more important was the paradoxical way in which the economic development worked in favor of the laboring classes. It has been noted that the boom years ended in 1873, bringing on a depression that lasted until 1896. However, the drop in prices was not accompanied by a cut in wages.[60] In reality, the purchasing power increased to the point that the wage earner was in a better position than he had been before. Likewise, there was no widespread unemployment in Germany or in Berlin. The protective tariffs introduced by Bismarck in 1879 contributed to a constant growth in industry, and the benefits of this policy were felt throughout Germany, Berlin being no exception. In other words, if Germany had suffered a protracted period of depression, the chances for a successful outcome of Bismarck's policy might have been realized. If the working classes had been confronted with shrinking wages, long periods of unemployment, the spectre of hunger, they may possibly have turned deaf ears to the siren songs of Marxism and rested their hopes on some form of state socialism. But since they were not confronted by these conditions, they concluded that the Marxian dogma of unrelenting class struggle had been confirmed while, concurrently, their own economic circumstances were slowly but surely improving.

Let us now take a look at the actual situation of the Berlin worker. We can say little more about housing conditions. Throughout the second empire this problem constituted the most glaring blemish on the social record of Berlin. The "rental barracks" continued in use with no significant improvement during the entire period. The average working-class family occupied a flat of two airless rooms, for which high rents were demanded, obliging the wife to seek additional employment either in the garment industry or by taking day jobs as a cleaning woman.[61] The work day was long, anywhere from ten to twelve hours, and wages ranged from eighteen to twenty-five marks a week. Female labor netted considerably less, reaching only 60 percent of the wages accorded to males. There is no doubt that the situation of the working-class family was dismal, but it was not desperate. The actual income was frequently above that of the small craftsman or even the underpaid public employee. The difference lay in the fact that the civil servant was protected from sudden dismissal, a danger which continued to threaten the worker.

As we have said, there were several levels of the working class. At the top were the highly skilled foremen in the great industrial enterprises; these formed an elite and tended to set themselves apart from the mass of their fellow workers. Their living standards and their outlook on life were those of the petty bourgeoisie rather than of the proletariat.[62] The next layer was made up of an enormous agglomeration of working men and women, some of whom were skilled and others who were not. Still lower on the social ladder was the lumpenproletariat, which merged with the criminal fringe of society existing in all great cities. Berlin was neither more virtuous nor more corrupt than any other large metropolis. It had its share of pimps, whores of both sexes, thieves, informers, and fences. Vice becomes monotonous when rendered into statistics, and we will spare the reader the dreary enumeration of police reports.[63]

Some aspects of the social picture, however, are significant. The industrial revolution had brought in its train a considerable increase in alcoholism, and the corner pub became an institution in Berlin. English observers noted that Berlin rated one *Bierstube* for each 148 inhabitants, whereas Birmingham had only one for each 258 residents. The Berlin pubs were called *Kneipe*, and their importance in the lives of the proletariat should not be underrated. The *Kneipe* became the confessional of the worker, and the social-democratic party was not slow to recognize the dangers inherent in this tendency and to fight it with great energy but with small success.[64] One of their watchwords was, "Workers, abstain from alcohol," and they recommended that the workers turn their attention to such diversions as Sunday outings, sports, reading, and study. It would be unreasonable to expect a worker to devote his few hours of leisure to a perusal of the socialist classics, yet more was done to improve the educational level of the working-class family than a cursory survey might indicate.

There were evening courses for adults and there were libraries, although, as might be expected, everything was oriented toward a strengthening of the utopian belief in a glorious future which would dawn when capitalistic exploitation had been overcome. During the 1870's, William Liebknecht issued a pamphlet entitled, "Knowledge is power; power is knowledge." It was widely read and set the tone for most of the adult education.[65] It was a far cry from the educational ideal of the bourgeoisie. Its answers were practical and pragmatic, and its appeal was to a class rather than to the individual. In contrast to Alexander Pope, it asserted that a little knowledge is better than none. However, certain educational programs were set in motion, and they were always carried out under purely secular principles. The ties that had once linked the underprivileged to the Protestant church had been severed. Religious life had never been predominant in Berlin; the Enlightenment and Hegelian philosophy had exerted the major influence. In the second empire Berlin became an a-religious city. Among Protestant marriages, only 27.3 percent were sanctified by the church; of all new born babies only 65 percent were baptized. And the number of children who received religious instruction and were confirmed reached a much lower percent. The Lutheran state church had failed to come to grips with the problem of the urban proletariat, and as a result the proletariat had turned its back on the church, though it must be said that the workers were not so much antireligious as a-religious.[66]

In 1880 the church made an attempt to regain the confidence of the working class, an endeavor which is closely linked to the figure of Adolf Stoecker.[67] This man was the son of a sergeant who had risen to the position of prison warden. Adolf Stoecker grew up during the period of reaction, and his background and education were Prussian. He studied theology first in Halle and later in Berlin. During the war of 1870, he served as chaplain with a Prussian division in Lorraine, a position which led to his appointment as court chaplain. He was ambitious, intelligent, and a gifted orator, but lacking in any critical appraisal of the forces he wished to serve. Doubts, he said, are the work of the devil; there are certain thoughts which one must kill (*die man einfach totschlagen muss*).[68] Socialism, he believed, was one of these, at least in its Berlin form.

The Christian churches had not altogether ignored the social problem. The Catholics had been eminently successful in keeping the workers of West and South Germany in the fold.[69] The Protestant church had embarked on a movement called the Internal Mission (*die innere Mission*), the goal of which was the alleviation by means of charity and Christian teachings of the sufferings of the poor. Its efforts were somewhat hampered, however, in that the Lutheran church was a state church and an indivisible part of the establishment.

Stoecker assumed the direction of the Innere Mission in 1877 and joined an association for social reform in the same year. He realized that the Innere Mission could not hope to overpower the social-democratic party; this could be accomplished only by another political party with a social program of its own. Such a party was launched on January 3, 1878, and became known as the Christian Socialist Workers party.[70] Stoecker himself took the floor and defended the hallowed ideals of the fatherland—Christianity and the Gospel against nihilism and the social-democratic party. He admitted the necessity for social reform, but for him the social question was only "the baited hook" that could be used to lure the working class away from the abyss of social agitation and toward the foot of throne and altar.[71]

The powers that were, especially Bismarck, took a skeptical attitude toward the court chaplain's movement, and it goes without saying that the working class did not swallow the baited hook. From another point of view, however, the movement has an additional interest, since it marks the beginning of anti-Semitism as a mass movement in Berlin. In an election pamphlet of 1881, Stoecker declared, "I have emphasized that the social revolution has to be overcome by healthy social reforms, built on a Christian foundation. I want a culture that is Germanic and Christian. That is why I am fighting against Jewish supremacy."[72]

The reader will remember that there had been an undercurrent of anti-Semitism ever since the foundation of the "Christian Germanic Circle" in Berlin. It was alive in the upper circles of the aristocracy and in the institutions which it controlled, but it was a religious, rather than racially determined anti-Semitism. Among the lower classes anti-Semitism had never died out and had retained many primitive phobias which had characterized medieval peoples in their attitude toward the Jews. Economic competition or hardships for which the lower bourgeoisie desired a convenient scapegoat provided the tinder for any ferment.

During the nineteenth century, the Jewish population of Berlin had risen steadily. As long as the army, the bureaucracy, and the diplomatic service remained closed to them, they could still better their condition in the free professions as lawyers, doctors, and journalists, not to mention the open field of economic activities. With the foundation of the German empire, the German Jews received a full measure of economic emancipation. It was out of the question for the constitution to grant them religious equality under the existing state-church system. But the economic legislation passed by the Reichstag between 1870 and 1874 which lessened restrictions on corporate growth and extended the principle of limited liability also encouraged the formation of joint stock companies. It was to be expected that some of the gifted Jewish entrepreneurs would take advantage of the opportunities thus opened to them. We have already noted some of their names: Strousberg, Bleichröder, Fürstenberg, Mosse, Ullstein, and there were many more.

The economic rise of the Berlin Jewry was accompanied by the appearance of Jewish parliamentarians, Lasker, Simson, Bamberger, to name only the most prominent. Heinrich von Friedberg was Prussian Minister of Justice from 1879 to 1889; Wolfgang Strassman was chairman of the city council of Berlin, and the list of university professors, editors of magazines, publishers of newspapers, who were members of the Jewish citizenry of Berlin, is a long one.

The immigration of Jews into Berlin increased at a rapid pace. Between 1871 and 1910 the number of Jewish inhabitants of Berlin rose from 47,489 to 151,256, representing a large percentage of Jews living in Germany.[78] Thus the concentration of Jews was greater in Berlin than anywhere else in the Reich. The process was natural and irrepressible, and the reaction to it was to be expected. It began in 1873 and rose to a sinister pitch in the 1880's.

Although the rise of anti-Semitism in Germany cannot be given any comprehensive discussion here, we must consider it at some length in view of its impact on Berlin. The spectre of anti-Semitism, once raised, never disappeared from the Germanic scene, and the holocaust of "the final solution" was in many ways the logical outcome of the anti-Semitic wave that swept Berlin for the first time in 1875.

Many minds, those of victims and onlookers alike, have wrestled with the question of German anti-Semitism: why did it reach such catastrophic proportions; why was it so savage; why was it so unappeasable? No satisfactory answer has yet been found. The phenomenon of anti-Semitism has always arisen wherever a Jewish minority reached a certain proportion of the host population. It was stronger in central and eastern Europe than in the West, and by the same token the incorporation of this minority into the body politic presented greater problems in Germany, Austria, Poland, and Russia than it did in Italy, Holland, England, or France. Moreover, the rise of a minority from a barely tolerated or even despised position to a level of some distinction or pre-eminence could be expected to rouse antagonism. This hostility was bound to increase when it blended with economic rivalry, as was undoubtedly the situation during the Gründerjahre. When the crash came in 1873, it was only too tempting to blame "the Jew" for the incredible speculation that, in reality, had been supported by a large portion of the population.

One point should, however, be clear: the desire to find a scapegoat for the excesses of a capitalistic development which the Germans were unable to control provided only the impetus for a movement which included a great number of heterogeneous elements, some archaic, some quite modern. Thus "The Jew" became an invention of German anti-Semitism, a mythological figure who was transformed into a social stereotype made up of mixed components. As a result, each group that harbored feelings of hostility toward the Jew was able to single out the element which it resented most bitterly.[74] For any comprehension of the phenomenon of anti-Semitism in Germany, it is essential to understand this stereotype. One must know the different ingredients that went into this witches' brew, and one must also recognize its impact on the various layers of German society, and how it could appear to be extinct in one decade, only to become virulent in the next.

Perhaps an observation made by Friedrich Nietzsche in 1885

may be appropriate here. "I have not met one German," he said, ". . . who was well disposed toward the Jews; and however unconditionally all the cautious and politically minded repudiate real anti-Semitism, even this caution and policy are not directed against the species of feeling itself, but only against its dangerous immoderation . . . about this one should not deceive oneself."[75]

The oldest emotion that flowed into German anti-Semitism stemmed from the early Middle Ages when the coexistence of Christian and Jew in one commonwealth was severed. "The missionaries of Christianity had said in effect: you have no right to live among us as Jews. The secular rulers who followed had proclaimed: you have no right to live among us." Only the French Revolution removed the age-old prejudice.[76]

Most European countries followed the example of France, removing the restrictions of ghetto life from their Jewish communities. But it is common knowledge that new legislation does not automatically remove deeply ingrained social habits and psychological prejudices. That the Jews in large part clung to their religious beliefs was but one of the many factors that set them apart. Beneath the surface simmered countless fears which had carried weight with the Germans for decades: the Jew could not be trusted in business deals; he was given to trickery and cheating; he practiced the ritual murder of Christian children; he had a sexual desire for blond and blue-eyed women.

It is difficult to assess the degree of animosity felt against the Jews in the different social groups. Certainly it was strongest in rural areas and among the lower-middle class who knew the Jews only as peddlers or usurers. The conservative party, to which these groups inclined, remained anti-Semitic. The Catholic party did not take an open stand, but its official Berlin publication, the *Germania*, frequently took sides against the Jews. There were only two parties in Germany which could be called free of anti-Semitism: the social democrats and the liberals. The social democrats were opposed to anti-Semitism, because, as Bebel put it, the petty bourgeoisie and the small farmer must understand that the enemy was not the Jewish capitalist but capitalism as a whole. Socialism alone could liberate them from their misery.[77] Jews were, therefore, welcome members, and the Jew, Paul Singer, a Berlin textile manufacturer, became one of the leaders of the party.

The attitude of the liberals differed from that of the socialists in certain important aspects. According to the liberal creed, citizenship was indivisible and could not be restricted by religious belief. The liberals had been the champions of political equality for the Jews in Germany as they had been elsewhere, and since Berlin was a liberal city and consistently voted the liberal ticket, most of Berlin's Jewry tended to support the liberal parties: the progressives and the national liberals. It follows that any setback of liberalism was bound to hurt the social and political status of the Berlin Jews. As we know, such a situation arrived in the wake of the 1873 crash and Bismarck's turn to a conservative economic policy. Even earlier, a host of pamphleteers had spoken out against Jewish influence in the new Germany. Some were merely rabble-rousers or fanatics whose voices carried little weight, but others belonged to the prophets of "cultural despair," such as Paul de Lagarde who equated liberalism with materialism and both with the influence of the Jews.[78]

Nevertheless, de Lagarde was a lone spokesman until 1879. Most Germans, and especially the Berliners, looked upon open anti-Semitism as a scurrilous aberration which was bound to succumb eventually to ridicule.[79] In 1879, however, one of the leaders of the German intelligentsia raised his voice against the Jews and his strictures could not be ignored. In this year Heinrich von Treitschke, professor of history at the University of Berlin and editor of the renowned *Preussische Jahrbücher*, published an article entitled, "Our Perspectives" (Unsere Aussichten). In it, he claimed that there was a Jewish problem in Germany, and that the great majority of his compatriots considered the Jews to be Germany's misfortune (die Juden sind unser Unglück).[80]

Treitschke's arguments present a mixed bag. He asserts that the Jews should become Germans without reservations, but while conceding that the emancipation of the Jews following the French Revolution could not be retracted, he still insists that the gulf between Germans and Semites can never be bridged, and quotes the famous words of Tacitus: "Odium generis humani."[81] Thus Treitschke backed Stoecker's arguments against the Jews with the force of his enormous prestige and contributed greatly to the agitation of the Christian-socialist movement in Berlin. Of more moment perhaps was the fact that Treitschke had reopened a question that seemed to have been solved by the foundation of the empire, and, in addition, gave it social status.

In the main, Treitschke's attack was answered by Jews: rabbis or Jewish intellectuals. There also appeared, however, a Declaration of Notables: professors of the University of Berlin, high-ranking liberal politicians and industrialists, who called the anti-Semitic propaganda "a national disgrace" and alerted the German people to the danger of reviving "an ancient folly."[82] The most important response came from the pen of Theodore Mommsen, Treitschke's colleague at the University of Berlin.[83] In a long and thoughtful essay, Mommsen admitted that the Jews formed an element of "national decomposition," but he claimed that such processes were not only inevitable but wholesome in that they facilitated the amalgamation of all Germans in a national state. In retrospect, the controversy sounds the prelude to the tragic fate which the Third Reich meted out to the European Jews. Had there been no Hitler we might pay scant attention to Stoecker's and Treitschke's diatribes.

As far as Berlin was concerned, the anti-Semitic movement was a failure. In the elections of 1881, the progressives won all six seats to the Reichstag, and Stoecker's effort to win a seat in Berlin came to nought. The situation remained unchanged during Bismarck's regime, nor did the anti-Semitic party prosper under William II. By then the movement had changed complexion and adhered openly to the ideas of racial purity. The leader in this campaign was a crank by the name of Wilhelm Marr. From the little we know of him, he was himself the son of a Jewish actor. After a brief career as a journalist, he devoted his time and energy to the fight against Judaism. He is credited with having coined the term anti-Semitism, and in 1879 he founded the "Anti-Semitic League," the aim of which was to save the fatherland from total Judaization.[84] Other eccentrics could be mentioned but they would add nothing substantial to the picture.

Nevertheless, the movement cannot be dismissed as insignificant. Even though it failed to succeed on the political scene, it served to keep the stereotype of "The Jew" alive and gave impetus to its acceptance among the petty bourgeoisie. From the days of Stoecker and Treitschke, the slogans of anti-Semitism were a recognizable undercurrent in the conservative party. Above all, the

Jewish question had been given the status of a major domestic issue in the sociopolitical fabric of the new Germany. A great many people who were in no way swayed by the anti-Semitic propaganda have borne witness to its influence. A few instances will serve to prove the point. Theodore Fontane wrote to a friend as follows: "I have been philosemitic since my childhood and have never experienced anything but kindness from Jews. Nevertheless I have the feeling of their guilt, their unlimited arrogance, to such an extent, that I not only wish them a serious defeat, but desire it. And of this I am convinced, if they do not suffer it now and do not change now, a terrible visitation will come upon them, albeit in times that we will not live to see." On another occasion, he wrote, "I love the Jews . . . but I do not wish to be ruled by them."[85]

Another observer of the Jewish phenomenon and its inherent danger was Jacob Burckhardt. He expressed himself in even stronger terms: "To the Semites I would recommend a great deal of sagacity and moderation, and even then, I do not believe that the present agitation will die out again. . . . The Semites will have to atone for their totally unjustifiable interference in all sorts of affairs, and newspapers will have to rid themselves of their Semitic editors and journalists if they want to survive. Such a thing [as antisemitism] can break loose suddenly and contagiously from one day to the next."[86] The same premonitory accents were heard from foreign diplomats stationed in Berlin.[87] The Jews themselves were in a state of turmoil, some admitting openly that they were not without blame when accused of "arrogance, vanity, and unspeakable insolence." Others faced the newly awakened *furor teutonicus* with utter bewilderment.[88]

Even so, those who pointed toward the gathering clouds of an anti-Semitic tornado were a minority, and by 1900 the menace seemed to have subsided. Several reasons can be given for this reversal. To begin with, Germany had entered a new cycle of prosperity in 1896, which put a damper on the economic envy aroused by the Jews. Moreover, in the era of *Weltpolitik*, the great number of external enemies served to blot out the problem of the Jews.[89] The government itself seemed to be more kindly disposed toward the Jewish population, and the Kaiser displayed a frankly philosemitic attitude. Among his trusted advisers were

Ballin, of the Hamburg-American Line, Karl Fürstenberg of the *Berliner Handelsgesellschaft*, Walter Rathenau, Friedländer-Fuld, and many other prominent Jewish figures. Officially, conversion to one of the Christian denominations was still the ticket of admission to the higher echelons of Berlin society, but there were even exceptions to this rule. The general trend seemed to point to assimilation rather than toward segregation. Statistics bear out this appraisal. The number who relinquished their membership in the Jewish community increased from fifty-one in 1873 to 1055 in 1913; mixed marriages doubled between 1875 and 1914.[90] By and large, mixed marriages were more acceptable among the aristocratic upper class and the bourgeoisie, whether propertied or educated, than among the lower-middle class. Since there had never been a ghetto in Berlin, the Jewish population was scattered throughout the different sections of the city, with income being the decisive factor in choice of abode. Under the circumstances, it is not surprising that a critic of the status quo, such as Bebel, could assert in 1906 that anti-Semitism "has no prospect of ever exercising a decisive influence on political and social life in Germany."[91]

In retrospect, we realize that this was just one more of the many illusions upon which the era seemed to thrive. Anti-Semitism had not disappeared; it had merely retreated momentarily and was bound to spring forth again when conditions were more favorable for its success. Recognizing this, we return to our initial question: what explanation can be given for the survival of the social stereotype we have been considering? There is no lack of clichés that attempt to account for the stereotype. In the case of "The Jew," they range from a condemnation of his arrogance and aggressiveness to an assertion that he is destined to succeed in any and all circumstances, that "he always gets what he wants." This phrase was heard again and again in Berlin, and for proof the speaker need only point to the Jewish ability to survive great crises and to rise from a state of penury to fantastic riches. Certainly there was a large number of rich Jews in Berlin, but there was also a large Jewish proletariat, just as there was in Warsaw or Vienna.

On the whole, it would appear that Jewish wealth was a factor rather than the cause of the survival of the social stereotype; this becomes clear when we remember that the poor Jews as well as the rich Jews were the targets of the stereotype. And though one is inclined, in view of the Hitler period, to blame the Germans alone for the continuance of anti-Semitic attitudes in Berlin, we must avoid this pitfall if we hope to reach the truth. Was there not something in the attitude of the Jewish minority that accommodated the antagonism of their anti-Semitic opponents, something that ultimately foiled the process of assimilation that, as we have said, was well on its way? For lack of a better word, let us call this "something" the *visibility* of the Jewish population. By visibility we refer in the first place to the concentration of the Jewish population in a few selected professions, such as banking, medicine, and the law. As we know, the Jews themselves were not responsible for this situation, but they were, nonetheless, the victims of its critics. Second, there was an undeniable preponderance of the Jewish element in the Berlin press. Furthermore, Jews exerted a tremendous influence in financial circles, especially in the great banks with their many branch offices which exercised a controlling power in the economic life of the capital. We come to a fourth fact: many of the large department stores of Berlin were owned and managed by Jewish families, and they presented an economic danger to the small shop owner and the artisan, neither of whom could compete with their mass produced articles. Fifth, there was a preponderance of Jews in the performing arts, especially in the theatre, the concert halls, and even in vaudeville, of which we shall speak later. In one way or another each of the professions that we have mentioned continually faced the lime-light, where writers, managers, entrepreneurs, actors, conductors, could bask in the public eye, a natural compensation for the long night of their oppression.

The reaction to this so-called visibility was, of course, heightened and sharpened by the fact that these positions of distinction or importance had been acquired over a surprisingly short space of time, in most cases in one generation, a flagrant rise from rags to riches. It is difficult to say whether the Jews controlled such a great proportion of the capital's wealth as their anti-Semitic opponents asserted. There were, without doubt, a fair number of Jews or Jewish converts in the list of millionaires residing in Berlin. Moreover, the Jews paid more taxes percentage-wise than any other of the three denominations.[92] But the whole story is never to be found in statistics, especially when one is considering a phenomenon as complicated as the growth of anti-Semitism. We have mentioned the large Jewish proletariat situated in eastern and northern Berlin. In certain ways they too shared in the stigma of visibility, that is, they clung to their long black gowns, their hairlocks and beards, which made them conspicuous among the non-Jewish population. (The reader may recall that Hitler traced his anti-Semitism to the encounter with members of the Jewish proletariat whom he met in Vienna.)

The phenomenon that we have termed *visibility* did not, however, apply to the many Jewish middle-class families whose greatest ambition was to be recognized by the Germans as one of them —as belonging. By 1914 the process of assimilation had made great progress, and without doubt it was a process that was greatly desired by the majority of German Jews who identified themselves with imperial Germany in an often sentimental and touching manner.[93] Zionism had no great hold in Berlin and was rejected by all those who wished to become members of the German bourgeoisie either in its propertied sector or among the educated *Bildungsbürgertum.*

One further observation may help to explain the survival of the anti-Semitic virus in Wilhelminian Germany. The autocratic structure of imperial Germany made the process of assimilation more difficult than did the same process in England, Holland, the United States, or France. Nevertheless, even in France, the country was obliged to suffer the infamies of the Dreyfus case before anti-Semitism was defeated. But it can be said that Berlin itself never became an anti-Semitic city. Although much of the criticism of Berlin found an easy target in its large Jewish community, the capital as a whole never embraced this creed. Even under Goebbel's influence, the city did not vote the national-socialist party into power.

Let us close this unhappy chapter of Berlin's history with another observation from Nietzsche, penned by him in 1885. "That Germany has an ample number of Jews, that the German stomach, the German blood has difficulty (and will have difficulty for a long time) digesting even this quantum of 'Jew'—as the Italians, French, and English, have done, having stronger digestive systems —that is the clear testimony and language of a general instinct . . .

the instinct of a people whose type is still weak and indefinite, so it could easily be blurred or extinguished by a stronger race. The Jews, however, are beyond doubt the strongest, toughest, and purest race now living in Europe. . . . Meanwhile, they [the Jews] want and wish rather, even with some importunity to be absorbed and assimilated."[94]

To summarize our survey of Berlin society, let us say that it mirrored the hierarchical structure of German society in microcosm. In an age characterized by rapid industrial development and urban growth, Berlin society still adhered to the old order established when Prussia was not a state that had an army, but an army that had a state. At the time of the founding of the empire, the Hohenzollern dynasty enjoyed a prestige unparalleled among the reigning houses of Europe. "The emperor William I," wrote a diplomat, "is . . . the most popular prince of his people in our time."[95] Yet this great reservoir of admiration and devotion was squandered in reckless fashion by his grandson, the Kaiser. William II often referred to his grandfather as "William the Great," and to the statesmen and officers who had been responsible for the unification of Germany, as his handymen (Handlanger). The imperial office became a stage across whose boards the "abominable showman" of Europe strutted, provoking fear among his peers and panic among his people. When he fled to Holland in 1918 to escape the German revolution, hardly a handful lamented his departure. Intelligent men had prophesied these events and had foreseen that Prussia's onetime glory would be the seed of its defeat.[96]

Berlin society was controlled in the main by an alliance between Junker aristocracy and bourgeoisie. "The people" were given little voice and less power, and in retrospect one can only marvel that the power structure lasted as long as it did. The answer must lie in the fact that, until 1914, it was not put to the test. So long as peace and prosperity reigned in the land, the Germans were willing to endure a superannuated form of government, albeit the more enlightened were well aware that a change in favor of a more popular, more representative division of power was inevitable. And there was an additional factor of some importance. Even among those who were opposed to the imperial government—the social democrats and the more progressive of the liberals, such as Fried-

rich Meinecke, Friedrich Naumann, Max Weber, and others—
there existed an intense national sentiment which obliged them
to sympathize with the expansionist, imperialistic policy of the
Kaiser's regime, even while they deplored his interference, his lack
of tact, and his frequent faux pas.[97] The average social democrat,
likewise, though he professed to be an internationalist and a re-
publican, succumbed to the thrill of his country's growing might.
Even the most insignificant Berliner could not fail to be proud
of his citizenship in the strongest nation of continental Europe,
or fail to share the Bismarck cult and the all-pervasive militarism
with which he had been indoctrinated during his years of service
in the army. There was something schizophrenic about the society
of imperial Berlin, and no one sought a remedy. Only the most
radical of the social democrats, such as Karl Liebknecht and Rosa
Luxemburg, were ready to advocate revolution, and as 1914 revealed, they had no backing.[98]

In my own recollections, I can call up no more than a handful
who admitted to any premonition of the catastrophic course upon
which Germany had set forth. To be sure, Bebel and his disciples
predicted the imminence of the great Kladderadatsch (breakdown) which would come, not as a movement of the working
class but as a result of the failures and blunders of the ruling
establishment. But these words fell on the imperturbable Junker-
bourgeois alliance that supported the government in most of its
actions.

Another facet of Berlin society is exposed when one explores
the activities of court society. Here can be found accounts of innumerable scandals which reached the ears of interested individuals
in an amazingly short time. It goes without saying that every
society has its catalogue of indiscretions; there will always be
those who refuse to abide by the rules. But the indecorum of
Berlin society was extraordinary; it was riddled with intrigue, sexual deviations, and monetary corruption. The contrast between
the pretensions of the imperial government and the unvarnished
chronicle of aristocratic life was so glaring that an enterprising
journalist like Maximilian Harden thought to topple William's
imperial regime by exposing the existence of homosexuality in the
Kaiser's entourage. But though Harden succeeded in tearing the
veil of Christian hypocrisy in which the Kaiser chose to drape

himself, he failed to disturb the dynastic loyalty of the populace.[99]
What few voices were lifted in a cry for change and repentance
went unheard in the general ebullience. In *Quay*, a poem in his
Seventh Ring, Stefan George sounds the note of doom:

> Who can regard this whirl with other thoughts
> (The thud of many feet, of hoof and hub)
> Than those the emperor had who ordered brought
> Ten thousand spiders gathered in a tub.

In another poem called *Citysquare*, he says:

> You—whether kings or hoi-poloi—pursue
> An idol who transforms your gold to cheap
> And common coin. My people, I shall weep
> When you atone with bondage, need, and rue.[100]

Berlin society produced, however, an offshoot which should be
briefly mentioned—the youth movement which started in 1896 in
a Berlin suburb. Steglitz was a section inhabited in unequal proportion by well-to-do patricians and a large number of white-collar
workers, civil servants, and merchants. A student at the University
of Berlin, Karl Fischer, rebelled against the stuffiness and arti-
ficiality of the life of the prosperous middle class and decided to
lead the German youth back to nature. He yearned to rediscover
the fields and forests, the brooks and meadows, from which the
suburbanites had become alienated. He wanted to feel rain and
sunshine, wind and snow on his skin; he wanted to walk rather
than be carried by train, to sleep in haystacks or in tents, and to
cook his own frugal meals. Needless to say, he abstained from
nicotine, alcohol, and the other stimulants which the bourgeoisie
used to maintain its flagging vitality. Here, then, was a movement
that was definitely antibourgeois, but it did not have a political
program. It was a cultural and an emotional protest and soon
created its own ritual of greetings and costume to set its members
apart from the despised middle class. It was a voice of dissent,
dissent from the urbanization and industrialization which was so
dominant in Berlin. The youth movement made its contribution,
however small, to German culture and subscribed to many of the
ideas which Stefan George professed in his poetry. But in its vociferous protest it undermined the culture of the German middle

class, rather than rejuvenating it, which had been its professed goal.[101]

The general mood of the city, however, was far removed from such feelings. In 1898 the *Berliner Illustrierte Zeitung* put out a questionnaire entitled *The Balance of the Century*.[102] It asked twenty-seven questions the answers to which were supposed to represent public opinion on various matters. There was general agreement that the nineteenth century should be called the century of inventions; that Lord Lister and, following him, George Stephenson were the greatest benefactors of the age. Prince Bismarck was named as Germany's greatest statesman, and Goethe her greatest poet. To the question as to the greatest thinker, there was a startling reply: Moltke was ranked above Darwin, Kant, Schopenhauer, and Nietzsche. The same chauvinism placed the painter Adolf Menzel above any of the French masters; the second-rate sculptor, Begas, was named, whereas neither Rodin nor Maillol were mentioned. Richard Wagner got the vote of the majority over Beethoven and Brahms, and Napoleon I received the crown as the best strategist. The most significant cultural achievement was voted to be the abolition of slavery. Other entries give still further evidence of Berlin's parochial and nationalistic perspective: the greatest hero of the age was William I; the most important woman, Queen Louise of Prussia; the most important historical event, the unification of Germany; the greatest Berliner, either Alexander von Humboldt or William I. But we may take heart at one correspondent's answer to this last question: "There is no such thing as a great Berliner." (Grosse Berliner gibt es überhaupt nicht.)[103] This typical Berlin reply gave evidence that in the midst of arrant nationalism and flagrant arrogance, at least one Berliner had not lost his most endearing trait, his sense of humor.

[5]

"World City?
Perhaps"

THE German language makes a distinction between *Grosstadt* (great city) and *Weltstadt* (world city). It is sometimes difficult to determine just when a large city becomes a world city. Numerical criteria are of no help, since both count their inhabitants in the millions; both may have architectural beauty, large parks, museums, theatres, opera, concerts, music halls, and night life. The world city, therefore, must offer all these attractions, but on a superlative scale, together with individual attributes not to be found elsewhere.

Before 1870, Berlin could not even have been called a big city; at best, it was a large town.[1] When it became the capital of the German empire, it underwent many rapid changes, and there were those who believed it might one day equal Paris. Yet despite its precipitous growth, Berlin continued to be a provincial city for some time, failing to reach the level of such older metropolises as Paris, London, Rome, or Vienna, though it surpassed Vienna in number of inhabitants.

In 1896, the city arrived at a turning point in its history. In that year Berlin held an unusually large and imposing trade-fair. Like other trade-fairs which had preceded it, the old-fashioned name *Gewerbeausstellung* continued in use. Now, at the end of the century, the Berliners wanted to prove that their city could hold its own with other metropolitan centers, and they seized upon the idea of organizing a world's fair after the model of the London, Paris, and Philadelphia fairs. As early as 1892, the chancellor, Caprivi, had approached the Kaiser, suggesting that the project be taken up. The Kaiser, however, rejected the idea summarily.[2] At the time he was on one of his junkets, and he wrote from Trondhjem, in Norway: "The glory of the Parisians robs the Berliners of their sleep. Berlin is a great city, a world city (perhaps?), consequently, it has to have an exhibition. It is easy to understand why this argument is . . . acceptable to the restaurants, the theatres and vaudevilles of Berlin. They would profit from it." However, he continued, Berlin is not Paris. "Paris is the great whorehouse of the world; therein lies its attraction independent of any exhibition. There is nothing in Berlin that can captivate the foreigner, except a few museums, castles, and soldiers. After six days, the red book in hand, he has seen everything, and he departs *relieved*, feeling that he has done his duty. The Berliner does not see these things clearly, and he would be very upset, were he told about them. However, this is the real obstacle to an exhibition."[3] The remainder of the letter is filled with the customary rodomontades without which His Majesty could not allow an epistle to leave his desk. For once, he was more modest than his subjects, and the exhibition became a reality four years later. Instead of attempting a world's fair, however, the Berliners contented themselves with demonstrating to the world what German industry, diligence, and expertise had accomplished during a quarter of a century. Those who visited the *Gewerbeausstellung* of 1896 were overwhelmed by this demonstration of Germany's industrial potential, and the beginnings of Berlin's existence as a world city date from this event.[4]

Two sites were considered for the fair, one to the west in Charlottenburg, the other to the east in Treptow. The latter was finally chosen, and an enormous stretch of land, almost 1,000,000 square yards, was given over to the fair.[5] Such an enterprise had to be guaranteed financially, and the amount of four and half million marks was set aside, a modest outlay by today's standards. The sum was speedily contributed by the merchants and industrialists who were backing the fair. A branch line connected the fair grounds with the main railway tracks, and the management even built a special station in Treptow. Catching fire from the general enthusiasm, the city appropriated six million marks for the paving of roads and the building of bridges. In keeping with the social and political structure of the empire, a Hohenzollern prince assumed the protectorship of the enterprise. This combination of the archaic and the modern is so characteristic of imperial Berlin that we will take advantage of it in dealing with the growth of

"World City? Perhaps"

Berlin's industrial power, which is, of course, only part of the amazing industrial expansion of Germany prior to 1914.

The fair was announced to the world by means of a poster, commissioned by the directors, and portraying the powerful arm of a workman raising a hammer over a distant landscape.[6] It resembles the posters of the Russian revolutionaries following 1917. However, the mood of the fair was not revolutionary, and indeed intelligent observers, such as Friedrich Naumann, insisted that the workman had not been given his rightful place in the exhibition.[7] In reality, the fair was dominated by the giants of Berlin's industry, the first place being appropriated by the machine-building industry. We have already taken note of the Borsig factories, and they and their steam engines were much in evidence. Next to the Borsig display were the great boilers produced by the Julius Pintsch corporation. Like Borsig, the Pintsch enterprises had risen from very modest beginnings: a small workshop where Pintsch and his four sons had started their experiments. Prominent also were the power-brakes, the giant cranes, and the pumps of other companies, all of them demonstrating how close was the link between German industrial growth and the sprawling railway system. Berlin owed much of its economic position both to its excellent railway connections and to the many waterways which joined the city with the great rivers to the east and west.[8] The railroads, most of which had been nationalized, were the best customers of the machine industry. But Berlin could not have concentrated 7 percent of the industrial output of Germany within its confines had it specialized in machine production alone. It is difficult to assign any one industry to second place, but in all likelihood it should be given to the electro-industry, which has continued to play an important role in the Berlin of today.

Like the Borsig enterprise, the beginnings of the electro-industry point back to the mid-nineteenth century. In 1847, a young artillery officer, Werner Siemens, had joined forces with a mechanic, Johann Georg Halske. The establishment of Siemens and Halske soon enjoyed an international reputation in the production and laying of cables. Its initial success in telegraphy was eventually surpassed by the invention of the electro-dynamo which directed Siemens toward the lighting of streets and theatres and led later to the construction of electric trains. Although electric trains were not yet employed for extended journeys, they became useful in city traffic as streetcars and for the transportation of commuters, which assumed ever greater importance as Berlin outgrew its narrow confines.[9] It is characteristic of the general trend that the Siemens enterprises, which began as the fruit of private initiative and invention, were eventually transformed into a joint stock company, attracting foreign capital for its constant expansion.

As in the case of Siemens, private initiative was the decisive factor in the founding of the second giant of the electro-industry: the Allgemeine Elektrizitäts Gesellschaft (AEG). Its founder, Emil Rathenau, is one of the most attractive figures in the industrial world of the period, both because of his accomplishments and because of the modesty of his personal behavior. Born in Berlin, he was trained as an engineer and tried his hand at machine production. The enormous growth of American industry attracted him, and he went to the United States, where he came into contact with Thomas Alva Edison.[10] Returning to Berlin, he wanted to set up a telephone company, but ran into opposition from the minister for post and telegraphy, who claimed the telephone as part of the state monopolies. Rathenau, benefiting from this experience, organized instead the German-Edison Company, later named AEG. His plans were far-reaching and aimed at nothing less than the electrification of the German economy. Rathenau succeeded in convincing one of the wizards of the financial world to support an enterprise which to a man of narrower vision must have appeared as sheer phantasy. His champion was Carl Fürstenberg, the head of the Berliner Handelsgesellschaft, a bank that concentrated on great industrial ventures, whether national or international. Fürstenberg advanced Rathenau the capital to introduce Edison patents in the German market.

The combination of technical knowledge and business acumen which Rathenau commanded was characteristic of many of the great entrepreneurs of the nineteenth century. He built an immense power plant in Oberschöneweide, on the outskirts of Berlin, thus enlarging the radius of the capital. Like Siemens, the AEG experimented constantly with new methods in the use of electricity, such as sending messages by short-wave, radio-communication, etc. Again following the pattern laid down by Siemens, the

AEG was organized as a joint stock company the shares of which were quoted on the stock market, and, like Siemens, the management lay in the hands of the Rathenau family. The name of Walther Rathenau is remembered more for his martyr's death as minister of the Weimar Republic than for his achievements as an industrialist, but it was in the electro-industry that he got his start. As long as his father wished it, the control of the corporation remained firmly in his own hands, and the son was obliged to look for other fields wherein to exercise his great gifts. In view of the close cooperation between the AEG and the Handelsgesellschaft, it was only logical that Walther should join the board of directors of this bank before taking over the family business.

This is not the place to give a fair estimate of this extraordinary man who rose to heights of excellence in many fields of human activity. He was not only a leading industrialist, but also a writer of repute, an art collector of note, and a distinguished statesman. Yet Walther Rathenau was not well liked in any of the circles where he moved, and no biographer has so far succeeded in solving the riddle of his personality. Few denied the superior intelligence, the phenomenal memory, the manifold artistic gifts that drew this man hither and yon, but the number of those who felt a close attachment to him was small, and Rathenau deliberately cultivated his inaccessibility. His fellow industrialists smiled at his literary ventures, such as his diagnosis of the times in *Of Things to Come*; at the stock exchange he was nicknamed "Jesus Christ in tails."[11] In spite of the animosity provoked by his personality, however, no one denied that he was well versed and experienced in international finance and that his activity in the field was beneficial for the expansion of the electro-industry.

It might appear that Siemens and the AEG had complete control of the electro-market, but this was not the case. Other enterprises, such as the Bergmann corporation or the Union Elektrizitätsgesellschaft (UEG), plus a host of smaller companies found plenty of opportunities to advance in the field. In keeping with the political tendencies of the period, Berlin became the center for all the various organizations which lobbied for the electro-industry, both for the personnel it employed and for its national and international interests. The growth of this branch of Berlin's economy continued uninterrupted until the outbreak of World War I, at which time its activities became dislocated in many countries.[12]

The chemical industry occupies a third place in our list of Berlin's economic affairs. It, too, had emerged from modest beginnings in private laboratories and apothecary shops; for example, the firm of Schering had its origin in the Grüne Apotheke (the Green Pharmacy), founded by Ernst Schering in 1852. It soon developed into a vast enterprise, putting into production not only such discoveries as chloroform and cocaine but also succeeding in the manufacture of synthetics which obviated the necessity of importing raw materials. In many instances the pharmaceutical industry benefited from the work of, and close contact with, the chemistry professors at the University of Berlin.

The pharmaceutical industry was firmly allied with two others: the producers of cosmetics, and those companies that put out certain specialities in the chemical field. Both had a large number of factories in Berlin and their products were entirely creditable. Of course, the cosmetic industry was no match for the French manufacturers of perfumes and soaps, but it sufficed for the domestic market. The chemical companies specialized in a number of products, among which synthetic dye was the most important. It was called Anilin, and the corporation manufacturing it was listed on the stock exchange as Aktiengesellschaft für Anilinfabrikation (AGFA). It is well known that the invention of synthetic dyes revolutionized a number of industries both in Germany and abroad. AGFA was also the leader in another wing of the economy, which was constantly gaining in volume: photographic materials. AGFA became later one of the six companies that merged in the famous dye trust, I. G. Farben, which survived until World War II.[13]

The progress in photography was a result, in part at least, of the production of optical instruments and the making of precision tools. Berlin had a fair number of such establishments producing microscopes, nautical equipment, surgical instruments, and materials required in the practice of dentistry. It is interesting to note that the fair of 1896 put on display for the first time the materials employed in taking X-ray pictures. One year earlier, Wilhelm Röntgen had made his pioneering discovery, but had refused any economic benefits which might accrue from it. German industry was not slow to take advantage of the new field.[14]

The chemical industry supplied the domestic market and also sent its goods out into the world market. As far as the domestic market was concerned, Berlin easily absorbed a large portion of the products, especially synthetic dyes. As we have noted, the textile industry had been one of the oldest branches of manufacturing in Berlin. During the early part of the nineteenth century there had been a shift from the capital to the provinces; both spinning and weaving factories found conditions to be financially more advantageous outside of Berlin in towns like Brandenburg, Cotbus, and others. However, the finished goods were returned to the city, where they were processed by the garment industry, and during the second German empire, Berlin became the center of the German garment industry, called *Konfektion* in German parlance. Beginning with the manufacture of lingerie and ladies-wear, the business soon expanded to include men's shirts and, eventually, ready-to-wear for men, women, and children. Thus Berlin became Germany's fashion capital, if one can call it that. In the main, the women were presented with copies of Parisian models, and the men were obliged to follow the preferences of Savile Row.

The garment industry used and abused female labor to a large extent. Women took the cut material to their homes and returned with the finished garment. The American invention of the sewing machine gave added momentum to the industry. A few women managed to save enough to buy their own machines, but many were forced to work in sweat shops for starvation wages and in degrading conditions. The prices of German textiles were low, and export increased to distant countries, such as the United States and Latin America. At the end of 1895 there were 495 wholesale garment dealers in Berlin, of which roughly one-third worked for the export trade. But the workers paid for the boom with their health and often with their lives. It has been estimated that women engaged in sewing or pressing reached an average age of only twenty-six.[15] Just before the fair of 1896 got under way, a strike in the garment industry called attention to the shocking conditions that prevailed.

The synthetic dyes may not have been as good as the older

vegetable and animal dyes, but they allowed the ever-changing fashion industry to offer its customers new patterns and new models with every season. In this manner one branch of the economy facilitated the expansion of others, and all together formed an enormous network of industrial plants which extended from the center of Berlin to its farthest limits. As early as 1862, an economist had noticed that Berlin was rapidly becoming a factory town which maintained an existence quite independent of the court.[16] During the second empire the process gathered speed at a rate that amazed most Europeans and could be compared only to the growth of the American industry. Walther Rathenau said that his city was a factory town which no one seemed to know, "perhaps the greatest in the world."[17]

Like most capitals, Berlin attracted the printing industry and all that went with it including the binding of books and the manufacture of illustrative material. The existence of a metropolitan press assured the printers of steady employment, and the publishing industry found a willing audience in so large a city. Many printing houses set up headquarters in Berlin, as did the publishers of musical scores. In a very short time Berlin was rivaling Leipzig's traditional position as the printing and publishing center of Germany.

There are other industries that could be mentioned; for instance, plants that processed rubber for the popular sport of bicycling and that soon turned to the production of tires for automobiles. But this is not an economic history of Berlin, and we cannot hope to present a complete picture of the transformation of the city from a royal residence to one of the industrial capitals of the West. But it should be clear that the socioeconomic change was of such magnitude that it affected almost all aspects of human life.

It has been mentioned that the industrial growth brought with it a rapid increase in population, mostly immigrants from the East Elbian provinces. Seen in the wider perspectives of the twentieth century, this was part and parcel of the constantly increasing trend toward urbanization. However, the growth of Berlin was so fast that it parallels the growth of the great American cities, such as New York and Chicago. The latter city has always appeared nearer to Berlin in style and speed of pace. Berlin passed the two million population mark in 1910. The suburban districts, Charlottenburg, Wilmersdorf, Lichtenberg, Spandau, which legally and administratively did not belong to Berlin, reflect in their statistics the same influx of people as does Berlin proper. When finally an urban unit called Great Berlin was established in 1920, Berlin became, overnight, a city of four million inhabitants.

The greater number of these millions lived in apartment houses of five or six stories, which varied considerably in space and comfort. Those who could afford high rents might have anywhere from seven to twelve rooms; the lower-income groups were obliged to content themselves with two or three. Elevators were to be found in only a few houses, even in elegant districts, and many still preserved the tile stoves which had heated German dwellings for hundreds of years. Facilities such as running water and bathrooms could by no means be taken for granted (the reader will find this subject treated with considerable humor in Fontane's *Stechlin*). The aristocracy and the bourgeoisie, of course, kept household servants, generally two or more maids who slept in, and did the cooking, cleaning, and other such chores. Conditions varied from heartless exploitation to patriarchal devotion. The upper-class German home was conducted along these lines in more or less the same manner up until World War I, when women found more satisfactory employment in factories and the social structure itself was undergoing unprecedented changes.

Berlin's building industry followed a see-saw course during the second empire, but on the whole it prospered and the returns on invested capital were high. This happy state of affairs also came to an end during World War I, when labor and materials were not available, and the price ceilings set up by the government on rents discouraged the construction of private dwellings.[18]

The traveler who came to Berlin by train passed through long corridors of dismal streets before reaching his destination. Writers of the day spoke of "a sea of houses" (ein Häusermeer) just as visitors to Wall Street write about "the canyons of New York." The Berliners were essentially apartment house dwellers; they had little love for the one-family house, and only in such suburbs as Westend, Dahlem, Zehlendorf, or Lichterfelde did this type of living quarters prevail. They were called "villas" and were usually of cement or brick construction. As we have said, the problem of providing adequate housing for the workers was as neglected in

133

Berlin as elsewhere and was approached with some interest and urgency only after the downfall of the empire.[19]

The industrialization of Berlin affected quite naturally many other aspects of the economy. We have noted the far-reaching influence of the department stores. The same tendency toward concentration of economic activity is noticeable in other fields. Food chain stores made their appearance, such as Carisch, Kaiser Kaffee, Gerold, and many more. In a short time they were competing with the corner grocer on whom the Berliners had depended for so long. Mechanized bakeries were introduced, and they likewise threatened the independent baker with their greater output and their improved production methods.[20] All these changes were a natural consequence of the industrial development, and there is no cause to bewail them, but for the people who were obliged to live through the process, the adjustment to new economic forms was not always easy. Many novels of the period express the nostalgia and sense of deprivation occasioned by the innovations of industry.[21] However, the Berliner is not overly sentimental, and it seems fair to say that the convulsions which accompanied the growth of the city were accepted in a more or less philosophical spirit. Most of the people soon came to realize that it was useless to resist the inevitable; moreover, it was evident that society as a whole benefited in one way or another from the changes. For instance, prior to 1870 Berlin had a limited number of good eating places. The few there were could be found along Unter den Linden or in the banking district, such as Dressel, Hiller, Borchardt. Their clientele was made up of diplomats, high-ranking bureaucrats, officers of the guard, brokers, and well-heeled visitors to the capital. These establishments continued to flourish throughout the empire, surrounding their guests with the comfort and attention which is the distinguishing mark of the expensive restaurant.

As the financial well-being of the middle class increased, however, it became evident that this group also would spend more on food and the privileges of restaurant dining than had previously been possible for them. The man who anticipated this development was an entrepreneur by the name of Kempinski, and he put his foresight into motion by building a showplace on one of the main shopping arteries, the Leipzigerstrasse. Moved in part by patriotic motives and in part by a well-calculated snobbism, he decorated his dining rooms with tiles produced in one of the Kaiser's own factories, and it followed as the night follows the day that the Kaiser lent the grace of his presence at the gala opening of the Kempinski restaurant. But the Kaiser's gesture was not alone responsible for the success of the venture. Kempinski's was a restaurant for professionals as well as for shoppers or visitors. Its prices were modest; it offered both everyday fare or delicacies, as the customer desired. One could have half a dozen oysters for seventy-five pfennige (twenty cents) or a glass of German champagne for the same amount. Kempinski's was close to the newspaper district, to theatres and the opera, and the name of the establishment soon became a household word for the Berliners. When the Nazis expropriated the Kempinski holdings, the family opened an eating place in London, but returned to Berlin after 1945 and once more set themselves up as the best restaurateurs in the city.[22] There were a great number of good restaurants that prided themselves on their vintage wines, like Habel, on Unter den Linden, where one was served on the bare wood. Situated close to the university, the opera, and the royal castle, Habel was host to many famous guests over the years. Another Weinstube, the Schwarze Ferkel (the Black Piglet), was patronized by writers, actors, and journalists, August Strindberg among others.

Bierstuben could be found at every corner, and the food served in these places was as cheap and as plentiful as the beverage. All the great breweries had their own restaurants, and the customer frequented those whose brew he preferred; this was a serious choice for the Berliner—once made, it was rarely changed. Aschinger was an innovation among the Bierstuben; it was a chain that had some forty outlets in the city. These were famous for their low prices: a sandwich could be had for ten pfennige and a warm dish for thirty pfennige. Those who ordered a beer only were allowed as many rolls as they cared to eat; every table was supplied with them, and one could make a meal on rolls if one wished. The Aschinger Bierstuben were neat, the food was appetizing, and people flocked to them from morning to night.[23] They were a haven for the petite bourgeoisie and the white-collar worker who could not afford Kempinski.

The increase in the number of hotels parallels that of the restaurants. The phenomenon of tourism, as we call it today, made its appearance during the period of the second empire's rise to power. A great increase in the mobility of life had been brought about by railways and steamships, and most European countries responded to this trend by allowing their citizens unrestricted freedom of movement. In providing adequate accommodation for the thousands of travelers who moved through Europe, the hotel industry developed into an important part of the economy. No capital could be called a world city that could not boast of a string of first-class hotels.

Some of the foreigners who visited Berlin came for amusement; some came on business, and some for educational reasons, or for medical treatment. Since every guest was required to fill out a registration form which was filed with the police bureaus, we have exact data about tourism in Berlin. In 1883, 351,914 foreigners came to Berlin; in the year of the trade-fair, the figure had more than doubled, 717,986. During 1906, a million strangers visited the German capital, and by 1914, their number reached 1,187,-483.[24] With the outbreak of the war the trend was halted, and only in the 1920's did Berlin regain its attraction for visitors from abroad. Among those who came from foreign countries, Austrians and Russians held the lead; however, visitors from the United States were frequent, as were those from Scandinavia and Holland. Among the travelers were some interesting personalities: Karl Marx, incognito, since he was officially banned; Nietzsche, on a furtive visit, the purpose of which has remained a secret; Lenin, who spent his time reading at the Royal Library. Not one of them stayed at the elegant hotels which had been built in Berlin after 1870.

Berlin's hotel industry had a late blooming. Only after the founding of the empire did it begin to flourish. Following the successful conclusion of the Franco-Prussian war, however, we find Baedecker and guide books listing no less than eight categories of accommodation for the traveler, to wit: first-class hotels, inns, hotel garnis, pensions, furnished rooms, boarding houses, *Hospize* (the equivalent of the American YMCA), and finally, *Gesellenhäuser*, which provided a place of rest for traveling journeymen.[25]

Since we are here concerned with Berlin's rise to the stature of a world city, we will confine our attention to those hotels which attracted the well-to-do visitor. These were located on Unter den Linden or on the Friedrichstrasse, the center of imperial Berlin, except for Der Kaiserhof, a luxury hotel built in 1875 and situated in the Wilhelmsplatz, opposite the imperial chancellery. The Kaiserhof was opened on the first of October, destroyed by fire ten days later, and then rebuilt with an even greater display of comfort and elegance. The old emperor, William I, is said to have remarked when he inspected the building, "I have nothing like this in my own home."[26] And, indeed, he spoke the truth. Every Berliner knew that the imperial residence was even minus a bathroom. When the old gentleman wished to take a bath, six footmen went to the nearby Hotel de Rome, and carried a tub from there into the imperial quarters. Just how the rest of the royal family managed their toilettes is a matter of speculation. The Kaiserhof possessed an excellent cuisine and an equally good cellar. In later years Hitler and Goebbels made it their headquarters, since it was only a step from the chancellery.

The modern hotel has a fascination all its own, and has intrigued many a novelist all the way from Arnold Bennett to Vicki Baum. In its way, it is a symbol for many features of modern life, its anonymity, its opulence, its sophistication, but also its unconcern, its callousness, a place where the guest soon becomes a room number. The great European hotels, such as Vienna's Saacher, Rome's Excelsior, Paris's Ritz, were landmarks of their cities and evidences of development. In Berlin this place was assumed by the Adlon, and much of the social life of the second empire rotated about it.[27] He who today views the charred ruins which stand at the entrance of Unter den Linden will find it hard to believe that this heap of rubble was once an internationally famous hotel. Like so many economic achievements of the period, the Adlon was a result of personal aggressiveness and initiative. A relentless energy and an unflagging interest had perfected Lorenz Adlon in the fundamentals of inn-keeping, and when it occurred to him that Berlin needed a hotel that could compete with the Savoy of London or the Crillon of Paris, he had a choice location already in mind: Number I, Unter den Linden, and the story of its acquisition is worth telling.

Unter den Linden, Number I, was the address of one of Schinkel's famous houses built by him for Count Redern early in the nineteenth century. It was part of the entailed estate of the Redern family, and as such, was protected from speculation or transference. But the current holder- of the title was a reckless gambler and had lost his entire fortune in one week to the king of England. He wanted to sell his palace to satisfy his creditors, and Adlon was eager to buy it. But the destruction of a building by Schinkel was an almost impious act in Berlin, and Adlon had to engage the support of the Kaiser to gain his point. Luck was with him and the Kaiser approved the project. Not only did he overrule the office entrusted with the preservation of architectural treasures, but he also used his influence to facilitate the financial arrangements for the construction of the hotel, which climbed to fantastic heights; twenty million marks were laid out for the building and its equipment. But the results surpassed all expectations and dazzled even the Kaiser. Every room was soundproofed by means of double doors, each room had its own bath, and the old-fashioned system of bells was replaced by light signals. The staircases, lobbies, and parlors displayed an abundance of oriental rugs, and the Kaiser could not repress a feeling of envy when he compared the opulence of the Adlon with the shabby furnishings of the imperial palace. The Adlon was henceforth used to accommodate those guests of the Hohenzollern who, for one reason or the other, were not housed in the palace. Needless to say, it became a prestige address for industrialists, prima donnas, actresses, and for those writers who were unduly conscious of their social status, such as Gerhart Hauptmann or Hugo von Hofmannsthal. Lesser snobs took pleasure in displaying the Adlon crest on their letters, though many of them could ill afford a dinner at Adlon prices. The Adlon served the very best in the way of food and wine, and the facilities for weddings, receptions, and coming-out parties were more than ample.

Five years after the appearance of the Adlon, the Esplanade furnished Berlin with one more luxury hotel. It, too, was located near the center of town, at the entrance to the Tiergarten, and its style was scarcely less than that of the Adlon. It catered to members of the ruling German dynasties and to other aristocrats on their visits to the capital. The outlying sectors of the city, such as Wilmersdorf and Charlottenburg, could boast of very few hotels. The Eden, however, opposite the entrance to the Zoo, was in the first rank. By 1914, Berlin had twelve hotels which could be classed as outstanding, with a total of 3,355 rooms.

We shall speak later of the attractions which Berlin offered its visitors—the museums, the opera, concerts, theatres, and cabarets. There were a fair number of dance halls, frequented by the demimonde, and foreigners were warned about pickpockets and con artists.[28] Another innovation was the tour bus, the Rundfahrt, which took the curious to places of interest. These are still active in today's divided city and take visitors from western countries on a jaunt through Checkpoint Charlie into East Berlin.

So much for Berlin's visitors. The inhabitants of the city had their own methods of recreation and relaxation. The aristocracy, even the Junkers, had always made it a practice to travel abroad, and they continued to do so; the middle class, on the other hand, were slow to take up the habit. For many years they had been content to rent a cottage in the country districts surrounding Berlin. The shores of the Havel and the Spree offered respite from the heat and dust of the city during July and August. Most families took their servants with them, and this type of vacationing was called *Sommerfrische* (summerfreshness). It carried with it many inconveniences. Country cottages, like country inns, had no indoor plumbing. Fontane, who loved Berlin, but hated to spend the summers there, has described the dilemma with some candor.[29] As time passed, even the bourgeoisie traveled to distant lands, either alone or in groups arranged by travel agencies. For the comfort or the entertainment of the dear ones left behind, they sent picture postcards from their various ports of call.[30] For the workman, his forced vacation arrived on the date of his unemployment, and was spent in a neighboring park or in search of other work. His ordinary relaxation was the Sunday outing—a picnic with the family, a fishing expedition with a friend, or a swim in one of the many lakes.

The many changes brought about by Berlin's expanding economy necessitated a corresponding increase in the city's administrative functions. Industrialization had created a host of problems in all European countries, and Berlin was no exception. Perhaps the most distressing situation to require investigation was housing, especially in an age that looked upon the question of subsidized housing with extreme distaste. But other matters were scarcely less urgent:

an adequate water supply, the construction of power plants, improvements in street cleaning, garbage disposal, sewer systems, fire prevention—the list seems endless. In addition, food markets needed supervision, hospitals and asylums were understaffed, and desperately short of space. Conditions in Berlin were further complicated because the city was not only the site of the municipal government, but also the seat of the powerful Prussian bureaucracy and the newly created imperial government. The spheres of influence of these three power structures were not clearly defined and overlapped in many instances. Two Prussian offices exercised particular influence in Berlin, that is, the president of the police and the director of finances and buildings. Of these the office of president of police carried the greater weight, since it was not limited to the keeping of law and order, but also exercised the right of censorship, the control of passports, and the licensing and supervision of businesses. In a word, the incumbent was one of the most influential men in the city.[31]

Berlin had enjoyed a certain amount of self-government since 1808. In 1850, its legal basis had been revised to include as citizens all inhabitants with an income of 1200 marks. Although this measure gave citizen status to Jews, it also considerably reduced the total number of eligible voters. To make matters worse, the three-class electoral system was introduced in Berlin at the same time that it was imposed on Prussia (1850). It was a complicated arrangement whereby the highest taxpayers in a given district belonged to the first class; those who paid the next highest taxes belonged to the second class; the remainder of the taxpaying population was relegated to the third class. The system resulted in the exclusion of the majority from active participation in the electoral process and rendered all but impossible any participation of the working class in political activity. Moreover, the application of these rules varied from district to district and any clear-cut explanation of the workings of the electoral system is impossible in the space at our disposal. In 1853 a further hindrance to self-government was added when city officials were placed under close supervision by the all-powerful state bureaucracy.[32] Another legal provision was purely antidemocratic. Half of the members of the city council were required to own real estate in Berlin, a provision clearly designed as a measure of protection for the large taxpayers.

"World City? Perhaps"

As may be imagined, these various ordinances throttled the initiative of the city government. In many instances class interest prevailed over the actual needs of the fast-growing city, and the state authorities took advantage of the situation to intervene. The *Polizeipräsident* in particular found many opportunities to overrule the parochialism of the city-fathers whenever he found them delinquent in the pursuit of their duties. A similar state of affairs existed in Paris where much of the modernization of the city is owed to the autocratic procedures of one of its prefects, the Baron Georges Hausmann.

Under the circumstances, there is little cause for wonder that Berlin did not produce politicians of great talent. In England, Birmingham's mayor was Joseph Chamberlain, Vienna had its Lueger, Konrad Adenauer distinguished himself as mayor of Cologne.[33] Berlin has no similar claim. Its mayors were conscientious public servants; the majority of them were liberals, but their names are largely forgotten. Some, it is true, wrote their memoirs, some have the honor of a biography, but these documents fail to impress the reader with any show of strength or social foresight. During the time of the constitutional conflict with Bismarck, Seydel held the office of mayor; Arthur Hobrecht followed him; Hobrecht yielded the title to Max von Forckenbeck, one of the leaders of the liberal party in the Reichstag; still later came Martin Kirschner and Adolf Wermuth.[34] Even for the student of German history these are but names, with the possible exception of von Forckenbeck. One reason for the mediocrity of Berlin's mayor was the stipulation that he had to be confirmed in his office by the king of Prussia.[35] William II, especially, used this weapon to let the city government feel the weight of his displeasure whenever he disapproved of its policies. A kind of guerrilla warfare was carried on between the Prussian government and the city of Berlin, which had been liberal ever since 1848, and continued to be so under Bismarck and later under the Kaiser. The city council had many distinguished members of the educated bourgeoisie among its representatives, but their influence on the administration of the city was limited.

In 1881 Berlin was permitted to form an administrative district of its own, yet this did not include complete autonomy in managing its affairs. On many issues it was necessary to compromise between

the interests of the city and the demands of the Prussian government. However, we must emphasize the fact that the Prussian
government was not always at fault in holding up progressive
development; frequently the city fathers themselves succumbed to
narrow class interest, especially in matters of taxation.

The principal source of revenue had been indirect taxes and the
tax on houses and rents, which were insufficient to meet the
growing expenses that the development of the capital demanded.
Only gradually did Berlin yield to more advanced forms of taxation for the financing of its most pressing problems. In 1876 the city
took over the care of streets and bridges, but public buildings and
monuments remained under the control of the Prussian government. On the other hand, street lighting and transportation came
under the jurisdiction of the municipality. The horse-drawn omni-
bus, originally a private enterprise, was replaced by the streetcar
and the elevated. Finally, in 1908, the first section of the subway,
the famous U-bahn, was opened. Here, too, the selfish interests of
house owners and real estate developers had delayed progress.

The building of urban hospitals was greatly accelerated after
the introduction of sickness insurance in 1883. The majority of the
new hospitals were built in the working class districts; the
Friedrichshain, the Virchow, and the Urban hospitals were constructed at this time. The heads of departments were selected by
the city magistrates and were chosen with commendable objectivity. As a result, these positions were much coveted by physicians
and attracted a goodly number of outstanding men. In addition to
the city hospitals, there were state hospitals: the Charité, which
also served as the university clinic, and a number of denominational hospitals, Jewish, Catholic, and Protestant, where needy
patients found admittance. The evaluation of these efforts to care
for the sick will differ according to the viewpoint of the observer.
Medical care in Berlin did not, of course, measure up to today's
standards in such countries as Sweden, Russia, England, or Germany
itself, but for the period which we are considering, it was unusually
good, and easily surpassed anything offered in other European capitals, let alone the United States. Nevertheless, it must be admitted
that the wards were crowded, the treatment of the patient superficial and mechanical, but these drawbacks were so general at the

time that the situation in Berlin was still superior to that of any other metropolis.[36]

The educational facilities of Berlin are worthy of note. They showed a great deal of improvement during the period, possibly because industry needed educated workers. The grammar schools (*Gemeindeschulen*) increased in number from 22 in 1861, to 122 in 1881, and to 300 in 1909. The financing of schools absorbed almost 25 percent of the city's income. Berlin's budget, incidentally, had risen to 300,000,000 marks, surpassing that of several federal states. The city also moved into the field of secondary education. The Prussian state supported two gymnasia, and Berlin opened eight new ones, in addition to two real-gymnasia, where Latin but not Greek was taught, and two *Oberrealschulen*, where the emphasis was on natural science. The central city library was very good, and there were local libraries in the outlying sectors.[37] In certain fields the city and private initiative cooperated. The city gave its aid to the establishment of a museum for the "cultural history of Berlin" by offering suitable quarters for the project. During the same period the first of the popular academies were opened, the Humboldt and the Lessing academies. These, too, counted on the city for housing, heating, and light. They rarely charged admission and were basically institutions for adult education. They were open to anyone who wanted to broaden his intellectual horizon, but they did not confer degrees.

The charitable organizations represented another field in which city and citizenry cooperated, especially those that were engaged in the care of children. Homes where sick children could be nursed back to health were provided, and needy children were sent to the sea or to the mountains during the summer months.[38] The *Ferienkolonien* could not cure the ills of the capitalistic system, but at least they made an effort to mitigate them. There were associations whose job it was to supervise the homework of the working-class children and to provide them with a nourishing supper (*Kinderhorte*). The city offered the classrooms which were not in use during the afternoons, while the association paid the teachers who proctored the work of the children, and also paid for the food that was supplied. This work was supervised by well-to-do women, who were responsible for the proper functioning of the institutions under their care. The municipal administration and private initiative also worked together on the supervision of juvenile delinquents. Social workers, as such, did not exist, but many women with a social conscience undertook to see that the youthful offenders were shown the straight-and-narrow path.

Many men and women of Berlin's bourgeoisie lived by the principle of "richesse oblige"—Marianne Weber (Max Weber's mother), Lilli Braun, Helene Lange—but there were others who labored in these fields without recognition, recompense, or public acclaim. It is, of course, easy to belittle these endeavors. Writers of socialist persuasion dismiss them by declaring that they were paternalistic on the part of the donors and degrading to the recipients. Here again, we must beware of applying today's standards to an earlier period.

The charitable activities of society during the second empire must indeed seem ludicrous to the convinced socialist; he is unable to accept them since they were aimed at the perpetuation of a system that he thought doomed to extinction. The position of the working classes on the nethermost rung of the social ladder and their fight to better themselves have already been discussed. However, there is a chapter in the history of the labor movement that we have not touched: the penetration by the working class of Berlin's power structure. Given the peculiar set-up of the city, where imperial, Prussian, and municipal offices overlapped, the conquest of the capital was a prolonged affair which resisted any effort to accelerate it.

With the failure of the Socialist Law and its repeal in 1890, the social-democratic party found it easy to send its representatives to the Reichstag. Berlin was divided into six electoral districts, and those of the north and east (Numbers four and six) were held firmly by the socialists. Wilhelm Liebknecht was the deputy from the sixth district, while the fourth district was represented by a textile-manufacturer-turned-socialist by the name of Paul Singer. Gradually the party conquered three more districts, and it became possible to call the capital "red Berlin." The same process holds good for the suburbs, where, little by little, the socialists overpowered their liberal and conservative opponents. It is characteristic that one of the most fanatic of all socialists, Karl Liebknecht, the son of Wilhelm, should enter the Reichstag in 1912.

"World City? Perhaps"

In the Prussian parliament and the city council, where the three-class electoral system prevailed, the situation was different. Voting was based on income and was indirect and public; as a result, many socialists who feared reprisals in case their political faiths became known refrained from voting. In some years as many as 58 percent did not visit the polls. The party did not give up the fight, however, and eventually succeeded in sending some of their best men to the city council. Karl Liebknecht was a member of the city council before he was elected to the Reichstag.[39] Admission to the Prussian parliament (*Landtag*) was also fraught with difficulties, and although the social democrats scored a number of victories, they were not able to break the stranglehold of the three-class electoral system.

The history of Berlin's social-democratic party faithfully reflects the struggle between orthodox Marxists and revisionists which was splitting the party right down the middle during these years. Their controversy belongs to the history of the socialist movement rather than to a history of imperial Berlin. In spite of the fact that the party maintained its allegiance to the doctrine of orthodox Marxism, its greatest efforts went toward the improvement of existing conditions among the working classes through the unions. Many a union official forgot his revolutionary persuasion when he could obtain tangible concessions from employers. "We have too many officials and too few revolutionaries," sighed one of the social democrats.[40] There began a process of arteriosclerosis in the socialist movement which led to the tragic dilemma of the party in 1914.

The older generation of fighting socialists faded slowly out of the picture—the Bebels, the Liebknechts, and the Singers. Whenever a death occurred in the ranks of the socialist leadership, the party used the opportunity to give evidence of its power and turned the funeral into a mass meeting to impress the Junker-bourgeois society, whose structure was not so near the brink of collapse as they could have wished.

In spite of the fact that the number of social democrats increased in Berlin, the city refused to fall into a revolutionary mood. Berlin was not St. Petersburg, and there had been no revolutionary upheaval to frighten the upper classes. There are several reasons for this: for one, the party was recognized and legally represented in the Reichstag and in the municipal parliament. In the second place, the system of social security, much as its enemies belittled it, gave the worker the feeling that he was not really the forgotten stepchild of society and caused him to be receptive to evolutionary propositions. In the main, the leadership of the party was composed of politicians who had risen in the relentless day-by-day struggle of union affairs and were unwilling to risk all on the gamble of a violent uprising. As the years 1918 and 1919 were to prove, Karl Liebknecht and Rosa Luxemburg had scant following among the workers of Berlin. Strikes occurred, of course, and were often prolonged and full of hardship for the worker, but in the prewar society there were too many safety valves to make an uprising inevitable. Employment was high, and for those who despaired of the existing society, emigration was always a possibility. If Bebel rose in the Reichstag to announce the imminent *Götterdämmerung* of bourgeois society, he was heartily applauded by his fellow socialists, but the statement in itself seemed to make an uprising unnecessary. As we have said, Berlin was not the Russian capital, and we would look in vain for a Lenin, a Trotsky, or a Stalin. The average worker often displayed a divided loyalty. In his modest parlor one might see portraits of Marx and Engels side by side with pictures of Bismarck and Moltke. Germany as a whole, like Berlin, was a-revolutionary if not anti revolutionary. (Germany's only successful revolution was the Nazi revolution of the petite bourgeoisie, ordered from above.)

Thus the visitor to Berlin received contradictory impressions. He saw a world city, one of the citadels of modern industrialism concentrating within its borders a great conglomeration of people. Yet he also saw a city which was the home of a regime proclaiming "the divine right of kings," a city that was both militaristic and authoritarian. If these two opposing forces had confronted each other in uncompromising hostility, the outcome would have been preordained. Revolution would have been the only possible solution. But the ruler and the militaristic power structure in Berlin depended on the rapidly growing economy, not only for its financial support, but even more for its armaments, its weapons, and last but not least, its manpower. Thus the archaic superstructure of the empire was tied to the continued existence of a modern industrial economy on which its world prestige was founded.

The results of these striking contradictions were conspicuous on the façade of the German capital and found expression in a peculiar restlessness. One observer complained that it seemed to be Berlin's fate to be "always becoming and never being."[41] The streets were constantly torn up and rebuilt; familiar landmarks disappeared and were replaced by architectural horrors chosen by the nouveaux riches. Berlin itself seemed to be a parvenu when compared with the settled beauty of Paris and Vienna, or the grandeur of Rome and London. Various American cities present a modern parallel.

Hand in hand with the restlessness of Berlin went a certain aggressiveness both in word and action which became the mark of the Berliner, at least in the eyes of the foreigner. Even Austrians and South Germans felt the distinction when they visited the city. How much more ingratiating was life in Munich, or Stuttgart, or Vienna, when compared with the perennial drive and turmoil of Berlin. Hofmannsthal tried to sketch these characteristics of the Prussian, which were nowhere more distinctive than in Berlin.[42] He found the Prussians a disciplined mass held together by authority and noted that there was more than a superficial affinity between the army and the scientific socialists. They were, he said, strong in abstractions and incomparable in executing a preconceived scheme, full of self-confidence, given to harsh exaggeration, arrogant, pedantic, and quite incapable of accepting any viewpoint other than their own. Another poet, and this time a Berliner, confirmed Hofmannsthal's diagnosis: "What does it mean," he said, "to have a career, but to live in Berlin, and what does it mean to live in Berlin, but to have a career."[43] This poet, Fontane, also saw and portrayed the arrogance of the Berliner who knew everything better and did everything better than anyone else. As a matter of fact, this arrogance became proverbial inside of Germany and penetrated the speech of the police officer and the waiter, the bourgeois and the workman. Very few understood that this apparent self-confidence concealed a great deal of insecurity, and even some envy of older cities. The bite of the Berliner was not as bad as his bark. "Herz mit Schnautze" was the Berliner's assessment of himself, which roughly translated, means "a heart of gold under the insolent behavior," or still more freely, underneath its veneer of metropolitan sophistication, Berlin still preserved many of the homely virtues of bygone days. Thus we find that we must add still another contradiction to the many we have already noted: the discrepancy between the cosmopolitanism of a world city and the exaggerated self-esteem by means of which the new arrival defends itself against the claims of the old and well-established.

A paradoxical situation of this kind will find expression in many ways. We have spoken of literature, but there is one sphere in which it manifested itself still more trenchantly: the deep, irrepressible humor of a city. Humor is various; there is English humor, Jewish humor, American humor. All manifest certain psychological traits which make use of humor to reveal themselves. The humor of Berlin is famous, and rightly so. It has a broad and inclusive character in which banker and taxi driver, butcher and newsboy, street sweeper and artist all participate. It is not like the humor of the London cockney or the New York Jew, and it is not easily defined, being quite difficult to translate into any other language. The Berliner loves a pun, and a pun loses its punch in translation. Frequently it refers to a situation which only the native is able to appreciate, and the essence of the joke would be lost in the explanation. However, we will offer a few samples here, well aware that they may fall quite flat. Volumes could be filled with the quips of taxi drivers, of delivery boys, bakers, butchers, bank clerks, bus drivers, etc. At the stock exchange one day a broker asked the banker, Fürstenberg, "Herr Fürstenberg, did you hear who died this morning?" "No," replied the banker, "but anyone is all right by me." Liebermann once painted the portrait of a brewer whose vulgarity disgusted him intensely. When it was completed, the brewer gazed admiringly at the picture and exclaimed in a tone of deep satisfaction, "Wonderful! what a close resemblance!" Answered Liebermann, "Yes, indeed. Nauseatingly so." ("Ja, ja! Zum kotzen ähnlich.") An elderly spinster once visited the painter in his studio at the Pariser Platz. She was deeply impressed, and turning to Liebermann, said, "How wonderful it must be to sit in this room and paint until the sun throws its last rays over the city!" But Liebermann only snapped, "You must be crazy! I shut up shop at five o'clock." ("Um fünf mach ich Kasse.") Another Liebermann story concerns a fellow painter who boasted that he gave the final touch to Liebermann's work. A friend of Liebermann's urged him to protest the statement, but the painter only laughed. "If he wants to tell the world that he does my painting, he is

welcome, but if he ever says that I do his, he had better watch out."
One rarely boards a bus or visits a shop in Berlin without being
treated to a sharp repartee or a witty remark. "Is there room on
top," asked a pretty girl, as she entered a crowded bus. "Sure, sure,"
answered the conductor. "You can lie down and stretch out in all
directions." A very old lady, widow of a famous historian, had an
olympian contempt for anything that was not in some way
connected with the university and always referred to engineers as
"those diggers in the sand-box." Like any other capital, Berlin
had its political jokes, and they were rife during the Hitler period.
I was riding in a taxi down the Kurfürstendamm one day in 1933
when we passed a group of brownshirts. "Are you a Nazi?" I asked
the driver. "Oh, no, sir," was the reply. "I am not that radical. I am
just a communist."

It was this humor that took some of the sting out of the megalomania which visitors to Berlin so deplored. If it failed to make life
in the capital pleasant, at least it made it tolerable.[44]

[6]

Writers, Journalists, and Scholars

By 1900 Berlin had become the political and economic center of the second empire. As an intellectual center it did not rate so high. For two generations little Weimar had been the home of the finest minds in Germany, but its splendor had vanished with the death of Goethe in 1832. And Weimar's preeminence had not been undisputed; Vienna and Munich, Heidelberg, and Berlin itself were qualified rivals.

Berlin's harvest was reaped in the fields of philosophy rather than poetry. The seeds of the enlightenment had taken root in Berlin and had never completely perished. In a peculiar way, they mingled and blended with the romantic movement which followed and opposed their growth.[1] There were many romanticists in the capital between 1800 and 1830; some were visitors or birds of passage, such as the brothers Schlegel; others were permanent residents, Schleiermacher and Tieck, de la Motte Fouqué and Chamisso, Kleist and Arnim. During a brief period Berlin was one of the focal points of German romanticism, and the sober and prosaic town attracted such extravagant minds as E. T. A. Hofmann and Clemens Brentano.

In her famous book on Germany, Madame de Staël garnered a great deal of information in Berlin as well as in Weimar. However, the impetuous lady never grasped those intricacies of German idealism that merged with romanticism in a unique synthesis evident in the writings of Berlin's thinkers and novelists. The first writer in whose work we recognize this amalgam was Schleiermacher, soon to be followed by Fichte and eventually by Hegel. Hegel was by no means a romanticist, but the undercurrents of romantic thought that color his system cannot be denied. Until the time of his death in 1831, this man's influence in Berlin overshadowed

153

all others regardless of the opposition of his colleagues. Romanticists continued to visit Berlin, but their sojourns were short. Hegel
had led Berlin's intellectuals back to the disciplines of philosophy,
and the literature of any other persuasion was relegated to second
place. Then came the great Götterdämmerung of the 1830's; in rapid
succession Hegel, Niebuhr, Goethe, and Wilhelm von Humboldt
died. A new generation stood on the threshold: Herwegh, Börne,
Gutzkow, Arnold Ruge, Karl Marx, and Friedrich Engels. They
marched under the banner of Young Germany, writing and living
in opposition to the existent power structure, and they were shortly
sent into exile. Heine took Paris for his haven; Marx and Engels
went to England; August von Platen, the finest lyrical talent of his
generation, lived as an expatriate in Italy. The few poets who
remained in Berlin gradually disappeared. Many of the young were
still attracted to the Hegelian school, and they came to the city
from all parts of Germany, Denmark, and Russia; Kierkegaard,
for instance, and Turgenev. But the poets turned away; for them,
Berlin was only a good town to visit.

ĭ

Berlin's literary position in the 1830's and 1840's shows considerable difference from that of London or Paris. For the French
writer, whether Lamartine, or Balzac, Musset or Hugo, Baudelaire
or Gautier, Paris, and only Paris, was the place to live and work.
This same attitude is true of the greater number of Victorian
writers; they gravitated naturally to London. Germany followed a
different pattern. In the first place, the country could boast of few
great writers, and in the second place, even these few did not seem
to prefer Berlin as a place of residence. After many wanderings,
Hebbel settled in Austria where the aging Grillparzer and Stifter
were living. Theodor Storm only felt at home in his native Husum,
in Schleswig-Holstein. Gottfried Keller and Konrad Ferdinand
Meyer remained in Switzerland. Schopenhauer took up residence
in Frankfurt am Main. Jacob Burckhardt rejected with some
vehemence an offer to come to Berlin as Ranke's successor at the

university. Nietzsche first became a citizen of Basel, then a perpetual wanderer, a "good European," forever en route. Brahms and Wagner did not feel that Berlin had the proper climate for an artist.

Much of this trend "away from Berlin" must be attributed to the reactionary attitude that prevailed in Prussia prior to 1866. And it might even be argued that there was something healthy in the desire for a decentralized culture which could spread itself with equal vigor from the North Sea to the Alps and from the Rhine to the Danube. But the student of imperial Berlin is interested in a different question. Was the centrifugal tendency of which we have spoken reversed after the founding of the new empire; did the young nation-state exercise a power of attraction beyond that offered by the individual states? In short, did Berlin become the literary and intellectual capital of Germany, as it had become its political and economic capital? There are no clear-cut answers to these questions.

None of the men we have mentioned made Berlin his home after 1871, neither Nietzsche nor Burckhardt, neither Brahms nor Wagner. The older poets such as Hebbel, Stifter, and Grillparzer, died before Berlin could draw them away from Austria, and Storm remained in Husum. But there is one notable exception to this general avoidance of Berlin, and that is Theodor Fontane.[2] For this novelist, we must reserve a special place in our study. Theodor Fontane has emerged gradually as the greatest literary figure of this period, and his work has received recognition in both East and West Germany. Beyond the borders of Germany, however, his reputation is restricted to those who have an empathy for Germany's problems. Moreover, a rather good reading knowledge of German is necessary, and since Fontane's style is unique, there are few translations available.

Born in Neuruppin in 1819, Fontane was of French Huguenot descent, the son of an apothecary. The drugstore-age will not easily comprehend the aura of mystery that surrounded the apothecary of other centuries. He combined the secretiveness of the alchemist with the curiosity of the scientist. M. Homais in *Madame Bovary* is a good example of the type, and Fontane has also pictured a lovable pharmacist in *Effi Briest*. His own father, however, was more interested in gambling than in the dispensing of miraculous cures, and the family suffered many hardships from his diversions. They moved from town to town, from Brandenburg to Pomerania, and were never allowed to feel the sense of security that was the shield of the middle class in the nineteenth century. But poets are a special breed and are often nourished by the very food which poisons others. The impressions of his childhood sank to the bottom of Fontane's soul and would later rise to color the novels of his maturity.

As a boy Fontane participated in the liberal enthusiasm of the 1830's; he believed in constitutions, in liberty for all, and whatever else was to be found on the liberal agenda. Together with most students of the gymnasium, he signed a petition demanding these rights. Because of the limited resources of his family, Fontane was unable to continue his studies beyond his fourteenth year and was sent to a trade school in Berlin where he pursued the profession of his father, apparently oblivious to the call of his own genius. He practiced his trade first in Berlin and later in Leipzig, but also joined the literary associations which existed in most German towns. Accepting the duty of every Prussian, he served for a year in one of the regiments of the guard, an experience which he put to good use in later years.

In 1844, Fontane joined a literary club in Berlin which called itself *The Tunnel*. The name might seem to suggest some form of underground activity, but actually The Tunnel was conservative in its beliefs.[3] Most of its members were already in the service of the state, or aspired to such positions; accordingly, their literary productions were late romanticist, nationalistic, and thoroughly mediocre. Fontane's contributions are no exception. He tried his hand at ballads, sometimes inspired by Scottish models, but more often by the exploits of Frederick the Great and his generals. For many years his reputation rested on these poems, which were set to music and sung in many a German home. They fail to arouse our interest today. There were, nonetheless, some advantages in being a member of The Tunnel. He encountered other poets, such as Theodor Storm, who outdistanced Fontane in the certainty of his vocation. Fontane matured slowly, and it is quite possible that his initial success as a patriotic lyricist delayed rather than advanced his intellectual development. There were, however, other factors to be considered. He married a Huguenot girl, and the responsibility of providing a home became a heavy burden. He had no means by which to support a family, and economic difficulties soon jeopardized his married life. His wife had "her merits," as Fontane put it; she copied his articles and later his books; she was a hardworking housekeeper and a good mother. But she lacked any understanding of her husband's gifts and had no faith in his ability as a writer. In her old age, she still spoke with derision of Fontane's belief that he was born to be an artist.

The circumstances being what they were, Fontane felt obliged to find some kind of solution. Newspaper work in Berlin was scarce and unreliable. The idea of emigrating to America occurred to him, as it did to many Germans before and after 1848, but he could not bring himself to cut loose. "I love German art; it is where I am at home. To give it up, I would have to abandon myself." So he compromised and accepted a position as a newspaper correspondent in London. His family stayed behind and he saw them only on occasional visits.

Fontane remained in England until the end of the 1850's, and the sojourn widened his horizon considerably. Most German writers of the period suffered from a parochialism that limited both their production and their audience. If Fontane was in danger of giving in to this tendency, he overcame it during his years in London. Like many another, he objected to English food, but he learned to admire English people and English society, though he never became an anglophile. He was not content with his life and despised the nature of his work, which often obliged him to conceal his political convictions, but he realized that he was releasing himself from the provincialism that marred the work of his German peers. "One may pay dearly for this knowledge," he said, ". . . but not too dearly."[4]

In Fontane's next undertaking, however, he seems to have discarded his belief in the value of panoramic vision. While still eking out a meager living as a journalist on the most conservative of Berlin newspapers, the famous *Kreuzzeitung*, he began an enterprise which had occupied his mind for some time. During his years in England, he had written about the stretch of land "around which the Havel curves and draws its blue ribbon." Now he started in earnest to investigate the Mark Brandenburg; on foot, by boat, sometimes alone, sometimes accompanied by a friend, he journeyed through the Mark until he knew every nook and cranny of it. Influential friends interested the Prussian government in this labor of love, and Fontane was granted the modest subsidy of 300 Taler (about $250) to complete the work. The first volume appeared in 1860, and was entitled *Wanderungen durch die Mark Brandenburg*. In the end, the *Wanderings* filled five volumes.[5]

Fontane had made an effort to blend the beauty of Berlin and its surroundings with the history that had washed across it and molded it. He was not a historian; anecdote and detail were to him of greater interest than the rise of the Prussian state; the Hohenzollern and the Junker inspired the storyteller and the poet in him rather than the patriot. For those who are not native to this region, or who have never visited it, the book holds scant interest. Yet today Fontane's *Wanderings* deserve to be unearthed and read; He wrote of a world that has forever disappeared. The storied castles of the Hohenzollern have either been destroyed in the flames of World War II or, behind the Iron Curtain, are put to use as museums of "the people." The manor houses of the aristocracy, the churches, and monasteries have also disappeared along with many villages and farmhouses. For those who wish to evoke the memory of this once beautiful land, Fontane's book supplies the background. It is a melancholy kind of appreciation, one which the author would not have expected and which would have given him little satisfaction, since the decade during which Fontane was engaged in writing the *Wanderungen* promised only a successful future to Prussia. Bismarck had been appointed prime minister and was advancing on his daring gamble to unite Germany by means of a policy of warfare and expansion. Fontane, still on the payroll of the Prussian government, accompanied the army in the war with Denmark and even attempted to write an official history of Bismarck's military enterprises. The work fills more than 3,000 pages. It is the most tedious piece of writing Fontane ever produced; uninspired, paid labor, and not very profitable at that.

During the Franco-Prussian war, Fontane became a war correspondent. When he arrived at the front, the empire of Napoleon III had already collapsed, but the Third Republic had been proclaimed and continued the fight. Just why Fontane ventured to go behind the French lines is not clear; he said that he followed an impulse to visit the village of Joan of Arc, Domrémy. Whatever the case, he was arrested as a spy by irate French soldiers and sent to Besançon. The penalty for espionage was execution, and the news of his arrest produced a frenzy among his friends who appealed to the Swiss government and even to Bismarck to intervene. As a result, the French minister of justice ordered Fontane to be freed, adding the comment, "Ce n'est pas à nôtre chère France qu'il faut recommender l'humanité." One shudders to think that Fontane might have become a victim of war psychosis. Not one of his novels had yet been written.[6]

He was now more than fifty years old, and his reputation, such as it was, embraced his activities as a journalist who drifted from assignment to assignment. During the period of the *Gründerjahre* when everyone was making his fortune, he seemed a leftover from a time long past. Most Germans harbored but one desire: to become rich in the shortest possible time, and Fontane found it difficult to resist the everlasting nagging of his wife who clamored for better circumstances. Once more friends came to the rescue, and in 1876 he was appointed first secretary of the Academy of Fine Arts. This position included not only a steady income but the promise of a pension, a perspective that few Germans have been able to resist. But Fontane found the office unbearable. He could not bring himself to flatter the president of the academy and refused to join any one of the various cliques. After three months he resigned. He felt he was on the point of losing his self-respect; freedom meant more to him than a steady salary. His wife called him irresponsible and suffered a nervous breakdown; few of his friends understood his motives. As for Fontane himself, there is the barest hint in his letters that he was conscious of his innermost intentions. "I have to prove by deeds that I have not acted irresponsibly."[7] There is little doubt that his resignation was the result of a conviction, as yet unrealized, that he was born to be a writer. It was late, very late, to fulfill his ultimate ambition. He wrote to his publisher: "It may sound ridiculous . . . but I may say, alas, I am only beginning. There is nothing behind me; everything is before me."[8]

At the time he made this statement he was almost sixty years old and close to being a failure. As he confessed, he had no fortune, no knowledge, no strong nerves to master life, and he should never have married or sired children; an apothecary who thought he could live on the proceeds of his poetry was a lunatic, etc., etc. But in spite of his self-doubts, he knew he had something to say that only he could say, something that had never been said before, and he was more than ever convinced that he should say it in the pages of a novel. Very few, if any, real talents held back by years of economic hardship have reached such a remarkable fruition in old age. Moreover, Fontane was not fortified by any feeling of belief in his ability to write a novel; he had never tried to express himself in the genre, and the annals of German literature carry a goodly number of examples of writers who misunderstood their true vocation. How then could Fontane be sure that his capacities went beyond the composition of mediocre ballads and travelogues possessing a strictly local interest?

Nevertheless, Fontane set forth on his career as a novelist, and twenty years later had some seventeen novels and stories to his credit. In addition, he wrote two autobiographical volumes, various literary criticisms, continued his journalistic assignments, and kept up a voluminous correspondance, which is among the most refreshing readings in German letters. His health left much to be desired, and more than once he succumbed to nervous disorders which brought him close to despair. Yet he endured all his difficulties, including his domestic troubles, in a spirit of resignation and ironic tolerance. Fontane's importance for the student of Berlin is twofold: his entirely original portrayal of the capital's society, and secondly, his critical assessment of the empire.

The first of these achievements carries the most weight because it has stood the test of time. Nearly all of Fontane's novels are as engaging today as they were at the time of their writing; only a few have grown stale with the passing years and fail to hold our interest. His best work concerns itself with Berlin and Berlin society.

Any evaluation of Fontane's position in German literature must take into account the fact that the social novel has always been a stepchild in Germany. The genre in which the German novelists distinguished themselves was called *Entwicklungsroman* and pictured the development of an individual through his trials and tribulations.[9] Its history goes back to the Middle Ages and Wolfram von Eschenbach's *Parsifal*. It appeared again in the baroque of *Simplicius Simplicissimus* by Grimmelshausen, where the Thirty Years' War provided the backdrop. Goethe revived it in *Wilhelm*

Meister, and in the twentieth century, Thomas Mann has proved its longevity in *The Magic Mountain.*[10] In none of these do we find German society used as subject matter.

During the nineteenth century the novel outside of Germany took on a new character: it became the mirror of modern, capitalistic society and of the struggle between the classes. Balzac is the foremost example, but all outstanding novelists of the century show some social awareness which was not to be found before the Age of Revolution. The English, French, and Russian novels reflect their respective societies with considerable clarity, whether the author be Jane Austen or Trollope, Dickens, Thackeray, Stendhal, Flaubert, Gogol, Turgenev, Tolstoi, or Dostoievski. Germany proves the exception, and her atypical development is not easily explained. Her literary tradition hindered rather than favored social consciousness. The German romanticists, Novalis and Achim von Arnim, for example, turned to the philosophical or the historical novel. Or they indulged in the idyl of a never-never land, as did Eichendorf in *Aus dem Leben eines Taugenichts* (From the Life of a Good-for-nothing). As the young German writers replaced the older generation, some attempts were made to give the novel social content and political significance; Gutzkow's *Ritter vom Geiste* (The Knights of the Mind) bristles with hatred against the court and the aristocracy.[11] As the industrial revolution penetrated deeper into Germany, writers from the middle class tried to give a picture of the solid virtues of the bourgeoisie. Such were Gustav Freytag's *Soll und Haben* (Debit and Credit), or Spielhagen's *Hammer und Amboss* (Hammer and Anvil). These books found large audiences, but they dealt in social clichés and have scant literary value.[12]

The real talents of the age remained faithful to the tradition of the *Entwicklungsroman.* Gottfried Keller wrote the story of his own tortuous development in *Der Grüne Heinrich* (Green Henry), and even more enlightening is the case of Adalbert Stifter, whose *Nachsommer* (Indian Summer) may be called the last novel in the Goethean tradition.[13] Stifter wanted to counterbalance a simple great ethical force against the wretched degeneration of the period.[14] He failed in his purpose; instead *Nachsommer* reasserts the unity of art, science, and ethics (a true Goethean ideal) and turns all three inward toward self-cultivation.[15]

In short, when Fontane began his career as a novelist, the social novel scarcely existed in Germany. Many years earlier he had made it clear that he was committed to the principles of aesthetic realism. Realism, he said, is as old as art itself; nay even more, it is art itself. His interest in depicting human beings and his search for the truth in their portrayal were inseparable.[16] As a result, his novels are realistic without being naturalistic. He knew the work of his contemporaries: Dickens, Thackeray, Flaubert, Zola, Ibsen, Turgenev, and Tolstoi, but it is hard to say whether he learned from them or ever made them his models; he tried to do them justice, but often failed to appreciate their true greatness.[17] One aspect of his work shows him as inferior to his European counterparts: he was no storyteller. His novels rarely have a plot, and they are entirely lacking in suspense. These defects are balanced, however, by his ability to portray human beings from all walks of life and from all layers of society. He describes the aristocrat and the bourgeois, the artist and the craftsman, not as social types, but as individuals. It is for this particular gift that he has been called "the sociologist of the human heart."[18]

Certain themes appear and reappear in Fontane's work: the problems of marriage and adultery, the conflicts between the imperative of the heart and the conventions of society, the commands of honor, the confrontation of the educated and the propertied bourgeoisie, and last but not least, the chasm which separated the aristocracy from all other social groups. Such an enumeration, however, does not take complete stock of Fontane's genius. Our response to his work comes as a result of our affinity toward his human creations, and not because they are centered around ideological concepts.

We must call attention to one other detail of Fontane's intellectual profile, since it was decisive in his mastery of the social novel. He did not belong to any class. He had met members of the aristocracy and had found the association pleasant, but obviously he was not born to this caste. For the German bourgeoisie, he had an unmitigated contempt. "I hate the bourgeoisie as much as though I were a member of the social-democratic party," he said.[19] Yet it is apparent that he did not belong in the world of the proletariat. Nor was he a bohemian. Nietzsche might have counted him among those free spirits who have a knowledge of the "human, all too human" side of life.

Thomas Mann has said that Fontane experienced a process of

steady spiritual rejuvenation, and it is indeed a fact that he became ever more radical with the advancing years. He made no public confession of this change of heart and even in his novels recorded it only in a symbolic way. Yet the man who had once been the chronicler of Prussia and its aristocracy wrote in 1897, "Our aristocracy must be eliminated; one may look upon it as one looks upon the relics in an Egyptian museum . . . but to favor the aristocracy in the rule of this country . . . would be our misfortune."[20]

The novels dealing with Berlin society were conceived as a cycle and were designed to present a complete picture of the capital.[21] *Irrungen, Wirrungen* (Error and Confusion) depicts a set of circumstances that must have been common among the young officers of the Guard.[22] Botho von Rienäcker, a lieutenant in the regiment of the imperial cuirassiers, lives a pleasant life. He has a flat near the Tiergarten; he likes his military duties and has time to indulge in the collection of paintings on a modest scale. However, he does not command the means to continue this standard of living and knows that sooner or later he will be obliged to make an advantageous match, one which his parents have planned for a long time. When we meet Botho, nevertheless, there seem to be no clouds on his horizon. "It is one of the best of all possible worlds," he says.[23] Only one element in his life fails to fit the parental plan: he has fallen in love with a girl from the working class. Her name is Lene Nimptsch, and she supports herself and her mother by working for the garment industry. The two women live on the western outskirts of the city near a nursery and are friendly with their landlords, a gardener and his wife. Botho visits her as frequently as he can and is quite at ease with the mother and the couple who own the nursery. One day he takes his beloved on an outing, and we are given to understand that they have become lovers. Botho loves Lene for her candor, her lack of pretense, her inability to dissemble or to lie. But both realize that their love is doomed, and after a brief struggle, Botho submits to the demands of society and marries his mother's choice, Kaethe von Sellenthin. She is all a man could wish —rich, pretty, and entertaining, but as one of Botho's friends says, "something of a silly."[24]

Lene faces the situation with the strength of character that stamps all her actions. She moves to a part of the town where she is not likely to run into Botho, and she agrees to marry a man of her own class, Gideon Franke, an industrial worker who has risen to the rank of foreman. In his younger years he traveled a good deal and joined a fundamentalist sect in the United States. Before she consents to marry him, Lene makes a full confession of her past, which Gideon accepts. Their marriage is announced in the newspaper, and Kaethe, reading the notices aloud to Botho at the breakfast table, is overcome with merriment at such names as Nimptsch and Gideon and breaks out in the giggle which is so irritating to Botho. "What do you find so funny?" he asks. "Gideon is better than Botho."[25] This is a simple story, but told with all the grace, understanding, and charm of which Fontane was capable. It is neither tragedy nor comedy, merely one of those incidents that are part of the Irrungen and Wirrungen of human life.[26]

The counterpoint in the Berlin cycle is entitled *Stine*, although Fontane maintained that the central figure is Stine's sister, the widow Pittelkow, a strapping woman of the working class who freely admits her origin and her mode of life. She has an affair with an old count for whom she doesn't care in the least. She calls him *"ein Ekel,"* a horror, and despises both the old man and herself.[27] Stine lives with her sister and works for the garment industry. She does not approve of her sister's ways, and when she meets the count's nephew, and the young man falls in love with her, she discourages his advances. But the count's nephew insists, and against the wishes of his family, proposes matrimony to Stine. She refuses again, and the young man commits suicide. We are not told about the fate of Stine but are given to understand that she too will die.

The novels are two sides of the same coin: the chasm that exists between the classes that may lead to tragedy if the individual is too weak to rise above social discriminations or to conquer them. Goethe treated the same theme in *Werther,* and Schiller in *Kabale und Liebe.* Fontane's novels present it as a daily occurrence accompanied by neither "pity nor terror." Nor should we assume that his sympathies were entirely on the side of the suffering individual. He knew that the demands of society are not ignored with impunity. "Society," says one of his figures, "is sovereign; what she allows is permissible; what she rejects must be rejected."

The demands of society were not always directed against the heart. There were times, and Fontane knew them well, when they were economic, and they were just as hard to bear. This theme is found in another novel, *Die Poggenpuhls*.[28] The Poggenpuhls are a noble family that has fallen on hard times. Major Poggenpuhl has died leaving his widow with a meager pension and five children. Two sons are in the army, the only possible career for a male Poggenpuhl. The mother and three daughters live in Berlin and find it next to impossible to meet the financial problems that beset the family at every turn. Eventually everything is satisfactorily taken care of, thanks to the generosity of an aunt by marriage, a member of the bourgeoisie who knows how to cope with money matters. This seems very slight in the way of a story, yet because of its sensitivity and humor, it is one of Fontane's most delightful tales.

The problems of the bourgeoisie form the theme of the fourth novel in the cycle: *Frau Jenny Treibel*.[29] The propertied bourgeoisie was as sharply separated from the educated middle class as the aristocracy was from all other classes. Frau Jenny Treibel is the wife of a wealthy industrialist who has made a fortune in Prussian blue, a dye which was much in demand. The Treibels have risen from very humble beginnings, but all this lies behind them. They occupy a villa furnished in the style of the Gründerjahre, and Herr Treibel aspires to a seat in parliament while his wife has her heart set upon an elegant house and a suitable match for her younger son, Leopold. The social circle of the Treibels is also enjoyed by the Schmidt family. Professor Schmidt is a former suitor of Jenny's, whom she had forfeited for the more advantageous union with Herr Treibel. Schmidt's daughter, Corinna, is a charming young woman who has made up her mind to marry Leopold. She has no love for him and feels little more than a mixture of pity and contempt when she thinks of him as a husband, but the riches of the Treibel family offer a fairer prospect than marriage with her father's choice, a cousin, and like her father, a teacher of classics. Leopold is quite willing to further Corinna's wishes, but though he proposes, his mother disposes. Her objections to Corinna are not based on rank or family, but solely on her lack of dowry: "She will bring nothing but her bedstead into the house."[30] She confronts Corinna with questions about her motives and assures her that "the house of Treibel will not grant you a villa in Capri for your honeymoon."[31]

As in most of Fontane's novels, the outcome is preordained. Leopold is too weak to oppose his mother successfully and consents to marry the heiress she has selected for him. Corinna is too much her father's daughter to continue the pursuit of a dream that could only promise ennui. She marries a cousin whose vocation is archeology and who is about to follow Schliemann to Troy and Mycenae.

Frau Jenny Treibel condemns the bourgeoisie through ridicule rather than by accusation. Fontane's contempt for the bourgeoisie centered around their eternal prattle about the Good, the Beautiful, and the True, which they carried on while making obeisance to the Golden Calf. However, his condemnation of the propertied bourgeoisie did not lead him into open censure. He took them for what they were and reduced their pretenses to absurdities.[32]

Still another novel of Fontane's to which he gives the name of a woman is *Effi Briest*. It does not lend itself to classification, since it belongs with novels that deal with the aristocracy, but also takes up the problems of marriage and adultery as well as the problem of honor as it was understood by the Prussian upper class.[33] Effi is the daughter of Herr von Briest, a well-to-do Junker in the Mark Brandenburg. She is eighteen years old when the story opens and is still half child. Nevertheless, she agrees to marry the man of her parents' choice: Baron Gert von Instetten, who is twenty years her senior and a former suitor of her mother's. These facts do not alarm or deter Effi, and to her friends' questions, she merely answers, "Anyone is the right one, providing, of course, that he is a nobleman, has a position, and is good-looking."[34] Instetten possesses the requisite qualifications; in addition, he is very manly and is also *"Landrat"* in Pomerania, i.e., a high government official. It is here, in this eastern province, that Effi takes up her married life. The house that Instetten has chosen is a mysterious one abounding with tales of ghosts and harrowing events. Effi is not happy in her new home and fails to understand why she must live in a house that gives her nightmares, but she accepts her husband's decision with good grace. In due time a daughter is born, and everything points to a happy marriage. Effi takes her place in the social life of the province and at a Christmas ball meets Major von Crampas, an officer in semiretirement, and like Instetten, many years her senior. Soon Effi and von Crampas are taking horseback rides together, and the officer finds it pleasant to flirt with the pretty girl. He wins her affection, and during the long hours when her husband is working in his office or traveling about the country, she welcomes Crampas and eventually becomes his mistress. Fontane gives no indication that she is in love with the Major; she yields to his entreaties because she is bored, because she is curious, and because she has some deep-seated aversion to her husband whose pretense of superiority offends her.

Adultery is one of the prominent themes of the nineteenth-century novel. In *Madame Bovary*, it is the major interest, and Tolstoi shows the full impact of its tragic entanglement in *Anna Karenina* (1877). But Effi does not pursue a romantic vision of the unattainable, as did Emma, nor is she deeply in love, as Anna is with Vronski. Throughout the affair she is quite conscious that she has no other justification than a desire to experience pleasure or excitement, and she is fully aware of her guilt. When her husband is promoted to the post of ministerial councilor in Berlin, she breaks off the affair.

Seven years pass, and Effi could be happy in her new home were it not for the memory of her transgression. On a day when she is absent from Berlin, Instetten finds the letters which Crampas has written her. In accordance with the Prussian code of honor, he is obliged to challenge her lover to a duel. He discusses the problem with a colleague, who advises against the duel. He asks if it is necessary for Instetten to take a life in retaliation for a misstep that occurred so long ago. It would not restore a lost happiness, and he suggests that there might even be a statute of limitations for affairs of such a nature. But Instetten does not take the attitude of Anna Karenina's husband. He feels he must live by the code he has inherited.

Instetten's conversations with his friend constitute the core of the novel; it is here that Fontane gives voice to the most edifying aspect of his philosophy; tolerance, forgiveness, and humanity are the only remedies of the afflictions that torment us. It is here that Fontane uses a phrase which Freud liked to quote: "Es geht nicht ohne Hilfskonstruktionen." (Life is unbearable without auxiliary supports.) [35]

Instetten kills Crampas in the ensuing duel and then divorces Effi. Her life is in ruins; she has lost husband, daughter, home, and honor. The society of which she had been a part forgave many things but not scandal. Even her parents turn their backs on her. She goes to live in a small apartment in the city with only her maid, Roswitha, as companion. When her health declines, her parents agree to take her in, but the tuberculosis from which she suffers cannot be arrested, and having made peace with herself, she dies. On her tombstone, only the name Effi Briest is carved.

Fontane came in for a good deal of criticism for having written a novel whose heroine is an adulteress, but he also received many letters expressing sympathy for Effi. This game of pro and con amused him, but as for himself, he would have supported Instetten, whom he called "an excellent human being."[36]

Fontane's last book is his human and artistic testament. Again the aristocracy forms the nucleus of the novel. The title, *Der Stechlin*, may refer to the family or to a lake on their estate.[37] The lake has subterranean connections with distant parts of the world; if there is an earthquake in Java or a spring flood on the shores of the Atlantic, a geyser spouts up from the depths of the lake.[38] It is a symbol for the coming social revolution that Fontane predicted, but the novel itself is more than a prophecy of coming events; it is a tableau of Prussian society at the end of the century. The principal figure is Herr von Stechlin, one of the most endearing characters in the whole galaxy created by Fontane. He is quaint, whimsical, good-natured, and deeply human. The plot is reduced to a minimum. "At the end an old man dies and two young ones get married; that is about all that happens on these five hundred pages."[39] But this is not wholly true.

Herr von Stechlin is surrounded by a cross-section of Berlin society: officers of the guard, members of the bureaucracy, painters and musicians, two enchanting women, Armgard and Melusine, together with the entire group that associates with them—a pastor who is an outspoken socialist, a princess who has married a head-forester, the coachman, the butler, the maids, and the physicians who attend the old Stechlin in his mortal illness. As Stechlin enters upon his final agony, he says, "The ego is nothing. Something eternal and lawful takes place, that is all, and this something, even if we call it death, should not frighten us. To submit quietly to it makes the ethical man and lifts him up."[40]

All of Fontane's novels are written in an inimitable style, epigrammatic, light, scintillating, and full of esprit. He himself believed his style to be his forte and attributed it to his French heritage.[41] From what we have said, it should be clear that Fontane established a new genre in German literature, the social novel. And we are fortunate that in the process he gave us a lively and detailed description of society in imperial Berlin. Even so, it cannot be denied that there are some gaps. Fontane was not at home in the milieu of the petite bourgeoisie, and he failed in his attempt to describe it.[42] Likewise, industrial labor has no place in his world, even though he was in sympathy with the workers, and wrote, "The new, better world begins only with the fourth estate. . . . What the workers think, speak, and write surpasses the old ruling classes. Everything is more real, truthful, and vital. The workers not only have new goals, they have new ways [to reach them]."[43] But in spite of such utterances, Fontane never tried to picture the life of the working class. Few writers have attempted it, and fewer still have succeeded. In general, socialist realism tends to make very tedious reading.

Fontane was not only the portraitist of Berlin society, he was also one of its most perspicacious critics. He knew that the days of the old regime were numbered, that the aristocracy was leading Germany to her ruin, and he had no hope that the bourgeoisie would be able to turn the tide. His opinion of Bismarck, of the Kaiser, and of many issues that split the new Germany asunder are remarkable for their foresight. Nor was his clairvoyance limited to the German scene. He predicted the downfall of the colonial empires, England's as well as Holland's. "The whole policy of colonization is madness," he wrote to an English friend in 1897.[44] And again, "It is imperative to break immediately with militarism, because it has become unbearable."[45]

With his foreboding of approaching disaster, and his clear perception of the ills that afflicted the second empire, it might be expected that Fontane would be a rallying point for the intelligentsia that stood in opposition to the new Germany, the Kaiser, and "the Junker-bourgeois coalition." But this was not the case. A man of seventy may change his opinions and become a radical, but it is not likely that he will lead an attack on the status quo. Furthermore, Fontane had always been a lone wolf and would have felt out of place as the speaker of a party. In addition, he was not openly hostile to the powers that were. He resented the neglect he had suffered at the hands of Prussian officialdom and found it ludicrous that he had his most faithful admirers among the educated Jews of Berlin, but that was not enough to make him take over the office of tribune for which he was ill equipped. He restricted his criticism to private remarks, and only after his death, when his letters were published, did it become apparent that the man whom many had considered the celebrant of the old regime was in reality one of its severest critics. And even in his criticism there is some ambiguity, the ambiguity of a man who finds himself too closely allied with the old society to advocate a revolutionary break. His attitude is best expressed in one of his letters when he refers to the Junker: ". . . these fellows are unbearable and charming at the same time."[46] This equivocal attitude characterizes many of his commentaries and is inherent in his novels. His stand on social and political problems is neither as firm nor as outspoken as that of Zola, or Shaw, or Chekhov. With all the affection we feel for him, we miss an element of universality. He remains the chronicler of Berlin society.

As a social historian, however, he is far ahead of other writers of the period. There were those like Ernst von Wildenbruch, who was related to the Hohenzollern dynasty and who exalted the virtues of the ruling house with a sovereign disregard of historical truth. He was the Kaiser's choice for poet laureate of the new Germany, but fortunately there were limits to the imperial power when it came to matters of taste. Many writers, of course, took Berlin society for their subject matter: Arno Holz, Georg Hermann, Fritz Mautner, Max Kretzer, and a fair number of gifted women, Adele Gerhard, Gabriele Reuter, and others, who tried to capture the spirit of Berlin, but today their books gather dust on back shelves.[47] Time is a merciless filter that separates what is merely consumer-product from the true work of art.

The spirit and style of Fontane's social novels were continued by Thomas Mann, who acknowledged his indebtedness to the older master.[48] But Thomas Mann's knowledge of Berlin was superficial compared to his familiarity with Lübeck and Munich, and he made no attempt to portray the new metropolis. His brother, Heinrich Mann, wrote a novel about a climber who comes to Berlin to make his way into the circles of the nouveaux riches; it is called *Im Schlaraffenland* (Fool's Paradise). It is one of his weaker books and not up to his other satirical descriptions of Wilhelminian Germany.[49] Jacob Wassermann also undertook to picture the disparate lives of the upper and working classes in

Berlin in his novel, *Christian Wahnschaffe*, a work which owes much to Dostoievski. But the synthesis which Wassermann had in mind is not achieved, and the book is more of a crime story than a picture of society.[50]

Germany's most significant literary productions after 1890 were in the field of lyrical poetry. However, none of the most prominent authors was a native of Berlin: Stefan George came from the Rhineland, Hugo von Hofmannsthal from Vienna, and Rainer Maria Rilke from Prague. All were in Berlin at one time or another, but they never remained there for long. George leaned toward Munich and Heidelberg, Hofmannsthal toward his native Vienna, and Rilke toward Paris.[51] They were drawn to Berlin by the presence there of friends and publishers, the theatre, and congenial artists, not by the city itself. The new German capital provoked in them a feeling of hostility rather than affection.

There is one field in which Berlin holds a very special place; this is the drama—to be exact, the naturalistic drama. Its triumph was not only a literary event; it was as much, or even more, a political and social victory for the ideas of the educated middle class, as well as their mode of expression. At the time the success of the naturalistic drama was celebrated in Berlin in 1889, naturalism was already recognized as a style; Zola and Ibsen enjoyed international reputations. But it was not an easy matter to bring this new mode of expression into the German theatre. The censor could not prevent the public from reading naturalistic books, but he could prevent the performance of dramas that "threatened the public morals." The staging of such works was a public affair and could only have taken place in Berlin, where pressures and counterpressures were strongest.

The successful performance of Gerhart Hauptmann's *Vor Sonnenaufgang* (Before Dawn) punctured the official armor. The story of this first night belongs with the history of the Berlin theatre, where we shall deal with it. Here we will restrict ourselves to Hauptmann's literary position and his relation to Berlin. Hauptmann was not a Berliner; he came from Silesia, and never lost touch with his native soil. Nevertheless, Berlin attracted him "like a magnet," and he knew he had to conquer it or consider himself defeated.[52] His fame as one of the great dramatists of his generation is indissolubly connected with Berlin, where the *Freie Bühne*

(Free Stage) was formed as an association of devotees of avant-garde literature. Its express purpose was to circumvent the strictures of the censor and to allow the performance of such "decadent" works as Ibsen's *Ghosts* or Hauptmann's *Before Dawn*.

Between 1890 and 1900, Hauptmann became a European celebrity in spite of the venom and hatred with which his work was received by German officialdom. His plays were performed all over Europe and translated into many languages. Some of his scenes are taken from localities near Berlin, but only one has the life of the city as its theme. It is called *The Rats*.[53] It was written in 1911 and deals, as its title suggests, with the seamy side of Berlin. It takes place in one of those rental-barracks of which we have spoken; the time is 1884, and the theme is the hopelessness of life in a metropolis where murder, kidnapping, starvation, alcoholism, and every form of vice are the order of the day. The people who are herded together in these slum-dwellings live like rats; they dig, and nibble, and devour everything that comes their way, but are themselves the victims of a callous and oppressive social order that denies them both decency and self-respect. It has been debated whether *The Rats* is one more naturalistic drama, or an attempt to show the decay of the antebellum world, a world already undermined by the ruthless activity of *The Rats*.[54]

Whatever the truth, Berlin as a city was as little of an inspiration for Hauptmann as it was for George or Rilke: it "oppressed him like a nightmare."[55] Nor did Berlin inspire Hauptmann's contemporary, Sudermann, whose plays provoked almost as much discussion as Hauptmann's, but which today are well-nigh forgotten. As Fontane said to Storm, Berlin was not a poetical city, and those who tried to press a drop of poetry out of its heartbreaking style of life were doomed to failure. There were the brothers Hart, Julius and Heinrich; there were the poets, Holz and Schlaf, who wished to capture the essence of metropolitan life; there was Richard Dehmel, who tried to inject Nietzsche's dionysian style into his poems. The list is endless. It should be clear, however, that Berlin did not inspire poets as Paris inspired Balzac or Baudelaire or Proust. It should also be clear that German literary criticism of Berlin society had little influence on reality. It had no contact with the life of the political groups that opposed the second empire, and the ruling class was impervious to the philippics levelled against it. The search for any other medium in which discontent with existing conditions might have found an outlet leads us into the discussion of journalism as practiced in Berlin.

ii

It has been said that every nation has the press it deserves. It would be more accurate to say that the press is a true mirror of the social conditions which it records. We have taken note of the appearance of a metropolitan press in Berlin. Its raison d'être was, more than anything else, the fact that daily newspapers had become big business. The influence exercised by these papers on politics is a different matter. In a society as castelike as that of Berlin, public opinion had a limited influence. Consequently, the newspapers addressed themselves to specific groups in society whose political and economic interests they made it a point to express.

The conservative papers, such as the *Kreuzzeitung* or *Die Tägliche Rundschau*, reflect the idiosyncrasies of the Junkers and those elements of the bourgeoisie who identified themselves with the Prussian aristocracy. Next in line was *Die Zeit* which, under the leadership of Friedrich Naumann, continued the agitation initiated by Stoecker, advocating an aggressive naval and colonial policy in common with the *Deutsche Zeitung*.[56] Neither paper displays a great amount of originality.

The liberal journals were more interesting and showed a higher level of intelligence in discussing the issues of the day. The *Berliner Tageblatt* was the prestige paper of the Mosse family, and the Ullsteins took over the renowned *Vossische Zeitung*, which dated back to the eighteenth century. The latter made no profits and was supported by subsidies, and by income from other papers which catered to mass audiences, to whose tastes for entertainment, gossip, etc. they gave full attention. The third member of the great triumvirate of newspaper publishers was August Scherl, who recognized the need for a journal which would devote itself to the cultural aspirations of the German upper classes. Scherl founded *Der Tag*; it appeared in two versions: the red *Tag* and the black *Tag*. The red *Tag* carried no advertising, giving itself over entirely to political and cultural commentaries.

The German newspapers of this period were in many ways different from the newspapers of today.[57] News was not the paramount consideration; of equal significance and interest were the articles in any field that might appeal to their audiences. Consequently the political editorials were prominently displayed on the first page. In the main they were written by the editor-in-chief and signed with his initials. The *Berliner Tageblatt* carried the editorials of Theodor Wolff, a member of the Mosse family who had considerable international experience. His opinions were noticed but rarely heeded. The by-line, G. B., in the *Vossische Zeitung*, stood for Georg Bernhard, whose opinions represented the politics of the Ullstein press. *Der Tag* was officially without political ties, but was decidedly more conservative than the two other prestige papers. Its editor was Paul Marx, one of the most attractive figures of Berlin journalism. A tall, proud man, of strong national feelings, Marx conducted his paper with great impartiality and permitted a variety of opinions to be expressed on its pages.[58] The political judgment of these pundits aroused extraordinary interest in Berlin, but again, carried scant weight with those who made the decisions. Political journalism in the second empire, and especially in Berlin, was an ungrateful task, a Sisyphean labor. The socialist press was, of course, still less influential, its main assignment being to guard the doctrines of Marxism and to pump fresh blood into the heart of the class struggle.

A large portion of Berlin newspapers was taken up by a section called *"Unter dem Strich"* (Below the line). Everything "below the line" was strictly apolitical, ranging all the way from novels to theatre criticism, from poetical sketches to art reviews and reports on musical events. Unter dem Strich articles were the equivalent of the French *feuilleton*, and it was in keeping with the apolitical orientation of the German upper class to give this section of the paper as much attention as was given to the political articles.[59]

The novels were published in daily installments as bait for the subscribers, especially their wives and daughters. Many novelists looked upon serialization as a monetary reward greatly to be desired. Of equal importance to the reader, however, were the theatrical and musical criticisms. These journalistic features were fully justified by the large variety of theatres and the extraordinary number of concerts and opera performances which were to be found in Berlin, and the high level of criticism with which they were received. Among the theatre critics were Theodor Fontane, who wrote for the *Vossische Zeitung*, Paul Schlenther, Otto Brahm, Alfred Kerr, and many lesser lights. The impact of this daily discussion of dramatic art on the reading public was considerable and was largely responsible for overcoming the parochialism of Berlin's educated classes.[60] It also led to a close cooperation between theatre criticism and management; there were a number of instances when a critic became a director and seized the stage to bring his ideas to light. Musical criticism and the discussion of art exhibits were likewise on a high level: Max Marshalk, himself a composer, was one of the chroniclers of musical events; Karl Scheffler and Julius Meier-Gräfe were outstanding in the field of art criticism.[61]

The significance of the feuilleton was not limited to the subjects on which these men reported, nor were their labors directed exclusively toward the enlightenment of the general public. Given the particular place of literature and the arts in imperial Berlin, the critical appraisal of a drama, an opera, or an art exhibition was, more often than not, a pioneering piece of work. Not only was the critic obliged to fight the ignorance or stupidity of the philistines, but he had also to oppose the reactionary taste of the upper classes and, more important still, the artistic dictatorship of the Kaiser. The hostility aroused by any innovation in the realm of literature and the arts was so violent that it required a good store of courage to praise the men and women who dared to open new windows on the world. When the dramas of Gerhart Hauptmann were first performed, incredible epithets were hurled at the author. A deputy to the Prussian parliament called the Free Stage "an intellectual brothel," and others insisted that "the fellow should be put behind bars."[62]

It is a perplexing feature of the second empire that political stagnation existed side by side with intellectual and cultural renaissance. In all of Germany, wrote Friedrich Meinecke, one could sense something new around 1890, not only in politics but also in the cultural world. But whereas the movement in politics was marked by a descending curve, there was an ascending spiral in the intellectual life.[63]

It is customary today to give the Weimar Republic the credit for an intellectual blossoming and to contrast it with the sterility of the Wilhelminian period. But such a perspective misses the fact that most of the remarkable accomplishments of "Weimar" were already gestating during the second empire, even though their birth may have been violently opposed.[64] And it is here that we begin to appreciate the obstetrical miracle performed by the liberal press of Berlin. The verbal battles which were fought *"unter dem Strich"* facilitated the triumph of contemporary poetry, the modern drama, impressionist and expressionist painting, the music of Richard Strauss—in short, the triumph of those fresh aspects of the arts which were atuned to the spirit of the epoch. One might almost say that the educated German middle class looked upon this struggle and its accomplishments as a substitute for the political successes that were denied them, or that they had too easily relinquished. Here again the parallel to the Weimar Republic is striking. The second empire and the Weimar Republic both reveal the educated bourgeoisie in a similar quandary engendered by their habitual preference for engaging in intellectual or ideological struggles rather than going into battle with their political opponents.

The Berlin press did not confine its activities to the dailies. Almost as important were the weekly and monthly magazines. In a way, they were perhaps more representative of certain groups in Berlin society and show their mood with greater clarity than did the newspapers which appeared day by day. From a sociological standpoint, this is easy to understand: by its very nature, the weekly or monthly magazine appealed to the educated classes, and only they were likely to form a reliable nucleus of subscribers. Berlin occupied the first place among all German cities in quality as well as quantity of its magazines. In 1890, no less than 604 weeklies, biweeklies, monthlies, or quarterlies were published in the capital, representing 19 percent of all such publications in Germany.[65] They had, of course, a wide audience, and their readers were not limited to Berlin. Among the most renowned was the *Preussische Jahrbücher*, which had been founded in 1858 by Rudolf Haym and later flourished under the leadership of Heinrich von Treitschke. Following Treitschke's death, Hans Del-brück, another historian from the University of Berlin, took over. The *Preussische Jahrbücher* was a serious magazine devoted to political, historical, and social analysis. It steered a middle course between the publications which addressed themselves to scholars and the so-called educated public. Another important magazine was the *Deutsche Rundschau*, which for many years held a leading position among German reviews. Established in 1874, it was, even more than the *Preussische Jahrbücher*, the voice of Berlin's intellectual and cultural elite. Its founder, Julius Rodenberg, had traveled widely and written on many subjects before he undertook the organization of the magazine. What he hoped to bring into being was a review like the *Revue des deux Mondes* or the *Quarterly Review*.[66] Both of these dated from the earlier part of the nineteenth century, and Berlin had nothing that could compare with them in the way of distinguished publications.[67] It was to Rodenberg's credit that he was able to assemble a group of contributors, the list of whose names reads like a *Who's Who* of 1880: Sybel, Schmoller, Mommsen, Dilthey, Hermann Grimm, Fontane, Storm, Gottfried Keller, C. F. Meyer, the Danish novelist Jens Peter Jacobsen, Georg Brandes, Wilhelm Scherer, Otto Brahm—and many, many others.

Politically, the *Deutsche Rundschau* stood in the right wing of the liberal party, a position which did not protect it from Bismarck's ire when the editors published documents which the chancellor considered detrimental to his reputation.[68] Artistically, the *Deutsche Rundschau* shied away from avant-garde movements both in music and in literature. It made its peace with Richard Wagner, but did not support the naturalistic vogue of the 1880's. The editors spoke out against Zola, the champion of naturalism, and belittled Hauptmann as "an immature talent which will suffocate in the swamp it attempts to picture."[69]

Although the *Deutsche Rundschau* continued its existence until it was suppressed during the Third Reich in 1942, its opposition to the more experimental or audacious forms of aesthetic production provoked a reaction. Those who saw in contemporary art and literature the promise of a spiritual renewal began to found journals of their own. *Die Freie Bühne für modernes Leben* (The Free Stage for Modern Life), founded in 1890, was devoted to the interests of the theatre. Its editor was Otto Brahm, about whom we shall have more to say in the following chapter. In 1905, Siegfried Jacobsohn established *Die Schaubühne* (The Theatre), which was changed to *Die Weltbühne* (The World Theatre) after World War I and became one of the most controversial publications of the Weimar Republic.

Of still greater impact was the *Neue Rundschau*, a review that gathered in most of the authors sponsored by the publisher, Samuel Fischer. This publication had more literary style and was more liberal than the *Deutsche Rundschau*. It attacked imperial Germany without hesitation or camouflage and must be considered one of the great publications of the second empire. If it did not actually inspire the founding of the *Nouvelle Revue Française* and Ortega y Gasset's *Revista del Occidente*, it easily ranks with both.

The foregoing rapid survey of German magazines and reviews confirms our earlier assertion that cultural interest and awareness outdistanced political and social consciousness in Berlin. Strictly political reviews were few and far between. The Pan-Germanic League (*Alldeutscher Verein*) began to beat its noisy drums in the *Alldeutsche Blätter* (1895), calling for colonies, a large navy, and *Lebensraum*, though the word itself was not yet in use.[70] At the other end of the political spectrum were the *Sozialistische Monatshefte* (the socialist monthlies), also founded in 1895; these did not, however, have the approval of the party and were actually subsidized by capitalistic money.[71]

In the list of political reviews, perhaps the most interesting venture was Friedrich Naumann's *Die Hilfe*. It attempted to bridge the gulf between capital and labor by means of a program of national socialism. Naumann aroused little response on the part of the working class which remained faithful to its Marxian creed and rejected all attempts at reconciliation as so much empty talk. Among the middle-class youth, however, Naumann acquired a large following. Here may be found several famous names: Max Weber, Friedrich Meinecke, Theodor Heuss, who saw in Naumann the leader of a magnificent youth movement and approved the idea of a great national party occupying a place between the antagonistic extremes.[72] The national-socialist concept promised to bring internal harmony to the national scene, a mutual understanding which Germany had not known since the founding of the empire. However, the cleavages in Germany were too deep, or the barriers between the classes were too high, and Naumann's agitation came to naught.

The most prominent journalist of this period in Berlin was Maximilian Harden, and it is not much of an exaggeration to say that he illustrates all of the tendencies we have noted. Although such a judgment could be substantiated, it might also be questioned, since Harden was not only individualistic in the extreme, but also possessed a personality of such unusual grain and color that he does not lend himself to facile generalizations.

Maximilian Harden was born in Berlin in 1861, the sixth son of a Jewish merchant, Arnold Witkowski. At the age of fifteen he broke away from his family, converted to Christianity, changed his name to Maximilian Felix Ernst Harden, and became an actor.[73] He preserved an affection for the theatre throughout his life; he was one of the god-fathers of the Free-Stage movement and later kept in close contact with Max Reinhardt. It seems more than possible that his choice of the acting profession may have been born of a deep-seated tendency toward exhibitionism. Certainly much in Harden's career can be understood only in this light.

However, the stage could not hold him for long; perhaps his talent did not reach to stardom, or possibly the lure of literary fame was more attractive. Whatever the reason, he switched to journalism, and from literary subjects he moved on to politics in 1890. The date is significant; it is the year of Bismarck's dismissal. Harden began to sign his articles with the name 'Apostata'; it is difficult to say from whom or from what he was breaking away.[74] In 1892 he established connections with Bismarck, who was then living in Friedrichsruh. The former chancellor received him and made him a confidant of his resentment against the new course and the men he held responsible for his dismissal, the Kaiser and his clique. Harden made the most of these revelations, going so far as to call one of his articles, "Kollege Bismarck" (My Colleague, Bismarck).[75] From 1892 on, he lived in opposition to official Germany, hostile not only to the public façade of his country, but to almost anything initiated by the new government. It is much easier to understand what Harden was fighting against than what he was fighting for. The imperial government was only one of the targets that provoked his fury. The bourgeoisie was another, and the social-democratic party still another, though his enmity stopped short of the working class. Although his polemics contained some brilliant insights, they were basically rhetorical and consistently negative: opposition for the sake of opposition.

His arena became more and more the domestic and international politics of Germany, but he had neither a clear conception of what Germany could or should accomplish, nor any sound proposal as to how her goal might be reached. Though he criticized the rule of William II for its personal nature, he was himself extremely personal in his attack on the abuses of the regime, attributing them to human failures rather than to structural flaws in the body politic. In a curious way, he became afflicted with the very illness which he wanted to cure: the substitution of personal solutions for objective ones.

Harden forged his own weapon for his fight against the status quo. He founded a weekly which he controlled and, in large part, wrote himself called *Die Zukunft* (The Future).[76] Its first issue appeared in 1892, its last in 1922 when his public career was cut short by attacks from national hooligans. During these thirty years, it was widely read, feared, censored, confiscated, but never effectively silenced. Exact figures as to its circulation are hard to come by. Around 1900 *Die Zukunft* sold some 10,000 copies; at the height of its notoriety the figure reached 22,000.[77] Few serious reviews could boast of such success, and its circulation figures came close to those of the Berlin dailies. *Die Zukunft* was Harden's most personal creation in style and purpose, but he could not write every issue himself and gathered in several distinguished contributors from various professions and with varied interests, such as the physicians, Robert Koch, Paul Ehrlich, and Schweninger; the economist, Sombart; the historian, Karl Lamprecht; the philosopher, Vaihinger; the critic, George Brandes; also other personalities which are more difficult to classify: Martin Buber, Rainer Maria Rilke, Walther Rathenau, and a host of writers from England, France, and Russia.

A publication such as *Die Zukunft* was possible only in Berlin, and it displays both the virtues and the flaws of the youngest of

the European metropolises. Its basic function was to criticize—
to criticize Berlin, the Hohenzollern, the bourgeoisie and its timor-
ous attitude toward the ruler, but also to criticize the tasteless
showmanship that prevailed in Berlin, the architectural and sculp-
tural atrocities that defaced the streets and the public squares of
the city; in a word it criticized everything that was tawdry, vulgar,
garish, or gross. Logically, its attitude attracted critical minds that
did not fear to strike out at the conditions which exposed Germany to the world's ridicule. But it was Harden who chose the
quarry, mapped the course, and listed the priorities for attack. To
guarantee the success of the enterprise, a number of qualifications
were necessary. In the first place came professional integrity, and
to the best of my knowledge, Harden was never accused of venality.
It cannot be said whether he was equally scrupulous in regard to
the sources of his information. He protested that he did not look
for privileged information, that he spent his days in his little
house in the *Grunewald* working on his review, but at the same
time he admitted that he had a wide circle of acquaintances who
kept him informed. Among these, he counted the painter, Liebermann; the bankers, Dernburg, Warburg, and Carl Fürstenberg;
industrialists, like Walther Rathenau, and later the Baron von
Holstein. Needless to say, he knew the leading journalists of the
capital, Theodor Wolff and Georg Bernhard, and bohemians from
the theatrical world. For some of his articles, he needed nothing
more than the information he gleaned from the official news
service, but for others he must have tapped undisclosed sources.
It was often said that he kept a dossier of all persons who might
one day become grist for his press, and that he was not squeamish
as to the manner in which he acquired his information.

This leads us to another question: what moved Harden in his
constant campaign against the Kaiser and the new Germany? Was
it a patriotic fear for the future of his country? Was it a moral
disgust with the prevailing hypocrisy and sham? Or was it something more personal, something at the wellspring of his being, an
irrepressible desire to occupy the limelight and to make the world
conscious of his power?[78] No one has yet solved the enigma of
Harden's personality. Without doubt, he possessed great courage;
he was accused three times of lèse majesté and was twice sentenced to prison; he challenged the most sacred taboos of imperial

Germany, the moral integrity of the officer corps and the aristocracy. Certainly this required fortitude and self-reliance. Yet one cannot suppress a sensation of uneasiness if one reads the accusations that he hurled in the face of imperial Germany. Some kind of verbal hysteria is apparent, a vindictiveness and hatred which is not in accord with his vaunted role of objective censor.

Surely he was entirely justified in railing against the liberal writers who were the self-appointed guides of public opinion in Berlin and were controlled by the financial interests of the newspapers. He was equally in the right when he attacked German foreign policy as it was pursued after Bismarck's dismissal, on the ground that it was motivated by dangerous illusions. Like his mentor, Bismarck, Harden favored a return to an alliance with Russia, but the diplomacy he advocated was fraught with as many perils as the policies he condemned. Envisioning England and France as Germany's principal enemies, Harden suggested a number of harebrained projects to improve Germany's international image. During the Boer war, he proposed a great continental alliance against England, and during the first Moroccan crisis he brought forward the idea of a preventive war against France.[79]

In domestic affairs he was a most vociferous champion of true constitutionalism; that is, he insisted there should be some effectual check on William II and his constant interference in the nation's politics.[80] Indeed, Harden went as far as anyone could in exposing the weaknesses of the regime, but even his most iconoclastic outbursts show a strange mixture of insight and incongruity. Perhaps Harden's shoulders should not be made to carry all the blame. As the price of his independence, he forfeited auxiliaries to man his directives. He failed to see that a political writer needs a following as well as an audience, but Harden prided himself on belonging to no clique, pressure-group, or party; by the same token, his words remained words, which his pen inscribed with ease, and the paper accepted with patience. They could warn of danger, but they could not incite to action. Harden himself must have recognized that the echo of his voice did not reach beyond the circle of his readers, and that if he was to demolish the citadel of Germany's autocracy, he would have to call up heavier ammunition. In 1906, he began his assault on the entourage of the Kaiser. This famous campaign is known as the

Eulenburg affair, and after more than sixty years and much painstaking research, its background is still shrouded in mystery.

In 1906, the Baron von Holstein was dismissed from his post in the foreign office.[81] Whether he merits the title of architect of German foreign policy following the dismissal of Bismarck is a moot question; no one can doubt that his influence on Germany's international relations was tremendous. Nor can it be denied that he was a vindictive, suspicious man, whose character bordered on the pathological. Harden had assailed his influence and his position in *Die Zukunft* and had made him the prime culprit for Germany's declining power throughout the world.[82] Holstein responded to this accusation, and Harden published the letter. There began a relationship between these two representatives of Wilhelminian Germany that would be called extraordinary in the extreme did we not know that politics makes strange bedfellows. To judge by his public declarations, Harden accepted Holstein's views in regard to his activities in the foreign office at face value.[83] Holstein's attitude toward Harden is not so transparent; his objective may have been to use Harden as a medium through which he might avenge himself for his dismissal.[84] That he conveyed information to Harden is certain, but the private vices of those in high office are rarely inviolate, and informers are legion. The decision to launch an attack on the personal retinue of the Kaiser was surely Harden's alone, but Holstein planned to use Harden's revelations in his scheme for vengeance.

The time seemed propitious. Others joined Harden in their condemnation of governmental policy. In his *Memoirs*, the chancellor, Hohenlohe, had thrown some light on the pernicious intrigues which accompanied every major decision in Berlin. During a debate in the Reichstag, von Bülow (Hohenlohe's successor) had called the "camarilla" a poisonous plant which should be uprooted. Thus Harden felt that the time was ripe for unmasking the dangerous men in the Kaiser's court. He began his denunciations by accusing Prince Philip Eulenburg and Count Kuno von Moltke of homosexual tendencies.

Von Moltke was aide de camp to the emperor and the commanding general in Berlin. Philip Eulenburg belonged to the highest echelon of the Prussian aristocracy and had held important diplomatic positions, but his real influence was a corollary of his intimacy with the Kaiser. He was a dilettante, dabbling in music and poetry and encouraging the Kaiser to do likewise. Although he was without personal ambition and had no desire to advance himself with the emperor, he nevertheless had a pernicious influence on William, supplying him constantly with the adulation he craved. Bismarck had given Harden some facts about Eulenburg and had referred to him as a "Prussian Cagliostro."[85] Actually, the influence of Eulenburg was on the wane by 1906, but Harden did not recognize this shift in the situation and asserted further that there were secret affiliations between Eulenburg and the French foreign office and that, knowingly or unknowingly, Eulenburg had passed on highly confidential information to French diplomats, thus contributing to Germany's defeat in the Moroccan crisis. Whatever the truth of the accusation, it was not the main issue. The Eulenburg affair rose to the questionable rank of a 'cause célèbre' on the basis of Harden's disclosure of sexual aberrations among a small but powerful group at the Berlin court.

The scandal moved from the pages of *Die Zukunft* to the halls of justice. Count Moltke announced his intention to sue Harden for libel, and nothing could have pleased Harden more. His information was unassailable; the Berlin police had for a long time been in possession of the facts.[86] The trial began in 1907, dragging on through appeals and retrials into 1908 and giving Harden an echo chamber far beyond what his own magazine could provide. When the curtain was finally lowered on Berlin's most sensational law-suit, Harden stood vindicated, and four members of the aristocracy, one of whom was a Hohenzollern, were forced into oblivion; a number of officers had also been gravely compromised.

In retrospect, it seems questionable whether Harden's strategy had been either wise or salutary. Was the homosexuality of certain Prussian grandees really a political issue of prime importance, or had Harden merely played a part in Holstein's vendetta? The disclosures made during the trials had indeed exposed the moral decadence that afflicted Berlin's upper circles. Whether there had been, as Harden asserted, political indiscretions, cannot be strictly verified, but in any case they were neither so grave nor so impor-

tant as he contended. Harden's own statements about the affair
are contradictory. We may accept his word that he had not intended to drag his paper through the dirt, but he is less convincing when he wrote that he felt impelled to warn the Kaiser of the
perverts who surrounded him. Had this been his intention, it
seems curious that he postponed his good deed for so many years;
Bismarck had informed him years before of Eulenburg's influence.

Harden's action seems intelligible only in the light of a desire
to discredit the personal regime of the emperor himself; since
he could not attack William II outright, it is possible that he
intended to discredit him by assaulting his friends. But the Eulenburg affair did not become another Diamond Necklace scandal.
When the Kaiser committed the blunder of the *Daily Telegraph*
interview in 1908, the moment appeared to be right for a constitutional revolution, but, as we know, it did not occur. Harden
was of the opinion that it had already taken place! "The empire,"
he wrote, "is sovereign, not the emperor . . . the constitution
does not need to be changed . . . it offers the people enough."

The statement sounds confident, but it was, alas, untrue. The
constitution was very much in need of alteration, but no one had
the courage to tackle the problem. Moreover, it is not certain that
a constitutional revolution was feasible in a country like Germany; it is possible that it would have resulted in a military dictatorship in dynastic disguise.[87] In any case, it was not in Harden's
destiny to lead it.

The peak of Harden's influence had been reached in the Eulenburg affair. The remainder of his life was anticlimactic. During
World War I, the *Zukunft* was frequently censored because of its
failure to follow the line of the High Command. In 1916, for
example, Harden praised President Wilson as a statesman of high
ethical principles; this was an opinion which the German foreign
office welcomed, but which the military authorities disparaged.
It must be admitted that his voice was no longer representative
of any significant trend in Germany.

When the empire collapsed in 1918, Harden had the bitter
satisfaction of seeing his warnings confirmed, but he was no admirer of the Weimar Republic and attacked Rathenau and President Ebert almost as vehemently as he had once denounced the

emperor. During the summer of 1922, he became the gang victim of nationalistic rowdies who beat him up severely, but did not kill him. Once more Harden's case was in court, but in those days of miscarried justice, his rhetoric reverberated hollowly. He left Germany and made his home in Switzerland where he died in 1927.[88]

Precisely because Harden had more courage and greater journalistic gifts than other critics of the political and social world of Berlin, he proves our point that the power of the press in the capital was limited. Its influence lay in the field of culture; in the realm of politics and social reform it was impotent. If we compare Berlin with other European capitals or with great American cities, the difference becomes apparent. Berlin did not have a metropolitan paper of the stature of the *London Times*, the *New York Times*, or even Buenos Aires' *La Prensa*. Nor were the newspapers owned by press-lords of the calibre of Northcliff, Beaverbrook, William Randolph Hearst, or Joseph Pulitzer. The impact of the press on the public mind was, therefore, commensurably less puissant.

Berlin did not spawn spectacular journalistic careers like that of Theodor Herzl, who utilized the press to initiate a movement of worldwide interest: Zionism.[89] Nor does one find in Berlin a journalist in command of such verbal magic as the Viennese, Karl Kraus. Kraus has sometimes been compared to Harden and *Die Fackel* to *Die Zukunft*, but Kraus felt nothing but contempt for Harden and was enraged when the latter was called the genius of the opposition.[90] However, Kraus wielded even less influence in Vienna than did Harden in Berlin and was heard only by those who belonged to a literary fringe made up of unconventional, roving spirits proud to be bohemians. Such groups flourished in Paris, in Vienna, and in Munich, but Berlin had nothing comparable. To be sure, there was *Das Romanische Kaffee* where a few unpublished writers discouraged each other by reading their rejected manuscripts; the anarchist, Erich Mühsam, who founded a journal with the appropriate name, *Der arme Teufel* (The Poor Devil), is one of the typical figures of this bohemia. Berlin was a city of hard work and no nonsense, with no room for a Latin Quarter or the coffee houses of Vienna.[91] Her lack of this particular adjunct of literary life gives us one explanation of the third element that determined the intellectual profile of Berlin: the institutions of higher learning, symbols of mental discipline and tangible achievements, qualities which the Berliner admired.

iii

The University of Berlin was the youngest of the great European universities, but in a comparatively short time it had taken its place with the universities of Oxford, Paris, and Heidelberg, even surpassing them in certain fields. At the beginning of the century, the influence of speculative philosophy had been all powerful; after 1840, Berlin had followed the flow of the tide and had replaced the older ideologies by an empirical approach. The "positive philosophy" of France and England had gained some following, though its reach was never undisputed nor as widely accepted in Berlin as it was in western Europe.

In viewing the institutes of higher learning, we must first consider the structural changes that the turn toward a more pragmatic science brought with it. As a focal point of Germany's industrial growth and in an atmosphere of technological progress and economic prosperity, the neohumanism on which Wilhelm von Humboldt had built the University of Berlin seemed antiquated and bloodless. At the very least, it was necessary to complement the traditional offerings by new disciplines which would be aligned with the rapid expansion of Berlin's industrial establishments. As a result of this demand for scientific institutions in tune with the Zeitgeist, a quiet revolution took place in German education. This struggle began at high-school level and gradually engulfed the universities and academies.

The gymnasium, as established by Humboldt, had held its monopolistic position in German education until 1870. Only the diploma attesting graduation from the gymnasium, called the Abitur, could be given as the credential for acceptance in the university. In 1859 a new type of high school had been introduced which still preserved intensive training in Latin (nine years), but omitted Greek, thus making room for the teaching of mathematics, physics, and chemistry. Gradually, this type of school, called *Realgymnasium*, gained ground; along with it there also appeared the *Oberrealschule* and the *Realschule* whose diplomas opened the doors to a limited number of professions. The universities insisted that only graduates of the gymnasium were qualified to enter any one of the four traditional faculties: law, theology, medicine, and philosophy.[92] The fight between the old institution and the new and more experimental ones was carried on for decades. In 1882, Germany had seven different types of high school, and the competition between these institutions necessarily involved the institutions of higher learning. Polytechnic institutes had been introduced in France in 1795, and both name and curriculum had been taken over in a number of European countries. In the United States polytechnic schools had long enjoyed university status. But the German universities turned a cold shoulder toward those establishments which were devoted to the teaching of the applied sciences and refused to lend their approval to the polytechnic institutes.

It has been said that the Kaiser approached every question with an open mouth, but there were some problems where he showed an open mind. As far back as 1890, he had initiated a conference for the reform of the gymnasia with a speech criticizing the formalism of their training. A second conference to debate the necessary reforms met in 1900. Among those invited to attend were some of the most distinguished names from the University of Berlin, but there were also representatives from industry and agriculture, and not long after this conference the faculties of law, philosophy, and medicine opened their gates to graduates of the *Realgymnasium*.

The next step was the recognition of the polytechnic institutes as equal partners in the process of higher education. The universities continued to insist that the institutes did not have the right to confer academic degrees; their graduates might receive diplomas only. The right to grant the Ph.D. degree was specifically denied. This dictum not only closed many doors to the graduates of polytechnic schools, but in a country as title-conscious as Germany, gave them inferior rank in the intellectual world.[93] On his own initiative, the Kaiser decided to break the resistance of the universities by appointing some members of the polytechnic schools to the Prussian upper chamber, the Herrenhaus. Heretofore, this privilege had been extended to the universities only, and they raised strenuous objections to the change. In writing about the situation, the Kaiser remarked, "There followed a violent struggle against the scholarly classical pride until my will was made to prevail by decree."[94] The initiative of the emperor was upheld and supported by the officials in the ministry of education. The men who occupied this position in the second empire were, by and large, aristocratic nonentities of conservative leanings.[95] They were not the master minds of German educational policy, and except for Friedrich Althoff, their names would add little to our study.

Friedrich Althoff was in charge of university affairs, and for more than twenty-five years his influence had been decisive not only in the selection of personnel, but also in the general proposals for the institutions of higher learning.[96] Althoff has been accused of prejudice in his choice of appointments, and brutality in his treatment of the university's representatives.[97] Whatever may be the truth of these allegations, it is also true that Althoff viewed the German university, especially the University of Berlin, in a much wider perspective than his colleagues in the ministry. Had his plans carried weight, Berlin might have been able to boast of the most advanced educational plant in all Europe.

Humboldt had intended that the university should be based on a union of research and instruction where each would benefit and fertilize the other. This union should find its institutional embodiment in a three-fold design of university, academy, and research institute. Only the university and the academy had materialized, and Althoff was very much aware of the need for institutes of advanced studies dedicated to pure research. He had reached this decision partly because he was aware that certain brilliant scholars are not proficient teachers, but he also had in mind the great demands made on the individual scholars as a result of the autonomous structure of the German university. In his endeavor to free them from this burden, Althoff conceived the idea of an institute in which distinguished scholars would devote their full time to research. These institutes are today a permanent feature of the academic world; when Althoff originated the project sixty years ago, they were unknown.

Althoff had his eye on an enormous plot of land in Berlin-

Dahlem belonging to the Hohenzollern dynasty. It was called at the time a *Domäne* (domain) and was given over to agriculture. (Some of the farms that dotted the area are still in operation today.) Althoff hoped he would be able to convince the Kaiser to donate this valuable land for the purpose of erecting buildings that would house his research institute. His plans, however, did not end here; his ultimate objective was to construct a university city in Dahlem, "a German Oxford," as he called it.

The University of Berlin and the Academy of Science were located in the center of Berlin in buildings which had not been designed for pedagogical purposes; some had been palaces and some were additions to state buildings which had been given over to university use. The clinics of the medical faculty were scattered over the northern sector of Berlin and at some distance from the lecture rooms. It was Althoff's inspiration to unite everything pertaining to the university, offices, classrooms, lecture halls, libraries, etc. in a great university community on the Dahlem property. This was not a simple matter; one obstacle was the desire on the part of rival offices to sell the Domäne in small lots. But in 1906 Althoff convinced the most distinguished professors of the University to petition the emperor for a centralized organization of all scholarly pursuits in Berlin.[98] The emperor received the suggestion with considerable interest.

Although Althoff died in 1908, his plans were not forgotten, and when the university celebrated its centennial anniversary in 1910, the Kaiser called for a foundation which would insure financial support for the research institute. The imperial appeal received the anticipated response, and on Founders' Day of the same year the Kaiser announced the establishment of the new institute.[99] It was, of course, called the Kaiser-Wilhelms-Gesellschaft, and one of the most extraordinary men of Wilhelminian Germany was selected to be its president. Adolf von Harnack was a great theologian and at the same time an experienced organizer. He was, perhaps, the last German scholar with the encyclopaedic knowledge and the administrative faculties required to preside over such an enterprise. Although he did not have the stature of the great founder of the academy, he was the closest to Leibnitz that Berlin had to offer.[100]

The Kaiser-Wilhelms-Gesellschaft became the research institute

Writers, Journalists, and Scholars

of the natural sciences and numbered many distinguished scholars on its roster—Fritz Haber, Otto Warburg, Lise Meitner, Fritz Strassmann, Otto Hahn, and many more. It has survived the onslaught of two world wars, and exists today as the Max Planck Institutes in West Germany. The institute did not fully correspond to Althoff's plans; he had not, for instance, intended to make it the exclusive domain of the natural sciences, and the vision of a "German Oxford" was never realized. Althoff died; the war erupted; and finally the German inflation put an end to the dream.

The academic institutes of higher learning, such as they were, demand some attention. Two new schools were set up during the second empire: Die Technische Hochschule and Die Handelshochschule.[101] As their names indicate, they were devoted to the teaching of the applied sciences and business administration respectively. The university, however, continued to be the trunk from which most scholarly endeavor branched out. It had changed complexion since 1810; following the trend of the times, the most notable transformation had taken place in the field of the natural sciences. The entire nineteenth century was a period of scientific advancement, and Germany was rapidly catching up with its neighbors to the west: France, Holland, and England. In this process, the University of Berlin played a significant role, and as was natural, there was some difference of opinion about the importance of the new disciplines. The naturalist, Rudolf Virchow, was confident of a transition from a philosophical age to an age of the natural sciences.[102] Others were not so optimistic, and the famous physiologist, Dubois-Reymond, tried to show the limits of human knowledge in a speech entitled: *Ignoramus, Ignorabimus.*[103] The real problem, however, concerned the reach of human knowledge and the position of man in the cosmos. Nowhere was this controversy so clearly reflected as at the University of Berlin. The principle upon which the university had been founded was *Die Einheit der Wissenschaft* (the unity of science), but by 1900 this unity had well been lost.

It has become the vogue to speak of "the two cultures," and C. P. Snow has made this the subject of a much discussed lecture. Actually this antithetical position of the humanities and the natural sciences was clearly visible in the intellectual structure of the University of Berlin and was discussed in scholarly treatises, although the consequences of the situation were not fully comprehended.

The positive philosophy of Auguste Comte and his disciples maintained the existence of only one science, though it was hierarchically ordered and supported by the law of the three stages which had been formulated by Comte. But German scholarship moved in a different direction. Speculative philosophy had fallen into disrepute in Germany as elsewhere. In its place, German scholars proclaimed a dualism of the cognitive approach; that is, they distinguished between the natural sciences and the cultural sciences, or humanities. Most of the scholarly achievements of imperial Berlin may be summarized in one or the other of these two categories.[104]

The dichotomy that existed between the natural sciences (*Naturwissenschaften*) and the cultural sciences (*Geisteswissenschaften*) was brought into the open by Wilhelm Dilthey, imperial Berlin's only great philosopher. Dilthey had felt obliged to defend the science of the mind against the effort of the natural sciences to impose their categories on the creations of the human spirit.[105] Dilthey conceived of man as a historical being first and foremost, and he tried to comprehend him as such. During his long life he engaged in a giant undertaking to "understand life on its own terms." He endeavored to develop the philosophical and psychological tools by means of which this could be accomplished. At the same time he wanted to demonstrate over what roads the human mind had traveled to reach the point from which the world could be comprehended in scientific terms. In other words, Dilthey planned to write the geneology of scientific thinking in the Occident.

His work was never completed, yet Ortega y Gasset has called Dilthey the most important thinker in the second half of the nineteenth century. Dilthey ushered in a new form of *Weltanschauung*, that is, historicism, a philosophy which looks at the human world in historical terms and denies the validity of absolute value to any single historical phenomenon. Historical relativism was the result, to which Dilthey freely admitted.[106] Weary but undaunted, he pursued his odyssey to the end of his life.

Dilthey was not a popular teacher of philosophy. Only a small group of devoted disciples knew his work and its superhuman trajectory. But his fame has grown since his death in 1911, and his thought has reached into many minds both in Germany and elsewhere. Dilthey did not claim to have a system; in fact he distrusted any theory which asserted a knowledge of all life. His colleagues at the University had even less of a system, and the students said quite frankly that philosophy in Berlin had been destroyed, root and branch.[107]

There were two lecturers who attracted the more sophisticated: Georg Simmel and Ernst Cassirer. Both were Jewish and could not, therefore, hope to become full professors under the Prussian system. Simmel was fascinated by the variety of forms in human life; he was interested in society and the individual, in the arts, and in money. One could be sure to find a new shade of meaning or a new twist to an old problem in his work. Ernst Cassirer came into his own only after the downfall of the empire.

The most impressive accomplishments in the cultural sciences followed the pattern outlined by Dilthey. They cut across the traditional boundaries of the faculties. In the theological faculty, Adolf von Harnack applied the same historical consciousness to the evolution of the Christian dogma, and even more decisively to Christianity itself in his famous *Essence of Christianity*. "Dogma," he said, "must be purified by history."[108] Anyone who had the good fortune to listen to this extraordinary man is not likely to forget the impression he made as one of the few scholars of the late nineteenth century still able to encompass most of the disciplines of the cultural sciences.

In a more remote field, the history of the arts, Heinrich Woelfflin progressed from the study of the Italian and the German Renaissance to a study of the Baroque. It is no exaggeration to say that his *Renaissance and Baroque* and *Principles of Art History* rediscovered this forgotten period.[109]

The greatest achievements, however, took place in the various fields of history, in the traditional meaning of the word. Berlin had been a center of historical studies since 1825 when Ranke joined the University faculty.[110] His philological-critical method combined with a desire to obtain a godlike objectivity and to relate history "as it actually happened" (wie es eigentlich gewesen) had created an environment highly propitious for the development of historical studies. Ranke's seminar became the training ground for many gifted historians, among them Jacob Burckhardt. Ranke's well-known *Primacy of Foreign Policy*, however, remained a typical German, not to say Prussian, premise that European and American historians rejected.[111]

The historians who followed Ranke preserved his methodological approach and his emphasis on the power-state as the most suitable object of history, but abandoned Ranke's demand for a passive objectivity. Instead they claimed that history should become the teacher of the nation in its political struggle. It was their aim to use history as a weapon in the fight for German unification under Prussian leadership. These writers gravitated naturally to Berlin, and a great deal, if not all, of their work was concerned with German or Prussian subjects. There was Droysen, who gave up his research on the history of Alexander the Great and Hellenism in order to concentrate on the rise of Brandenburg-Prussia.[112] There was Sybel, who used the history of the French Revolution to emphasize the necessity of Prussian hegemony in Germany, and who condemned Germany's imperial policy during the Middle Ages as erroneous and misguided, a barely veiled attack on the Austrian monarchy that had become the heir of medieval tradition.[113] Finally, there was Treitschke about whose influence at the university we have already spoken. He was not Prussian-born, but in spite of great reservations about the city, he made Berlin his home. The influence he had as a writer and as editor of the *Preussische Jahrbücher* matched the authority he exercised from his chair at the university. His *Historical Political Essays* and his *German History* became the classical expression of the meaning the new Germany wanted to bestow upon its genesis.[114]

Treitschke's model in style and presentation was Macaulay. Just as the English writer had forged the typical Whig interpretation of English history, so did the German writer attempt to block out the Prussian, or *kleindeutsche*, exposition of German history. It was in the nature of a myth, but a very persuasive myth in the light of Bismarck's successful foreign policy. Luther, Frederick the Great, and the reformers of 1813 were Bismarck's forerunners. The state signified power, power, power. Treitschke, who had begun his career as a liberal, did not deny his earlier convictions, yet the older he became, the nearer he moved toward a glorification of the *Grosstaat* (Great state), and his only criterion in judging the historical process became success. Racial overtones crept into his writing; the Germans were the Chosen People carrying out the *"gesta Dei per teutones."*

Treitschke's *German History* is not an analytical work; like Macaulay, he wanted to evoke rather than to dissect. The book is one long passionate argument, *cum ira et studio*, in which those whom he considered the enemies of German unity stand condemned, and those whom he considered constructive are unduly praised. Though the *German History* was never completed, it set the tone for much of the thinking of the educated German middle class.

The Prussian school had a tremendous influence in Berlin, and through Berlin, on the rest of Germany. Its most distinguished members occupied the chairs for modern European history at the university. Treitschke became Ranke's successor, and Sybel was made director of the Prussian archives. Sybel also edited Germany's most prestigious historical review: *Die Historische Zeitschrift*.

It is not surprising that the next generation of historians fell under the spell of these men. A recent book, *The Ranke Renaissance*, attempts to show that the younger historians shied away from the Prussian persuasion of Sybel, Droysen, and Treitschke, and returned to the universal and objective position of Ranke.[115] But this thesis must be viewed with caution. The younger historians, Erich Marcks, Max Lenz, and Friedrich Meinecke, did indeed admire the old master and were less parochial in their choice of subject matter; they wrote about Queen Elizabeth I, Coligny, and Napoleon I, but their historical criteria were Treitschke's: the national state and its emergence in European history were their ultimate goals. Only after 1914 did Friedrich Meinecke overcome the innate bias of the Prussian interpretation of history.[116] It is interesting to note that all three—Marcks, Lenz, and Meinecke —began and ended their careers in Berlin.

It should be remembered that there was at least one eminent historian among the many which Berlin called its own who did not join in the adulation and glorification of the Prussian power-state. Theodor Mommsen's scholarly achievements match those of Ranke and surpass those of his contemporaries, Sybel and

Treitschke. Mommsen taught and wrote in Berlin from 1858 until his death in 1903. We will not try to summarize the extraordinary scope of his investigations; they reach beyond the limits of this study, but a word should be said about his *Roman History*. Next to the work of Ranke, it is the greatest accomplishment of any German historian. Unfortunately, Mommsen completed only the story of the Roman Republic; he did not write the history of the Roman emperors, giving instead a description of the provinces of the empire from Caesar to Diocletian. Yet the work is a masterpiece in form, style, and the analysis of historical material, from written sources to inscriptions and coins.[117]

Mommsen's famous portrait of Caesar has sometimes been misunderstood as a panegyric to military dictatorship, but nothing could have been further from his mind. He was a sincere democrat and manifested his convictions as clearly and as often as the situation warranted. He condemned Treitschke's anti-Semitism as vehemently as he censured the authoritarian methods employed in the building of the second empire. There is a tragic note in his last will and testament, written in 1899: "I have always been a political animal and have wanted to be a citizen. But this is not possible in our nation in which the individual, even the best one, can never entirely transcend military subordination and political fetishism. This inner estrangement from people to whom I belong has made me decide as far as possible not to appear before the German people for whom I have no respect."[118]

His voice remained that of a prophet crying in the wilderness. Mommsen's successor at the University of Berlin was his equal in scholarship, but lacked Mommsen's artistic and literary talent. Eduard Meyer may have been as great a historian as Mommsen, but his work was the work of a specialist, whereas Mommsen was avidly read by the general public, perhaps the last historian of whom this may be said. Meyer, moreover, was an ardent nationalist, and his lectures were often marred by anti-Semitic interpolations. Together with Eduard Norden and Ulrich Wilamowitz, he upheld the time-honored classical tradition of the university. Wilamowitz was a peculiar mixture of aristocrat and actor who captured his academic audiences by means of a dramatic presentation; in his scholarly pursuits, he followed Mommsen in method and perspective.[119] Other names could be added to prove the enormous influence that the historical approach exercised on all humanistic disciplines: in political science, Gustav Schmoller; in economics, Werner Sombart; in comparative history, Otto Hintze and Gustav Breysig.

In the last decade of imperial Berlin, the philosophy of historicism received a new impulse through the powerful personality of Ernst Troeltsch, who came to Berlin from Heidelberg where he had associated closely with Max Weber. His *Social Teachings of the Christian Churches* was an attempt to bring the old theological and the modern sociological perspectives together. Troeltsch had been a member of the theological faculty in Heidelberg, but had left the boundaries of dogmatic Christianity behind. Among German scholars, he was one of the few who knew the Anglo-Saxon world through personal experience. He was an extraordinary teacher and orator and drew great numbers of students to his classroom who appreciated both the tremendous erudition and the earthy vitality of his lectures. His appointment to a chair of philosophy at the University of Berlin was passionately contested by his enemies, but eventually his undeniable traits of genius prevailed, and the Berlin appointment was confirmed.[120]

Troeltsch's contact with Max Weber had widened his horizons to a great extent; Weber's *Sociology of Religion* had been conceived on a global scale, and Troeltsch was quick to grasp the universal perspective. He had, moreover, a gargantuan intellectual appetite and a comparable capacity to digest great masses of material in short order. He was heir to the entire realm of German philosophy from Leibnitz to Hegel and Dilthey, and he was animated by the conviction that "world history had rational meaning and was motivated by an invincible ethical driving force."[121] Troeltsch's teaching career in Berlin coincided with the outbreak of World War I, and he was aware that the conflict had brought into the open a deep-rooted crisis in Western civilization.

Troeltsch hailed from southern Germany, and he observed the excesses of nationalism emanating from the war with misgiving. It was clear to him that some of the wellsprings of German imperialism were her glorification of the "national spirit," the idolatry of the state, and the complacent acceptance of the status quo; all of these had led Germany to the denial of a universal idea of humanity. He presented the first seeds of his thought on historicism in 1916 in an address, *Standards for Judging Matters Historical*.[122] Seven years later, and but a few months before his death, these thoughts had grown into an imposing volume entitled *Historicism and Its Problems*.[123] Like Dilthey, Troeltsch confessed to the anarchy of opinion, or, shall we say, to the relativity of values. Unlike Dilthey, he hoped for a new cultural synthesis which would extricate Western man from the nihilistic swamp in which he was mired.[124]

The preceding observations and reflections must suffice to prove our point that the historical disciplines were the best the University of Berlin had to offer in the humanities. Other universities excelled in philosophy, Marburg and Freiburg, for instance; Heidelberg was superior in sociology and literature. But no university equalled Berlin in the variety and depth of its presentation of human history.[125]

This writer cannot speak with authority about progress in the area that Dilthey had set apart from the cultural sciences, i.e., the natural sciences. The achievements in this field were perhaps still more impressive than those in the humanities, and even the layman should take note of the most outstanding accomplishments. In medicine the paramount advancement was in bacteriology, and was due, almost exclusively, to the work of Robert Koch. In 1876 Koch produced a pure culture of the bacillus anthrax and was able to come up with a preventive inoculation against the disease a few years later. He was made professor of medicine in Berlin, and it was here that he isolated the bacillus of tuberculosis in 1882. The young Paul Ehrlich was among his listeners at the institute for physiology and has described how Koch explained in a simple direct fashion, the etiology of this illness: "Everyone who attended the lecture was moved, and I must say that I remember this evening as the greatest scientific experience of my life."[126] Other discoveries followed, such as the identification of the comma bacillus as the cause of Asiatic cholera. The work of Robert Koch parallels that of Pasteur in the fight against infectious diseases and their prevention or treatment. Many scholars carried on the ideas that Koch had launched. The most gifted of them was Paul Ehrlich who, like his great teacher, was a master of the experimental approach. He applied the new science of chemistry to medicine. Ehrlich got his start in Koch's institute for infectious diseases and was appointed director of a new Institute for Serum Investigation in 1896. His genius conquered a series of different though related fields, such as histology, immunology, hematology, and chemotherapy. Both the theoretical discoveries and the practical results were extraordinary. Ehrlich used the synthetic dyes produced by German industry for the tinctorial analysis of tissues, a prime example of the collaboration between the chemical industry and medical science which proved to be an immense methodological advancement in the exact diagnosis of certain diseases.[127]

Ehrlich's most spectacular discovery was salvarsan, which promised a cure for syphilis, the curse of metropolitan life in the nineteenth century. For his work on immunology he was awarded the Nobel prize. Although he was frequently attacked, he also found devoted followers, especially in Berlin, where physicians who shared his experimental daring applied his findings.

In singling out Ehrlich we do not wish to give the impression that he was the only scholar who was forging ahead in new and sometimes unorthodox procedures. In general, standards were high and the school of medicine had a large and competent staff. In 1895, there were eighteen full professors, forty-four extraordinary-professors (associate professors), and one hundred and seventeen *Privatdozenten* (lecturers).[128] The philosophy which animated the medical school was materialistic and was frequently expressed by Dubois Reymond: "There is no other form of knowledge than the mechanical one and no other form of scientific thinking but the mathematical physical."[129] The most formidable embodiment of this thought was provided by Hermann von Helmholtz, who through his various investigations belongs to medicine as well as to physics, and who came to Berlin in the year of the founding of the empire.

The names of the great physicists who taught in Berlin have found worldwide recognition; in addition to Helmholtz, there were Max Planck, Albert Einstein, Max Laue, and Walther Nernst, all recipients of the Nobel prize. The Quantum Theory as well as the General Theory of Relativity were formulated in Berlin. These theories revolutionized Newton's conception of the world and ushered in the "new physics." Although the general public may not comprehend in detail the newborn concepts, they have become all too familiar with their practical results in the nuclear age. During the period which constitutes the subject of this study, no one envisaged these results. There was in Berlin, as in Cambridge and Copenhagen, an infectious enthusiasm for the great advances being made by theoretical physics. The list of internationally famous names in the new field is long: James Frank, Gustav Hertz, Peter Pringsheim, Max Born, to mention only a few.[130]

Our bird's-eye view cannot hope to do justice to all the disciplines that were available to the student at the University of Berlin, but it should be evident that the institution occupied a distinguished position among the European centers of higher learning, and, of course, first place among German universities. Many of the discoveries we have mentioned could, without doubt, have been made elsewhere, yet it is not accidental that they were made in Berlin. Imperial Germany, whatever its faults, maintained a friendly attitude toward scholarship and science, holding to a tradition in its capital which had been evident since the days of Frederick the Great.

The question of a single theory, or philosophy, or ideology which might be representative of imperial Berlin can receive only a qualified answer. Berlin produced no theory with its roots deep in the native soil, such as Vienna brought forth in Freudian analysis; nor was there a philosophy that could have competed with Bergson's Creative Evolution and its impact on the literary world of Paris.[131] In truth, it would seem that the only school of thought to bear the identity of the German capital was historicism. Here are the traces of Prussia's adulation of power, and here is the overestimation of the individual and his unique position as opposed to the universal commands of law and ethics.[132] Even so, historicism in itself was not an exclusively German product; it was manifested quite as potently in Benedetto Croce's Italy and in Carl Becker's America. It was the extraordinary assemblage of so many fine minds, all devoted to the pursuit of truth in both the natural and the cultural sciences, that gave the University of Berlin its marked eminence.

There was, however, one specific German quality to be noted in Berlin. The university was burdened with a political tradition to which most of its members adhered without reflection or compunction. The professors and, under their influence, the students shared a naïve belief that their country had no parallel, and that it could count on a cloudless future. There was a deep seated complacency in the University of Berlin which played down the flaws of authoritarianism, militarism, and thinly veiled absolutism that characterized the second empire.[133] Those who felt the necessity of social reform were few and far between, and even these few succumbed easily to the siren song of German imperialism.

It is true that most European countries in the period before 1914 were weighed down by tradition, but nowhere was tradition so heavily biased in favor of bourgeois-Junker rule together with its militaristic superstructure. It seems paradoxical that the same men who proudly proclaimed their objectivity in the pursuit of science should have been hoodwinked by the political slogans and nationalistic propaganda which brought the empire to its knees in World War I.[134]

[7]

Berlin and the Arts

B ERLIN has been referred to as "Athens on the Spree" as far back as the eighteenth century, and the Berliner himself as a "Spree-Athener." There is something baffling, even ludicrous, in these expressions; the status of the arts in Berlin could scarcely be compared with its enshrinement in the Greek capital. If we are to arrive at an accurate assessment of the conditions under which the arts flourished in imperial Berlin, we must again beware of generalizations. Although it is impossible to apply the same yardstick to all branches of the arts, one assertion may be made at the outset: in no other field is the tension between official and actual Berlin reflected in as clear a light as in the world of art.

i

As we have noted, the Kaiser considered his museums to be among the city's most interesting treasures, and indeed there were few institutions in Berlin that deserved such unstinting praise. Most of the museums were located on an island in the Spree near the imperial castle called the museum-island. A number of buildings, quite disparate in character, housed the extraordinary treasures which Berlin could call its own: the collection of Italian, Dutch, French, and English paintings of the period preceding the nineteenth century; German sculpture and painting of the same period; the magnificent assemblage of Egyptian, Babylonian, and Greek art, which included the famous Pergamon Altar; the National Gallery devoted to contemporary art of the nineteenth century; and the splendid collection, ignored by many, of graphic art that went by the name of *Das Kupferstichkabinett.*[1]

This astonishing concentration of great art had been acquired over the centuries, but in the main it was the creation of imperial Berlin. Like most European museums, those of Berlin had their beginnings in a dynastic collection. As we know, the Hohenzollern did not play a prominent role prior to the eighteenth century and had neither the money nor the inclination to assemble art treasures after the fashion of Philip II of Spain, the Austrian Hapsburgs, or England's Charles I. Munich and Dresden had much firmer foundations whereon to build their reputations in the realm of art.

During the Reformation the Hohenzollern purchased a few pictures by Lucas Cranach, and in the seventeenth century the Great Elector set up the "schöne Kammer" (beautiful chamber) in his castle, but it was Frederick the Great who first acquired a number of outstanding paintings. The fact that his taste had been formed by France dictated his acquisition of some of the finest Watteaus to be seen in Europe.

After the Napoleonic wars, Karl Friedrich Schinkel was commissioned to undertake the architectural planning of the museums in earnest, and the Museums Insel thus came into being. One gallery which Schinkel himself designed and which was intended to house paintings later became the home of ancient art, the Alte Museum, one of his most accomplished achievements in the classic style. Frederick William III and Frederick William IV bought a number of private collections, among them the famous Altar of Ghent by Jan and Hubert van Eyck.[2] But the museums of Berlin were still no match for the galleries of Dresden or Munich, to say nothing of the Louvre or the Uffizzi. The situation changed for the better after the Franco-Prussian war.

William I had yielded to Bismarck's wishes in the conflicts which arose between the chancellor and the crown prince and princess. Their influence on German politics has been limited to a great extent, but it was still necessary to keep them occupied, preferably in a field where they could not interfere with Bismarck's operations. To accomplish this bit of palace diplomacy, the crown prince was put in charge of the royal museums. He realized full well that he had been put on ice and cut off from the inner council of German politics, but he took his new duties seriously. He ordered the foundation of two new museums, those of Völkerkunde and Kunstgewerbe (ethnology and artistic crafts), but located them at some distance from the Museums Insel. In the area that he gained by this arrangement, a building for European painting and sculpture was to be erected. Upon its completion it bore his name: the Kaiser Friedrich-Museum. Its architecture was not the most felicitous, imitating as it did the baroque style of the seventeenth century, but its content placed it in the forefront of the great museums of the world.

Wilhelm Bode was chosen to direct the galleries of Berlin, a position which he held for two generations, and his merits were recognized far beyond the frontiers of imperial Germany. Bode was born in Brunswig in 1845 and had studied law in Göttingen and Berlin. He abandoned his career in the courts to obtain his Ph.D. in the history of art.[3] His twofold training stood him in good stead when he entered the administration of the museum in a double capacity: as director and as art expert. It was this unique combination of talents which made him an unquestioned master among the small circle of connoisseurs who conducted the growth of the European and the American museums.

The latter part of the nineteenth century marked the last period during which great collections of art might be assembled in Europe. After 1900 the American tycoons, such as Mellon, Frick, Huntington, Bache, and Lehmann, began to buy classic art on a grand scale, with the museums not far behind—the Metropolitan of New York, the Fine Arts Museum of Boston, etc. Advising them were such experts as Bernard Berenson, perhaps the greatest expert in Italian art, and the British art dealer, Duveen. Berlin would have found it impossible to meet the prices that Duveen could demand. But Bode had begun his work three decades earlier, having entered the career of museum-organizer in 1872.

Bode's vision was universal, spanning both Occident and Orient, but there can be little doubt that his heart belonged to European art. Nevertheless, it was his hope to leave behind him museums which would encompass the great art of all mankind. When he died in 1929, half-blind and paralyzed, he had come as near his goal as was humanly possible under the circumstances. World War II sundered his life work, and today's visitor to Berlin must look for Bode's acquisitions on both sides of the Wall.

As we have said, Bode was an art expert of the highest rank, but he also possessed the sensitive nose of a bloodhound when it came to searching out hidden treasures. In those days few countries protected their national treasures by prohibiting the export of works of art. Thus Bode was able to assemble an unbelievably rich harvest; perhaps those best known to the world are Rembrandt's *Man with the Golden Helmet,* Dürer's *Hieronymus Holzschuher,* Franz Hals's *Hille Bobbe,* and the famous *Nefertiti.* Berlin's collections of Botticellis, Titians, Raphaels, and Rembrandts were of the highest order, to say nothing of the Flemish masters and the English painters of the eighteenth century.

Part of this harvest, such as the Pergamon Altar, must be credited to other interested researchers. The Kaiser himself had a lifelong regard for archeology, and he favored the excavations of scholars such as Conze and Dörpfeld. Germany's friendly relations with the Ottoman empire facilitated these enterprises, which brought to light not only the Pergamon Altar, but also the Gate of Milet and the architectural remnants of Baalbeck. The display of their findings was delayed by a chronic lack of space and the disruptions occasioned by World War I, and they were not shown to the public until the days of the Weimar Republic. The final complex which comprised and housed Berlin's art was all a part of Bode's original vision as he approached the problem of the Museums Insel.[4]

Plans of such magnitude as Bode conceived called for large financial resources far beyond those at his disposal, since he was obliged to operate within the limited confines of the Prussian budget. He attempted to secure additional funds by organizing the Association of the Friends of the Kaiser Friedrich-Museum, which advanced capital when he needed it. The secret of his success, however, lay in his personal diplomacy. Bode was a fund raiser that any American university would have envied, and his methods might be borrowed to advantage. To the vain and the snobbish he held out the promise of a decoration, or if this gambit was not successful, he advanced the prospect of a personal visit by the Kaiser. His Majesty was a great friend of Bode's and had made him *Generaldirektor* of the museums of Berlin in 1906. A visit from the emperor was a very effective lure and might even lead to the granting of a title, or in the case of a large gift, to

Berlin and the Arts

the bestowal of a knighthood. Some friends of the arts came to fear these visits of William II; they were aware that a *Kaffeeklatsch* with His Majesty might prove to be an expensive pleasure.[5] Another method employed by Bode in the furtherance of his purposes was even more effective. A number of wealthy industrialists and merchants in Berlin engaged in the noble pastime of building up private collections. It was only natural that they should turn to Bode or to his able assistant, Max Friedländer, for advice. Both were glad to be of help, though perhaps not entirely without calculation. It would be ridiculous to accuse Bode of any thought of personal profit, but there is no doubt that he hoped for the day when some of these collections would become the property of the Berlin museums. His hopes fed on the promises of grateful collectors that their treasures would be left to the Kaiser Friedrich-Museum, and this was reward enough for Bode. Unfortunately, the German inflation of the 1920's upset some of his expectations. Eduard Simon's *Titian* was sold to an American dealer, and Hulschinsky's gallery was auctioned off in 1928. Nevertheless, some of the promises were kept, and they helped Bode to realize his dream: a museum for German art.[6]

Many Berlin collectors' names are still famous; others will be recognized only by those who have some link with Berlin and its society. There was the banker, Oskar Hainauer; the mining magnate, Hulschinsky; the coal baron, Eduard Arnold; the newspaper tycoon, Rudolf Mosse; Oskar Oliven, whose wife was the granddaughter of Ludwig Loewe. Not all of these men were interested in art for art's sake, and even Friedländer considered the collecting of art as the only tasteful way of displaying one's fortune. Some collectors were most interested in the size of the painting; others were eager to display as many canvases as their purses would allow. But there were, nevertheless, those who became willing disciples of Bode, and who learned to distinguish between showmanship and connoisseurship. Hulschinsky's gallery, for instance, included a Raphael, a Botticelli, a Rembrandt, a Franz Hals; Eduard Simon specialized in Italian Renaissance works and counted among his possessions a Titian, a Bellini, and works of the della Robbias. And, of course, the purchase of such important pictures required the services of an expert; Bode's advice was invaluable, not alone for the individual collector, but for the future fame of the Berlin museums. The following anecdote gives an example of the situation in the Berlin art markets of the early twentieth century. A friend of the author once found in an antique shop a picture that he thought might be valuable. He asked the price and was told it was fifty marks. Not wanting to show too great an interest, my friend asked if he might take the picture home to judge how it might look in his drawing room. "To be sure," answered the dealer, "but if you come back tomorrow and want to purchase it because Friedländer has told you it might be a Breughel, the price will be 5,000 marks."

One of the fringe benefits which Berlin received from Bode's activities was the impetus given to the traffic in works of art. A whole generation of art dealers settled in Berlin where they could count on the advantage of Bode's opinions and those of his trained staff. As for the student of art, there were few places where he could so profitably engage in his chosen discipline. After a lecture by Wölfflin, Werner Weissbach, or Oskar Fischl he could, at the end of a five-minute walk, be standing before the masterpiece that the professor had just discussed in the classroom.[7] Several teachers actually held their classes in the Kaiser Friedrich-Museum and taught the unexperienced how to look at a work of art. The student could likewise visit the collection of graphics and ask to see a Dürer drawing, a Rembrandt etching, or the famous Botticelli illustrations for the *Divina Comedia*. Within minutes an attendant would show him the original for which he had asked.

Bode made few mistakes in his evaluation of art works, but it was only natural that certain of his decisions were questioned. He had, for instance, attributed the sculptured head of a young woman which he had purchased for the museum, to Leonardo da Vinci. His opinion was not accepted by many art historians, who frankly declared the work to be a forgery. The emperor gave Bode a free hand, however, and even made valuable contributions from time to time, for instance, the Islamic palace façade which the Sultan Abdul Hamid had presented to the emperor as a token of his esteem.

There was one field, however, in which the emperor's taste was both undiscerning and obtuse, and here he refused to bow to the advice of even the most erudite art critic; this was the field of contemporary art. Bode was either too much of a diplomat or too indifferent to attempt any improvement in the Kaiser's judgment, and he would rather have lost one of his best collaborators than cross His Majesty's pronouncements on modern, especially modern French, art. In 1909, a conflict occurred between the Kaiser and the director of the National Gallery, Hugo Tschudi. Since the reputation of the French masters was by then firmly established even in Germany, Tschudi considered it his duty to purchase not only German, but also French impressionists.[8] The Kaiser, however, vetoed the director's decision, and Tschudi resigned.

The emperor's opposition to contemporary art was an evidence of his bigotry, and was in part the result of nationalistic prejudice, and in part lack of taste. The effect of his interferences would not have been so catastrophic had he not set himself up as an *arbiter elegantarium* whose word was final. Upon one occasion the emperor delivered a speech which expressed his artistic canon with startling candor:

"An art which transgresses the laws and barriers outlined by Me, ceases to be an art; it is merely a factory product, a trade, and art must never become such a thing. The often misused word 'liberty' . . . leads to . . . license and presumption. . . . Art should help to educate the people; it should also give to the lower classes (den unteren Ständen) after their hard work . . . the possibility of lifting themselves up to ideals. To us, to the German people, ideals have become permanent possessions, whereas among other peoples they have been more or less lost. Only the German nation is left, and we are called upon to preserve, cultivate, and continue these great ideals, and among those ideals is the duty to offer to the toiling classes the possibility of elevating themselves to the beautiful and of raising themselves above their ordinary thoughts. If art, as so frequently happens now, does nothing more than paint misery more ugly than it is, it sins against the German people. The cultivation of the ideal is, moreover, the greatest work of civilization (Kulturarbeit); if we wish to be and to remain an example for other countries, the entire nation must cooperate. If culture is going to fulfill its task, it must penetrate into the deepest layers of the people. This it can do only if it proffers a hand to uplift, instead of to debase."[9]

The foregoing outburst took place at the solemn inauguration of the Siegesallee (the avenue of victory) in 1901. Even before the Kaiser had conceived this project, Berlin had been invaded by a collection of monster monuments celebrating the heroes of the unification: William I, Bismarck, von Roon, and others, but the Siegesallee superseded all previous attempts at official magnificence. The Kaiser was, of course, convinced that Berlin owed its greatness to the drive and genius of the Hohenzollern, and no one will question the grain of truth that may be found in this belief. Inspired by the idea that he was the descendant of a long line of heroes, the Kaiser conceived of a wide avenue on both sides of which there should be placed a number of white-marble monuments commemorating the achievements of his forebears. Thirty-two of these enormous creations were designed and placed between the Königsplatz (where the Reichstag was located) and the Rolandsplatz near the Tiergarten. These thirty-two "stations of national pride" glorified thirty-two princes; the monument of each prince was surrounded by a low semicircular wall which was further enhanced by busts of two of the prince's advisers who were considered worthy of the honor. The Siegesallee, when completed, was a gift of the monarch to the city, which, he prophesied, would place Berlin at the head of the most beautiful cities of the world. What it did, however, was to make Berlin the laughingstock of the world, and the first to laugh were the Berliners. They called the Siegesallee the avenue of the puppets, and Max Liebermann said he needed dark glasses to look at this crime against good taste. But the Siegesallee was there for good, and Liebermann could not lay aside his glasses—"a life sentence," as he put it.[10]

The whole project manifested the hubris of the Kaiser—his nationalism, his dynastic pride, his pretense of ruling by divine right in an age of technology, science, and the upward march of the masses. The Siegesallee was a symbol of the inherent contradiction from which Wilhelminian Germany suffered, the illusion which drew her to her perdition.

In all fairness, it must be said that Germany had no monopoly on bad taste. Rome's monument to Victor Emmanuel is as offensive as the Siegesallee. Massive monuments and heroic sculptures are without meaning and function in the twentieth century, but the Kaiser was as impervious to this change as he was to any innovation in the field of aesthetics. The same stubborn conservatism characterizes his directives for the architectural improvement of the capital. In this case, however, his aesthetic dictatorship was restrained by the fact that the city government had considerable authority in architectural projects. Some of the features of Berlin's architecture have already been noted, especially those occasioned by its rapid expansion. At this point we will consider the artistic characteristics of Berlin's architecture as they became manifest between 1870 and 1918 in both public and private buildings.

ii

The public buildings adhered without exception to the inherited patterns of historical style, the architects adapting them as best they could to modern purposes. In large measure, the construction of public buildings was given over to the erection of churches. Although the mood of the population was increasingly secular and church attendance was on the wane, the government chose to ignore the trend. The church near the imperial castle which had been the official place of worship for the dynasty and the court was replaced by a copy of Michelangelo's St. Peter's. The intention was the same as it had been in the erection of the Siegesallee, that is, to show the "grandiose development of Brandenburg-Prussia since the assumption of Hohenzollern leadership."[11] The official church had been built in baroque style, but the majority of churches copied gothic or romanesque models. The most famous of these was the Kaiser Wilhelm Memorial Church, erected at the entrance to the Kurfürstendamm and dedicated to the emperor's grandfather. In earlier days churches and cathedrals had been named in honor of the Trinity, the Virgin Mary, or the saints; in the second empire, the Hohenzollern preempted this distinction. The empress, Augusta Victoria, who refrained from interference in political matters, was particularly interested in furthering the growth of religious buildings. The propertied bourgeoisie were encouraged to make contributions, and many donated stained glass windows in exchange for a decoration or a title. For the average Berliner, however, the Kaiser Wilhelm Memorial Church became one more target for their sarcasm.[12]

For other public buildings the emperor and his government relied on the court architect, Ernst von Ihne, who designed the Kaiser Friedrich-Museum and, shortly before the war, the new royal library. The old library, opposite the opera, had become quite inadequate. The site chosen for the new building was on the avenue Unter den Linden, only a block from the university and would also house the Academy of Sciences. After the style of the seventeenth century, it was heavily constructed, with imposing staircases, marble lounges, and vast amounts of wasted space. The main reading room, however, was an improvement over its predecessor. It was a copy of the well-known reading room of the British Museum, with a high cupola over the circular arrangement of desks.[13] Each desk was provided with a reading lamp, which the student could turn on and off at will, instead of waiting for the momentous decision of the presiding official, a practice still observed at the Bibliothèque Nationale in Paris. Following the downfall of the empire, the royal library became the Staatsbibliothek, a name which it still holds in East Berlin.

The great majority of official buildings came under the jurisdiction of the city government, or, as we should say, the city governments, since Spandau, Steglitz, Schöneberg, and Charlottenburg still preserved their municipal autonomy. The city halls which every section felt it necessary to erect were given gothic façades, with the result that a certain mask-like appearance characterized their decor.[14]

Ludwig Hofmann was a leading figure among Berlin's city architects, and he was responsible for the design of the greater number of public buildings constructed after 1895. Hofmann leaned heavily on traditional forms and patterns while avoiding duplication. His creations reveal a moderate eclecticism, solid in the execution of floor plans and the use of building materials, but without noticeable daring or invention. One of his conceptions was the museum for the Mark Brandenburg, a curious combination of church, city hall, tower, and patrician mansion.[15] Being a public servant, Hofmann was obliged to cater to the taste of the magistrates and the city fathers, and would not have been permitted to venture into bold experiments after the fashion of his American contemporaries, Frank Lloyd Wright and Louis Henri Sullivan. In short, the public buildings of the second empire in Berlin were, at best, tradition-bound; at worst, copies of famous models which they could not hope to equal.

Berlin's private buildings offer a more interesting problem. Until the end of the nineteenth century private dwellings were captive to the same pattern that we encountered in public buildings, that is, the emulation of established styles or the tasteless combination of various stylistic elements in the same building. The well-to-do preferred palaces copied from Roman, Venetian, or Florentine originals. The French "hotel" of the Faubourg St. Honoré was also much in demand, as were likewise the patrician houses of Nuremberg.

The apartment house, home of the majority of Berliners, remained unchanged throughout the period of the second empire, for the very good reason that the floor plan of these buildings precluded any substantial improvement. Most of the apartment houses displayed an impressive entrance hall equipped with marble columns and large mirrors. In general, the apartments had two or three rooms on the street side where reception and drawing rooms were located. Since all such houses were built around courtyards, the connection between the rooms facing the street and those facing the courtyard was established through a gateway room lit by one large window opening on the courtyard. This usually dark and forbidding chamber served as the dining room in most apartments. Further along were bedrooms, bathroom, pantry and kitchen. Frequently the kitchen was at the very end of a dark corridor, and at considerable distance from the dining room. It would be difficult to design a more inconvenient arrangement, yet the Berliner clung to this layout with a stubborn insistence worthy of a better cause.[16] He also preferred his apartment to any dwelling on the outskirts of the city, very likely because of the transportation problem. Only at the end of the century was there any change in the situation.

At the approach of the new century, artists all over Europe became inspired with a desire to get away from the pompousness and prolixity of ornamentation which had characterized late nineteenth-century architecture. Their movement went under different names in different countries, i.e., *art nouveau* in France, *Jugendstil* in Germany.[17] In retrospect, the advent of the new style was only the beginning of the traumatic encounter between industrial production and the artistic imagination. Thinkers such as John Ruskin and William Morris had maintained that industry and art were antipathetic, and that art should reject commercialism and should dedicate itself to natural reproduction and handmade products. Their beliefs were a reaction to the mediocrity of industrial productions, especially in regard to such articles as furniture, rugs, curtains, etc. Morris's crusade was continued on the continent by the Belgian architect, van de Velde, who thought as Morris did, but believed in the possibility of a collaboration between the artists and the manufacturer whereby the artist would design the forms of industrial goods which the manfacturer would produce according to market demand. Van de Velde's motto was: "The strength is in the line," a creed which was in accord with the beliefs of the *Jugendstil* artists.[18]

Van de Velde's great success lay in the field of interior decoration. In 1900 he designed the interior of Count Harry Kessler's apartment in Berlin, brushing aside the traditional copies of Renaissance furniture, the heavily brocaded curtains with their golden tassels, and replacing them with simple functional pieces. On the whole, however, van de Velde was not a spectacular success at reforming the private dwellings of the Berliners. But he had made a beginning, and at the recommendation of Count Kessler he was called to Weimar to direct the art school which was the forerunner of the *Dessauer Bauhaus*.[19]

His place in Berlin was taken by the young architect, Hermann Muthesius. As cultural attaché at the German embassy in London, Muthesius had become a great admirer of the English one-family home. He had been deeply impressed by Howard's *Garden Cities of Tomorrow*,[20] and on his return to Berlin he advocated the introduction of a type of housing entirely new to the Berliners: the English-style garden cottage.[21] Although favored by the Kaiser and appointed head of the industrial crafts, Muthesius did not get ahead very fast with his reform program. In the first place, real estate in the outlying districts of Berlin had been bought up by speculators, and it followed that one-family homes would be more expensive than anything similar in England. The lower-middle and working classes were thereby automatically excluded from his project. Thus Muthesius's impact was limited to those who believed with him that apartment house living was a poor substitute for the one-family home which might return man to the "happy quietness of rural life" and preserve the strength of every new generation in its struggle against the destructive turmoil of the metropolis.[22]

Muthesius built his own house in the region where the Grune-wald borders on the chain of lakes surrounding Berlin. His example was followed by those whose financial resources permitted this luxury, but he was not able to break the prevailing housing pattern in Berlin. Nevertheless, his indefatigable agitation left its mark; like van de Velde, he was a pioneer.

Muthesius's drive to bring industrial production and artistic imagination together was perhaps more significant than his efforts to initiate a new style of housing. He organized the *Werkbund*, an association of artists, writers, craftsmen, and industrialists, using all his influence to induce them to avoid repetition of the "shop-worn forms of the past." This was the first time in Germany that the problem of industrial design and its relationship to traditional art forms had been raised. More intricate questions were to follow: was modern technology the master or the servant of man, and how, in modern life, could the proper proportion of means and ends be reestablished? Muthesius's ideas were received with some protest, but he prevailed and was able to draw a group of the most gifted artists to Berlin.

In the wider perpectives of the twentieth century the guide lines of Muthesius are seen to parallel those of architects in other countries. In the United States, Sullivan and Frank Lloyd Wright carried out similar programs. Adolf Loos in Austria expressed kindred ideas when he stated: "It is the goal toward which all mankind moves, to search for beauty in the form only and not to make it dependent on ornament."[23]

At least one architect was already moving toward this goal. He was Alfred Messel, who had taught architecture at the Polytechnic University in Berlin since 1885. Messel had constructed a number of private residences in keeping with the classic style which had determined the architectural face of Berlin for so long. In 1896, he completed the construction of a new department store, Wertheim's, at Leipzigerstrasse, giving Berlin its first functional building. Wertheim's was conceived according to the purpose it was asked to fulfill. It was eminently desirable in the case of a department store to present it, not as though it were a warehouse, or an oriental bazaar, but with a façade designed in such a way that it would facilitate the display of merchandise in an attractive manner, that is, with light, air, and space. Messel solved the problem by replacing the traditional solid wall that had encased buildings until then by great glass surfaces interrupted by columnar stone buttresses. To the student of contemporary architecture this may not seem a daring undertaking, but it was the first step on the road to the "new international style" whereby the building is composed of a rhythmical combination of glass and steel, or glass and concrete. Messel's innovation was soon copied by other department stores with an even larger expanse of glass for the purpose of display.[24]

More significant still was a dawning understanding among architects that design in an industrial age must abandon old norms and create new ones, that the construction of railway stations, or subway entrances, or suspension bridges offered a challenge to the artistic imagination unknown to preindustrial times. The process was not, of course, a one-way street. Industry itself had to recognize the need for close cooperation with architecture and artistic design.

The Allgemeine Elektrizitätgesellschaft was the first to appoint an artist of rank to design street lamps and other similar conveniences. In 1907, Peter Behrens was invited by Emil Rathenau to take over this limited assignment, but his range was soon extended to the building of great halls of glass, steel, and enforced concrete. These structures are still extant in Wedding and Moabit; their functionalism and clear design made them models in the twentieth-century architecture. Behrens had his counterpart in Paris, where Auguste Perret proved the effectiveness of concrete as building material. The creed of all these men was, "Form follows function."

Peter Behrens attracted such extraordinary students as Le Corbusier and Walter Gropius. He also called together a group of architects who worked first and foremost in Berlin: Hans Poelzig, Bruno Taut, and Paul Mebes. Even more than Gropius or Le Corbusier, they were fascinated by the older institutions of cultural life, such as the theatre and the church. Like Gropius and Le Corbusier, however, they applied a new architectural direction to these ancient centers of communal gathering. One of the most remarkable examples was Poelzig's transformation of a circus into a modern theatre—the *Grosse Schauspielhaus* of Max Reinhardt.

One thing should be clear: the tradition which links Messel with Behrens, and Behrens with Gropius and Le Corbusier made imperial Berlin one of the focal points of modern architectural planning. Gropius was only twenty-eight years old, newly graduated from Behrens's studio, when he built his first factory, the Fagus factory, with a sheet of glass stretched over a frame of steel.[25]

With architecture progressing in such a revolutionary manner, we are not surprised to learn that the architects of Berlin turned toward a problem that had been sadly neglected in the history of the city: urban planning. The existing regulations had not been revised since 1863,[26] and although far-sighted men had called time and again for a new master plan which would take into consideration the industrial development of Berlin, no fresh ideas had been set in motion.[27]

Inspired by a feeling that Berlin was falling behind both England and America in developing solutions to the problems of metropolitan life, the Association of Berlin Architects launched a contest in 1910, calling for an urban blueprint that would bring into being a new and greater Berlin.[28] The first prize was given to Hermann Jansen, a professor of architecture at the Polytechnic University. The contest provoked a lively, even passionate, discussion among architects, laymen, and the state officials who had so far controlled building activities in Berlin. The details of the plan need not delay us here; their basic features were adopted after World War I. It seems amazing that the Kaiser raised no objections to the idea of a master plan for Berlin. In former years he had scorned the idea that committees, artistic contests, and prizes could produce appreciable results.[29] Ten years later, he remained silent in the midst of the fervent controversy provoked by the new plan for Berlin. It is hard to say whether he had matured or grown resigned. In any case, World War I made the execution of the project impossible, leaving it for the Weimar Republic to find the time and means for its completion.[30]

iii

In general, painting and sculpture met the same difficulties and achieved the same successes in Berlin as did architecture. Sculpture had been admitted under the aegis of the architect and sculptor, Schlüter. At the beginning of the nineteenth century, there were at least two masters whose efforts secured for Berlin an honorable place in this field: Schadow and Rauch. Schadow was the creator of the Chariot of Victory crowning the Brandenburg Gate and of several monuments attesting to his mastery of the classic style. His works were not, however, imitations of classic antiquity; instead they gave evidence of a realism that accorded well with the practical down-to-earth spirit of the city with which he was entirely familiar. His disciple, Rauch, gave Berlin one monument with which every citizen was well acquainted, the equestrian statue of Frederick the Great which commanded a stretch of Unter den Linden near the university and the opera.

Painting, on the other hand, was a late-comer to the scene, and it was not until the romantic movement invaded the Prussian capital that it took its place among the established arts. Even then, Berlin did not attract the best of the German painters; Philipp Runge and Caspar David Friedrich worked and taught in Dresden.

The Berlin romanticists failed to measure up to the unique creations of Friedrich, though Schinkel has left us some charming paintings, among which his designs for Mozart's *Magic Flute* are the most prized. His student, Karl Blechen, too, tried his hand at sketches for the operatic stage and revealed his romantic imagination in a series of somber landscapes.[31]

The paintings of the Biedermeier period hold a quaint attraction for all who are familiar with the German capital. The most gifted representative in this era was Franz Krüger, who specialized in painting horses in varied positions and backgrounds. As a result, he became the darling of the officers and of the court and advanced to painting parades and military pageants. These give an excellent idea of the Berlin of his days, at least, of official Berlin.

Berlin also possessed a group of painters who concentrated on the capital itself, continuing the tradition of such eighteenth-century masters as Canaletto and Belotto. The most appealing among them was Eduard Gärtner, who preserved in his pictures the face of a city destined to disappear under the onslaught of what goes by the name of "progress."[32]

Compared with other German cities where the fine arts flourished —Düsseldorf, Dresden, Munich—Berlin could hold its own. However, when compared with Paris or London, Berlin's painters had, at best, a local interest; there was only one in Berlin who could match Turner, Bonnington, or Constable, to say nothing of such masters as Ingres or Delacroix.

The great exception is Adolf Menzel. For two reasons Menzel is a test case when we attempt to make some assessment of painting in imperial Berlin: his extraordinary gifts lift him well above the average painter of the period; in addition, his long life (1815–1905) is almost entirely coincidental with imperial Berlin.

Menzel was born in Breslau, but moved to the capital in 1830, and most of his work is, in one way or another, connected with the city. His father had been a lithographer, and young Menzel took charge of the workshop. He had a self-taught talent for all the media of the graphic arts, and from them he advanced slowly to larger enterprises, especially oil paintings. The little man, almost a dwarf in stature, became a professor, finally a celebrity with the title of *Excellenz*. He was decorated with the order of the Black Eagle, the highest Prussian mark of distinction, and when he died the Kaiser walked behind his funeral cortege.

Menzel's talent as a lithographer was soon recognized, and the art historian, Franz Kugler, asked him to illustrate an edition of the works of Frederick the Great with woodcuts, an assignment which gave the twenty-four year old aspirant a solid economic basis. He produced no less than four hundred illustrations for Kugler's enterprise. They were based on an intensive study of the eighteenth century, yet Menzel's approach was thoroughly modern, thoroughly realistic.[33]

This realistic trend became even more apparent when he turned to painting, and produced in the 1840's a series of landscapes, interiors, and portraits which are astounding in their modernity. He anticipated the *pleinair*-ism of the French impressionists by twenty-five years; he conquered atmosphere and color and combined these techniques with his mastery of line. His "Room with

Balcony," his "Houses in the Snow," his "Woman Reading in the Evening," have become famous. They are companion pieces to Courbet's realistic paintings and to Corot's landscapes, which Menzel admired. On a visit to Paris in 1856, during a performance of the "Théâtre Gymnase," he was caught by the fantastic play of lights and shadows and later committed them to canvas. In a certain measure, Menzel's career parallels that of Fontane; both took their start from Prussian subject matters, and both were avowed realists. Yet, whereas Fontane gradually freed himself from the prejudices which were the inseparable traits of Prussianism, Menzel, as time went by, was swept deeper and deeper into this world of ephemeral glory, and eventually became its pictorial chronicler. It would be unfair to accuse him of sacrificing his artistic integrity or of having been dazzled by the pageantry of Prussian success. He remained open to new and fresh encounters with reality, witness his painting of an iron rolling mill (1875), or his drawings of bricklayers and construction workers whom he observed during the boom-years. Yet, a close look at Menzel's output after 1860 testifies to a constant fascination with the themes of Prussian history. There are the monumental pictures, "The Flute Concert" and "The Round Table," in which the figure of Frederick the Great dominates the scene, and there is the painting that transfixed on canvas the occasion when William I, seated in his carriage, rode through Unter den Linden before his departure for the front in 1870. This last is a masterpiece in which pictorial realism and the memory of a historical moment are kept in delicate balance.

After 1870, however, Menzel was drawn more and more into the social sphere of imperial Berlin. Invited to attend the official court functions, he began to paint the ceremonious suppers, the gala dances, or any other occasion when the glitter of uniforms, the decolletage of the ladies, and the constant movement attracted his eye. One cannot suppress a sense of disappointment in looking at these canvases; there is something photographic, a lack of imagination, and a certain artistic stagnation that force themselves on the observer as he compares these later works with Menzel's earlier productions. Moreover, Menzel bestowed on the official society of Berlin an importance which it did not possess. Both the occasions and the people who attended them were a veneer that flaked off as time went by; an attempt to halt the process only encouraged a historical falsehood. The monumental pictures of European aristocracy had reached and passed their zenith.[34] Thus Menzel became the prisoner of his environment and surrendered to a genre that the best artists of his day had already abandoned. He seemed to have forgotten his beginnings when his work was so close to that of the French impressionists, and in fact, he became blind to qualities that had formerly characterized his best work. Max Liebermann relates that Menzel was one day shown some impressionist paintings that a Mrs. Bernstein had collected, among them a Monet, a Degas, and a Manet. Menzel looked them over, and turning to the owner, asked, "Have you really paid money for this trash?"[35] Thus Menzel, who seemed destined to lead German art out of its parochialism, failed to rise to the challenge. Perhaps he was too old, but more than likely he accepted the imposition of an official art with equanimity.

Official art in Berlin represented more than the forces of conservatism and inertia which oppose innovations everywhere. It was backed by a powerful group that had the approval of the Hohenzollern and saw its principal function as the manufacture of incense so constantly demanded by the dynasty, the aristocracy, and the army. The head of this group was Anton von Werner, a painter from South Germany who had accompanied the crown prince in the Franco-Prussian war and who knew how to court favor with the princess Victoria. He was made president of the Academy of Fine Arts and specialized in what might be called illustrative pictures of Prussian history. He was very popular in Berlin and was continually swamped with commissions of all kinds. His influence was especially pernicious in the capital because it enjoyed the support of the authoritarian regime. As a result, a large sector of the bourgeoisie was brought to believe that these painted photographs were the epitome of art. (It is not to be wondered at that the word *Kitsch* was coined in Germany.*) The thirty-year rule of Anton von Werner over the Academy of Fine Arts and the aesthetic dictatorship of the Kaiser complemented each other in refusing sanction to what William II had called "the art from the gutter." Thus the element of au-

---

* *Kitsch:* an almost untranslatable word, meaning something trashy, showy, in bad taste, gaudy.

thoritarianism and oppression prevailed even in the realm of the arts, and it took a palace revolution to shake it off.

An accurate evaluation of the academy's position under the presidency of von Werner must take into consideration the finality of the academy's choice of works for the annual art exhibition, where some 3,000 were presented to the public. Moreover, the academy, and through it the Kaiser, had a voice in deciding which works should receive a prize, and, still more important, which would be purchased by the museums. In Berlin, it was the National Gallery which was entrusted with the acquisition of contemporary art.

When this writer was first introduced to the hallowed halls of the National Gallery, he was exposed to the pseudopaganism of Arnold Böcklin, the pseudohistory of Piloty, the pseudoreligion of Max von Uhde, and was instructed to admire these counterfeits as true art. The gallery had fallen behind. More and more as the age advanced, the times came under the influence of a group of artists who had refused to be chalked off by von Werner's judgments and had set themselves up as an independent group. They seceded from the academy; hence the name *Sezession* (1898).

In truth, the arts in Berlin were one generation in arrears. In 1890 French impressionism had triumphed over all its opponents and had become the dominant style of European painting. This fact did not escape some of the German painters, especially those who, like Liebermann, had studied abroad. Liebermann's style was formed by the French masters, especially Manet, and like Manet by some of the Dutch painters, notably Franz Hals. His work showed the new approach in his brushstrokes, in his choice of color and light, and in his preference for the contemporary and the human above the historical or religious subject.[36] His "Asylum for Old Men," his "Women Plucking Geese," his "Flax Spinners" were recognized as masterpieces and even awarded the official prizes. But Liebermann realized that an individual triumph meant little in view of the concerted effort of official Germany to curb "the art from the gutter." This became only too evident when the Association of Berlin Artists invited the Norwegian painter, Edvard Munch, to exhibit his work in Berlin (1892). The exhibition produced a storm of indignation among the critics, who accused Munch of lack of form, brutality, crudity, and vulgar emotion. The exhibition was forced to close after two days. The incident was the beginning of a schism in the ranks of Berlin painters which instigated the *Sezession* movement. Its leaders were Liebermann and Walter Leistikow. The latter, though not a born Berliner, had fallen in love with the landscape surrounding Berlin and tried to capture its charm in countless paintings. Today, they are, at best, period pieces, but his sincere enthusiasm for modern art and his disgust with official German painting cannot be questioned.[37] Liebermann and Leistikow were joined by a third painter, Lovis Corinth, who expressed the impressionist creed in words which Monet might have used: "Everything in this world is beautiful if seen by a painter, incredibly rich in color and brilliant light.[38]

Although Berlin was by no means the only place where such movements occurred (there were parallels in Dresden, Munich, and Vienna), the capital became the vortex of a growing artistic unrest and discontent. Max Slevogt, Ludwig von Hofmann, Lesser Uri, Franz Skarbina, Käte Kollwitz, and others like them joined in the thrust for recognition. The work of these artists was exhibited from May to September in a salon on the Kurfürstendamm. Liebermann, leader of the group, was already internationally recognized, his paintings being purchased by such galleries as the Tate in London.

The reaction of imperial Berlin was predictable. In fact, it was the breakaway movement of the secessionists which caused the Kaiser to deliver his speech on "the art from the gutter," a phrase which soon became familiar to the intellectuals of the capital. It is not difficult to understand why His Majesty became so irritated by the secessionists. To him, their movement smelled of treason; it negated the official optimism which stressed the well-being of Germany and the assurance that the Kaiser was leading the country toward a glorious future. These new fellows were rocking the boat; they questioned his omniscience, and he would have none of it. Käte Kollwitz, who had illustrated Gerhart Hauptmann's *Weber*, a work that was in disrepute at the court, was denied the golden medal which the jury of the art exhibition had awarded her.[39] Officers who wished to visit the exhibition of the secessionists were advised to wear mufti.[40] All this could be dismissed as the laughable or ludicrous attitude of the older and conservative element had it not been followed by the maniacal deeds of the Nazi period—the burning of "decadent books," the removal of "decadent" art from the museums, the ban on painting. Perhaps it is not quite cricket to cast the shadows of Hitler and Goebbels over the smaller figure of the Kaiser since his megalomania was, on the whole, merely verbal, but within this category he was unsurpassed. He rejected Leistikow's landscapes on the ground that he, William, was, after all, a hunter and was better acquainted with nature than the painter.

The German impressionists were not to be held up by the imperial harangues, however, and fortunately the buying public paid little heed to William either. The art dealers opened their galleries to them, even the long-established concerns such as Schulte, Unter den Linden, and Fritz Gurlitt. One art dealer committed his efforts entirely to the propagation of modern art. This was Paul Cassirer, husband of the famous Berlin actress, Tilla Durieux.[41] The close cooperation between the artists and the art dealers served still another purpose. Cassirer organized exhibitions of the French impressionists and avant-garde artists such as van Gogh and Cézanne.[42] The effect on the German art world was extraordinary and produced repercussions which were felt far beyond the expectations of the organizers. The secessionists felt themselves to be the true representatives of German art, and they took care to bring some of the best painters, past and present, to the attention of the public. The work of Leibl and of Trübner was exhibited; Menzel alone refused to be shown in the salons of the secessionists. It seems obvious that this group of modern artists was responsible for the emergence of Berlin as the artistic capital of Germany, and this they accomplished in the face of the Kaiser's hostility and those sycophants who catered to His Majesty's taste.

A foreign visitor to Berlin has furnished us with a vivid description of this abnormal situation: "A visit to the National Gallery of Berlin," wrote James Huneker, "makes me gnash my teeth. The sight of so much misspent labor, of the acres of canvas deluged with dirty, bad paint, raises my bile."[43] When Huneker finally discovered the French masters, he found them on the top floor of the building in a badly lighted room. They had been bought against the express wish of the Kaiser, who would have preferred to dismiss the director of the national gallery rather than consent to further acquisitions of the kind. "The masters," Huneker goes on to say, "who have thus fallen under the ban of official displeasure are Monet, Manet, Pissaro, Renoir, Sisley, and Cézanne." To find the work of an artist he could admire, Huneker was obliged to make a trip to Berlin's Sezession Gallery, where he found the pictures of such men as Liebermann and others.[44]

Perhaps the situation was not quite so bad as it may have appeared to the sensitive American critic. There were artists such as Hans Baluschek, whose work had a ringing note of social protest; there was Käte Kollwitz, whose charcoal drawings and prints stir the onlooker not only because of their human pathos, but by means of the strength of their lines. There was, last but not least, the master of the social cartoon, Heinrich Zille, who earned a living by drawing for such magazines as *Simplicissimus* or *Die Jugend* and who exhibited at the Sezession Gallery. Zille is a remarkable figure in the Berlin art world, a species of German Daumier, whose deft pencil revealed the misery of the working class, the struggle against the ubiquitous police; in a word, the seamy side of imperial Berlin, whose plight was made manifest through his humor.[45] The secessionists were not, however, in any sense a revolutionary group; such a description would be both artistically and socially untrue. Liebermann's style was conservative and restrained when compared with the French masters; design was as important for him as light and color. Slevogt and Corinth were possibly more exuberant, but they can hardly be called experimental, and as for their manner of living, it was much the same as any other member of the upper bourgeoisie. Liebermann, for instance, occupied a townhouse at the Pariser Platz adjacent to Friedländer-Fuld and the French Embassy.

It was ironic that the secessionists caught up with the French impressionists at a time when modern art had advanced to a new frontier far beyond the position so recently conquered by the German painters. Once more France had taken the lead. The artists whom we call the postimpressionists, van Gogh, Gauguin, Cézanne, Seurat, had come to believe that new avenues to reality were to be found beyond the beautiful surfaces of Monet and Renoir. Cézanne strove to create something "durable and solid" from impressionistic art, and Gauguin aspired to penetrate "the mysterious center of thought."[46] The reaction to impressionism took different forms in different countries. In Germany it goes under the name of expressionism.[47] Although Austrian and Russian artists made substantial contributions to the movement, expressionism is a typical German product. It coincided with the appearance of cubism in France and Italy, but is linked to Marinetti, Picasso, and Braque only in its desertion of the impressionist art forms.

Expressionism was not born in Berlin. Before it converged on the German capital it had two distinct focal points, one in Dresden, the other in Munich. Certain beliefs were held in common by the two groups: "We look today beneath the veil of appearances for the hidden things in nature . . . we look for and paint the inner, spiritual side of nature." The roots of expressionism go back to German romanticism, to Nietzsche and perhaps to such ephemeral prophets as Julius Langbehn. The latter's book, *Der Rembrandtdeutsche*, had called for a spiritual renewal in Germany. Germany, the author declared, has been militarized, now let her be civilized, and he seemed to envisage no contradiction between the country's martial preparations and the fostering of an artistic education.[48]

The expressionists depended on inner vision, on intuition; they freed themselves from the conventional use of form, color, line, and space. These props were unnecessary, they maintained, in the revelation of a reality that was entirely subjective, buried in the soul of the artist where it craved release in expression—hence the term 'expressionism.' Many of the expressionists avowed their belief in instinct, intuition, and in a religious participation in the hidden processes of life. "There is a fire blazing in the bowels of the earth," said Emil Nolde, ". . . and it influences us mortals." A Viennese critic expressed himself differently; to him expressionism was less a style than "a cry of anguish."[49] The expressionists shared van Gogh's belief that colors have a life of their own capable of revealing emotional realities which cannot be manifested in any other fashion. Thus, they demanded complete freedom in the use of line and color for bringing their inner drives to the light. The range of their emotions was wide and stretched from mysticism to cynicism.

Berlin and the Arts

The Dresden group was the older of the two expressionist centers. It included Ernst Ludwig Kirchner, Karl Schmidt Rottluff, Erich Heckel, Max Pechstein, and (after 1906) Emil Nolde. They called themselves *Die Brücke* (the bridge), since they hoped to unite "all the revolutionary and surging elements."[50] The Munich circle was more international in its composition; its members were Kandinski, Franz Marc, Lyonel Feininger, August Macke, and Paul Klee. The group became famous under the name *The Blue Rider*.[51]

For our study *Die Brücke* is the more interesting of the two centers because its members felt the attraction of Berlin far more than did the painters of *The Blue Rider*. By 1911, the entire group had drifted to the capital and had attempted to exhibit their work in the salon of the *Sezession*. But the older artists did not see eye to eye with the young revolutionaries, and the secessionists split over the question of exhibiting the work of the *Brücke*. The *Sezession* broke apart, one group in favor of the young artists, the other opposing them. The rejected painters organized their own exhibition, giving Berlin its "salon des refusés." Leading art critics like Karl Scheffler were drawn into the debate. Scheffler now raged against the expressionists as fervently as he had once championed the impressionists.[52] On the other hand, there were critics who entered the lists on the side of the expressionists. Herwart Walden launched a journal, *Der Sturm* (The Storm), in 1910, and soon acquired a salon where he put the expressionists on display. Franz Pfemfert followed his lead with *Die Aktion* (1911), which had stronger political undertones.

Walden's *Sturm* was the first to use the term expressionism consistently in characterizing the new movement.[53] An extraordinary feat was accomplished by Walden in 1913; he sponsored an exhibition in which ninety artists from fifteen countries displayed some three hundred works. He opened the exhibition with an address: "Art," he said, "is presentation, not representation . . . the painter paints what he visualizes with his innermost senses . . . every impression becomes for him expression from within."[54] The artists who were promoting these revolutionary changes in contemporary painting had varied objectives and adopted quite different techniques, but one quality of their work emerges simultaneously: an eruptive, explosive vision demanding the most intense pictorial presentation, obliterating any reminiscence of optical realism or any objective imitation of nature.[55]

Perhaps only those who have lived through the beginnings of German expressionism can fully appreciate the shock of its impact on the prewar world. But the painters were also exasperated by the prewar world. They felt a deep hostility to the mechanized Prussian respectability which surrounded them in Berlin, and, as Kirchner expressed it, they had the audacious idea of renewing German art, and through that art, of renewing German life.[56] It was a typical German illusion, though no doubt a noble one.

The life they presented in their paintings was, more often than not, the very life they abhorred—the overwhelming loneliness of the individual in a great metropolitan city. Nolde and Kirchner have painted the "human condition" in scenes of lonely streets and slovenly interiors. Kirchner tells of sleepless nights when he walked the streets searching in vain for a God among men. In his pictures he captured the desolate aspects of the city, its towering buildings, the masklike faces of men and women who resembled the figures in a wax museum.[57]

Of course, the expressionists offered other fare. There were the powerful portraits of Kokoschka, who had joined the expressionists; there were the flower pieces and landscapes by Schmidt-Rottluff. But it was obvious that reality was no longer the essence of the picture, which now obeyed its own laws of color and shape in their relation one to another. The paintings were often executed in a ruthless style, even bordering on crudity, with the idea of giving vent to the artist's emotion. Many of these works which once startled the observer have found their way into the museums and are gazed upon with equanimity by the general spectator; however slowly, the expressionists succeeded in gaining the attention of the public and of the directors of the museums. When Ludwig Justi began to acquire expressionist pictures for Berlin's National Gallery, the scoffers said he was "sailing with the Storm."[58] By 1914, Berlin had become the hub of Germany's most progressive painting. Though it had not started in Berlin, it reached maturity there.

It is difficult to estimate its immediate influence on the intellectual climate of the capital. If it be true, as some historians maintain, that the expressionists were aware of the frailty of the bourgeois era, that they sensed the advent of great revolutions, and that art for them was only meaningful as a revolutionary action, we can be certain that such insights were entirely wasted on the great mass of Berliners.[59] Expressionism was an avant-garde movement, and the great majority looked upon it as a *jeu de théâtre*. Only during the war and after 1919 did expressionism become a trend of significance in the cultural conduct of Berlin and of Germany.

We can deal briefly with the role of sculpture. By its very nature it was more closely tied to the ruling powers. The Kaiser in particular favored sculpture as a symbolic expression of imperial might. One of Berlin's sculptors, Reinhold Begas, had become the Kaiser's protégé. Begas was not without gifts and had produced at least one monument that attested to his taste: the Schiller statue before the Royal theatre. But he was not the man to stand up to William II, and when the Kaiser commissioned him to do a monument for his grandfather, William the Victorious, Begas produced one of the most appalling sculptures imaginable. Begas had chosen to show the old emperor on horseback, guided by the goddess of victory. On the steps leading to the statue was a profusion of angels, horses, and lions. This monstrosity was promptly dubbed "William in the Lion's Den" by the Berliners, and they would add, "That's the amount of bronze you can buy for four million marks." Begas was responsible for yet another disaster—the Bismarck statue before the Reichstag building—but he was still the Kaiser's choice when it came to designing the Siegesallee. One assumes that the sculptor's conscience had been silenced by imperial hypnosis.

Even if the relationship between sculptor and sponsor had been less encumbered by imperial megalomania, the position of this art in an industrial age could no longer be held in the same regard it had enjoyed during the days of the Renaissance and the Baroque. Great monuments can be produced only by public mandate and must command genuine public acclamation to merit their existence. Very few such memorials have been erected in the twentieth century. In Berlin neither the mandate nor the requisite talent was forthcoming.

In France, Rodin still reached greatness in his statues of Balzac and Victor Hugo, and there was Maillol who returned to the simplicity of Mediterranean beauty unfettered by historical settings, expressive through its own grace. In Berlin, a few sculptors trod the same path as Maillol—George Kolbe and Gerhard Marcks, in whose work we find at least a recollection of ideal plasticity. But such beauty as these artists achieved cost them any sympathy with those restless drives which marked their own period.[60]

Eventually sculpture made contact with the aesthetic code of expressionism. The tragic figure of Wilhelm Lehmbruck comes to mind. Though inspired by French sculpture, his work is highly individualistic. His elongated female forms, which remind us of El Greco, express an unforgettable melancholy, a brooding beauty; they seem somehow to predict the artist's early death by suicide in 1919. Another sculptor who moved close to the expressionists and joined *Die Brücke*, was Ernst Barlach. His goal was the re-establishment of a lost tradition with the religious sculpture of the Middle Ages. For the most part, he worked in wood, and his statues resemble the work of medieval masters such as Riemenschneider.[61]

It has often been observed that there is a close relationship between the expressionist arts and expressionist literature, a kind of consanguinity. Expressionist poets broke the molds of established form and style at the same moment as did the painters and sculptors. Kirchner's *Street Scene* finds a startling echo in Gottfried Benn's *Nachtkaffee*.[62] Georg Trakl, and even more Georg Heym, reveal a cosmic vision trembling with the premonition of an approaching catastrophe.[63] The voices of these poets were not heard until the storm had broken over Germany; only during the war years did the expressionists receive the attention of larger audiences. Not until 1916 did they conquer the stage.

iv

In Berlin, the performing arts reveal a sharp division between those serving cultural purposes and those which had no other goal than entertainment. One might be inclined to explain this division by Berlin's class cleavage and to ascribe the more elevated forms to the higher classes, the aristocracy and the bourgeoisie, and the more popular forms to the lower classes, but such an assumption would not be accurate. The division cut across the classes. Berlin, like most German cities, adhered to the aesthetic canon established by Goethe and Schiller according to which the theatre was an important part of the process of acculturation (*Bildung*) and necessarily moved on a high level. The natural instincts of showmanship, playfulness, and gaiety, which are indigenous to the performing arts, looked for different outlets, and found them in the popular types of entertainment. In other words the division in the performing arts was governed by taste, not class, and this became even more true during the period with which we are concerned. The cleavage between the two types of representation was not bridged in any cultural center, but it was more marked and more defined in Berlin than it was in Vienna, or Paris, or London where the works of Johann Strauss, Jacques Offenbach, or Gilbert and Sullivan helped to merge the two fields of entertainment.

Since the end of the eighteenth century, Berlin had cultivated the performing arts with assiduity. During the second empire, the city became the leading theatrical center of Germany, possibly of the world. We shall begin our brief survey with the role of musical life in Berlin.

Music came to Berlin through the interests of Frederick the Great. His building of the opera house in 1742 was only the most tangible expression of his belief in its importance. He himself was a composer of some merit, and he was successful in drawing musicians of rank to his court. Operatic music, however, was exclusively an Italian import. During the eighteenth century, German music, both spiritual and secular, began to make a place for itself. Private theatres offered German *Singspiele* and French *opéra comique*; these attracted larger audiences than the official Royal Opera. The educated middle class became the main sponsor of operatic and concert performances, although the court continued to show an enlightened interest in opera. Unlike the aristocracy of Vienna, Berlin's upper class was never devoted to the art of music.

A new type of musical offering had considerable success: choral singing.[64] Whether this was a secularized form of choir singing in which the congregation often joined is hard to say; in any case, group singing as such was much more popular in Protestant than in Catholic countries and occupied a place of great distinction in

Berlin. Karl Friedrich Zelter, a mason by profession, founded Die Singakademie in 1809, and soon devoted all his energies toward making this institute a center of concert performances. Zelter, one of the few men to whom Goethe spoke and wrote in the familiar second person singular, secured a home for his institute opposite the Opera House, and eventually the singers were given orchestral accompaniment. Zelter's student, Felix Mendelssohn-Bartholdy, rediscovered Bach's *Passion after St. Matthew* in 1829, and its performance marked a historic step in the appreciation of Johann Sebastian Bach. This was soon to be followed by Haydn's *Creation*, Beethoven's *Missa Solemnis*, and the oratorios of Mendelssohn.[65]

Thus Berlin became a city of many singing groups, all amateurs, who participated in the presentation of secular and sacred music from sheer enthusiasm in their performance. It is quite unlikely that there was another city in Europe where one could hear as many oratorios as could be enjoyed in Berlin. At Easter time the music lover might attend the two great Passions by Bach, the St. Matthew's and the St. John's; at Christmas time there was Bach's *Christmas Oratorio* and Händel's *Messiah*; throughout the year the less well-known oratorios, such as *Israel in Egypt* and *Judas Maccabeus*, were performed; and, of course, Bach's *Mass in B Minor* and Mozart's *Requiem*. These offerings transcended denominational barriers and were often given in Lutheran churches. The orchestral parts were frequently played by amateurs, and the solo parts were taken by singers who had specialized in sacred music.[66]

An Academy of Music had been founded shortly before the rise of the empire, and the violinist, Joseph Joachim, had been appointed director (1869). Joachim was on intimate terms with most of the great musicians of his day, Johannes Brahms, Clara Schumann, and Franz Liszt, and appeared constantly on the concert stage. Moreover, he introduced Berlin to chamber music with a standard of excellence that was unsurpassed. As his biographer said, he played the violin in the service of an ideal. He founded the "Joachim Quartet," and at its performances one would find Menzel, Moltke, and Helmholtz in the audience, to say nothing of most of the capital's musicians. A tradition was thus established which was carried on in Berlin by Schnabel, Flesch, and Grünfeld.[67] In most of these enterprises, it is evident that the initiative had passed from the court into the hands of the educated bourgeoisie who formed by far the greater part of the audiences at these concerts.

The development of orchestral music follows a similar pattern. A royal orchestra had come into being in 1842, conducted briefly by Felix Mendelssohn. Upon Mendelssohn's resignation, a mediocrity by the name of Wilhelm Taubert took the baton. In the meantime, private initiative had created a symphonic orchestra. Its conductor was the former head of a military band, Benjamin Bilse, who put on popular concerts attended in great numbers by an enthusiastic middle class. The ladies brought their needle work, the husbands their pipes; children were also admitted and coffee was served. It was not unlike the English music hall except that for the most part the programs were made up of classical music. Gerhart Hauptmann was among the many who came to hear Haydn, Gluck, Mozart, Beethoven, Schubert, and Brahms, and who thus became thoroughly familiar with the great masters.[68]

A rift between Bilse and some members of his orchestra led, in 1882, to the founding of a new organization which called itself the Philharmonic Orchestra. Brahms appeared as its conductor and so did Richard Strauss. The philharmonic became great, however, only after Hans von Bülow accepted its permanent conductorship. Bülow was a man of unquestioned integrity who had proven both his love for contemporary music and his immense knowledge of classical works. He taught the Philharmonic Orchestra discipline and respect for musical detail as well as love for the symphonic sweep of the great masterpieces. He never failed to give voice to his opinion, whether he spoke to Nietzsche or to some Berlin courtier. He referred to the concerts of the Royal Opera as "circus performances," and was thenceforth forbidden to set foot within those hallowed halls. Richard Strauss confessed that he owed to Bülow whatever he knew about the art of conducting. Bülow always conducted entirely from memory and once told Strauss, "You should have the score in your head, not your head in the score."[69] He resigned his position in 1892 and was followed by Arthur Nikisch who, like Bülow, enjoyed an international reputation; he knew how to attract young talents like Eugen d'Albert and Ferruccio Busoni who eventually made Berlin their home. Both d'Albert and Busoni were composers of note, but the public of Berlin knew them better as pianists and interpreters of Bach and Beethoven.[70]

The meteoric rise of the Philharmonic Orchestra brought about a major change in the concerts given by the Royal Orchestra. Felix Weingartner became its conductor in 1891 and revolutionized the stereotyped programs of his predecessors by performing Berlioz's *Symphonie Fantastique* on the night of his debut. When Weingartner left Berlin, he was replaced by Richard Strauss, who remained the conductor of the Royal Orchestra until the end of the empire. While preserving the classic-romantic core of the programs, he extended their range to include such masters as Reger and Mahler.[71] To see and hear Strauss conduct the orchestra was an experience never to be forgotten. His poise and his calm, almost nonchalant manner were entirely different from the sterile exhibitionism of some of the younger conductors. As in many other cities, the orchestra rehearsed in public in the forenoon at modest prices and played at night for a more elegant audience. I remember well what must have been the final concert of the Royal Berlin Orchestra on the night of November 8, 1918. From my place among the standees, I watched the maestro conduct the *Egmont Overture* with the same composure that I had admired many times before. But when I left the opera house, soldiers with machine guns were guarding Unter den Linden. On the following day the empire collapsed.

The Royal Opera was, of course, the most representative among the musical establishments of Berlin. As the oldest, it also commanded a more generous share of the royal subsidies than any other theatre. Certain disadvantages accompanied this largess. The royal theatres, the opera and the theatre for dramatic production, were under the direction of an 'intendant,' a manager appointed by the ruler. He belonged traditionally to the court aristocracy, and it was often hard to say what qualifications, if any, had led to his appointment.[72] Subject to the intendant and often at cross purposes with him were the conductors of the opera. During the *Biedermeyer* era, the most outstanding conductor was the Italian, Gasparo Spontini, whose activities in Berlin were accented by a passionate rivalry with two other composers, both of whom were more gifted than he: Karl Maria von Weber and Giacomo

Meyerbeer. Weber's *Der Freischütz* was first performed in Berlin
in 1821. With its mixture of romantic witchcraft, its incorporation
of folklore motives, it made a direct appeal to the hearts of the
German people, and Weber's melodies became part of the German folklore itself, especially in Berlin. The public was divided
between those who admired Weber and those who favored Spontini, but in the end Spontini came out ahead, and Weber, as a
rival for the conductorship, was no longer a threat. Spontini's
luck did not hold when it came to Meyerbeer. One of the few
composers who had been born in Berlin, Meyerbeer had been
captivated by the Italian style, especially by Rossini who was then
at the height of his fame. From the two elements, his German
heritage and his Italian predilection, he created a new type of
opera which enchanted first his French and soon his German contemporaries. Upon the accession of Frederick William IV in 1840,
Spontini fell from grace and, for good measure, was thrown into
prison for a declaration which the Prussian government chose to
term lèse majesté.[73] Meyerbeer stepped into his shoes, and as
Generalmusikdirektor in Berlin, he was instrumental in producing
Wagner's *Rienzi* and his *Flying Dutchman,* a service acknowledged
by Wagner with his customary lack of gratitude. Meyerbeer's
tenure in Berlin made the opera there an important center of
musical art in Europe. His tastes were catholic and included the
bel canto of Bellini and Donizetti as well as the German *Spieloper*
of Lortzing and Nicolai. Many of these became favorites with the
Berlin public.[74]

The ensemble of singers was uniformly good and from time to
time was highlighted by famous stars such as Pauline Lucca whose
performance swept the Berliners off their feet.[75] Nevertheless, it
cannot be maintained that Berlin was a pacesetter for operatic
music. The fight for Wagner was won in Paris and Munich before
the German capital capitulated. *Die Meistersinger* still provoked
a furor when it was performed on April 1, 1870, but soon after
this episode the *Ring* was presented in its entirety. By 1875, the
Wagnerites had triumphed.

There is a certain temptation to speak of Richard Wagner as
the incarnation of the artistic traits marking the second German
empire; Heinrich Mann has yielded to this temptation in his novel
Der Untertan (The Subject). One recognizes in Wagner the

same ardent nationalism, the same anti-Semitism, the same historicism that links the present with the medieval German past. But one should not disregard the deep-seated revolutionary fire in Wagner's music, the anarcho-socialist message contained in *Siegfried* and indeed present in the entire *Ring*. It is only with his superficial or, if the word be allowed, his phony side that Wagner belongs to the second empire.

Erich Leinsdorf has made the attempt to classify Richard Strauss as the clearest manifestation of Wilhelminian traits, but this ascription also stands in need of qualification. Richard Strauss was a Bavarian by birth and a prodigy at the age of four. Despite some dazzling success, he had not found himself before he was well into his twenties. His gifts as a composer had come to light in a number of symphonic poems, and among these his *Zarathustra*, completed in 1896, caused a sensation. The composition made its way through Europe and America where James Huneker called it 'dangerously sublime.'[76] Many of Strauss's symphonic poems are inspired by literary motifs; *Till Eulenspiegel*, for instance, or *Don Quixote*. Most of his operas were based on dramas, such as Wilde's *Salomé* or Hofmannsthal's *Electra*. The Strauss-Hofmannsthal collaboration is unique in the history of the fine arts—a union of enchanting poetry and superb music that produced such masterpieces for the operatic stage as *Der Rosenkavalier*, *Le Bourgeois Gentilhomme*, *Die Frau ohne Schatten*, and *Arabella*.[77]

Strauss's preeminent position among conductors of the Berlin opera is in itself a note in cultural history. The Kaiser did not care for his music and made this clear in no uncertain terms. Yet, by the end of the nineteenth century, Strauss was the most talked-of musician in the world, and it was imperative that he should direct the Berlin opera, just as it was that Mahler should conduct the opera in Vienna.

It would be a mistake, I believe, to inject political meanings into Strauss's acceptance of the conductorship. He was first and foremost a musician and looked upon the political scene with the indifference of the egotist who measures political events by the effect they may, or may not have, on his work. He could even, therefore, tolerate the insolence of a Goebbels, since the only thing that mattered to him was his work. This may not be an admirable attitude, but it must be regarded in its proper perspective. As Strauss wrote to Romain Rolland, "I am no hero . . . I am not made for battle . . . all I want is to make sweet and happy music."[78] In this exclusive preoccupation with his own productions, he blissfully ignored the work of his contemporaries such as Puccini, but this was not the result of envy or spite. He was far too convinced of his own gifts.

With such a man at the head of the Berlin opera, the institution soon became one of the leading operatic centers of the world. Yet we must not assume that Strauss identified himself with Wilhelminian Berlin.[79] His own operas were first performed in Dresden under the direction of Ernst von Schuch, who did not attempt to emasculate either Strauss or Hofmannsthal and carried *Salomé* and *Electra* to a resounding success.[80] In spite of Strauss's commanding position in Berlin, the performance of *Salomé* ran into opposition not so much from the Kaiser as from the empress. The situation was not new to Strauss; his early work, *Feuersnot*, had produced a violent disagreement between him and the administration which made Strauss decline "once and for all" to have his dramatic work performed at the Berlin Opera House.[81] Nevertheless, *Salomé* was given in Berlin after the composer had made certain concessions to the pious empress: the star of Bethlehem was to rise on the nightly sky after Iokanaan and Salomé had ended their lives. This was a ludicrous, face-saving device, and we have no information as to whether it immunized any of the spectators against the sadistic decadence of the Wilde-Strauss combination.

A similar state of affairs awaited *Rosenkavalier*. It had been performed in Dresden in 1911 with unprecedented success. Both the emperor and his intendant, Count Hülsen Haeseler, were impressed by the number of special trains that had been ordered to take music lovers from Berlin to Dresden to attend the performances, and as a result, *Der Rosenkavalier* was accepted for the next season in Berlin. However, strings were attached: Count Hülsen insisted that his "mild and refining hand" should be allowed to guide the performance. What seemed to have scandalized the Kaiser and Hülsen was the uninhibited lustiness of Baron Ochs von Lerchenau. "An imperial chamberlain should not act like a vulgar fellow." Strauss was under no misapprehension as to the motives behind the objections to his work, but he agreed to the proposed cuts.[82] In spite of this aristocratic prudishness, *Der Rosenkavalier* received as much applause in Berlin as in Dresden, and Strauss considered Berlin's opera "the finest artistic institute of Germany" in the years before 1918.

Thus opera continued to flourish in Berlin. Enrico Caruso and other famous singers appeared on its stage; in general the quality of the performances was high. Many other conductors, some of them as accomplished as Strauss, such as Leo Blech and Max von Schilling, maintained the standard of the institution in their every night performance. The Royal Opera house had little to fear in the way of competition from privately owned companies because of the high maintenance cost. A few there were, but their life span was brief. Following the example of the *opéra comique*, one enthusiastic manager opened the *Komische Oper*.[83] Its director, Hans Gregor, tried to overcome a few traditions by coaching the singers in a more natural manner of acting. Although his intentions were applauded, it took another fifty years before the dramatic style of operatic singing yielded to realistic presentation. Shortly before the war, an opera house was opened in Charlottenburg where today West Berlin's opera house has been rebuilt. Its beginnings gave little promise, but it rose to fame under the leadership of Bruno Walter during the Weimar Republic.

The gap between the serious musical performance and that devoted solely to entertainment, which we have already noted, held good for imperial Berlin. A type of farcical comedy, called *die Posse*, became popular in the capital. Song and dance were interspersed with strong local color sketches and the genre had great success, but its origins are obscure and its longevity surprising.

Along with such forms of amusement came the operetta imported from Paris, London, and Vienna. Offenbach, Gilbert and Sullivan, Johann Strauss, Millöcker, Suppé, and Léhar were regular fare in Berlin, but they were not native products, and their success speaks for the general mood of the period rather than that of the capital. Musicals were also popular. These were a blend of dazzling show, hit tunes, and acting. The composers of these "revues," as they were called, were personalities well known to everyone in Berlin: Paul Lincke, whose song about the little glowworm made him famous, Walter Kollo, and Jean Gilbert. And these revues had their stars among which at least three became part of the Berlin scene. Josef Giampietro became famous through a song which glorified and parodied the guard officer; Fritzi Massary was an idolized feminine star, a combination of erotic charm and personal grace; Claire Waldoff specialized in songs written and performed in the argot of the Berlin gamin.[84] A remark of Grillparzer holds true for all of them; he said, "Talking about music is like describing a banquet; the listener hears the words, but he does not taste the food." To convey the flavor of these entertainments is well nigh impossible, and doubly so if one attempts a translation. The hits, which were named *Schlager*, were very much a part of everyday living. The Kaiser and the crown prince favored certain composers and performers with their attentions, and the revue, surviving the downfall of the empire, stepped into great popularity after 1919.

Today Radio Berlin frequently plays one of the revue songs which every Berliner knew by heart: "So lang noch Unter den Linden/ Die alten Bäume blühn,/ Kann nichts uns überwinden,/ Berlin bleibt doch Berlin." (As long as the old trees continue to bloom Under the Lindens, nothing can conquer us; Berlin remains Berlin.) But an Austrian by the name of Hitler cared nothing for the warning that lay beneath these words. As chancellor of the Third Reich, he ordered the removal of the linden trees, the better to view his marching hordes. And Berlin ceased to be Berlin; the "divided city" took its place.

While the Philharmonic Orchestra and the Royal Opera were moving toward world acclamation, the Berlin theatre was also making strides toward fame. Its rivals in the race for the top rank, Vienna, Munich, Hamburg, and Leipzig, seemed to have a better chance to claim the lead, and at first glance Berlin's success appears paradoxical. As an artistic and as a sociological phenomenon, the development of the theatrical arts in Berlin is both interesting and significant.

During the first two-thirds of the nineteenth century the theatres of Berlin were provincial in style and insignificant in number; until 1848 there were only two worthy of mention. One was the Royal Theatre and the other was the Königstädtische Theatre, located in the old center of the city near the Alexander Square. But by 1897, Berlin had some thirty theatres, not counting vaudeville or the summer theatres, all of which were making their way without much effort. The most immediate reason for this sudden rise was the liberal legislation that had come into being with the founding of the second empire. Since 1867, any energetic person could obtain a license to open a theatre; the policy of laisser aller, laisser faire paid little heed to qualifications; success or failure would speak the final word in due time.

The foundation of the empire renewed a desire which the Germans had harbored since the days of Lessing, Schiller, and Goethe; a national theatre, they thought, was the logical accompaniment of the political unification. One might even say that the demand for a national theatre preceded the desire for political unification; it is certainly true that the great poets of the classical-romantic period had set their hopes on the educational mission that a national theatre might fulfill. Yet it was not until 1890 that any one of the many theatres that had been founded lived up to expectations. The situation in Berlin was a true reflection of the general political condition. At the beginning of the nineteenth century the Royal Theatre was called Das National Theater; but to the extent that reaction and oppression prevailed, it became more and more a royal theatre, its policy dictated by the court. A lieutenant of the guard had been named royal intendant by Frederick William IV. His name was Botho von Hülsen, and for thirty-five years he ran the theatre (now again the Royal Theatre) with military efficiency.[85] Although it could afford some of the most gifted actors, it lacked any spirit of dramatic adventure or innovation; it was tame, stuffy, and tedious in its performances. The repertory was burdened with classical literature, which served only to check the progress of the arts, to quote Oscar Wilde.[86] The public viewed the Royal Theatre as a court appendage which in no way corresponded to its dream of a national theatre.

The history of the theatre in Berlin is basically an account of the efforts of the bourgeoisie to find a means for expressing its aspirations. The aristocracy was, on that score, amply satisfied with the Royal Theatre, and the proletariat was as yet a long way from setting up a playhouse that might give form to the nebulous and contradictory aesthetics of Karl Marx. There were, however, certain goals the Germans hoped to reach in the founding of a national theatre. They wanted to present not only the German classics but all the great dramatists of the world, both past and present. The dramatists of rank in the 1870's and 1880's were Scandinavian or Russian, but this should not bar them from the German stage; the national theatre should not foster chauvinism.

A second prerequisite was the high artistic level demanded for all performances, and the agreement of the actors about principles of style and presentation. During the last decades of the century, only two theatres in the German cultural landscape aspired to such homogeneity: the famous Burgtheater in Vienna, and the company organized by the Duke of Meiningen. The latter, a typical German product, had grown out of one of the court theatres cultivated by all small German principalities. Duke Georg II, of Saxe-Meiningen, assembled a group of actors who agreed to work in unison rather than starring certain individuals. His guiding idea was authenticity, and he visualized a stage which would produce a near-perfect illusion.[87] To this end he paid scrupulous attention to details of costuming and stage settings. He insisted that these should be faithful replicas of the period of the drama itself. When he presented Schiller's *Wallenstein*, Bohemian goblets from the time of the Thirty Years' War were among the props.

Though one may argue that Duke Georg violated a principle of dramatic art, namely, that the imagination of the spectator must be engaged, his stage directions were nevertheless aimed at the utmost realism. He rehearsed his company with the greatest care and was very demanding in the preparation of his performances. This necessarily strained the finances of the small dukedom, and he could maintain his company only by "going on tour," so that the "Meininger" were on the road most of the year. Their appearance in Berlin in 1874, where they gave Shakespeare's *Julius Caesar*, made a deep impression; the funeral oration of Marc Antony and the mass scenes at the forum were loudly applauded.[88]

Vienna's Burgtheater still cultivated the style of a by-gone day; the actors declaimed their lines and moved about the stage like automatons. Yet Vienna was a city in which the enthusiasm for the theatre was almost obsessive and in which the great actors were worshipped as nowhere else. Neither the "Meininger" nor the Burgtheater fulfilled the German ideal of a national theatre, the former because it adhered to a false conception of reality, the latter because it clung to an outmoded form of dramatic presentation. Both were, however, superior to the Royal Theater in Berlin, which more and more became the target of the critics. As for the private enterprises, they were the object of financial speculation.[89] In order to compete successfully with their rivals, they specialized in different types of entertainment: the French parlor comedy of Dumas, Sardou, or Scribe; the *Posse*, which was sheer entertainment and often quite vulgar; the foreign actor who often provided a sensation for the audience. In 1889, the situation changed dramatically. "1889," wrote Otto Brahm, "was the year of the German theatrical revolution, just as 1789 was the year of the revolution of humanity."

The political undertones of this declaration will not be wasted on the reader; yet the apparently pretentious claim held some truth. The revolution in the theatre was the purpose of the Free Stage movement. Ten men were responsible for its appearance, some of whom bear names already familiar to the reader: Maximilian Harden; Theodor Wolff, future editor of the *Berliner Tageblatt*; S. Fischer, the publisher; the brothers Hart, well-known for their unrelenting criticism of conditions in the Berlin theatre; and, finally, the *spiritus rector* of the entire venture, Otto Brahm.[90]

The Free Stage movement was patterned after the Théâtre Libre of Paris and had as its principal goal a theatre free from conventions, censorship, or commercial aims. It hoped in Berlin to give modern plays of decided interest which the established stage could not or would not present.[91] It was organized as an association (Verein), thereby sidestepping police interference. One thousand passive members were entitled to attend the performances, and ten active members and the chairman, Otto Brahm, managed the association.

Brahm might seem an unlikely choice as the director of a theatrical venture. He was the son of a Hamburg merchant whose surname was Abraham. Otto had studied literature in Berlin and had germanized his name. He had written a number of biographies on Schiller, Kleist, and Gottfried Keller, for which he had received the coveted Kleist award. His real love, however, was contemporary literature, especially the work of Ibsen, Gerhart Hauptmann, and August Strindberg.

"The motto of the new art," he said, " . . . is the one word 'truth'; and truth, truth on every path of life, is what we strive for and what we demand."[92] The first performance of the Free Stage was given over to Ibsen's *Ghosts*, a play which had been barred from the German theatre because of its theme of inherited syphilis. This produced a scandal, but a more violent one occurred a few weeks later when Brahm presented Gerhart Hauptmann's *Before Dawn* (*Vor Sonnenaufgang*). This was the occasion of one of the most notorious events in the history of the Berlin theatre. Interruptions from the audience and the din of catcalls back and forth increased from act to act; only with the greatest difficulty could the play be brought to its conclusion. Friends and foes attacked each other not only with words but with their fists, and a general pandemonium filled the theatre.[93] But the scandal established both Hauptmann and Brahm's Free Stage in the eyes of the Berlin public and sealed the triumph of naturalism as a theatrical style.

This style was dubbed Brahm's style in literary circles and was characterized by a retreat from the old rhetorical manner of dramatic declamation; it also repudiated the illusionary realism of the "Meininger." It carefully avoided theatrical effect, the play for the gallery. Brahm was a puritan of sorts, and his direction of both actor and play was suited to the naturalistic drama alone, to the work of Ibsen, Hauptmann, Strindberg, Tolstoi, Gorki, and Schnitzler. The great classical dramas became drab and lifeless in his hands, and he soon refrained from presenting them on his stage.[94] However unfortunate this result may have been, it must be granted that the Brahm's style was an indispensable corrective, a necessary purge, which liberated the Berlin theatre from the hollow rant and bombast of bygone days.[95]

The Free Stage had been financed by some of the industrialists and merchants whom we have already met as art collectors: James Simon, Eduard Arnold, von Mendelssohn, and others. These men also advanced Brahm the money to branch out and to rent a theatre which would be under his direction. This theatre had been built by Adolphe l'Arronge, himself a playwright and actor, and was called Das Deutsche Theater. It was located in the center of town, in the Schumannstrasse, near the Friedrichstrasse, and the name was symbolic and prophetic at the same time; the Deutsche Theater came as close to achieving the dream of a national theatre as Berlin would ever come.

Before following Brahm in his career as director of the Deutsche Theater, it is necessary to speak briefly of another innovation which appeared concurrently with the Free Stage movement and which was intimately connected with it: the People's Stage or Volksbühne. The Free Stage movement had been the effort of a number of men of liberal persuasion, all members of the Berlin bourgeoisie. They had met with open hostility from official Germany, the Kaiser, the censor, and the greater part of the aristocracy, who looked upon the movement as a menace to the established order and its moral canons. The founders were accused of inciting "the masses" to revolt. Paradoxically, the workers did not identify themselves with the movement and thought the moment right to start their own theatre.

One of the foremost Marxian apologists, Georg Lukács, has called Marx's ideas on art and aesthetics a coherent system.[96] A less partisan observer will be unable to see the truth of this statement. Actually there are few aspects of Marxian thought that reveal its inherent contradictions so blatantly as Marx's scattered thoughts on the future of the arts in a proletarian civilization. As in other aspects of the proletarian culture, his views remained vague and nebulous. Marx's own predilections went clearly toward the great geniuses of the past, Aeschylus, Shakespeare, Goethe, Beethoven, Balzac. The art of the future presented Marx and his disciples with an unsolvable problem: would the class struggle, the dictatorship of the proletariat, and the ensuing classless society produce a new and revolutionary art, or would the forms that had been cultivated by the bourgeoisie be continued? Furthermore, what attitude could the working classes be expected to assume toward the culture of the past? Would they reject it, or would they affirm it, at least in part?

Marx left these questions unanswered, and Engels' attempt to deal with the obvious contradictions of the Marxian position presented no solution.[97] The social democrats in Berlin were obliged to find an answer, but were divided in their opinions. The leaders of the party, such as Bebel and Liebknecht, considered the problem a secondary one; without brushing it aside altogether, they contended that political power was the prerequisite for any cultural activity of the working class, and the theatre, or for that matter any one of the arts, was given low priority on their list of party goals. Yet even those who hoped for a proletarian culture found it difficult to adhere to the ideas and tenets of the Free Stage movement. One would have assumed that Marxism and naturalism were logical allies, since both were in opposition to the existing class structure; both rejected the idealism of the past and professed their belief in a materialistic philosophy. However, the leadership of the social-democratic party objected to the naturalistic drama of Hauptmann and Gorki, advancing arguments that were very like those of the Kaiser. Eduard Bernstein, for instance, reproved Hauptmann for portraying human suffering without advancing remedies for its relief. If Marxism were to be successful, it would be obliged to conjure up that silver lining without which the lives of the workers were all but unbearable. Naturalism was unable to deliver this order.[98] As a result, the majority of the socialists interested in bringing culture and the working class together occupied a somewhat conservative position. They shied away from the ugliness of everyday life as it was presented by the naturalists; the airing of sexual problems was considered licentious, and they refused to identify themselves with it, considering it a symptom of bourgeois decadence. In truth, the social democrats reflected the same philistine, petty-bourgeois prejudices on which Marx had heaped such scorn. The attempts to organize a theatre for the "toiling masses" revealed, therefore, the inherent contradictions of Marxian philosophy.

Die Freie Volksbühne came into being in 1890. Its most immediate *raison d'être* was the inability of the workers to pay the price of admission demanded by the existing theatres, and their consequent exclusion from any participation in the dramatic arts. Motivated by these considerations, Dr. Bruno Wille, a social democrat by conviction rather than by party affiliation, published an appeal: *Aufruf zur Gründung der Freien Volksbühne*.[99] His basic idea was the creation of a theatre for the working class; the price of admission was to be fifty pfennige, and the tickets were to be distributed by lottery among its members, thus avoiding any discrimination of income. The People's Stage was also to be set up as an association (*Verein*) to avoid police and censorship strictures.

But the principles underlying the effort to establish a theatre of, by, and for the working class was, from the beginning, subject to all manner of tensions. The founders of the Volksbühne disagreed about the use of the theatre as an instrument of propaganda, "the literary organization of the German working class"; should it not, instead, be considered as an artistic enterprise destined to establish continuity between the existing culture and the proletarian future?[100] The People's Stage split, and a New People's Stage movement was organized in 1892. But the party and the great majority of its members favored the traditional approach rather than the revolutionary, semianarchistic attitude adopted by the more independent faction. Pressure from the authorities also obliged the movement to advance with caution.[101] Thus it moved closer and closer to the bourgeois theatre until, in 1913, they closed ranks.

From the point of view of a proletarian culture the People's Stage was not a success, although a political theatre was started during the Weimar Republic by Erwin Piscator, Ernst Toller, and Bertolt Brecht. Nevertheless, neither in Germany nor in any other country has the problem of a culture inspired and maintained by the ideals of the working class reached any kind of solution. Nor can it be resolved in the manner predicted by Marx and his disciples. It is a dream which fades when confronted by the stark reality of a socialist society.

However, as an organization, the People's Stage came up with colors flying. By 1905, it had 11,000 members, and the number steadily increased. It has survived war and revolution, and today is the common foundation for most of Germany's theatres. Those who had hoped that the People's Stage would become the German National Theatre, however, were doomed to disappointment. It did not and could not fulfill this function for the ample reason that a proletarian culture did not exist.

When Otto Brahm took over the direction of the Deutsche Theater in 1894, it seemed possible that the gap might be filled. Brahm achieved two different, but related, aims; he brought about the triumph of naturalism as a theatrical style, and he was successful in defending the victory obtained by the Berlin bourgeoisie with the founding of the Free Stage. The former was a matter of artistic principle; the latter a political issue barely disguised under an aesthetic veneer.

Brahm planned to give the public both classical and contemporary fare. Moreover, the contemporary was not limited to the naturalistic drama of Ibsen and Hauptmann; it also embraced the symbolism of the *fin de siècle* as found in Maeterlinck and the neoromanticism of Hugo von Hofmannsthal. Brahm himself confessed, "I do not consider naturalism to be the last word of the arts." Altogether some forty-five modern authors were represented on Brahm's stage, yet there is no denying that his preference was for Ibsen and Hauptmann. Maximilian Harden criticized him severely for his omissions, but failed to give him credit for his commissions, one of which was the liberation of the Berlin stage from shopworn tradition. As one critic observed: "[Brahm's] pervasive intellectualism, together with his one-sided literary predilection, furnished the strength and unity of purpose leading to [his] notable achievements. On the other hand, intellectualism and literature also govern his limitations."[102] Eventually his style became outmoded and was replaced by a more expansive and flexible spirit.

The political side of Brahm's struggle, however, deserves unqualified approval. The test case again concerned a drama of Hauptmann's, *Die Weber* (The Weavers). In this work Hauptmann had dramatized the economic plight of the Silesian textile workers of the 1840's. Written in dialect, the play brought the masses and their problems to the stage and was considered an open attack on the existing social order. Actually, nothing could have been further from Hauptmann's intention; throughout his life he had found ways and means to accommodate himself to the powers that were. But the authorities were displeased. Berlin's president of police made the observation: "Uns passt die ganze Richtung nicht" (We dislike the whole trend), and he banned any public showing of *The Weavers* in Berlin on the ground that it was an open appeal to rioting.[103] The Free Stage and the People's Stage continued, of course, to perform the drama before closed audiences. The case came before the courts which refuted the police ban by saying that Berlin theatre prices precluded the attendance of any appreciable number of workers at the performances of the Deutsche Theater. As a result, *The Weavers* was presented on September 25, 1894, to an audience composed mainly of the Berlin bourgeoisie and was accorded a rousing success.[104] One would like to attribute Hauptmann's triumph to the poetical power of his work (it is one of his best plays), but it would be nearer the truth to admit that the public applauded because they could thereby express their displeasure with the efforts of the Kaiser and his agents to control the currents of literature.

There was no uncertainty about the Kaiser's attitude toward Hauptmann's work and its performance. He cancelled the subscription of the imperial box at Brahm's theatre and officers of the army and navy were counseled to avoid attendance there. The theatre, he told the actors of the royal establishment, should serve the cause of idealism and should fight against the un-German tendencies to which many theatres had succumbed.[105]

But, in line with his pronouncements on the visual arts, the Kaiser's words had little or no influence. The Deutsche Theater continued to maintain its leading role and indeed acted as a magnet for a great number of artistic talents both inside and outside of Berlin. Their names would mean little to anyone who did not live in Germany at the time, but to Brahm and his successor, Max Reinhardt, this plethora of great actors and actresses was the means by which they could build the national theatre for which the Berliners clamored.[106] Looking back, one realizes that Max Reinhardt's fame rested to a large part on the foundations laid by Otto Brahm.

The appearance of Max Reinhardt in Berlin marks a turning point in the history of the theatre. Reinhardt was born in Baden near Vienna, on September 9, 1873, with the name, Max Goldmann, and became the most outstanding director and theatrical producer of his era.[107] His beginnings, however, were modest and lacking in promise; he was a mediocre actor when he came to Berlin to learn his profession under the guidance of Otto Brahm. Reinhardt had very different ideas about the potentialities and possibilities of the theatre, and in 1902, he left Brahm and tried his hand at vaudeville in Germany's first cabaret called *Schall und Rauch*. He drifted from one theatre to another until he took over the direction of the Deutsche Theater from Otto Brahm in 1904. Brahm had run into various difficulties; some of his best actors had deserted him, and the public had tired of his puritanical style. The time was ripe for change, and the change was startling. Reinhardt was a wizard for whom the stage was not a moral, or an educational, and especially not a political institution;

it was a magical contrivance with which to ravish and enthrall an audience. His tastes had a much wider range than Brahm's, and were, moreover, notably catholic. During one season he would stage Maeterlinck, Gorki, Wedekind, and Wilde; in the next, it would be Tolstoi, Shaw, Lessing, Euripides, and Schiller; in a third, he would bring forth Shakespeare, Schnitzler, Chekov, and Ibsen; for a fourth it would be Kleist, Hofmannsthal, and Molière; and as a fifth, Goethe, Gogol, Hauptmann, and Hebbel. And so it went for season after season.[108]

Reinhardt has been compared with André Antoine and Stanislavski, but he surpassed both in the variety of his productive imagination, and it is here that we find the key to his being. His phantasy became as inflamed by Goethe's *Tasso* as by an Offenbach operetta, but there was, nevertheless, a great constancy in his lifework, a good deal of planning, even scheming, a vast ambition that took in the entirety of western civilization. All of this conspired to make Reinhardt the greatest theatrical producer of modern times.[109]

Light and music were used by Reinhardt with a profusion previously unknown. He also took advantage of technical inventions, such as the turnstile stage, which he used in the production of *Midsummer Night's Dream* and other romantic tales. However, the secret of Reinhardt's success lay in his ability to reach out to the actors, to see creative potentialities which the actors themselves failed to recognize, and to discover, even in nonactors, possibilities that lay hidden from the practiced eye. For him the world was indeed a stage, every individual a potential actor, and color, sound, and light the ingredients of the spell he cast over the audience. Like every actor he emphasized effect and recognized no limits in producing that effect. He thought of the actor as the core and the heart of the theatre; it belonged to him. True as this may be, it still took a magician like Reinhardt to stimulate the actors into giving their very best, even to surpass themselves in their roles.[110] He was a perfectionist whose greatest ambition was the creation of the mood, the *Stimmung*, as the Germans say, which emanated from his productions.

It has been said that he completed the theatre of the haute bourgeoisie, and that, as such, he was typical of the period in which and for which he worked.[111] Very likely, but this is meager recognition of his great talents and his valuable gifts to the stage. Those who were fortunate enough to see Reinhardt's Shakespearean productions, his *Othello*, his *As You Like It*, or his staging of Schiller's *Don Carlos* will not be content with this stinted estimation.

It was only natural that he attracted actors just as he was attracted by them, and that his Deutsche Theater became the foremost stage in Berlin and even in Germany. He soon branched out and built a small and intimate playhouse, Die Kammerspiele, adjacent to the Deutsche Theater. This little theatre consisted of a rectangular room, lacking decoration of any kind, and accommodating not more than four hundred people. Here he gave plays that demanded the lowered voice, the whispered word, and also a cultured audience which would respond to the pianissimo. As his fame spread, he was called upon to produce plays in Munich, to undertake the production of *Rosenkavalier* in Dresden, etc. Hofmannsthal lured him to Salzburg, where he staged *Everyman* on the steps of the old cathedral. Eventually even the People's Stage capitulated and, in 1913, became a part of the Reinhardt enterprises occupying a new theatre in the working class district.

The financial aspects of Reinhardt's work have never been explored. Officially, he left such sordid details to his brother, Edmund.[112] Shortly before the fall of the empire, Reinhardt attempted to reach out to a societal element which was beyond his depth. He dreamed of a theatre for the masses. The People's Stage no longer satisfied him, and he conceived the idea of an arena theatre to be constructed on a giant scale. We have already referred to the old circus which the architect, Bruno Poelzig, transformed into a theatre. This was the answer to Reinhardt's dream. The opening of the new house, Das Grosse Schauspielhaus, coincided with the last days of the empire. Reinhardt may have harbored the hope that the advent of the Weimar Republic would give added impetus to his theatre of the masses, but his venture was not a success. The actors' voices were lost in the vast reaches of the theatre, and no spectacular staging could remedy this defect. Reinhardt opened with Aeschylus's *Oresteia*, but even with the wonderful cast he had assembled, the handicaps imposed by space were not to be overcome. Still later Gerhart Hauptmann's dramatization of the conquest of Mexico by Cortéz suffered a like fate. Reinhardt and his followers blamed the Berlin critics for the failure and a verbal battle ensued, but no amount of words could save this last venture.[113] The great Schauspielhaus became the home of spectacular musicals, for which it was indeed far better suited. Although Reinhardt retained his position as director and owner of the Deutsche Theater, his career after 1920 was no longer limited to Berlin. He shifted the center of his operations to Austria and made his home in Salzburg, where the festival together with Reinhardt's international appeal allowed his art to survive for another fifteen years, at which time his light, like so many others, was snuffed out by the Nazis. Everything considered, however, Reinhardt must be seen as a product of the prewar world, and especially the prewar world of imperial Berlin. When, in the 1930's he tried to transfer his magic to another medium, the film, he failed, just as he failed when he set up a school of dramatic art in the alien atmosphere of Hollywood. He died in 1943.

As the strategist and projector of Germany's national theatre, Reinhardt's honor cannot be denied. It was ironic and at the same time tragic that official Germany continued to ignore his gift to the country. During World War I a last attempt was made to win the Kaiser's confidence to the point where he would allow Reinhardt's company to tour the front and entertain the soldiers. The crown prince and his brother, August Wilhelm, both of whom admired Reinhardt and were regular visitors at the Deutsche Theater, tried to break the Kaiser's resistance, but to no avail. The Kaiser was as unteachable in 1915 as he had been twenty years earlier.[114] The gulf between real art and official *kitsch* remained unbridged.

The theatres of Brahm and Reinhardt were, of course, not the only homes of the dramatic arts. As we have noted, intense competition forced the directors and the producers into a high degree of specialization on which they relied to secure an audience. There was the Hebbel theatre whose favorite dramatists were Wedekind and Strindberg; there was the Lessing theatre where the Brahm tradition was maintained by Barnowsky; there were the establishments which catered to more popular tastes and offered comedy and farce. Nevertheless, Berlin's position as the theatre capital of Germany rested squarely on the work of Brahm and Reinhardt. The other German cities, such as Frankfurt, Hamburg, Munich,

Dresden, or Bremen were close followers of the Berlin example. In many cases their offerings were as good, or even better, than those of Berlin. Yet Berlin kept its lead even after the downfall of the empire and into the days of the Weimar Republic. The arts had thus joined the other areas wherein Berlin had taken the lead; the city had become the true capital of Germany, and a metropolis of the first order.

[8]

War and Revolution

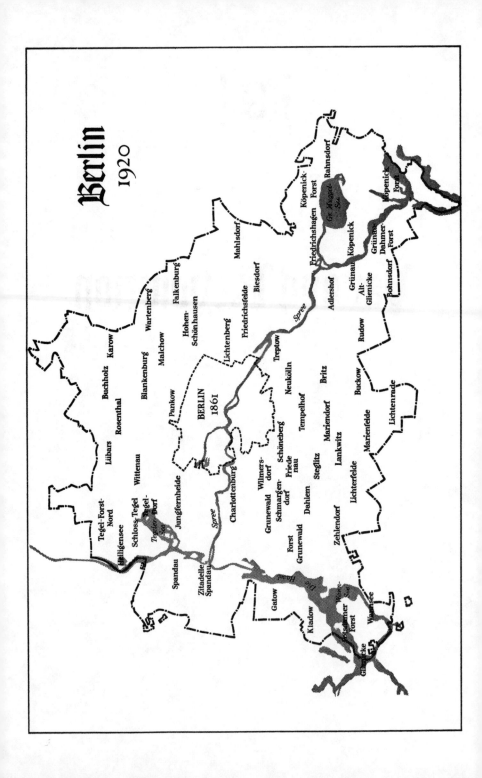

$\mathcal{T}$HE year was 1914, and forty-four years had passed since the founding of the second German empire. During this period Berlin had become one of the great cities of the world. Her growth had been precipitous, but in most fields the administration had kept pace with it. Disraeli once remarked that statistics belonged with the finer types of deceit; nevertheless, a few facts and figures may serve to prove our point.

The population of Berlin had risen steadily, likewise its budget, which by 1912, had reached the imposing figure of 350 million marks.[1] The largest part of this sum was spent on such basic items as gas, water, and transportation. In second place were the expenditures for education. Berlin now maintained eleven gymnasia, in addition to the *Oberrealschulen* and the *Realschulen*,[2] and there were also vocational schools for employees and workers.[3] In 1914, Berlin had six municipal hospitals of high medical standard, besides those serviced by the state or by private initiative.[4] The parks and public gardens, then as now, were among the most pleasing to be found anywhere.

Inevitably the increasing complexity of the administration required a large body of public officials, and it is symptomatic of the social structure of the capital that honorary officials who worked without pay surpassed the number of salaried city employees in the proportion of five to one.[5] This circumstance reflects, of course, the influence of the bourgeoisie. There is no doubt, however, that a great number of Berliners gained their livelihood in the city's countless factories.[6] Nevertheless, for most Germans and for most Europeans, Berlin's prominence derived from the fact that it was the nerve-center of the greatest military power on the continent. If we are to assess the changes which

Berlin underwent during the first world war, we must review those political and social forces which revolved about the city.

The forty-four years of empire had passed in peace. No single European power appeared ready to measure the German might, yet four years later its glory had vanished, its power had crumbled, and its political structure had been demolished. The leaders of the working class had predicted this ignominious finale, but the hostility of the workers cannot be blamed for the failure of the empire; on the contrary. The war was lost, first because its leadership disregarded Bismarck's warning that the secret of a successful foreign policy consisted in being *à trois* in a world of five; second, because German leadership failed to envisage what war would mean in an age of industrialization and technology; and third, because this same leadership insisted upon preserving its monopolistic grip on all important positions of power in the state, blinding itself to the growing strength of the socialist movement in town and country and the necessity of compromising with it.

The constant increase in votes cast by the German people for the "party of revolution" actually produced a kind of neurosis among the ruling class, a fear bordering on hysteria.[7] It escaped the elite that a revolution from below could have been countered only by one from above, i.e., a voluntary limitation of the privileges and prerogatives of the ruling class.

Any student of the history of Germany between the years 1870 and 1918 will be struck by the extent to which economic and class interest outweighed all other considerations. The very nation which until 1848 had indulged in unbounded utopian idealism now seemed determined to take heed only of its material interests. They were all good Marxists, even those who inveighed most vehemently against Marx. With the exception of the *Kulturkampf*, there was no issue in German public life that rose above the level of class war, which every group fought relentlessly for the maximum benefit possible.

We have spoken of Bismarck's shift to protective collectivism. Behind the shield of high tariffs the German industry had not only weathered the depression of 1873–1896, but had gained new ground. The accompanying social legislation, however, had failed to reconcile the working class with the new empire. When William II became emperor, he seized upon Bismarck's defeat over a renewal of the antisocialist law as a pretext to force the aging chancellor out of office. But William's efforts to become "the kaiser of the workers" came to naught, and the way was open for the social-democratic party to become the largest and best organized labor party in the prewar world.[8] A number of legislative measures were introduced protecting women and children and establishing courts of arbitration for industrial disputes. Bismarck's successor, Caprivi, brought down the price of bread by concluding a series of commercial treaties based on the principle of the most favored nations.[9]

That such steps would provoke the ire of the agrarians was predictable. The Junkers and their followers organized the Bund der Landwirte (Agrarian League), which became one of the most powerful pressure groups in Germany. Yet in the overall picture of German domestic policy, the appearance of an agrarian conservative lobby produced fewer changes than one might be led to expect. The Junkers had always known how to defend the economic basis of their elite position with stubborn cunning. Whatever differences they might have had with the commercial and industrial bourgeoisie were minimized by the common fear of socialism which united both groups. The horror of revolution was so prevalent that the old alliance of "steel and rye" was easily restored in the 1890's.

Numerically speaking, Germany's fate was thus governed by a small minority, but since it controlled the army, the navy, the diplomacy, and the bureaucracy, it could impose its will with little opposition. In the Prussian parliament the three-class electoral system guaranteed the survival of an outdated class rule, but the situation was different in the Reichstag. Although the prerogatives of the executive branch outweighed those of the legislature, the Reichstag had a budgetary control that even the emperor could not ignore. William, who claimed that he had never read the constitution, insisted that his chancellor should muster majorities willing to pass such laws as were necessary for the steadily increasing expenditures of the Reich.[10] Since Conservatives, Free Conservatives, and the National-Liberals, on which the government could rely, never obtained a solid majority, the chancellor was obliged to seek out other allies who would aid in passing the bills that were considered vital. In the 1890's, a policy of "concentration" was attempted, but it failed to gain the support of the middle class at which it was aimed.[11] The crucial role was therefore held by the Catholic Center party whose vote could swing in either direction. As a result, Hohenlohe, Bülow, and Bethmann-Hollweg were impelled to shift from one party combination to another to keep the ship of state afloat.

Inevitably, the instability of parliamentary support produced a considerable amount of wheeler-dealership, "cow-trading," in German parlance, which favored a type of politician able to excel in this kind of negotiation and compromise. This is not meant to indicate that Germany lacked parliamentary talents, but since constitution and tradition cut them off from any participation in governmental responsibility, they turned to a close cooperation with the mighty economic groups, i.e., the agrarians, the industrialists, and the merchants, and became their willing agents. What was good for "steel and rye," was good for Germany, or was made to give this appearance.

The most famous example of the type of politician bred by the circumstances was Matthias Erzberger, who rose from the rank and file of the Catholic trade unions to become the outstanding figure of his party. Frankly admitting his desire to amass a fortune, he did not avoid unscrupulous means to realize his ambition.[12] The leaders of the national-liberal party, to say nothing of the conservatives, followed this lead. The possibility of a conflict of interests, national versus corporative interests, did not appear to inhibit the deputies, yet the existence of such crosscurrents was common knowledge and did not enhance the prestige of the Reichstag in the eyes of the German people. When the leader of the Conservatives, Oldenburg Januschau, made the statement that the emperor should have the power to send the Reichstag packing at any time by dispatching a lieutenant and ten men into the halls of parliament, he did not speak for the extreme right alone.

However tempting such a step might have appeared to the Kaiser, and even more to the crown prince, it was never seriously considered.[13] Even if a coup d'état could have cut through the maze of Germany's domestic policy, it would have weakened her position in the world. And it was here that the Kaiser had elected to play a role. The "New Course" that had been initiated with

Bismarck's dismissal reached its apogee with Germany's claim to "a place in the sun."

Germany, under Bismarck, had already joined the race for colonies, and she now declared her determination to protect her commerce by the creation of a strong navy. Prior to this time, Germany's fleet had ranked seventh among the navies of the great nations; now she entered into competition with Great Britain. A glance at the map is sufficient to demonstrate the extravagance of this undertaking.[14] But here domestic and foreign policy were of one mind: pressure groups, such as the navy league, the Pan-German league, or the German colonial association, backed an enterprise from which only one stratum of German society could benefit—the heavy industry of the Ruhr, the Saar, and Upper Silesia, and of course, the great shipyards of Hamburg, Bremen, and Stettin.

The Kaiser embraced the venture with delight, and to his many bloomers added another: "Germany's future," he declaimed, "lies on the ocean." Alfred Tirpitz was appointed secretary of the navy; he was a man of great ambition and cunning, but like most German officers of the period, was sadly lacking in any realistic appraisal of Germany's true position in Europe. The first German naval bill passed the Reichstag in March of 1898, with the decisive vote of the Center party, 212 to 139. A second bill, which further increased the number of ships of the line, was approved in 1900.[15] Germany had embarked on a collision course with Great Britain.

The historian of imperial Berlin is under no obligation to unravel the complicated diplomatic web which finally brought the German nation to the brink of war. However, it must be understood that a series of external crises was added to the internal tensions which tore apart the social fabric of the body politic. Inevitably these circumstances influenced each other. Real or imaginary threats from abroad furnished fresh fuel to the demands for more and better arms; the armament race increased the tax burden; increased taxes that should have raised the power and stature of the Reichstag merely provided the incentive for the reactionary groups to return to an autocratic, absolutist regime.

Any observer who has pondered the aberrant fate of the German people must have wondered whether the road to perdition was preordained, or whether it was simply a matter of throwing the switches at the wrong moment. We know that there were inherent flaws in the Bismarckian constitution which resulted in pitting the imperial crown against the Reichstag, and the civil authority against the military.[16] However, the external position of the empire had been secure as long as Bismarck was at the helm. By 1900 affairs had taken a turn for the worse, though the diplomats in the Wilhelmstrasse pretended to be unaware of the deterioration. For them, Germany was sitting pretty; she had sufficient cover from her alliances with Austria and Italy to face any threat from the Franco-Russian front with equanimity. As a result, Germany pursued a policy of the "Free Hand." After some hesitation, she refused the British offer, tentative though it may have been, to bring about an Anglo-German understanding.[17] By building a powerful navy, insult was added to injury, and a strong anti-German sentiment was aroused in Great Britain, leading the *Saturday Review* to conclude an article in 1897 with the ominous words: "Ceterum censeo Germaniam esse delendam."[18] It seems patent that by 1900 Germany had no valid choice but to accept the British offer, or at the very least, to make sure of British neutrality in case of a continental conflict. The German diplomats closed their eyes to the brewing storm and paid little heed to the Franco-English rapprochement which was cemented in 1904. The first Moroccan crisis ended in defeat for Germany at the conference of Algeciras (1906), and in the following year the Anglo-Russian treaty became a fact, contrary to the calculations of those German diplomats who had wagered that the Russian bear and the British lion would never come together.

The formation of the Triple Entente was received with cries of injured innocence in Berlin. It was dubbed "the encirclement of Germany," and the world waited with considerable apprehension to learn what steps would be taken by the unpredictable German foreign office. The purpose of the entente was clear: it proposed to contain German imperialism. In 1908, Austria seized the opportunity of strengthening its position in the Balkans by the annexation of Bosnia and Herzegovina. But this was a gift of the Danaides in that it made the Dual Monarchy a prime target for Slavic nationalism. Nevertheless, though the symptoms were many and dangerous, a detoxification of the Anglo-German relations might still have been possible. In 1912, however, the Haldane mission gave final proof that Germany had no intention of limiting her naval expansion, any more than England was willing to abandon her commitments to France.[19] Each of these crises disturbed the European people deeply. As Bergson expressed it, they felt that war was impossible, but probable. Although it is entirely unlikely that they envisaged the tragic dimensions of the catastrophe that was approaching, they had fears for the future.

There were three groups in Berlin whose thoughts were centered on the problems of war: the military, whose duty it was to consider the possibility of a conflict; the diplomats, who by a peculiar sort of brinksmanship hoped to secure peace by rattling the sabre; and finally, the social democrats who opposed war on ideological grounds. The aristocratic and bourgeois parties did not consider war to be incompatible with their programs; some even welcomed it as an escape from domestic crises. The attitude of the social democrats toward the problem of an impending war was a significant part of the great discussion which kept the socialist parties of Europe in a state of turmoil. The disagreements arose from the ambiguities inherent in the Marxian doctrines. To the many contradictions and ambivalences of Marx an unsurmountable obstacle was added: Western capitalism stubbornly refused to adhere to the pattern which Marx had predicted. Consequently, the parties embracing the Marxian creed were confronted with the task of interpreting the master's statements in terms compatible with the socioeconomic realities of Europe. Engels, who survived Marx by more than a decade, tried to bend the Marxian doctrines, while still leaving the main body of theory intact.[20] But the full importance of the problem was felt only when Eduard Bernstein reopened the debate by calling for a revision of the Marxian dogma.[21]

The most crucial of all the issues was the method by which the victory of the proletariat could be achieved. Bernstein and his teachers, the English Fabians, advocated gradualism, a slow triumph of socialism through the irreversible ascendancy of the masses. The German social-democratic party rejected Bernstein's ideas, adhering to the belief in a revolutionary uprising which would put an end to capitalistic society. In theory, Bernstein was defeated; in practice, however, he prevailed, since the great majority of the German social democrats merely talked about revolution—*toujours en parler, jamais y penser.*[22]

One of the problems that Marx had not foreseen was the rise of imperialism, but by 1914, it had become clear that, in the words of Rosa Luxemburg "the questions of militarism and imperialism are the central axis of today's political life."[23] The socialist parties were internationally minded ("the workers have no country"); they rejected dynastic wars as much as expansionist wars, and they intended to obstruct the machinations of diplomats and militarists by all the means at their disposal. The Second International Congress, meeting in Basel in 1912, promised that the proletariat would reject all attempts to draw them into a conflict where workmen would be directed to fire at other workmen.[24] However, the summer of 1914 found the German socialists in a less determined mood.

In the elections of 1912 the socialists had acquired one hundred and ten seats in the Reichstag, thus becoming the strongest party. Had the social democrats and the radical liberals joined forces, they might have gained a majority. But though the socialist party as a whole retained its façade of "revolutionary respectability," it was doubtful that it would forsake the fatherland in its hour of need.[25] The German government was conscious of the intrinsic contradictions in the party's attitude and used the circumstance as a basis for their calculations in regard to the domestic situation.

Thus we come to the fateful six weeks preceding the outbreak of war, and one is tempted to enter the controversy raging around Germany's responsibility for the conflict. We will restrain ourselves to the comment that Berlin was, without question, the one capital where the decision for war or for peace was made.[26] There can be little doubt that after Sarajevo the German government had decided to seek a showdown with the powers of the entente at the risk of igniting a general conflagration such as Europe had not seen since the days of Napoleon. But neither civilian nor military authorities wanted to assume responsibility for such an action. In 1913, the chief of staff, von Moltke, had warned that in a coming war the voluntary sacrifice of the people (*Opferwilligkeit*) would be of prime importance.[27] In accordance with this view, the government operated with consummate skill in placing the blame for the outbreak of hostilities on Russia's doorstep. This accusation was fostered especially for the sake of the German worker who would be a vital element in the German war effort. The Kaiser wanted to arrest the social-democratic leaders "tutti quanti," and this was precisely what the party expected. On July 25, it had published an appeal to the people which ended with these words: "Down with war. Long live the solidarity of the people."[28] On July 30, the socialist leaders, anticipating dissolution by government action, sent their treasury to Switzerland. They were to feel a measure of relief when they learned that Bethmann-Hollweg did not plan any repressive measures and were therefore quite willing to accept the official version, i.e., Germany had been ruthlessly attacked and was the blameless victim of Russian expansionism. "We have been villainously assaulted," announced the Kaiser, and considering his psychological makeup, he may even have believed his claim.[29] With a few notable exceptions, the entire nation fell for this lie. Immersed in a process of self-delusion which has few parallels in history, Germany harbored the idea that the country had been the object of encirclement and attack. And this self-hypnosis started a chain reaction: since they were the victims rather than the perpetrators of criminal assault, they came to believe that they were entitled to compensations for the enormous loss of life and goods which they eventually suffered during the war; in turn, this belief fostered a demand that they be made secure against future onslaughts. Such compensations and precautions could only take the form of territorial annexations which would serve to guard Germany against further aggression. Thus began the intoxication with war aims from which few Germans were free.[30] That the parties of the right and the center embraced the imperialistic war aims without reservation is not surprising, but the attitude of the social-democrats amazed even their lifelong opponents.[31]

The party made a complete reversal of its previous stand against the war. It accepted without a qualm the famous declaration of the Kaiser, "I no longer know parties, only Germans." The party also applauded the proclamation of a "civic truce" (*Burgfrieden*) for the duration of the war. This somersault occurred in the days from July 30 to August 4 and has rightly been called a landmark in the Marxian calendar.[32] A party leader stated at a later date, "We all believed that Germany had been attacked."[33] In an atmosphere of frenzied chauvinism, the party voted on August 4 to grant the war credits requested by the government.[34] The declaration which the party leader read to the assembled members of the Reichstag gave no hint that the left-wing social democrats had greeted it with bitter opposition. Instead a deceptive unity of the whole German people was proclaimed. It was not long, however, before this stratagem was shattered, and the great schism which was to split the German socialists into two, and finally three, warring groups had begun.[35]

Berlin was not the only European capital where the idea of proletarian brotherhood had foundered. Jaurès had been shot in Paris; MacDonald preferred to go to prison rather than sacrifice his convictions to the waves of jingoism that engulfed England; Bertrand Russell followed his example. To a remarkable degree, indeed, the mood of the German capital was very much like that of the other great cities; an unbelievable enthusiasm swayed the population. The emperor, who had been so often the target of bitter criticism, became overnight the symbol of national unity. The great square before the imperial castle was, in those early August days, crammed with delirious citizens who waved caps and hats and kerchiefs until the imperial couple appeared on the balcony.[36] Earnest parents and their children attended the special services in the various churches, and raised their voices in unison to the strains of "A Mighty Fortress Is Our God." But in a small room in Kranachstrasse, Rosa Luxemburg sat and wept uncontrollably.

The railway stations were crowded with chaotic multitudes. All customary schedules had been suspended to transport the armies to the front and the reservists to their appointed stations. More than two million men had volunteered for military service, among them men who had passed the age of service together with young boys who had never undergone military training. Many thought that the great storm was clearing the air and that it would bring to the nation that feeling of unity so much desired by Bismarck. But this was only another illusion. Lemmings are not alone in their compulsion to commit collective suicide.

As an immediate result of the war, civilian offices, though they continued to operate, were superseded by the military, who took over supreme authority. Evoking an old Prussian law of 1851, a state of siege was proclaimed, and the empire was divided into twenty-four districts in which the deputy commanding general took over the task of maintaining "public safety."[37] This highly ambivalent expression was a euphemism allowing for the encroachment by the military on all human rights, especially in matters concerning censorship and freedom of assembly.

When the social democrats had accepted the idea of "civic truce," they had hoped it would furnish the occasion to set in motion various efforts for long overdue reforms, especially the democratization of the imperial government and the abolition of the three-class electoral system in Prussia. "We are defending the fatherland," said Scheidemann," in order to conquer it."[38] But the conservatives and their allies assigned a very different meaning to the words "civic truce"; to them it meant only the preservation of the status quo. Many had actually welcomed the war as a safety valve by means of which pent up pressures could escape and the elite be confirmed in its entrenched position. Had there been a group of determined parliamentarians, skilled in making use of their favorable position, they might have turned the situation to their advantage. But the Reichstag continued in its pusillanimous attitude, allowing the government and the military to solve all problems and considering the "civic truce" a convenient excuse for surrendering the responsibilities of certain of its prerogatives to the government.

The conversion of industrial raw material into the requisites of a nation at war presented the first and most pressing problem. General von Schlieffen and the younger officers of the staff had been convinced that the war would be brief, since long wars "were impossible in an age when the existence of the nation is founded upon uninterrupted continuation of trade and industry."[39] But Schlieffen was as mistaken in this calculation as he had been in his overall strategy. The first to face the situation squarely was Walther Rathenau. Though he was convinced that the Kaiser would not lead a victorious army through the Brandenburg Gate, he bent all his energies toward the problem of converting industry to war production.[40] Together with Wichard von Moellendorff, he convinced the Prussian Minister of War, von Falkenhayn, that an emergency existed which demanded unprecedented solutions. Against traditional prejudices, Rathenau was appointed to head the new office of the *Kriegsrohstoffamt* (Office for War Materiel), and with the help of a number of experienced industrialists, he set out to organize the new institution. The creation of this office is important in two ways. First and foremost, it allowed Germany to continue the war after the Schlieffen plan had failed; second, it greatly increased the trend toward centralization, thus modifying the constitutional structure of the second empire in a manner which resulted in a more unified form of administration. The office combined the private initiative of great corporations with strict governmental supervision. Although it is not correct to call Rathenau, or his successor, Colonel Scheüch, economic dictators, it is true that, lacking their services, a military collapse would have been unavoidable.[41] One of the by-products of this development was the strengthening of Berlin's position as the center of Germany.

In a related field, Berlin also proved its claim to be the scientific capital of the empire. Until the outbreak of the war, the nation had relied on the importation of Chilean nitrates for the manufacture of ammunition. Since this source was cut off by the British blockade, it was providential that Fritz Haber, professor of chemistry at the University of Berlin, together with the industrialist, Bosch, had perfected a process of nitrogen fixation from the air which made Germany independent of foreign imports.[42] Other synthetic products followed, giving the term *Ersatz* international currency.

Imperceptibly, however, the life of the capital entered a new phase. Not that there were many who questioned Germany's victorious emergence from the war; very few perceived that after the battle of the Marne, Germany's only hope lay in a negotiated peace.[43] Even fewer realized that her military efforts were like the tortures of Tantalus, that after every victory the final triumph appeared to be at a greater remove, that the government piled error on error, and that new enemies joined the allied powers as the war continued: Japan, Italy, Rumania, and finally, the United States. After all, the theatres were still crowded; musicals glorified the deeds of the army in "field grey"; the cafés were filled with men and women gorging themselves on rich pastries and whipped cream. Yet on the back drop of this gay and festive scene were written the daily bulletins from the front, the ominously increasing lists of casualties. In the newspapers more and more columns were devoted to the names marked with the Iron Cross, the emblem reserved for those who had died on "the field of honor." And gradually the stage darkened, the lights dimmed, the laughter faded.

The most significant change that occurred in the public life of the capital was occasioned by the absence of the Kaiser. Early in the war the emperor had decided that his place as commander-in-chief was at the supreme headquarters. He was following a tradition established by his ancestors, yet his step confirmed once again the superiority of the military over all branches of the government. "During the war," said the Kaiser, "Politics keeps her mouth shut until Strategy permits her to speak again."[44] He reserved to himself the last decision on all matters of importance, but he was easily swayed by the arguments of army and navy heads who used the imperative of dire necessity as a counter to political claims.

The emperor's absence from the capital affected the general atmosphere of the city, and sensitive observers like the industrialist, Ballin, argued that the Kaiser should maintain a more personal contact with his people.[45] Such murmurs were in vain, however, and the emperor remained the willing prisoner of the military, siding with them on all important issues.[46] Whether the presence of the Kaiser might have rekindled the embers of dynastic loyalty is problematical; he continued to be the same blundering busybody that he had been all his life, and his residence in Berlin may have provoked more antagonism than solidarity.[47]

In any case, Berlin was now a capital minus a ruler, and as a result, other institutions came to play a larger role. In the first place was the Reichstag; second, the imperial administration. But of increasing importance were the rapidly expanding and proliferating offices of the war economy with their interlocking branches which tied them to the large corporations and to the unions. Whereas the military decisions were, on the whole, made in the supreme headquarters, Berlin became the switchboard for most of the social and economic problems that beset the nation.

By necessity, the unrelieved tensions of the city found expression in new political constellations. New parties at the far right, the far left, and even clandestine underground activities of revolutionary character, came into being. The latter might have been dangerous for the status quo had they been better synchronized in their efforts to bring the war to a close. As it was, they were disunited, frequently quarreling about such matters as tactics and strategy, and many of their leaders were of little use, being imprisoned or held in protective custody. Their real impact was, therefore, of small import until the end of the war. In the Reichstag a small fraction of the social-democratic party established itself as an independent group and cooperated with the international congress that met in Zimmerwald, Switzerland, in September of 1915.[48] On May 1, 1916, Karl Liebknecht dared to organize a protest meeting in the center of Berlin and to hurl forth the words: "Down with the government! Down with the war!"[49] He was arrested on the spot, his immunity as deputy to the Reichstag revoked, and he was sentenced to four years at hard labor.

The right wing reacted in a different manner. The great economic associations, the Federation of Industrialists, the Central Association of German Industrialists, the Farmers' League, the Peasants' League, and various other pressure groups expressed their advocacy of an expansionist program on May 20, 1915.[50] They also supported an increased offensive in the conduct of the war, especially an unrestricted submarine warfare. The champions of this strategy were the secretary of the navy, Tirpitz, and his chief of staff, Bachmann. The case of Tirpitz is particularly interesting. During the year 1914, all his theories had been refuted. The fleet, built at such great expense, had proved to be useless. Its share in 'determining the outcome of the war was negligible. But Tirpitz did not see the mote in his own eye, only the beam in the eyes of others, reproaching the Kaiser and Bethmann-Hollweg for their lack of a vigorous war policy. Rumor has it that he even toyed with the idea of having the Kaiser declared incapable of governing the nation, favoring his replacement with a man of greater energy.[51] Whatever the truth, Tirpitz never lost the aura of the successful leader and became one of the founders of the *Vaterlandspartei*, an ultranationalistic assemblage of industrialists, professors, teachers, and military personnel bound together by imperialistic aims.

Significant as these innovations in the political life of Germany

may have been, they were less important than the economic consequences of the "civic truce." When the social democrats had decided to vote the war credits, they had been strongly influenced
by the attitude of the trade unions. Membership in these organizations had grown from 680,000 in 1900 to 2,574,000 in 1913.
Their leaders were practical, sober men who had always looked
askance at radical agitators such as Liebknecht and Rosa Luxemburg. When war was imminent and the extremists urged a general
strike, Carl Legien, chairman of the General Commission of the
trade unions, opposed the move as futile. "In a land with universal conscription," he said, "where one third of the men will
be taken into the army, and another third will be unemployed,
the thought of a mass strike is manifestly absurd."[52] In any case
the unions' support of the war would have been assured because
they believed it to be a defense against imperialist Russia.[53]

From these beginnings a close cooperation sprang up between
organized labor, management, and the army, which became increasingly significant as the war continued. It was obvious that
the conversion of Germany's industrial potential to war production could not be accomplished without the active collaboration
of the labor forces. Here again it was necessary to start from
scratch. Women, unskilled youths, and unemployed workers were
requisitioned to meet the increasing demands for weapons and
ammunition.[54] The details of this effort are unimportant here.
In general, the army acknowledged that the workers were performing their duties willingly and that they were supported and
encouraged by their leaders.[55]

Berlin's metal industry was of prime importance. Both labor and
management benefited from the enormous demands made on
them, the former by obtaining higher wages, the latter by reaping
greater profits. The situation was in the beginning quite chaotic,
since the various industries were eagerly competing for all available labor. Eventually the army was obliged to take a hand in the
matter and regulate the practices. A board for the metal industry
of Great Berlin was finally established on which both labor and
management were represented.[56]

The metal workers were not only better organized and better
paid, they were also the most radical members of the Berlin
proletariat. Although their chairman was somewhat conservatively

inclined, the rank and file did not necessarily abide by his orders. Since strikes were forbidden for the duration of the war, the shop stewards resorted to wildcat strikes to make their demands felt. At the beginning they were occupied with an increase in wages, shorter hours, and better food rations. However, the more politically minded were already looking forward to the formation of a revolutionary avant-garde that might topple the regime and bring the war to an end.[57]

Second in importance to the metal industry was the electro-industry, especially Siemens and the AEG, who were the most active producers of war materiel: field telephones, equipment for submarines, motors for airplanes, mines, even machine guns were among the articles manufactured by the electro-industry.[58] The chemical industry likewise had a boom; as Rosa Luxemburg observed "The dividends rise, and the workers die." (Die Dividenden steigen und die Proletarier fallen.)[59] But this comment was unjustified; the war struck all classes, and all classes suffered.

The food situation became increasingly critical as the war passed the six-month mark on which the military had counted. Here, too, the industrialists showed greater foresight than the authorities. Albert Ballin suggested that a private corporation should buy all the grain obtainable in foreign countries.[60] After considerable delay, a semiprivate corporation, the Central Purchasing Agency, was established in Berlin, but a great deal of time was lost before a general plan for the allocation and distribution of the food supply was worked out. In the meantime the large cities were left to fend for themselves.[61] A metropolis such as Berlin had necessarily more obstacles to overcome than smaller centers. At the end of 1914 the possibility of a famine situation could no longer be denied. Ceiling prices were introduced, and on January 25, 1915, bread was rationed, though for a short time fat, sugar, meat, and potatoes remained free from control.[62] The immediate result was a rapid rise in the price level, and the appearance of a black market which spread from one end of the country to the other. To secure the most basic staple, Berlin introduced in February of the same year a *Brotkarte* which guaranteed every inhabitant a minimum of bread or flour. Other cities followed suit, but there was no uniform regulation and the amount of bread allotted varied from city to city. Step by step, meat, sugar, potatoes, eggs, fat, and milk were also rationed. Many families tried to hoard non-perishable food, such as rice, barley, flour, dried fruit, tea and coffee, but only people of means could defend themselves in this manner, since both money and storage space were required. The Kaiser, munching a rusk, amply spread with butter and jam, maintained that he lived on soldiers' rations. In general, the headquarters of the army staffs were well provisioned, and the average soldier was better off than the civilian.

Black marketeering soon became a fine art in which both vendor and buyer needed a skillful hand and eye. Some food stores adopted the practice of selling more than the allotted ration at greatly inflated prices. Many people went to the railway stations and waited for the farmers to bring in their produce which would then be bought at fantastic sums. Still others journeyed out to the villages and farms to find food, but were obliged to face the suspicious eyes of the police upon their return. Long queues (*Schlangen*) formed in front of stores hours before they opened. Certain goods such as fish and game remained unrationed for some time, but were an additional source of nourishment only for those who could afford the price. Another way to bypass the strict regulations was to eat out. Although every guest was obliged to surrender his food coupons, a good tip to the head waiter could result in a larger portion of meat. Everyone knew about the black market and everyone who could patronized it, especially the German Hausfrau, who had little choice but to play the game or let her family go hungry. Occasionally soldiers on leave would arrive at their homes with large supplies of bread, eggs, or butter, whose manner of acquisition only they could know.

Workers in heavy labor were entitled to extra rations, and each cut in the bread or potato ration could provoke a riot. The entrepreneurs soon learned how to obtain foodstuffs for their workers by illegal means. Luxury goods, such as coffee, tea, cocoa, and tobacco disappeared altogether and were replaced by foul tasting *Ersatz*. Coffee was made from acorns, tea from the leaves of certain trees, and almost anything would serve for tobacco. There was synthetic honey, synthetic marmalade, synthetic bouillon cubes, synthetic lemonades. Soap was largely made of sand which left the skin raw and grimy. Wool and cotton likewise disappeared, except what was requisitioned for army uniforms and blankets. Bad as the situation was, however, it provoked the usual number of Berlin jokes, some unquotable and almost all untranslatable. It also produced a new type of profiteer whom the Berliners called Herr Raffke. There were endless stories about Herr and Frau Raffke, their crudeness, their greed, their lack of culture. But humor, at best, is a poor substitute for the necessities of life.

As in most situations of this kind, the chasm between town and country grew wider and wider. Peasants and Junkers refused to sell at ceiling prices, nor would they increase their production to overcome the shortages. It was the "scissor crisis" of which Trotsky later spoke during the Russian revolution. The steady growth of bureaucratic institutions with overlapping jurisdictions confounded rather than solved the problem. To no avail did the Reichstag deputies accuse the government of incompetence.[63] The root of the evil was the British blockade which Germany was unable to break.

The food shortage reached its climax in 1916–1917. The potato crop had yielded only half as much as in the preceding year. There was no one to work the farms; the horses had been requisitioned by the army. Turnips, a vegetable rarely appearing heretofore on German tables, replaced potatoes and were consumed in every form and description, leaving most Germans with an insurmountable distaste for this root. It is fair to say that as far as the food supply was concerned, the war was well lost in the winter of 1916–1917.

From a military point of view the year marks a critical period in both camps. The Central Powers had conquered vast sections of Poland, but had failed to break the western front at Verdun. Both coalitions were suffering incredible losses in human life. The Russian empire was at the brink of collapse. On the other hand, Italy and Rumania had joined the Allies, and the entrance of the United States was a growing possibility. Both groups felt that the final decision was hanging in the balance and that only by means of a supreme effort could a favorable outcome be achieved. In Germany, the situation brought about the appointment of Hindenburg and Ludendorff as chiefs of staff, with the expectation that Ludendorff's strategic genius and mastery of technical detail would turn the tables in favor of the Central Powers, while the unshakable determination of Hindenburg might restore domestic confidence. The appointment of Ludendorff was a desperate step. His allies were on the right, and he identified himself with the goals of the German imperialists and the domestic ideas of the élite minority that had dominated Germany since 1871. These groups, in turn, took advantage of Ludendorff's strong will to advance their claims. Germany began its drift into an undeclared military dictatorship which the parties of the center and the left did not care, or did not dare, to challenge.[64]

The first impact of the new leadership on the homefront was an attempt to mobilize all available forces for the war effort. Such a move had been long in the making. There were some, mostly civilians, who thought that the entire economy should be organized after the model of the army. The different interest groups in German society looked upon this idea of total mobilization from sharply divergent points of view. The unions asked for wage premiums to meet the rise in prices. They also demanded that management and labor should henceforth negotiate on a parity basis, and they wanted protection for their members against any hardship in the event of peace.[65] The government saw in the war an opportunity to win over the working class for the nation, expecting them to abandon their old hostility toward the state.[66] That this end could not be reached without pronounced reforms was well understood by Bethmann-Hollweg.[67] But the leading conservative clique sabotaged any effort toward drastic changes or had them watered down to vague promises. The more radical of the union leaders welcomed the delaying tactics of the government since they were thereby furnished with a pretext to step up the propaganda against the regime and the imperialist war.

On January 1, 1916, a group led by Liebknecht and Luxemburg severed ties with the social-democratic party and set itself up as the *Spartakusbund*.[68] They declared war to be the last phase of the political world of capitalism, and imperialism the worst enemy of the working class.[69] It was clear that an explosive situation was at hand which ordinary police methods could not handle. A member of the social-democratic party, E. David, declared in the Reichstag that political catastrophes were likely to occur "such as Germany has never seen."

In an effort to disentangle the war economy, a new office,

Wumba, was created for the procurement of weapons and ammunition on September 30, 1916.[70] A high-sounding ideological cover was concocted to explain the industrial needs from which the German economy was suffering: "a conscious, national-aristocratic-corporative-socialist orientation" of the entire nation.[71] The great number of offices which had sprung up were consolidated in one superoffice called the Supreme War Office, and a general of considerable acumen, Wilhelm Groener, was appointed to head it.[72]

The legislative instrument needed to make the mobilization of the civilian population operative was forged in heated debates in the Reichstag and was passed on December 5, 1916.[73] Every German male between the ages of seventeen and sixty who was not serving in the army was henceforth required to perform "auxiliary service" for the duration of the war. Free movement of the workers was severely restricted though not entirely prohibited. Female labor was not made compulsory. As compensation for these restrictions, committees were to be established in which the employees would be represented. It was also stated that "a good understanding . . . between the workers and their employers should be sought and that all wishes and complaints of the workers be given a fair hearing."

In spite of such mollifying phrases, however, the hopes which the German high command had placed on this law were not fulfilled. As many problems were created as were solved, and the German industry became even more dislocated.[74] One of its consequences was the great increase in female workers. Women had replaced men as drivers and conductors of street cars, mail carriers, and postal officers prior to 1916. Now they were also employed in ammunition factories. Perhaps the harrowing descriptions of working conditions in these factories should not be taken too literally.[75] Very likely they were no worse or more hazardous than similar work in peacetime, but the scarcity of food and the long hours made them more exhausting.

Evaluations of the auxiliary service law differed sharply: union leaders emphasized the gains the working class received from it, while Spartakus considered it as one more step to deprive the workers of their rights.[76] Such a law might have been effective had it been sponsored by a revolutionary élan, as was the case in revolutionary France in 1793 when harsh measures were imposed by the Committee for Public Safety. But Berlin and Germany were not in the upsurge of a revolutionary élan; they were nearing the breaking point.

When the bread ration was further curtailed, there were riots, and bakeries and butcher shops were looted in Berlin. The agrarian sector of Germany remained deaf to all pleas to come to the assistance of the urban population and continued to pursue its own selfish interests.[77] The government's price policy encouraged rather than curbed the activities of the black marketeers. The increasing number of offices where many clerks were employed became the object of constant mockery; there were in all forty such offices, most of them in Berlin.[78]

In view of these circumstances, the revolutionary shop stewards considered that the time was propitious for a strike. Although their leader, Richard Müller, was quickly arrested, the strike got under way. If we may believe Müller's account, 300 shops and 300,000 workers were involved. But the effort was scarcely more than a gesture. The government was empowered to draft any worker who did not fulfill his obligations as a civilian, and the political significance of the strike was blunted by an improvement in the rations of meat, bread, and potatoes.[79] Although parallel movements occurred in Leipzig, Halle, Brunswig, and Magdeburg, the strike never got off the ground.[80] For good measure, Hindenburg appealed to the workers' patriotism by calling any strike an unforgivable sin against the men in the trenches.

By 1917, the unrest had spread beyond the working class and had reached the educated bourgeoisie. This was manifest in the production of two dramas of strong pacifistic tendencies that escaped the eye of the censor: von Unruh's *Das Geschlecht*, and Reinhard Goering's *Seeschlacht*.[81] Goering's work, especially, had a deep impact on the younger generation, and the play was even circulated among high school students in Berlin.

It was a winter of discontent. Unrestricted submarine warfare had been declared, with the result that the United States had entered the war. Only clear-headed observers like Max Weber, however, understood that this event would tip the scales in favor of the Allied Powers. Since the declaration of war by President Wilson coincided with the collapse of the czarist regime, a prudent

German policy would have been to bring the war to an end before the impact of American participation was felt. But the German policy remained inflexibly annexationist in its war aims and repressive in its domestic affairs. It was in vain that Bethmann-Hollweg tried to steer a "diagonal policy" between the different factions.[82] He himself became the first victim of an attitude which attempted to placate everyone and that eventually alienated all.

The downfall of the czarist government brought the question of internal reforms once more to the fore. The "civic truce" vanished before the need to offer the people a ray of hope amid the ever-darkening clouds. Even Stresemann, the leader of the national-liberal party, called for some action that might take the people's minds off the strained food situation.[83] The chancellor convinced the Kaiser that a promise of reform must be proclaimed, and he obtained from the reluctant monarch the Easter Message of 1917, which declared that a change in the Prussian electoral system would take place after the war.[84] Even this meager bait appeared unacceptable to Ludendorff and the conservatives who called it a kowtowing to the Russian revolution.[85] On one side was the high command, still maintaining that the war must be ended by a military victory with large territorial acquisitions in the East and in the West. On the other side was the growing opposition in the Reichstag, where social democrats, progressives, the center party, and even the national liberals urged a peace by compromise, a reform of the Prussian electoral system, and the transformation of the imperial government into a parliamentary monarchy in which the cabinet would be responsible to the Reichstag.[86]

Matters came to a head in July of 1917. The spokesman of the Center party, Matthias Erzberger, who had been a rabid annexationist, reversed himself, and in two speeches, attacked both Germany's conduct of the war and her internal stagnation.[87] He stated unequivocally that Germany's only hope lay in a compromise peace, and he introduced a resolution calling for a renunciation of all annexations. The resolution was adopted on July 19, with a vote of 212 for, and 126 against.[88] Two weeks earlier an interparty committee (*interfraktionelle Ausschuss*) had been formed by seventeen members from the progressive, the social democratic, the center, and the national-liberal parties, with the express purpose of discussing all problems related to the war aims and to constitutional reforms.[89]

The stage seemed to be set for a confrontation between the forces which had prevailed in Germany for forty-seven years and the forces sponsoring a parliamentary democracy. However, the existing powers were too well entrenched to surrender their position to a resolution drawn up by a parliament they had long held in contempt. The first victim of their disdain was Bethmann-Hollweg whose policy of promising all things to all men had made him suspect in both camps.[90] In the choice of his successor, the interparty committee was not even consulted, and a civil servant bearing the name of Georg Michaelis, unknown to everyone, even the Kaiser, was chosen as one might draw a lottery ticket from a hat. He soon became the laughing stock of public opinion and was replaced by the seventy-five-year-old Count Hertling, a Bavarian diplomat, who accepted the office with reluctance, and who exercised even less influence over the arrogant Ludendorff than the hapless Bethmann-Hollweg had mustered.[91]

Militarism had become a naked reality in Germany. The Reichstag had gained nothing by the dismissal of Bethmann-Hollweg; the resolution with its call for a compromise peace was ignored, and the July crisis had turned into a defeat for the forces of reason. A brief analysis may clarify the situation. To begin with, there were no leaders in the German parliament who could have seized the banner of revolution and flaunted it in the face of the existing autocratic rule. The mercurial Erzberger was hardly the man to do it, and, as a Catholic, he would have been given little credence among the protestant majority of Germany. Stresemann, who later developed qualities of true statesmanship, had yet to learn his lesson and to forget much of his past. Ebert, or any other member of the social-democratic party, had lived too long in isolation to grasp the reins of government unless they were thrust into his hands. In short, there was no Mirabeau, no Jefferson, and indeed no Cromwell, among the German deputies. Even had there been such a leader, it seems most doubtful that any amount of determination could have prevailed in 1917. Germany had no revolutionary tradition, as did France and England. An uprising in time of war would have been branded as high treason. And can one believe for a moment that the Kaiser and his military advisers would have accepted with docility a power play bent on curbing not only their influence, but also their privileged position in state and society?[92] The stage was set, and the last act of the German tragedy was about to begin. When the efforts of the military dictatorship failed, and the civilian authorities were urged to obtain an immediate peace, no governmental office could be found with sufficient moral prestige to execute the demand. Revolution thus became unavoidable.

In the summer of 1917, a truce of sorts was achieved. The inter-party committee continued to press, though timorously, for a peace by compromise. It received some support from the educated bourgeoisie, especially in Berlin, where such luminaries as Friedrich Meinecke, Adolf von Harnack, and Ernst Troeltsch came out for "internal reforms."[93] On the other hand, the noisy annexationists were not sitting on their hands, and they demanded a "peace with compensations," rejected the proposed reform of the electoral system in Prussia, and found they could count on the support of the great industrial associations. One of the most curious devices to maintain the nationalistic frenzy was invented in Berlin. On the Königsplatz, near the Reichstag, a wooden statue of Hindenburg was erected. For the price of a mark, one was allowed to drive an iron nail into the unresisting giant. The income was to be devoted to some patriotic enterprise. But such attempts to change the mood of the civilian population were both fruitless and ludicrous. The food situation went from bad to worse, and some accurate information about the predicament of Germany was divulged by soldiers on leave from the front. One of them said in 1917, "To be sure we will conquer, until we are all dead" (*Wir siegen uns zu Tode*). During this period, the role of Berlin changed drastically. While the military decisions were made in the imperial headquarters which continued to shift from east to west, Berlin remained the nerve-center of all economic and political action. In an unforeseen yet highly significant manner, Berlin was, more than ever, the capital of Germany.

Between the summer of 1917 and the fall of 1918, the war followed along its inexorable path. By all standards, the greatest event was the fall of Kerensky and the seizure of power by Lenin, but only by hindsight was the world able to recognize in this circumstance the initiation of a new era in history. No prophet of the day comprehended or could comprehend what the entrance of America and Russia's withdrawal would mean to the issues of the war. The German government saw in Lenin's formula of "Peace and Bread" only another opportunity to further its megalomaniac plans. In vain did the Austrian emperor, Karl, and his foreign minister, Czernin, issue their warning: "We are fighting against a new enemy which is more dangerous than the Entente —against international revolution which finds its strongest ally in general starvation." Ludendorff had no fear that the German army would be contaminated by the poison of revolutionary brotherhood.[94]

At the peace of Brest-Litovsk, Germany extracted an enormous fee from Russia for the cessation of hostilities. Only Lenin with his unshakable belief in the ultimate victory of world revolution would have agreed to pay the price.[95] The separation of Finland, Poland, the Baltic provinces, and the Ukraine were the conditions imposed, and the German appetite for a greedy victory was not satiated with even this rich fare. Germany had always been enamored of great schemes directed toward the expansion of her power in the East. First had been the dream of a Berlin-Bagdad Railway, then Naumann's *Mitteleuropa*, and now the emperor's voraciousness went even further. He "emphatically endorsed" a proposal for incorporating the Russian province of Georgia into the Reich! He also amused himself with designing a personal coat of arms for the new dukedom of Courland.[96] The Austrian government entertained serious pretensions of placing an archduke on the Polish throne. In writing about these men and their projects, it is difficult to avoid the satirical note; in the words of Karl Kraus, they were figures from an operetta acting out the tragedy of mankind.[97] Even the social democrats, though officially on record for a peace without annexation, sanctioned the peace of Brest-Litovsk by abstaining from voting. An intellectual of the calibre of Rudolf Borchardt anticipated in December of 1917 that the final blow to the entente would soon be delivered.[98]

There were, of course, others who saw in the Russian revolution the dawn of a new day, and who believed that the time was not far off when Germany would follow the Russian example. The *Vorwärts* of December 1, 1917, published a radio message from Lenin and Trotsky addressed to all people appealing for an end to the carnage.[99] The response to their entreaty was instantaneous, at least in Berlin. Spartakus urged the workers to go on strike. The revolutionary shop stewards also agitated for a strike, in the hope that it would ignite the revolution, and the independent socialists backed their motion.[100] The resolution for a peace without annexation was spread throughout Berlin by leaflets, but the date of the walkout was kept secret.

On January 28, 1918, 400,000 men and women went out on strike, and elected an action committee in which the social democrats and the independents were represented. In order to maintain control of the masses, the social-democratic party was forced to support the movement.[101] The military reacted violently. *Vorwärts* was censored and certain ringleaders were arrested, while the commander of Berlin threatened to take over the factories. Spartakus wanted to take advantage of the situation and call an open rebellion. Such an action might have succeeded in Berlin, but would not have met with any success outside of the capital. On February 3, the strike was called off. Six men had died, and scores had been injured. Though there had been demonstrations of sympathy in other cities, the slogan, "Workers of the World, unite," rang hollow.[102] Even if the strike may not have been a general rehearsal, it was, at least, symptomatic of the general mood of the people. The military made the mistake of drafting some of the leaders into the army, where, of course, they merely spread the climate of agitation. It goes without saying that Russia tried to fan the flames, but there is no evidence that she was successful.[103]

In the spring of 1918, Ludendorff launched a new offensive designed to break the Western front, but after a few initial advances, the attack petered out. By summer the German fury had spent itself and the Allies could take the offensive. On August 8, the German lines were sundered; it was the beginning of the end. Germany could not match the firepower, the tanks, or the human reserves which General Foch threw into battle. Simultaneously, Austria was asking for an armistice and the Balkan front collapsed. It was at this moment that Ludendorff suffered his famous breakdown and urged the government to arrange for an armistice within twenty-four hours. He also urged the reorganization of the government on a democratic basis.[104]

Only those who lived through October of 1918 in Germany can

begin to understand the impact of these days of shock. For more than four years the people had believed in the promise of a great victory; now overnight they faced humiliation and defeat. Prince Max von Baden, a liberal and a relative of the emperor, undertook the thankless task of forming a government "that would have the confidence of the people." Included in it were members of the center and of the progressive parties, and for the first time the social democrats were represented. Whether it was a wise decision on the part of the latter to come to the rescue of the bankrupt regime is questionable. The nationalistic blowhards were thus empowered to hypnotize the people into a belief that they had been "stabbed in the back." Actually, the social democrats shared some of the responsibility for the war, since they had voted the war credits on August 4 and therefore felt that they were honor bound not to leave the workers in the lurch.[105] Ebert especially took this attitude, and those who have criticized him must admit that his only alternative would have been to agree that the floodgates of revolution be opened and that Germany join Russia in the communist experiment.

Germany was now obliged to swallow the same medicine she had forced down the Russian throat. Conditions for an armistice became more severe with every note from Washington. It soon was made clear that one prerequisite of peace was a change of ruler. The abdication of the Kaiser thus became a burning issue. The emperor, however, would not listen to such nonsense and continued to live in the world of fantasy which he had occupied throughout his life. When he finally was faced with defeat, history had already passed him by.[106] Revolution had erupted in Germany, and the word of an emperor had lost all meaning.

The events of November 1918 are called the November revolution, but to vary a famous phrase, they were more of a revolt than a revolution. The uprising was without plan or goal; it had little hope, but a great deal of hatred for the existing authorities. It was born of frustration rather than expectation, and was motivated by hunger. On October 12, the government had declared a general amnesty, and Karl Liebknecht was among the first to be released.[107]

Liebknecht took over the leadership of the Spartakus movement, and expressed his complete agreement with the aims of the

Russian revolution. A council of soldiers and workers was henceforth to run German affairs.[108] But Spartakus did not wield much power; the social democrats (SPD) and the independents (USPD) commanded a much greater following. Moreover, there were the shop stewards, who were the real activists among the socialist groups. As a result, Germany became engaged in a four-cornered fight for power in which the different groups paralyzed each other instead of advancing their common cause.

The November uprising had not begun in Berlin. At the end of October, councils of soldiers and workers had sprung up in various parts of the country. The spark that set off the final explosion flashed up in Kiel, Germany's principal naval base. After four years of inglorious passivity, the admiralty was bent on a last battle, and the fleet had received orders to put out to sea. This suicidal command was, however, resisted by the sailors, and their insurrection spread from ship to shore, easily overcoming what little opposition it encountered. A council of sailors was elected, and the government in Berlin declared its willingness to negotiate with the mutineers. The social democrat, Gustav Noske, naval expert of the party, was sent to Kiel and accepted the program of the sailors which was not in the least extreme.[109] The entire uprising was a spontaneous effort to end the war, and soon groups of sailors spread out from Kiel, to Hamburg, Munich, and Stuttgart. Wherever they appeared the old order broke down. All over Germany, the pattern was the same: councils of soldiers and workers assumed the authority of the state, though the personalities of those taking office differed widely. In Munich, the unfortunate Kurt Eisner became prime minister, a role for which he was ill suited even in the eyes of his party.[110]

Berlin, for a time, seemed to have lagged, but appearances were deceptive. In the capital the most important issues stood foremost on the agenda: the abdication of the emperor and the form of government for the new state. If the Kaiser had followed the advice of Prince Max, the monarchic rule might have been saved by a regency council, but the Kaiser's obstinacy was on a par with his lack of judgment, with the result that the SPD finally presented him with an ultimatum on November 7. The emperor's continued refusal to abdicate seemed to tilt the nation toward civil war, and in such an eventuality, not even the army could have been relied upon. In Berlin the garrison was fraternizing with the workers who were pouring out of the factories.[111] A last-minute attempt to preserve some continuity by making Friedrich Ebert the new imperial chancellor came to naught when a general strike was declared. The characteristic feature of this uprising, wrote one of its leaders, was in the elementary force of its eruption in all sections of Berlin. It was, he said, like the battle action of mass armies during the war.[112] The city had never experienced anything like it. Trucks filled with soldiers and workers rumbled through the streets displaying red flags that hailed the revolution. Officers were insulted and their insignias torn from their uniforms. There was little bloodshed, however; the bourgeoisie was nowhere in sight, and the armed forces offered only sporadic resistance.

Toward noon on November 9, Karl Liebknecht invaded the imperial castle and speaking from the balcony declared Germany a socialist republic.[113] But the SPD had no intention of surrendering to Spartakus. They knew only too well the meaning of Liebknecht's slogan: "Supreme authority for the workers and soldiers." Translated into terms of future action, it spelled out Germany's fate as a Russian province, a destiny the SPD was determined to avoid. Stealing Liebknecht's thunder, Scheidemann proclaimed Germany a republic.[114] In vain did Ebert, white with anger, insist that only a constituent assembly had the power to decide Germany's fate. The decision had been taken, and the only question now was: what kind of republic was Germany to be?

Imperial Berlin was no more, and the reader might well expect that our narrative would end at this point. But the forces which had made Berlin the capital of the German nation now flowed through new channels, and we cannot take leave of her until we understand why she remained the vital center of the country. The revolution that had not been initiated in Berlin was decided in Berlin, though four months of confused and apparently meaningless fighting were required, and the tug of war between the different socialist groups had a deep significance.

First in importance was the SPD, whose principal aim was to keep control of the revolution and to preserve its hold on organized labor. Though it may be criticized for having lost its original idealism, which called for "a socialization of the means of production," it must likewise be credited with a cold and realistic appraisal of

Germany's internal and external situation. The country was exhausted; it was depleted by hunger and war, and surrounded by enemies who were far from allowing it to undertake a utopian venture. The SPD believed in the democratic experiment, i.e., that only a constituent assembly could lay the cornerstone of the new Germany. Before the national assembly could meet, however, there would necessarily be a period of demobilization which would undoubtedly bring chaos to the land, since everyone's hand held a weapon, and all external discipline had come to an end. For mere survival under such conditions, the SPD must close ranks, that is, cooperate with the independents, the USPD that had seceded from the party during the war. Among the leaders of the USPD were some of the finest minds of the party: Karl Kautsky, Eduard Bernstein, Rudolf Hilferding, and others, who were not unmindful of the dilemma that German socialism was facing, and they decided to steer a middle course between the SPD and the extreme left.

The SPD and USPD reached an understanding of sorts by setting up a provisional government. After the Russian model, it was called the Council of the People's Commissars (*Rat der Volksbeauftragten*), and included Ebert, Scheidemann, and Landsberg from the SPD, and Haase, Barth, and Dittmann from the independents. The shoals that lay ahead will be apparent when we consider that the Council of People's Commissars had to be approved by a meeting of the council of workers and soldiers of Berlin. The most gifted politician in the Council of Commissars was, without doubt, Friedrich Ebert, and while the council was abrogating a number of unpopular laws, Ebert was busy securing the support of the armed forces. On November 10, he had a telephone conversation with General Groener, who had succeeded Ludendorff. Ebert agreed that officers would be allowed to retain their power of command and their badges of rank. In exchange, Groener decided to cooperate with Ebert "in order to prevent the spread of Bolshevism."[115] There are those who believe that the revolution lost its first great battle on the day of its decision to recognize the authority of the old officer corps.[116] But it is difficult to see that Ebert had a choice unless he had wanted to become another Lenin.

To follow Lenin's example was, however, the avowed purpose

of the two other revolutionary groups: Spartakus and the shop stewards. Both tried to use the council of soldiers and workers as a screen to seize direction of the revolution. Spartakus, whose leaders were Liebknecht, Luxemburg, and an odd assortment of Polish and Russian revolutionaries, had acquired its own newspaper, *Die Rote Fahne,* but the movement was sadly lacking in mass support.[117] Spartakus criticized the Council of Commissars mercilessly; they took upon themselves the role of Lenin in their eagerness to overthrow the Kerenskys of the German revolution. They did not recognize that the situation in Germany was essentially different from that in Russia, that Berlin was not St. Petersburg, and that Lenin's formula of communism as "Soviet power plus electricity" did not apply in a thoroughly industrialized society. The slogan, "All land should belong to the peasants," with which the Russian farmers were hoodwinked, had likewise little appeal for the rural population of Germany. That the Spartakus program would have made Germany a branch office of Russia was a prospect that held little alarm for Liebknecht.[118] Spartakus was, however, not the only group that urged revolutionary action. There were also the sailors, the People's Naval Division, who had established themselves in Berlin and who seemed willing to do the dirty work of the revolution. And there were also the shop stewards who promised to mobilize the factory workers for a takeover.

In retrospect, there appears to be no strategic planning behind the uprisings which took place in Berlin between December 1918 and March 1919. The armistice had been signed on November 11, 1918, the conditions of which were extremely harsh, since the Allied powers were determined to avoid a reopening of hostilities.[119] But the very fact of the armistice deprived the extreme left of one of its most powerful propaganda weapons, i.e., the demand for an immediate end to the war.

Whoever today investigates the motives of Liebknecht and his followers must come to the conclusion that these men were interested in preventing general elections and the gathering of a national assembly. In other words, Spartakus must have been conscious that it represented but a small minority of the German people; there are indeed proofs that Rosa Luxemburg knew full well the basic weakness of their position. "Socialism," she wrote, "cannot be made and will not be made by order ... it must be made by the masses."[120] But it is most doubtful that the starving masses were at this point ready to be stirred to action by the hope of a new social order. Nor had they any great interest in Luxemburg's mystique of the masses. Furthermore, Spartakus had no cadres of "professional revolutionaries" who could have guided a coup d'état.

The fight between the social democrats and the extremists of whatever color was reduced to a series of separate engagements for the control of Berlin. In themselves, these were not decisive, but they revealed the alternatives that loomed on the horizon. If the national assembly were not to meet, or if its opening were to be postponed, Germany would be plunged into civil war.[121] Russia was not only banking on the triumph of the Soviet system in Germany, but was actively supporting the struggle with arms and money.[122] On the other hand, it was highly unlikely that the victorious entente bent on destroying Bolshevism in its homeland would permit it to succeed in a bordering country. There would either have been open intervention, or the returning German army would have been ordered to suppress the socialist movement. In any case, a Spartakus victory would not have brought peace to Germany. The social democrats wanted peace and order, and the majority of workers manifested their agreement when the council of soldiers and workers decided that elections for the national assembly should not be delayed. They were set for January 19, 1919.[123] The selection of a specific date did not necessarily assure the convening of the assembly, however. The position of the SPD was weak and could have been shattered by a determined opposition, but two circumstances favored Ebert and his followers: his enemies were not only divided in their goals, but also in regard to timetable and procedures. They were lacking in organization and leadership; neither Liebknecht nor Luxemburg had ever given any proof of executive ability, to say nothing of the minor figures of the revolution. But of greatest importance to the SPD was the fact that they could count on the armed forces who by mid-December had retreated across the Rhine.

In some parts of Germany, especially in Hamburg, new demands were made to abolish the power of the officers in favor of the councils of the soldiers. The High Command rejected the requests with indignation. On December 20, Groener, accompanied by Mayor von Schleicher, attended a meeting of the Council of Commissars and made the standpoint of the High Command abundantly clear.[124] If the discipline of the army were to be further relaxed, it would cease to exist, and the High Command would be obliged to resign. Such a threat might have given Ebert pause, but not the more radical members of the Council.[125] They did, however, back away from the possibility of forming a revolutionary militia in Berlin. Just as there was no Lenin in Berlin, neither was there a Trotsky. At all events, it had become clear that Ebert and his colleagues preferred to collaborate with the army rather than yield to the revolutionary left. The following days were to prove how momentous this decision was.

The first open conflict occurred on December 23 and involved some thousand sailors from the People's Naval Division who had been quartered in the imperial palace and in the stables nearby. The main cause of the dispute appeared to be a demand for pay, but the disputants went further and threatened to arrest the government, i.e., the Council of the Commissars. They were not able to carry out this intention, but did succeed in seizing the civilian commandant of Berlin, a social democrat by the name of Otto Wels. He was rescued by a detachment of the regular army which shelled the palace, and the outcome was a draw. The sailors were given their pay and were allowed to leave, and Wels was freed.

This incident spelled the end of the uneasy coalition between the SPD and the USPD, the latter accusing Ebert of bad faith in using the regular army. Its members resigned from the council, thereby leaving Ebert and his friends in control of the situation. As Bismarck said, the state cannot stand still, and the vacuum created by the resignation of the independents was filled with majority socialists, the most important of whom was Noske.

The failure of the independents did not discourage Spartakus, which had constituted itself as the Communist Party of Germany. Luxemburg harbored grave doubts about the wisdom of an uprising without mass support. "Spartakus," she said, "will never undertake to govern other than through the clear and unmistakable wish of the great majority of the proletarian masses of Germany."[126] But, as her biographer has said, one should not look for traces of orthodox democratic thinking in Rosa Luxemburg.[127] If she questioned the mandate of Spartakus, she did nothing to discourage the action of the extremists. She may very well have thought that revolutionary action would propel the masses into revolutionary participation by spontaneous combustion.

Renewed fighting broke out in Berlin on January 5, 1919, and again the pretext was spurious.[128] The independents, Spartakus, and the revolutionary shop stewards called on the workers to refuse submission to a government which was stifling the revolution with bayonets. On the same day, the rebels took over the building occupied by *Vorwärts*. It is an example of the hopeless naïveté of the movement that it preferred to occupy a newspaper building rather than arrest the government or take possession of the telephone and telegraph offices, the railway stations, or other important strategic buildings.

The revolutionaries had, moreover, overrated the support they expected to receive from the workers. Neither the People's Naval Division nor the Council of Soldiers and Workers cared to be drawn into the melée, and as a result, the fight was lost from the beginning. In the meantime, Ebert and Noske had assembled a corps of volunteers (*Freikorps*) in the vicinity of Berlin, all in all, some 4,000 men, well-equipped and well-trained. While crowds surrounded the government buildings, the troops moved into Berlin. The *Vorwärts* building was recaptured on January 11, and the leaders of Spartakus went into hiding. A worse fate was reserved for Liebknecht and Rosa Luxemburg. On the same night, they were ferreted out, seized, and assassinated by officers of the *Gardeschützendivision* (sharp-shooter division).

Deprived of its leaders, the Spartakus uprising disintegrated. A mop-up operation was set in motion to clear the city, though the work had to be repeated after a second uprising in March. Four days after the murders of Liebknecht and Luxemburg, the people voted for the national assembly. The outcome confirmed Ebert's position. He had the majority of the people behind him; his party won 165 seats, which together with the 91 seats of the Catholic Center party, and the 75 seats of the new Democratic party, provided a workable coalition. It was decided that the assembly should meet in Weimar rather than in Berlin in order to avoid pressures from riotous mobs.

Although the new state was baptized the Weimar Republic, Berlin remained the capital. During these months of upheaval, it had proved again that it set the pace for the entire country. It is paradoxical that we must view imperial Berlin in the perspective opened by the November Revolution. The capital had known how to defend its position of preeminence. Defeat of the revolution in Berlin spelled defeat of the revolution elsewhere. The city of Bremen, which opposed the new government, was subdued, as was Brunswick. In the industrial districts of Westphalia, the army was called upon to reestablish "law and order." The most tragic events took place in Bavaria. There the election had shown a clear majority for the parties of the middle class, but Kurt Eisner insisted on retaining his position as prime minister of the state, contrary to the wishes of his own party. He had adopted the misbegotten idea of playing the council of soldiers and workers against the Bavarian parliament. The device did not succeed, and Eisner paid for the gamble with his life. He was killed by a radical nationalist, Count Arco, on February 21.[129] A period of panic and chaos followed during which a group of left-wing intellectuals proclaimed Bavaria a Soviet republic. Anyone familiar with the Bavarian psyche could have told them that they were courting disaster. The first Soviet republic was replaced by another, even more radical, whose government, if such it may be called, was prepared to fight to the bitter end. It was soon put to the test. On the first day of May, a Bavarian Freikorps, actively supported by the civilian population, "liberated" Munich. White terror now followed red terror. The reader will no doubt recollect that the Soviet system was nowhere successful in Europe at the close of World War I; it failed in Berlin as it failed in Munich, Budapest, Turin.

There is here no intention of exonerating Ebert and Noske for allowing the forces of the counterrevolution to operate at will. Ultimately, they had little choice and could only have jumped from the frying pan into the fire. Like the sorcerer's apprentice, they had called forth spirits which refused to retreat. By relying on the returning army, the social democrats paved the way for a revival of the forces of militarism.

After 1919, there were two types of militarism in Germany. The old Prussian type, organized and disciplined, was reestablished in the Reichswehr, where the short-sighted provisions of the Versailles Treaty made its survival an easy matter. General von Seekt became the incarnation of this trend, and under his influence, the Reichswehr became a state within a state.[130] Another type of militarism was made up of the thousands of returning veterans who could not or would not become a part of the civilian population, and for whom violence had become a way of life. Both types felt sympathetic toward each other; the official Reichswehr protected the black Reichswehr, as the Freikorps were called, and would take a stand against the mercenaries only if its own existence were challenged.

It would be unfair to blame the social democrats for all the blunders from which the Weimar Republic suffered. The German middle class made as poor a showing in 1919 as it had during the Second Reich. A perspicacious man like Friedrich Meinecke saw with misgiving the establishment of the mercenaries in Berlin and heard with dismay the whistled mockery of the republic in the old imperial hymn, "Heil Dir im Siegerkranz."[181] General Maercker, who commanded a Freikorps in 1919, had this to say: "Almost every time we entered a town, I had to ask myself the question: would our intervention have been necessary if everyone had been at his post? Where was the German bourgeoisie? . . . I have acquired in five months of activity . . . little respect for the constructive ability of the German bourgeoisie, but a high opinion of the organized workers."[182] Perhaps the general was not entirely objective. At least the upper bourgeoisie, the industrialists, were willing to come to terms with labor. The secretary general of the Free Trade Unions, Legien, and the representatives of industry, Hugo Stinnes and Karl von Siemens, signed an agreement on November 15, 1918, in which the eight-hour work-day was established, unions were recognized as the official agents of labor, and factory committees as well as mediation councils for labor disputes were created. It was a formal recognition of the partnership of labor and management, and since it was a voluntary agreement, it could have laid the foundation for a permanent reconciliation of capitalists and workers.[183] That this did not occur was due to many factors. Moreover, the representatives of industry were quite willing to ally themselves with other elements, such as the national socialists, if it suited their purposes. Large sections of the educated bourgeoisie remained hostile to the new republic, whereas the petite bourgeoisie, which had suffered greatly during the war and were destined to suffer even more during the period of inflation which followed, seemed at first inclined to throw in their lot with the social democrats. They soon became disappointed, however, and began to put their faith in the promises of a rabid megalomaniac from Braunau, who called himself Hitler.[134]

One other factor must be mentioned in discussing the failure of the Weimar Republic. The hostile bourgeoisie was entrenched in the bureaucratic apparatus and in the judiciary, while the aristocracy continued to dominate the higher echelons of the army. Both groups resented the new socialist masters and engaged in a long process of sabotage against the state. It has been argued that their resistance could have been broken if the Weimar Republic had used the councils of soldiers and workers to replace the recalcitrant bureaucratic machinery and the judiciary.[135] To be sure, the council movement was spontaneous, though it closely followed the Russian model. But the men in the councils were inexperienced, and it would have been disastrous to have placed the bureaucratic machinery of a state like Germany in their hands. There were the problems of demobilization, the reconversion of industry to peacetime production, and, of even greater importance, the pressing problem of finding food for a starving nation. Even if the councils of soldiers and workers had been used efficiently, the independence of the judiciary and the tenure of the civil servants would have had to be disregarded. Both of these were sacred cows in Germany, and any effort to put them in jeopardy would have stirred up new resentment and opposition among the bourgeoisie. Since the experiment was never tried, one may draw one's own conclusions. Following the ratification of the Weimar constitution, the government returned to Berlin. To the best of our knowledge, no other city was ever considered as a capital for the new state. During the fourteen years of the republic, Berlin was not only the center of all government operations, but the seat of Germany's financial and industrial power, and more important still, the very incarnation of her cultural productivity. Much of what goes under the name of Weimar should by rights be called Berlin culture.[136] Of course, other centers of culture, such as Munich, Heidelberg, and Dresden, continued their own authentic life, but it was in Berlin that a special flowering prevailed.

Perhaps one should not exaggerate its constructive value. There was much that was great and new, especially in architecture, painting, and poetry; the names of Gropius, Mies van der Rohe, Mendelssohn, and Paul Klee, come to mind. The theatre in Berlin kept its high standards and received an infusion of experimental daring from the expressionist drama that conquered the stage and presented the Berliners with the spectacle of a theatre committed to the hope for a better world.[137] There was at that time no other city on the continent where one could find an equal number of magnificent art exhibitions, concerts, or operas, as in Berlin. Yet, a good deal of license tainted the intellectual liberty which Berlin was enjoying. A wave of sexual permissiveness drove out the last vestiges of Wilhelminian hypocrisy, but the results were frequently offensive and scandalous. Christopher Isherwood has captured the atmosphere of this Berlin more accurately than anyone else. There was a smell of corruption in the air. Some of the journals, such as *Die Weltbühne* or *Das Tagebuch*, were acidly witty in their criticisms of the reigning powers, but their purpose was vague, and a chasm separated them from the values by which the average Berliner, be he bourgeois or worker, measured his conditions.

In the institutions of higher learning, the levels of discussion and production were as high or higher than they had been prior to 1918. But here, too, a wide gulf separated the thoughts of men like Max Planck, Albert Einstein, Carl Heinz Becker, Friedrich Meinecke, Ernest Troeltsch, or Werner Jaeger from the ideas that guided the man in the street. Tradition without intelligence, intelligence without tradition, are the characteristics that Hans Herzfeld has attached to those years.[138] Nevertheless, we who lived in Berlin during the 1920's are not likely to forget the enormous stimulation of those years. Perhaps we were too willing to overlook the malaise that began to churn underneath the glittering surface of this culture. The Berlin of this period was in almost every aspect the outgrowth of the Wilhelminian age—of the artistic, intellectual, and political opposition which had sprung up, in, and against the second empire. One might say that it was the antithesis of the thesis that preceded it. But such Hegelian terms should not drop lightly from the pen. No synthesis followed; its place was blocked by the Third Reich.

When on February 28, 1933, the Reichstag went up in flames; when on May 10, the best books that the Weimar Republic had produced were burnt, the Berlin that we have tried to picture on these pages ceased to exist. That Hitler toyed with the idea of making it the center of the Europe he planned to create meant nothing. Like so many things which he touched, and by touching, destroyed, the idea of a great arch of triumph and a glorious avenue of victory crossing the city from north to south were but mirrors to reflect his insatiable ego.[139] Nothing came of his delirious dreams but the destruction and the partition of Berlin, making it a living symbol of the tensions that tear our world apart.

Epilogue

$\mathfrak{I}$t is an author's melancholy pleasure to say farewell to a book he has just finished writing. He has tried to do his best, although his best has not satisfied even himself. He thinks he is aware of all the flaws in his work and will be surprised when the critics find others which have eluded him. In my own case, I feel that I owe the reader an apology, or at least an explanation, for failing to give certain subjects a full treatment, or indeed any treatment whatever. There is, for instance, my assumption that imperial Berlin was not essentially a religious city, and that in consequence that phase of Berlin life could be ignored without loss. I can only repeat my conviction that such was the case. I have also omitted to deal with the field of sport. Although gymnastics were practiced in Berlin since the days of Father Jahn, I am not of the opinion that Berlin developed a sport comparable as a national pastime to American baseball or English cricket. True, there was the *Sechs Tage Rennen*, a bicycle competition which was more of an endurance test than anything else, but it was a sociological phenomenon rather than a sporting event. As for horse racing, there was nothing in Berlin that could compare with the glamour or the enthusiasm produced at Epsom Downs or Ascot. Moreover, I still wonder whether sport is a proper subject for the historian, but this may be my own limitation. Finally, there is the world of film. There can be little doubt that films and television have achieved extraordinary importance, not only as an influence of mass media on mass audiences, but also as an artistic vehicle, the possibilities of which are seldom understood and rarely realized. Yet films were in their childhood when the empire collapsed, and their first appearance gave little promise. It was only during the Weimar Republic that

German films acquired worldwide recognition. No doubt there are other omissions of which I am not conscious and cannot therefore apologize for them here. I can only turn the last page, leaving my book in your hands.

Berlin, November 2, 1969

Notes

Bibliographical Note

Index

NOTES

Introduction

1. Heinrich Heine, *Reisebilder*, Part 3, "Sämtliche Werke" (Munich, 1964), 5:173. "Berlin ist gar keine Stadt, sondern Berlin gibt bloss den Ort dazu her, wo sich eine Menge Menschen, und zwar darunter viele Menschen von Geist versammeln, denen der Ort ganz gleichgültig ist; diese bilden das geistige Berlin."

2. Wilhelm Berges, "Das Reich ohne Hauptstadt," in *Das Hauptstadtproblem in der Geschichte* (Tübingen, 1952), pp. 1–2; Steen E. Rasmussen, *London, The Unique City* (Cambridge, Mass., 1967), pp. 37ff.; Lewis Mumford, *The City in History* (New York, 1961).

3. Berges, *op. cit.*, p. 19; see also G. Roloff, "Hauptstadt und Staat in Frankreich," in *Das Hauptstadtproblem in der Geschichte*, p. 249ff.

4. Gerald Strauss, *Nuremberg in the Sixteenth Century* (New York, 1966), p. 2.

5. *Ibid.*

6. E. Faden, "Berlin, Hauptstadt, seit wann und wodurch," in *Jahrbuch f. Brandenburgische Geschichte* (Berlin, 1950), pp. 20–21.

7. Quoted by Werner Hegemann, *Das Steinerne Berlin* (Berlin, 1965), p. 13; see also Mario Krammer, *Berlin und das Reich* (Berlin, 1935); Mario Krammer, *Berlin im Wandel der Jahrhunderte* (Berlin, 1956).

[1] To the Brandenburg Gate

1. *Berlin, Neun Kapitel seiner Geschichte* (Berlin, 1960); see especially, the articles by Johannes Schultze. "Entstehung der Mark Brandenburg und ihrer Städte," and Berthold Schultze, "Berlins Gründung und erster Aufstieg."

2. Berthold Schultze, *op. cit.*, pp. 65ff.

3. Otto Hintze, *Die Hohenzollern und ihr Werk* (Berlin, 1915).

4. Hans Rothfels, ed., *Berlin in Vergangenheit und Gegenwart* (Tübingen, 1961), p. 2.

5. E. Kaeber, *Beiträge zur Berliner Geschichte* (Berlin, 1964), pp. 6off. The official withdrawal from the Hanseatic League occurred only in 1518.

6. Kaeber, *op. cit.*, p. 119; Willi Hoppe, "Reformation und Renaissance in Berlin," in *Berlin, Neun Kapitel seiner Geschichte*, pp. 8off; H. Spiero, *Berlin in Geschichte und Kunst* (Munich, 1928), pp. 32ff.

7. Herbert Roch, *Fontane, Berlin, und das 19. Jahrhundert* (Berlin, 1962), pp. 9ff.

8. Adolf von Harnack, *Geschichte der königlichen preussischen Akademie der Wissenschaften*, 3 vols. (Berlin, 1900).

9. Rothfels, *op. cit*, p. 6; Walther Kiaulehn, *Berlin, Schicksal einer Weltstadt* (Berlin, 1958), pp. 47ff.

10. Moeller van den Bruck, *Der Preussische Stil*, 3rd ed. (Breslau, 1931); Paul O. Rave, *Berlin in der Geschichte seiner Bauten* (Berlin, 1964).

11. Quoted by Richard Dietrich, "Berlin und die Hohenzollern," in *Berlin, Neun Kapitel seiner Geschichte*, pp. 112–113.

12. Theodor Fontane, "Die Märker und das Berlinertum," in Josepf Ettlinger, ed., *Aus dem Nachlass* (Berlin, 1908), pp. 295–312.

13. Alfred Zastrau, "Im Zeitalter Goethes," in *Berlin, Neun Kapitel seiner Geschichte*, pp. 136–138.

14. Rothfels, *op. cit.*, p. 7; F. Meinecke, *Das Zeitalter der deutschen Erhebung* (Göttingen, 1957), p. 28.

15. Martin Hürlimann, *Berlin, Berichte und Bilder* (Berlin, 1934), pp. 177ff.

16. *Ibid.*, p. 243.

17. Fontane, *op. cit.*, pp. 309–310.

18. Quoted by J. Christopher Herold, *Mistress to an Age* (New York, 1962), p. 268.

[2] From Kingdom to Empire

1. Kurt von Raumer, "Deutschland um 1800," *Handbuch d. deutschen Geschichte* (Potsdam, 1935), 2:214.

2. Eduard Spranger, "Gedenkrede zur 150. Jahresfeier der Friedrich-Wilhelms Universität," in H. Rothfels, ed., *Berlin in Vergangenheit und Gegenwart* (Tübingen, 1961), p. 62.

3. Quoted by Meinecke, *Das Zeitalter der deutschen Erhebung* (Göttingen, 1957), p. 53. For a more critical appraisal of the Reform movement see W. Simon, *The Failure of the Prussian Reform Movement* (Ithaca, N.Y., 1955).

4. E. Kehr, *Der Primat der Innenpolitik* (Berlin, 1965), p. 31.

5. Dr. Clausewitz *Die Städte-ordnung von 1808 und die Stadt Berlin* (Berlin, 1908), p. 42.

6. Richard Dietrich, "Berlins Weg zur Industrie und Handelsstadt," in *Berlin, Neun Kapitel seiner Geschichte* (Berlin, 1960), p. 162.

7. Spranger, *op. cit.*, p. 62.

8. *Ibid*, p. 64; F. D. Schleiermacher, "Gelegentliche Gedanken über Universitäten im deutschen Sinne" (1808), reprinted in Wilhelm Weischedel, ed., *Idee und Wirklichkeit einer Universität* (Berlin, 1960), p. 123.

9. Wilhelm von Humboldt, "Über die innere und äussere Organisation der höheren wissenschaftlichen Anstalten in Berlin" (1809 or 1810), reprinted in Weischedel, *op. cit.*, p. 195.

10. Spranger, *op. cit.*, p. 65. There were many jokes told by the Berliners about the statues of Wilhelm and Alexander von Humboldt which flanked the entrance gate to the university. As for the arrogance of the Berliner the most amusing description is to be found in Fontane's, *Der Stechlin*.

Notes

11. To the whole problem see Friedrich Meinecke's classical book, *Weltbürgertum und Nationalstaat*, 1st ed. (Munich, 1908).

12. Franz Schnabel, *Deutsche Geschichte, im neunzehnten Jahrhundert* (Freiburg, 1964), 2: 44; Hans Kohn, *Prelude to Nation-States* (Princeton, 1967), pp. 252–278.

13. Gustav Parthey, *Jugenderinnerungen*, 2 vols. (Berlin, 1907), 1: 335–336.

14. A Zastrau, "Berlin im Zeitalter Goethes," in *Berlin, Neun Kapitel seiner Geschichte*, p. 145.

15. Günther Franz, *Staatsverfassungen* (Darmstadt, 1964), p. 124; Theodore S. Hamerow, *Restoration, Revolution, Reaction* (Princeton, 1966), p. 56.

16. Franz Rosenzweig, *Hegel und der Staat*, 2 vols. (Munich, 1920); Herbert Marcuse, *Reason and Revolution* (New York, 1941); Gerhard Masur, *Prophets of Yesterday* (New York, 1961).

17. F. A. Staegemann, *Briefe und Aktenstücke zur Geschichte Preussens*, 3 vols. (Leipzig, 1899–1902), 3: 18.

18. Reinhart Koselleck, "Staat und Gesellschaft in Preussen, 1815–1848," ed. Hans Ulrich Wehler, *Moderne deutsche Sozialgeschichte* (Köln–Berlin, 1966), p. 83.

19. Karl Georg Faber, *Die Rheinlande zwischen Restauration und Revolution* (Wiesbaden, 1966).

20. Hamerow, *op. cit.*, pp. 3, 11.

21. Ilja Mieck, *Preussische Gewerbepolitik in Berlin 1806–1844* (Berlin, 1965), p. 19.

22. *Ibid.*, pp. 43ff.

23. *Ibid.*, p. 72.

24. Walther Kiaulehn, *Berlin, Schicksal einer Weltstadt* (Berlin, 1958), p. 140.

25. Dietrich, *op. cit.*, pp. 173ff.

26. Bettina Brentano, *Dies Buch gehört dem König* (Berlin, 1921).

27. Gerhard Masur, *Friedrich Julius Stahl* (Berlin, 1930); Hoffmann von Fallersleben, *Mein Leben*, in *Gesammelte Werke*, 8 vols. (Berlin, 1890–1893), 8: 328.

28. Friedrich Sass, *Berlin in seiner neuesten Zeit und Entwicklung* (Leipzig, 1846), p. 46.

29. *Heimatchronik Berlin* (Köln, 1962). See especially the article by Konrad Kettig, "Berlin im 19. und 20. Jahrhundert," pp. 347ff.

30. Rudolf Virchow, *Briefe an seine Eltern* (Leipzig, 1907), p. 143.

31. *Heimatchronik Berlin*, p. 398.

32. F. Meinecke, "The Year 1848 in German History," *Review of Politics*, 10 (1948): 475–488.

33. The German text reads as follows: "Unter Deinen Flügeln kann ich ruhig bügeln," quoted by Theodore von Laue, *Leopold Ranke, The Formative Years* (Princeton, 1950), p. 61.

34. Heinrich Hefter, *Deutsche Selbstverwaltung im 19. Jahrhundert*, (Stuttgart, 1950), pp. 327–343; L. B. Namier, *Avenues of History* (New York, 1952), pp. 45–55.

35. Ludwig von Rochau, *Grundzüge der Realpolitik* (Stuttgart, 1853).

36. Hans Rosenberg, *Grosse Depression und Bismarckzeit* (Berlin, 1967); see especially, pp. 30, 37.

37. Hamerow, *op. cit.*, p. 207.

38. Werner Hegemann, *Das Steinerne Berlin* (Berlin, 1965), p. 234.

39. Dietrich, *op. cit.*, pp. 173–174.

40. *Ibid.*, p. 179; see also J. Clapham, *Economic Development of France and Germany* (Cambridge, 1966), p. 280.

41. Gordon A. Craig, *The Politics of the Prussian Army* (New York, 1964), pp. 136ff; Eugene Anderson, *The Social and Political Conflict in Prussia, 1858–1864* (Lincoln, Neb., 1954).

42. *Heimatchronik Berlin*, p. 409.

43. Otto Pflanze, *Bismarck and the Development of Germany* (Princeton, 1963), p. 265.

44. Johannes Ziekursch, *Politische Geschichte des neuen deutschen Kaiserreiches*, 3 vols. (Frankfurt, 1925), 1: 189.

45. Pflanze, *op cit.*, p. 400

46. *Ibid.*, p. 399.

[3] The Boom Years

1. The text of the constitution of the empire is reprinted in G. Franz, *Staatsverfassungen* (Darmstadt, 1964), pp. 168ff.

2. Otto Pflanze, *Bismarck and the Development of Germany* (Princeton, 1963), p. 344.

3. Hans Dietzel, *Die preussischen Wahlrechtsreformbestrebungen von der Oktroyierung bis zum ersten Weltkrieg* (Köln, 1934).

4. Pflanze, *op. cit.*, p. 9.

5. Hans Rosenberg, *Grosse Depression und Bismarckzeit* (Berlin, 1967).

6. Walter Bussmann. *Treitschke* (Göttingen, 1952), pp. 316ff.

7. Annemarie Lange, *Berlin zur Zeit Bebels und Bismarcks* (East Berlin, 1959).

8. Otto Glagau, *Der Börsen und Gründungsschwindel in Berlin* (Berlin, 1876). Although biased and violent in his accusations, Glagau is still one of our principal sources for the *Gründerjahre*. See also Rudolph Meyer, *Politische Gründer und die Korruption in Deutschland* (Leipzig, 1877); Maximilian Müller Jabusch, *So Waren die Gründerjahre* (Düsseldorf, 1957); Otto Wiedenfeldt, *Statistische Studie zur Entstehung und Entwicklung der Berliner Industrie* (Leipzig, 1898); Frieda Busch, *Tribute und ihre Wirkungen, untersucht am Beispiel der französischen Zahlungen nach dem Krieg, 1870–71* (Basel, 1936).

9. Henry Bethel Strousberg, *Dr. Strousberg und sein Wirken* (Berlin, 1876).

10. *Ibid.*, p. 33; see also P. G. Pulzer, *The Rise of Political Anti-Semitism in Germany and Austria* (New York, 1964), p. 20.

11. *Verhandlungen der durch die allerhöchste Verordnung vom 1. Februar 1872 einberufenen Häuser des Landtages;* Session of February 7, 1873, p. 934.

12. *Ibid.*

13. J. Kastan, *Berlin Wie Es War* (Berlin, 1907), pp. 9–10; Ernst Kaeber, *Beiträge zur Berliner Geschichte* (Berlin, 1964), pp. 293ff.

14. W. Hegemann, *Das Steinerne Berlin* (Berlin, 1963), p. 245.

15. *Ibid.*, p. 248.

16. Most books on Berlin condemn the speculation in real estate and consider its results harmful. An exception is the autobiography of Georg Haberland, *Aus meinem Leben* (Berlin, 1931). Haberland and his father were among the most active developers of Berlin-Schöneberg.

17. Hegemann, *op. cit.*, p. 253.

18. Kastan, *op. cit.*, pp. 18, 65–66.

Notes

19. There is a fairly large literature on the housing problems of the working class in Berlin. Still basic are Eduard Bernstein, *Geschichte der Arbeiterbewegung in Berlin*, 3 vols. (Berlin, 1907); Otto von Leixner, *Soziale Briefe aus Berlin* (Berlin, 1894), p. 178; Ernst Hirschberg, *Die soziale Lage der arbeitenden Klassen in Berlin* (Berlin, 1897), p. 29; Ruth Glatzer ed. *Berliner Leben, 1870–1900* (East Berlin, 1963), p. 317ff.

20. Bernstein, *op. cit.*, 1:261.

21. Alfred Döblin in his *Berlin, Alexanderplatz* and Jakob Wassermann in his *Christian Wahnschaffe*.

22. Peter de Mendelssohn, *Zeitungstadt Berlin* (Berlin, 1959), p. 69. Mendelssohn's book is the best book on the newspapers in Berlin, but concentrates heavily on the liberal papers. For Scherl, see Hans Erman, *August Scherl* (Berlin, 1954).

23. Gustav Dahm, *Das literarische Berlin* (Berlin, 1895).

24. L. Kantorowicz, *Die Sozialdemokratische Presse Deutschlands* (Tübingen, 1922); Dieter Fricke, *Die deutsche Arbeiterbewegung* (Leipzig, 1962); Dieter Fricke, *Zur Organisation der deutschen Arbeiterbewegung* (Berlin, 1962); Vernon Lidtke, *The Outlawed Party, Social Democracy in Germany in 1878–1890* (Princeton, 1966).

25. Quoted by Mendelssohn, *op. cit.*, p. 213.

26. *Ibid.*, p. 76.

27. Glatzer, *op. cit.*, p. 185.

28. Paul Weiglin, *Berlin im Glanz* (Berlin, n. d.), pp. 53–54; H. O. Modrow and Paul Wiegler, eds., *Berlin* (Berlin, 1936), pp. 60, 72, 127.

29. Walther Rathenau, "Die schönste Stadt der Welt," in *Nachgelassene Schriften* (Berlin, 1928), 2:259–80; Paul O. Rave, *Berlin in der Geschichte seiner Bauten* (Berlin, 1960), pp. 37–38; Karl Scheffler, *Berlin* (Berlin, 1931).

30. Rosenberg, *op. cit.*, p. 45.

31. Pulzer, *op. cit.*, p. 81.

32. *Ibid.*, pp. 76–86: Fritz Stern, *The Politics of Cultural Despair* (Berkeley, Calif., 1961).

33. Quoted by Pulzer, *op. cit.*, p. 84.

34. See the article by Wilhelm Wehrenpfennig, published in the *Preussische Jahrbücher*, quoted by Rosenberg, *op. cit.*, p. 64.

35. J. H. Clapham, *Economic Development of France and Germany* (Cambridge, 1966), pp. 278–338. For the details of the fight of the social democrats against the Socialist Law the reader may consult Lidtke, *op. cit.*, pp. 320–332.

36. Rosenberg, *op. cit.*, p. 78.

37. See the interesting chronology in *Berlins Aufstieg zur Weltstadt, ein Gedenkbuch* (Berlin, 1929), pp. 229–245.

38. There is, of course, a large amount of highly technical literature on the development of the banking system in Berlin. The human aspects are emphasized in Erich Achterberg, *Berliner Hochfinanz, Kaiser, Fürsten und Millionäre* (Frankfurt, 1965); Georg Bernhard, *Meister und Dilettanten am Kapitalismus* (Amsterdam, 1936); Karl Helfferich, *Georg von Siemens, ein Lebensbild*, 3 vols. (Berlin, 1921); Hans Fürstenberg, *Carl Fürstenberg, Die Lebensgeschichte eines deutschen Bankiers* (Wiesbaden, n. d.); David Landes, "The Bleichröder Bank," in *Leo Baeck Yearbook*, 5: 201–220; Walter Kiaulehn, *Berlin, Schicksal einer Weltstadt*, pp. 150ff.; F. Stern. "Gold and Iron, Bleichröder and Bismarck," *American Historical Review*, 75(1969): 37–46.

39. Wolfgang Zorn, "Wirtschafts-und sozialgeschichtliche Zusammenhänge der

deutschen Reichsgründungszeit, 1850–1879," in *Historische Zeitschrift,* 197(1963): 318–342.

40. Rave, *op. cit.,* p. 370.

41. Zorn, *op. cit.,* p. 265.

42. Thomas Nipperdey, "Interessenverbände und Parteien in Deutschland vor dem ersten Weltkriege," *Politische Vierteljahrschrift,* 2(1961): 262–280.

43. There are innumerable books on Old Berlin. To mention only a few: A Nalli Ruthenberg, *Das Alte Berlin* (Berlin, 1912); Kastan, *op. cit.;* Franz Lederer, *Schönes Altes Berlin* (Berlin, 1930); Hans Mackowski, *Häuser und Menschen im alten Berlin* (Berlin, 1923); Helene von Nostitz, *Berlin, Erinnerungen und Gegenwart* (Berlin, 1938); Frau von Nostitz, who was a niece of President Hindenburg, gives a good description of castles and parks in Berlin, but her book is marred by an unmitigated adulation of Adolf Hitler who was just then beginning the destruction of what was left of Old Berlin.

44. Heinrich von Treitschke, *Politics,* ed. Hans Kohn (New York, 1963), pp. 21, 236. "If Germany is to become a true monarchy, the capital city of its emperors must also be the capital city of the nation."

[4] Berlin Society

1. Theodor Fontane, *Der Stechlin,* Nymphenburg edition (Munich, 1954), p. 216 "Oberklasse gutt, Unterklasse serr gutt; Mittelklasse *nicht* serr gutt." The speaker is a Czech musician, Dr. Wrschowitz, living in Berlin.

2. H. Gollwitzer, *Die Standesherren* (Göttingen, 1964); Graf Paul Vassili, *Hof und Gesellschaft in Berlin.* (Budapest, 1884); N. von Preradovich, *Die Führungsschichten in Österreich und Preussen, 1804–1918* (Wiesbaden, 1955), pp. 75–189; Lysbeth Muncy, *Die Junker in the Prussian Administration under William II* (Rhode Island, 1944).

3. L. von Nordegg, *Die Berliner Gesellschaft,* 2nd ed. (Berlin, 1907); Ruth Glatzer, ed., *Berliner Leben* (East Berlin, 1963). The best information about society, with a capital S, can be found in the diaries and memoirs of the period. Among these documents the diaries of intelligent women, who belonged to "the happy few," occupy the first place. I will only mention those which I think are outstanding. R. Vierhaus, ed., *Das Tagebuch der Baron Spitzemberg* (Göttingen, 1960); Princess Marie Radziwill, *Briefe vom deutschen Kaiserhof* (Berlin, 1936); Mathilde Gräfin von Keller, *40 Jahre im Dienste der Kaiserin* (Berlin, 1935), Marie von Bunsen, *Die Welt in der ich lebte, 1860–1912* (Berlin, 1929); Bogdan Graf von Hutten Czapski, *60 Jahre Politik und Gesellschaft,* 2 vols. (Berlin, 1936).

The memoirs of personalities of the middle class are less revealing and less numerous, and we have only very few personal histories of members of the working class.

4. Vassili, *op. cit.,* p. 26; see also Jules Laforgue, *Berlin, La Cour et La Ville* (Paris, 1923). The young poet Laforgue occupied the position of Vorleser (reader) to the empress Augusta. His portraits of the imperial couple in the 1880's and of the court are very perspicacious. The book with which Laforgue hoped to make a fortune, was not published in his lifetime, since he died at the age of twenty-seven. About Laforgue see Warren Ramsey, *Jules Laforgue* (New Haven, 1954).

5. Vassili, *op. cit.,* p. 130.

6. Nordegg, *op. cit.,* p. 29.

7. *Ibid.,* p. 241ff.

Notes

8. Frederic B. M. Hollyday, *Bismarck's Rival, Albrecht von Stosch* (Durham, N. C., 1960). The book contains a comprehensive bibliography of the circle close to the crown prince.

9. The literature on the Kaiser is copious but of uneven value. Emil Ludwig, *Kaiser Wilhelm II* (London, 1926); F. Nowack, *Kaiser and Chancellor* (London, 1930); Erich Eyck, *Das persönliche Regime Wilhelms II*, (Zürich, 1948); Walther Rathenau, *Der Kaiser* (Berlin, 1921); Graf Robert von Zedlitz Trütschler, *Zwölf Jahre am deutschen Kaiserhof* (Stuttgart, 1925). There is a wealth of information in letters, memoirs, and biographies, which I cannot mention here.

10. Ludwig's book is based on the idea that the mistakes of the Kaiser can be explained by an "inferiority complex" for which he overcompensated.

11. Georg Kotowski, ed., *Das Wilhelminische Deutschland* (Frankfurt, 1963), pp. 9–10, 38.

12. Johannes Haller, *Aus dem Leben des Fürsten Philip zu Eulenburg*, (Berlin 1924), p. 154; Chlodwig, *Fürst zu Hohenlohe Schillingfürst*; K. A. von Müller, ed., *Denkwürdigkeiten der Reichskanzlerzeit* (Berlin, 1931).

13. Bernhard von Bülow, *Denkwürdigkeiten*, 4 vols. (Berlin, 1930); Bülow's truthfulness has been questioned by many historians. One other source of great importance for the period is Norman Rich and M. H. Fisher, eds., *The Holstein Papers*, 4 vols. (Cambridge, 1957–1963). They are composed of diaries and letters of the enigmatic privy councillor.

14. Theodor Fontane, *Briefe an Georg Friedländer* (Heidelberg, 1954), pp. 309–310.

15. Spitzemberg, *op. cit.*, p. 398.

16. Wilhelm II, *Die Reden in den Jahren 1888–1905*, 4 vols. (Leipzig, n. d.). This is an official publication purged of some of the most offensive expressions used by the Kaiser.

17. *The Daily Telegraph* affair is not entirely clear. The emperor granted the interview in the fall of 1908. It was published on October 28, 1908. In it the emperor claimed that he was anglophile at heart, while the German people, especially the middle and the lower classes, were harboring hatred against England. About the reaction in Germany, particularly in the Reichstag, see *Stenographische Berichte, Session of 1908*, vol. 233 of November 10, 1908.

The puzzling part of the affair is that the emperor submitted the text of the interview to the German Foreign Office where it was cleared. The reasons why the document was cleared are opaque. Some say that the officials failed to read it; others have assumed that Bülow allowed the interview to be published because he foresaw its effect and wished to embarrass the Kaiser and to expand his own power. If so, he failed, because the Kaiser never forgave Bülow and replaced him soon by appointing Bethmann-Hollweg as his successor. Wilhelm Schüssler, *Die Daily-Telegraph Affaire* (Göttingen, 1952).

18. Henry W. Fisher, *The Private Life of Wilhelm II* (London, 1906).

19. Trütschler, *op. cit.*, p. 8.

20. Alfred Graf von Waldersee, *Denkwürdigkeiten*, 3 vols. (Stuttgart, 1923), 2: 145.

21. O. von Leixner, *Soziale Briefe aus Berlin* (Berlin, 1894); Karl E. Born, "Der soziale und wirtschaftliche Strukturwandel Deutschlands am Ende des 19. Jahrhunderts," in H. U. Wehler, ed., *Moderne deutsche Sozialgeschichte* (Köln, 1966), pp. 271–284; Friedrich Meinecke, *Erlebtes, 1862–1919* (Stuttgart, 1964).

22. F. Achterberg, *Berliner Hochfinanz* (Frankfurt, 1965).

23. Ernst R. Huber, *Deutsche Verfassungs Geschichte*, 3 vols. (Stuttgart, 1963), 3: 91ff.

24. H. Rosenberg, "Die Pseudodemokratisierung der Rittergutsbesitzerklasse," in *Moderne deutsche Socialgeschichte*, p. 287; see also Lilli Braun, *Memoiren einer Sozialistin, Lehrjahre* (Munich, 1909), p. 240.

25. Braun, *op. cit.*, p. 345.

26. *Das Wilhelminische Deutschland*, p. 76ff; K. Demeter, *Das deutsche Offizierkorps*, (Frankfurt, 1962), pp. 196–229.

27. Fontane, *op. cit.*, p. 236.

28. Spitzemberg, *op. cit.*, p. 353.

29. Wolfgang Heidelmeyer, ed., *Der Fall Köpenick* (Frankfurt, 1968). The book contains excerpts from the most pertinent documents of the case as well as from the autobiography of Voigt.

30. A comprehensive study of the German educated middle class in the second empire is still missing. There are some monographs of the bourgeois critics of the Kaiser which contain pertinent information. See Anneliese Thimme, *Hans Delbrück als Kritiker der wilhelminischen Epoche* (Düsseldorf 1955), especially pp. 12–13. Theodor Heuss, *Erinnerungen* (Tübingen, 1963), pp. 13–45; Meinecke, *op. cit.* passim; Hermann Oncken, *Historisch Politische Aufsätze und Reden*, 2 vols. (Munich, n. d.).

31. Theodor Fontane, *Frau Jenny Treibel*, Nymphenburg Edition, 1954.

32. Vassili, *op. cit.*, p. 130.

33. Fritz Kaplan, "Jakob Burckhardt u. die Wiederbesetzung von Ranke's Geschichtsprofessur," *Historische Zeitschrift*, 168 (1943): 113–131.

34. About the influence of Treitschke on the younger generation, see Marianne Weber, *Max Weber, Ein Lebensbild* (Heidelberg, 1950), p. 112, also Thimme, *op. cit.*, p. 15.

35. Koppel Pinson, *Modern Germany*, 2nd ed. (New York, 1967), pp. 242–244.

36. Arnold Sachse, *Friedrich Althoff* (Berlin, 1928), pp. 214–215.

37. Nipperdey, *op. cit.*, pp. 369ff.

38. Leixner, *op. cit.*, p. 95.

39. Friedrich Meinecke, *Politische Schriften und Reden*, ed. G. Kotowski (Darmstadt, 1958); see also R. Sterling, *Friedrich Meinecke* (Princeton, 1958).

40. Annemarie Lange, *Das wilhelminische Deutschland* (East Berlin, 1967), pp. 79–80.

41. A. Damaschke, *Aus meinem Leben*, 7th ed (Berlin, 1928), p. 26.

42. Friedrich Lüdtge, *Deutsche Sozial– und Wirtschaftsgeschichte* (Berlin-Heidelberg, 1966), p. 363.

43. Leixner, *op. cit.*, p. 154.

44. Lidtke, *op. cit.*, p. 10.

45. *Ibid.*, p. 11.

46. Karl Marx, "Critique of the Gotha Program," in *Marx and Engels, Selected Works*, 2 vols. (Moscow, 1955), 2: 33.

47. Lidtke, *op. cit.*, p. 41.

48. Bernstein, *op. cit.*, passim, Lange, *op. cit.*, passim, E. R. Huber, *Deutsche Verfassungsgeschichte, seit* 1789, 3 vols. (Stuttgart, 1964), 2: 536–539.

49. Hans R. Fischer, *Was Berlin verschlingt* (Berlin, 1890), p. 4.

50. G. Roth, "Die kulturellen Bestrebungen der Sozialdemokratie im wilhelminischen Deutschland," in *Moderne deutsche Sozialgeschichte*, p. 342.

51. Lidtke, *op. cit.*, passim.

Notes

52. *Ibid.*, pp. 339–345.

53. Bernstein, *op. cit.*, 1: 389ff.

54. See Engel's letter to J. P. Becker, of May 22, 1883, quoted in *Berliner Leben*, p. 131.

55. See the statistics of the membership in German trade–unions between 1891–1913 in Koppel Pinson, *op. cit.*, p. 247. The Free Trade Unions surpassed their rivals, the Christian trade unions and the democratic trade unions, by almost two millions.

56. Reinhardt Höhn, *Die Vaterlandslosen Gesellen* (Köln-Opladen, 1964), introduction, pp. lxxii–lxxiii.

57. *Ibid.*

58. Carl Schorske, *German Social Democracy, 1905–1917* (Cambridge, Mass., 1955).

59. Egmont Zechlin, "Bethmann–Hollweg, Kriegsrisiko und SPD 1914," in *Der Monat*, January 1966, pp. 17–32.

60. Hans Rosenberg, *Grosse Depression und Bismarckzeit* (Berlin, 1967), passim.

61. Bernstein, *op. cit.*, 2: 272, gives a statistic of the weekly wages for a number of occupations. The locksmiths occupy the top with 21.85 marks, while textile workers commanded only 15.00 marks. However, there were certain skills that received even higher wages such as printers, slaters, the builders of tile stoves, and so forth.

62. Lange, *op. cit.*, p. 177.

63. Paul Lindenberg, *Berliner Polizei und Verbrechertum* (Leipzig, 1892).

64. Davis, Parks, Best, *Berlin und seine Arbeiter in englischer Beleuchtung* (Berlin, 1907); see also Bruno Bürgel, *Vom Arbeiter zum Astronomen* (Berlin, 1925), pp. 3, 44, 46; Leixner, *op. cit.*, passim.

65. Wilhelm Liebknecht, *Wissen ist Macht, Macht ist Wissen* (Leipzig, 1873). To the whole problem of the education of the workers, see also Gerhard A. Ritter, *Die Arbeiterbewegung im wilhelminischen Reich* (Berlin, 1959), pp. 218ff.

66. G. von Loebell, *Zur Geschichte der evangelischen Kirchengemeinden Berlins, 1875–1908* (Berlin, 1909), p. 11; Karl Kupisch, *Die deutschen Landeskirchen im 19–20. Jahrhundert* (Göttingen, 1966).

67. Walter Frank, *Hofprediger Adolf Stoecker und die christlich soziale Bewegung*, 2nd ed. (Hamburg, 1935).

68. *Ibid.*, p. 19.

69. *Ibid.*, pp. 24–27.

70. Karl Kupisch, ed., *Quellen zur Geschichte des deutschen Protestantismus (1871–1945)* (Göttingen, 1960), pp. 65ff.

71. Frank, *op. cit.*, p. 64.

72. Quoted by Pinson, *op. cit.*, p. 176; S. A. Kaehler, "Stoecker's Versuch eine christlich soziale Arbeiterpartei in Berlin zu begründen," in P. Wentzke, *Deutscher Staat und deutsche Parteien* (Berlin, 1922).

73. Arthur Ruppin, *Soziologie der Juden*, 2 vols. (Berlin, 1930), 1: 59.

74. Klemens Felden, *Die Übernahme des antisemitischen Stereotypes als soziale Norm durch die bürgerliche Gesellschaft Deutschlands, 1875–1900* (Heidelberg, 1963), p. 17.

75. F. Nietzsche, *Jenseits von Gut und Böse*, trans. Walter Kaufmann (New York, 1966), p. 187.

76. Raul Hilberg, *The Destruction of European Jews* (Chicago, 1961), p. 3. See also Gerhard Masur, *Friedrich Julius Stahl* (Berlin, 1930), chapter 1. There is a large body of literature on the problem of anti-Semitism following the "holocaust" and the atrocities of the Nazis. Inevitably, much of it is highly charged with emotionalism.

Eva Reichmann, *Hostages of Civilisation* (London, 1950); Hannah Arendt, *The Origins of Totalitarianism* (New York, 1955); and the rather questionable *Eichmann in Jerusalem* (New York, 1963); Adolf Leschnitzer, *The Magic Background of Modern Antisemitism* (New York, 1956).

77. E. Silberner, *Sozialisten zur Judenfrage* (Berlin, 1926).

78. F. Stern, *The Politics of Cultural Despair* (New York, 1965), pp. 95ff.

79. See the *Kladderadatsch*, one of Germany's "funny" papers, p. 10 of 1875: "Die grosse Judenverfolgung."

80. Treitschke's article is reprinted in Walter Boehlich, *Der Berliner Antisemitismusstreit* (Frankfurt, 1965). In the same book are most of the answers and refutations of Treitschke, and his reply.

81. *Ibid.*, p. 12.

82. Pulzer, *op. cit.*, pp. 337–338. The declaration was signed by Droysen, Gneist, Mommsen, Virchow, Siemens, Forckenbeck, and others.

83. *Ibid.*, pp. 98–99.

84. *Ibid.*, pp. 50–52.

85. T. Fontane to Count Philip Eulenburg: "Ich liebe die Juden, ziehe sie dem Wendisch–Germanischen eigentlich vor,—aber regiert will ich nicht von den Juden sein," November 21, 1880. *Gesammelte Werke*, second series (Berlin, n. d.), 11: 24.

86. Quoted by Stern, *op. cit.*, p. 94.

87. Vassili, *op. cit.*, p. 109.

88. B. Auerbach, *Briefe an seinen Freund Jakob Auerbach* (Frankfurt, 1889), pp. 269, 425, 427, 439.

89. Pulzer, *op. cit.*, p. 196.

90. Ruppin, *op. cit.*, 1: 211.

91. Pulzer, *op. cit.*, p. 197.

92. Werner Sombart, *Die Juden und das Wirtschaftsleben* (Leipzig, 1911), pp. 219–221; Richard Mun, *Die Juden in Berlin* (Leipzig, 1924), p. 115.

93. Ernst Ginsberg, *Abschied* (Zürich, 1965), p. 43; Felix Theilhaber, *Der Untergang der deutschen Juden* (Berlin, 1921); also the unpublished *Memoirs* of Dr. Heinrich Strassmann.

94. Nietzsche, *op. cit.*, p. 187; the italics are mine.

95. Vassili, *op. cit.*, p. 5.

96. *Ibid.*, p. 64.

97. F. Meinecke, *Erlebtes*, p. 114; see also Gerhard Masur, "Max Weber und Friedrich Meinecke in ihrem Verhältnis zur politischen Macht," *Studium Berolinense* (Berlin, 1961), pp. 707–725.

98. Ritter, *op. cit.*, pp. 195–196.

99. This aspect of the society of the second empire has been neglected, and is hard to grasp. However, any reader of the *Holstein Papers* will get an idea of these symptoms of moral decay. See also Fedor von Zobeltitz, *Chronik der Gesellschaft unter dem letzten Kaiserreich*, 2 vols. (Hamburg, 1922).

100. Stefan George, *Der Siebente Ring*, trans. Olga Marx and Ernst Morwitz (Chapel Hill, 1949), p. 207.

101. Gerhard Masur, *Prophets of Yesterday* (New York, 1961), pp. 352–380.

102. *Berliner Illustrierte Zeitung*, No. 52 (1899), "Die Bilanz des Jahrhunderts." The questionnaire was first published on December 25, 1898, the answers on February 1, 1899. Facsimile Reproduction of the *Berliner Illustrierte Zeitung*.

103. *Ibid.*, p. 48.

Notes

[5] "World City—Perhaps?"

1. Among those were observers as different as Sir Arthur Nicolson and the young Friedrich Meinecke.
2. The letter was first published by Hans Herzfeld in *Das Hauptstadtproblem in der Geschichte* (Tübingen, 1952), p. 168.
3. *Ibid.*, pp. 168–169.
4. This is the opinion of the philosopher Eduard Spranger; see his *Berliner Geist* (Tübingen, 1966).
5. Annemarie Lange, *Das wilhelminische Berlin* (East Berlin, 1967), p. 32.
6. *Ibid.*, p. 80.
7. Friedrich Naumann, *Ausstellungsbriefe* (Berlin, 1909), p. 47.
8. H. Herzfeld, ed., *Berlin und die Provinz Brandenburg im 19. und 20. Jahrhundert* (Berlin, 1968). See the contribution by E. Schmieder," Wirtschaft und Bevölkerung," pp. 335ff.
9. *Ibid.*, p. 372.
10. W. Kiaulehn, *Berlin, Schicksal einer Weltstadt* (Berlin, 1958), pp. 158ff; Georg von Siemens, *Geschichte des Hauses Siemens*, 3 vols. (Munich, 1947–1952); Felix Pinner, *Emil Rathenau und das elektrische Zeitalter* (Leipzig, 1918).
11. Harry Graf Kessler, *Walther Rathenau* (Berlin, 1928); for a more intimate picture of Rathenau see his *Briefe*, 2 vols. (Dresden, 1927); Ernst Schulin, "Walther Rathenau," *Der Monat*, June 1968, pp. 45–56.
12. Schmieder, *op. cit.*, p. 372; Georg Bernhard, *Meister und Dilettanten am Kapitalismus, im Reiche der Hohenzollern* (Amsterdam, 1936), pp. 147–157.
13. Lange, *op. cit.*, p. 40; Schmieder, *op. cit.*, p. 367.
14. Lange, *op. cit.*, p. 42.
15. *Ibid.*, p. 52; Schmieder, *op. cit.*, p. 358.
16. Herzfeld, *op. cit.*, p. 9.
17. *Ibid.*
18. Schmieder, *op. cit.*, p. 381.
19. W. Hegemann, *Das Steinerne Berlin* (Berlin, 1963), pp. 318ff.
20. Schmieder, *op. cit.*, p. 384.
21. See the books by Adele Gerhard, *Geschichte der Antonie van Heese* (Berlin, 1906), or her *Die Familie Vanderhouten* (Berlin, 1909); for an appraisal of the works of Adele Gerhard as expressions of her time, see Melitta Gerhard, *Das Werk Adele Gerhards als Ausdruck einer Zeitenwende* (Bern, 1963).
22. Kiaulehn, *op. cit.*, p. 225.
23. *Ibid.*, p. 222.
24. See *Statistisches Jahrbuch der Stadt Berlin* for the years 1883–1919, Berlin.
25. *Führer durch Berlin* (Berlin, n. d.), p. 270.
26. H. Ermann, *Weltgeschichte auf Berlinisch* (Herrenalb, 1962), p. 322.
27. Hedda Adlon, *Hotel Adlon* (Munich, 1961), pp. 5–102.
28. Kiessling, *Berliner Baedecker* (Berlin, 1893), p. 38.
29. Herbert Roch, *Fontane, Berlin und das 19. Jahrhundert* (Berlin, 1962), pp. 168ff.
30. Walter Benjamin, *Berliner Kindheit um Neunzehnhundert* (Frankfurt, 1950), p. 64. About the significance of Benjamin's childhood memories, see Hannah Arendt, "Reflections," *The New Yorker*, October 19, 1968, pp. 65ff.

31. R. Dietrich, "Verfassung und Verwaltung" in *Berlin und die Provinz Brandenburg im 19. und 20. Jahrhundert*, p. 252; Friedrich Karl Steffen, *Das Berliner Verwaltungsrecht* (Berlin, 1936); Harry Götz, *Die Verwaltungsorganisation der Weltstädte* (Berlin, 1931); A. Schinz, *Berlin, Stadtschicksal und Städtebau* (Braunschweig, 1964); Sarah Greer, *Outline of Government-Organization Within the Cities of London, Paris and Berlin* (New York, 1936).

32. Herzfeld, *op. cit.*, p. 66.

33. Carl E. Schorske, "Politics in a New Key," *The Journal of Modern History*, 39, No. 4, (1967): 355–365.

34. Herzfeld, *op. cit.*, p. 76. Martin Philippson, *Max von Forckenbeck* (Dresden, 1898); Georg Reicke, *Ein Bürger zwischen Welt und Stadt* (Berlin, 1923); A. Wermuth, *Ein Beamtenleben* (Berlin, 1922). I found most of these books disappointing and unrevealing.

On the other hand, there are a number of books by foreign journalists which can still be studied with considerable interest: Jules Huret, *Berlin* (Paris, 1909); Charles Huard, *Berlin Comme Je L'ai Vu* (Paris, 1907). Likewise some of the German journalists kept an open mind about the new metropolis: Paul Lindenberg, *Berlin als Kleinstadt* (Berlin, 1893); Julius Rodenberg, *Bilder aus dem Berliner Leben*, 3 vols. (Berlin, 1891).

35. For example, the emperor objected to the care of the graves of the victims of the revolution of 1848 that the city council had ordered.

36. I find it difficult to accept the value–judgments of Lange, *op. cit.*, in regard to the medical facilities that Berlin offered.

37. Herzfeld, *op. cit.*, p. 91.

38. *Ibid.*, pp. 90–91; Lange, *op. cit.*, p. 388.

39. Lange, *op. cit.*, p. 162. The German word for city council is *Stadtverordnetenversammlung*, and is not quite the equivalent of the American city council. The city council of Berlin was more like a parliament than a council and had 144 members.

40. *Ibid.*, p. 209.

41. It was the art critic Karl Scheffler, quoted by Herzfeld, *op. cit.*, p. 72.

42. Hugo von Hofmannsthal, "Preusse und Oesterreicher," *Ausgewählte Werke*, 2 vols. (Frankfurt, 1957), 2: 615–617. The essay was probably written during World War I but the problem occupied Hofmannsthal's mind for many years.

43. The poet is Fontane, as quoted by Herzfeld, *op. cit.*, p. 74.

44. There are several books which deal with the humor of Berlin and the Berliners. Herbert Günther, ed., *Hier Schreibt Berlin* (Berlin, 1929); Hans Meyer, *Der Richtige Berliner* 10th ed. by W. Kiaulehn (Munich, 1966); Maximilian Müller Jabusch, *Die Aussprüche des Bankiers Karl Fürstenberg* (Berlin, 1941); Elizabeth Jacham, *Bummelzug und Sechserbus* (East Berlin, 1965).

[6] Writers, Journalists, and Scholars

1. Josepf Nadler, *Die Berliner Romantik, 1800–1830* (Berlin, 1921); Renate Böschenstein–Schäfer, "Das Literarische Leben" in H. Herzfeld, ed., *Berlin und die provinz Brandenburg im 19. und 20. Jahrhundert* (Berlin, 1968), pp. 659ff.

2. A few of Fontane's novels have been translated into English and there are some monographs about him: J. Remack, *The Gentle Critic, Theodor Fontane and German Politics* (Syracuse, 1964). The best studies are naturally in German: J.

Notes

Förstenau, *Theodor Fontane als Kritiker seiner Zeit* (Potsdam, 1948); Mario Krammer, *Theodor Fontane* (Berlin, 1922); H. Reuter, *Fontane*, 2 vols. (Munich, 1968). There are several editions of Fontane's writings. The older edition is still indispensable for Fontane's letters and I have used it. For the novels I have depended on the more recent and more accessible Nymphenburg edition.

3. Fontane, *Von Zwanzig bis Dreissig*, and *Christian F. Scherenberg* in, *Gesammelte Werke*, 2nd series, vol. 2. H. Roch, *Fontane, Berlin und das 19. Jahrhundert* (Berlin, 1962), pp. 56ff.

4. Roch. *op. cit.*, pp. 91, 127.

5. An attractive selection from these five volumes has been published by Paul Fechter (Hamburg, 1952). See also, H. Fricke, "Fontane Dokumente," *Jahrbuch f. die Geschichte Mittel– und Ostdeutschlands* 6(1955): 88ff.

6. Fontane, *Kriegsgefangen*, Nymphenburg Edition, 3rd Section.

7. For the whole episode see Fontane's letters in *Gesammelte Werke*, 2nd series (Berlin, n. d.), 10: 360ff, 6: 234ff.

8. *Ibid.*, p. 418.

9. There is no English equivalent for the term *Entwicklungsroman*. For its history, see Melitta Gerhard, *Der deutsche Entwicklungsroman* (Bern, 1968).

10. See Thomas Mann's Epilogue to *The Magic Mountain*, Modern Library Edition (New York, 1952), pp. 716ff.

11. Ernst K. Bramstedt, *Aristocracy and the Middle Class in Germany* (Chicago, 1964), pp. 80ff.

12. *Ibid.*, pp. 154ff.

13. Carl E. Schorske, "The Transformation of the Garden: Ideal and Society in Austrian Literature," *American Historical Review*, 72, No. 4(1967): 1268.

14. *Ibid.*

15. *Ibid.*, p. 1297.

16. Fontane's letter to Julius Rodenberg, of March 2, 1896, *Gesammelte Werke*, 2nd series, 11: 381.

17. In volume 11 of the *Letters* are also Fontane's judgments of his French and Russian contemporary novelists.

18. Roch, *op. cit.*, p. 222.

19. See also, T. Fontane, *In Freiheit Dienen* (Munich, 1956), p. 94; Remack, *op. cit.* p. 40.

20. T. Fontane, *Letters to Georg Friedländer, April 5, 1897* (Heidelberg, 1954), p. 310.

21. Letter to his son Theo, May 9, 1888, *Gesammelte Werke*, 2nd series, 7: 174.

22. Fontane, *Kleine Romane*, Nymphenburg Edition, p. 95.

23. *Ibid.*, p. 122.

24. *Ibid.*, p. 194.

25. *Ibid.*, p. 232.

26. *Ibid.*, p. 233.

27. *Ibid.*, p. 260.

28. Fontane, *Drei Romane aus der Berliner Gesellschaft*, Nymphenburg Edition, pp. 287ff.

29. Fontane, *Frau Jenny Treibel*, Nymphenburg Edition, p. 7.

30. *Ibid.*, p. 130.

31. *Ibid.*, p. 141.

32. Fontane expressed his feelings about the German and especially the Berlin bourgeoisie without any inhibitions, in many of his letters.

33. Fontane, *Zwei Frauenromane*, Nymphenburg Edition, pp. 171ff.; some of his books, which I shall not analyze, treat the same problems: marriage and adultery in *L'Adultera* and *Unwiederbringlich*; the problem of honor in *Schach von Wuthenow* and *Cecile*.

34. *Effi Briest*, p. 182; Mary E. Gilbert, "Fontane's Effi Briest," in *Der Deutschunterricht*, 11(1959): 404.

35. *Ibid.*, p. 421.

36. Quoted by Roch, *op. cit.*, p. 236.

37. Fontane, *Der Stechlin*, Nymphenburg Edition.

38. *Ibid.*, p. 124.

39. Klaus Müller Dyes, "Das literarische Leben, 1850–1933," in Herzfeld, *op. cit.*, p. 714.

40. Fontane, *Der Stechlin*, p. 346.

41. Fontane's letter of August 22, 1884, *Gesammelte Werke*, 2nd Section, 7:22.

42. See the novel *Mathilde Möhring* in which Fontane tried to capture the spirit of a middle-class woman.

43. Letter of February 22, 1896, *Gesammelte Werke*, 2nd series, 2: 380.

44. *Ibid.*, p. 434.

45. *Ibid.*, p. 435.

46. *Ibid.*, p. 59.

47. See Klaus Müller Dyes, op. cit., pp. 711–714; see also Klaus Ziegler, "Die Berliner Gesellschaft und die Literatur, in Hans Rothfels, ed., *Berlin in Vergangenheit und Gegenwart* (Tübingen, 1961), pp. 43ff.

Some of the novelists who are of interest to the literary historian only are: M. Ring, *Ein Kleinstädter in Berlin*, 2 vols. (Berlin, 1873); A. Schulze, *Aus dem Notizbuch eines Berliner Schutzmannes* (Leipzig, 1887); M. Kretzer, *Meister Timpe, ein sozialer Roman* (Berlin, 1927).

48. Thomas Mann, "Der alte Fontane" in *Adel des Geistes* (Stockholm, 1948).

49. Heinrich Mann, *Im Schlaraffenland* (Berlin, 1916).

50. Jakob Wassermann, *Christian Wahnschaffe* (Berlin, 1919); English translation, *The World's Illusion* (New York, 1921).

51. For George, see Sabine Lepsius, *Stefan George* (Berlin, n. d.) for Hofmannsthal, his *Letters to Helene von Nostitz* (Frankfurt, 1965). For Rilke his *Gesammelte Briefe*, 6 vols. (Leipzig, 1936–1939).

See also, Oscar Handlin and John Burchard, eds. *The Historian and the City* (Cambridge, Mass., 1963), especially the essay by Carl Schorske, "The Idea of the City in European Thought," pp. 95–114.

52. H. Barnstoff, "Die soziale, politische und wirtschaftliche Zeitkritik bei Gerhart Hauptmann," *Jenaer germanistische Forschungen*, No. 34(1938); F. W. Behl, "Gerhart Hauptmann in Berlin," in *Berliner Almanach*, 1947, pp. 271–282; Behl, "Gerhart Hauptmann und Berlin," in *Berliner Blätter für Geschichte und Heimatskunde*, vol. 4:(1934).

53. Gerhart Hauptmann, *Die Ratten* (Berlin, 1913). There are several English translations.

54. Benno von Wiese, "Gerhart Hauptmann" in, *Zwischen Utopie und Wirklichkeit, Studien zur deutschen Literatur* (Düsseldorf, 1963), pp. 193–231.

55. K. L. Tank, *Gerhart Hauptmann in Selbstzeugnissen* (Hamburg, 1959),

Notes

p. 8: "Das ungeheure Lebewesen und Sterbewesen Berlin war mir alpartig gegenwärtig"; see also E. Dosenheimer, *Das deutsche soziale Drama von Lessing bis Sternheim* (Konstanz, 1949), pp. 128–175.

56. Emil Dovifat, "Das publizistische Leben," in *Berlin und die Provinz Brandenburg im 19. und 20. Jahrhundert*, p. 763.

57. *Ibid.*, p. 765; Harry Pross, *Literatur und Politik* (Olten & Freiburg, 1963).

58. Peter de Mendelssohn, *Zeitungstadt Berlin* (Berlin, 1959), pp. 505–507; Walther Kiaulehn *op. cit.*, *passim.* Adele Gerhard, *Das Bild meines Lebens*, reprinted in Melitta Gerhard, *Adele Gerhard* (Bern, 1963), pp. 229ff.

59. Wilmont Haake, *Handbuch des Feuilletons*, 3 vols. (Emsdetten, 1951).

60. About Fontane as a theater critic see Roch, *op. cit.*, 178; Alfred Kerr, *Die Welt im Drama*, 5 vols. (Berlin, 1917).

61. R. A. Schroeder, *Berlin, Einst und Jetzt* (Berlin, 1954); Karl Scheffler, *Berlin, Ein Stadtschicksal*, (Berlin, 1910).

62. Tank, *op. cit.*, pp. 28, 101.

63. Friedrich Meinecke, *Erlebtes*, p. 111, "In ganz Deutschland ist um 1890 nicht nur politisch sondern auch geistig etwas Neues zu spüren, und zwar beides zueinander in umgekehrter Kurve. Politisch ging es abwärts, geistig wieder aufwärts."

64. Peter Gay, *Weimar Culture* (New York, 1968).

65. Dovifat, *op. cit.*, p. 764.

66. Wilmont Haake, *Julius Rodenberg und die Deutsche Rundschau* (Heidelberg, 1950).

67. *Ibid.*, p. 30.

68. *Ibid.*, p. 117.

69. *Ibid.*, p. 136.

70. Dovifat, *op. cit.*, p. 764.

71. Lange, *op. cit.*, p. 187.

72. Meinecke, *op. cit.*, p. 237.

73. Harry F. Young, *Maximilian Harden, Censor Germaniae* (The Hague, 1959), pp. 5–6; see also "Bibliographical Note," pp. 274–279.

74. Maximilian Harden, *Apostata* (Berlin, 1892).

75. *Ibid.*, p. 19.

76. Harden was the responsible editor of *Die Zukunft*. His most interesting contributions are more easily accessible today in *Köpfe*, 4 vols. (Berlin, 1911–1924) and *Krieg und Friede* (Berlin, 1918).

77. J. Kürschner, *Handbuch der Presse* (Leipzig, 1902), p. 1250; Harden in *Die Zukunft*, 57: 372.

78. To the best of my knowledge few historians have tried to answer the psychological riddle of Harden's personality. The novelist Jakob Wassermann, has given a portrait of Harden in his novel *Josepf Kerkhovens Dritte Existenz* (Amsterdam, 1934), p. 162. He calls Harden's innermost motive: "Der Wahn des Tribunen, der Wahn von papierener Unsterblichkeit."

79. *Die Zukunft*, March 10, 1900, p. 418; June 10, 1905, p. 387.

80. *Ibid.*, December 31, 1892, October 15, 1892.

81. Normann Rich & M. H. Fisher eds., *The Holstein Papers* (Cambridge, Eng. 1957–63); see especially vol. 4.

82. *Die Zukunft*, June 23, 1906, p. 444.

83. *Ibid.*, June 22, 1907.

84. Helmuth Rogge, *Holstein und Harden* (Munich, 1959), pp. 7–8; Young, *op. cit.*, pp. 90ff.

85. Quoted in Georg Kotowski, ed., *Das wilhelminische Deutschland* (Frankfurt, 1965), p. 63.

86. Lange, *op. cit.*, p. 347; Harden's own defense is reprinted in *Köpfe* 3: 411–506.

87. See *Die Zukunft* of November, 1908; all issues of this month discuss the crisis provoked by the Daily Telegraph Affair. Wilmont Haacke, *Die Politische Zeitschrift* (Stuttgart, 1968), pp. 236–247.

88. Wolfgang Sauer, "Das Problem des deutschen Nationalstaates" in H. U. Wehler, ed., *Moderne deutsche Sozialgeschichte* (Köln, 1966), p. 433; Kiaulehn, *op. cit.*, p. 516.

89. Schorske, *op. cit.*, p. 365; Alfred Bein, *Theodor Herzl* (Vienna, 1934).

90. Karl Kraus, *Maximilian Harden* (Vienna, n. d.); Kraus, *Maximilian Harden, Ein Nachruf* (sic) (Vienna, 1908).

91 Erich Mühsam, *Unpolitische Erinnerungen* (East Berlin, 1958), p. 65.

92. Karl Helfferich, *Deutscher Volkswohlstand, 1880–1913* (Berlin, 1914), is a highly optimistic appraisal of Germany's industrial potential before the outbreak of the war. See also Friedrich Paulsen, *Geschichte des gelehrten Unterrichts auf deutschen Schulen und Universitäten*, 2 vols. (Leipzig, 1919–1921); Paulsen, *Das deutsche Bildungswesen* (Leipzig, 1906).

93. *Das wilhelminische Deutschland*, pp. 140–141.

94. Wilhelm II, *Ereignisse und Gestalten* (Leipzig and Berlin, 1922), p. 164.

95. Georg Kotowski, "Bildungswesen," in *Berlin und die Provinz Brandenburg im 19. und 20. Jahrhundert*, pp. 522ff. The Prussian Ministry of Education still went by the old fashioned name of *Kultusministerium*, reminiscent of the sixteenth and seventeenth centuries.

96. Arnold Sachse, *Friedrich Althoff und sein Werk* (Berlin, 1928).

97. Meinecke, *op. cit.*, p. 147.

98. Sachse, *op. cit.*, pp. 282–283. Althoff's memorandum and the official correspondence about the foundation of the Kaiser Wilhelm's Institut are reprinted in *Idee und Wirklichkeit einer Universität, Dokumente zur Geschichte der Friedrich Wilhelms Universität* (Berlin, 1960), pp. 487–523.

99. Eduard Spranger, "Gedenkrede zur 150. Jahresfeier der Friedrich Wilhelms Universität," in Hans Rothfels, ed., *Berlin in Vergangenheit und Gegenwart*, p. 70.

100. About Harnack, see Adolf von Harnack, *Aus der Werkstatt des Vollendeten* (Giessen, 1930), p. 26; Dietrich Gerhard, "Adolf von Harnack," *Jahrbuch der Stiftung Preussischen Kulturbesitzes*, 3(1964):65.

101. M. J. Bonn, *So macht man Geschichte* (Munich, 1954), p. 327; Franz Eulenburg, *Die Handelshochschule zu Berlin* (Berlin, 1930); Erich Blunck, *Die technische Hochschule zu Berlin* (Berlin, 1925).

102. Spranger, *op. cit.*, pp. 70–71.

103. *Ibid.*

104. For the problems involved see Masur, *Prophets of Yesterday* (New York, 1961), pp. 159ff. and H. S. Hughes, *Consciousness and Society* (New York, 1958). The history of the university has been described in great detail by Max Lenz, *Geschichte der Friedrich Wilhelms Universität zu Berlin*, 4 vols. (Halle, 1910–1918); see also *Studium Berolinense*, 2 vols. (Berlin, 1960).

105. About Dilthey, see Masur, *op. cit.*

106. Carlo Antoni, *From History to Sociology*, trans. Hayden V. White (Detroit, 1959), pp. 32ff.

107. The expression is a pun: the name of the two professors of philosophy in Ber-

Notes

lin were Stumpf and Riehl, the German phrase for root and branch is "Stumpf und Stiel."

108. Quoted by Gerhard, *op. cit.*, p. 293.

109. Antoni, *op. cit.*, pp. 207ff.

110. Ranke's opus is extraordinary in scope and depth; see Gerhard Masur, *Rankes Begriff der Weltgeschichte* (Munich, 1926); Theodor von Laue, *Leopold Ranke, The Formative Years* (Princeton, 1950). Lately Ranke's *Diaries* have been published (Munich, 1964).

111. Georg Iggers, *The German Conception of History* (Middletown, Conn., 1968), pp. 63ff.

112. Eduard Fueter, *Geschichte der neueren Historiographie*, 2nd ed. (Munich, 1936), p. 492; about Sybel, see Fueter, p. 535 and Theodor Schieder, ed., *Hundert Jahr Historische Zeitschrift* (Munich, 1959), pp. 1–105.

113. Fueter, *op. cit.*, p. 539.

114. W. Bussmann, *Treitschke* (Göttingen, 1952) is still the best book on Treitschke. See also Mario Krammer, "Grosse Geschichtsschreiber im Leben Berlins," *Jahrbuch d. Vereins f. d Geschichte Berlins, 1953*, pp. 19–69.

115. H. H. Krill, *Die Rankerenaissance, Max Lenz und Erich Marcks* (Berlin, 1962).

116. See my article on Meinecke, in *International Encyclopaedia of the Social Sciences*, also R. Sterling, *Friedrich Meinecke, Ethics in a World of Power* (Princeton, 1958); and Iggers, *op. cit.*, pp. 90–123.

117. Alfred Heuss, *Theodor Mommsen und das 19. Jahrhundert* (Kiel, 1956); Albert Wucher, *Theodor Mommsen* (Göttingen, 1956); Lothar Wickert, *Theodor Mommsen*, 2 vols. (Frankfurt, 1959).

118. Quoted by Iggers, *op. cit.*, p. 123.

119. Ulrich von Wilamowitz Möllendorf, *Erinnerungen* (Leipzig, 1928); see also the detailed analysis by Werner Jaeger, "Die klassische Philologie an der Universität Berlin von 1870–1945," in *Studium Berolinense*, pp. 459–485.

120. *Ibid.*, p. 507. Ulrich Pretzel, "Ernst Troeltschs Berufung an die Berliner Universität."

121. This was the opinion of Otto Hintze, quoted by Iggers, *op. cit.*, p. 174.

122. Ernst Troeltsch, *Über die Masstäbe zur Beurteilung historischer Dinge* (Berlin, 1916); *Der Historismus und seine Probleme* (Tübingen, 1923).

123. Iggers, *op. cit.*, p. 189; Antoni, *op. cit.*, pp. 73ff.

124. Iggers, *op. cit.*, p. 194.

125. For the law faculty, see R. Smend, "Zur Geschichte der Berliner Juristenfakultät im 20. Jahrhundert," in *Studium Berolinense*, pp. 109ff.

126. Quoted by Annemarie Lange, *Berlin zur Zeit Bebels und Bismarcks* (East Berlin, 1959), pp. 302–303.

127. See the article in the *Encyclopaedia Britannica*, 1961 edition.

128. See the various articles on the medical faculty in *Studium Berolinense*, p. 209.

129. *Ibid.*, p. 223.

130. *Ibid.*, pp. 774–790: "Ernst Brüche, Aus der Berliner Elektronenphysik."

131. Masur, *Prophets of Yesterday*, pp. 252ff.

132. Iggers, *op. cit.*, p. 174.

133. Pflanze, *Bismarck and the Development of Germany*, p. 497.

134. Hans Herzfeld, "Nationalsozialismus und deutsche Universität," in *Universitätstage, 1966* (Berlin, 1966), p. 16.

[7] Berlin and the Arts

1. Literally, the Copper etching-cabinet.

2. Walther Kiaulehn, *Berlin, Schicksal einer Weltstadt* (Munich, 1958), pp. 313ff.

3. Wilhelm Bode, *Mein Leben*, 2 vols. (Berlin, 1930).

4. Kiaulehn, *op. cit.*, p. 326–327.

5. *Ibid.*, p. 320.

6. There is no basis for the doubts which Annemarie Lange, *Das Wilhelminische Berlin* (East Berlin, 1968), p. 510, has cast on Bode's integrity.

7. Werner Weissbach, *Und Alles ist zerstoben, Erinnerungen aus der Jahrhundertwende* (Wien, Leipzig, Zürich, 1937).

8. See the correspondence between Hugo von Hofmannsthal and Helene von Nostitz, *Briefwechsel* (Frankfurt, 1965), p. 8, about the reputation of the French impressionists in Germany.

9. Ernst Johann ed., *Reden des Kaisers* (Munich, 1966), p. 102 (my translation).

10. Barbara Tuchmann, *Proud Tower* (New York, 1966), p. 303. It should be noted, however, that the *Siegesallee* was not unanimously rejected by the public. Critics like Karl Scheffler expressed themselves in *Die Zukunft* without reservation against the idea and its execution. But even liberal journals, such as *Die Grenzboten*, praised the avenue as a "piece of luminous beauty." See *Das Wilhelminische Deutschland* (Frankfurt, 1965), p. 133.

11. Paul Seidel, *Der Kaiser und die Kunst* (Berlin, 1907), p. 86.

12. Not very far from the Kaiser Wilhelm Memorial Church stood the famous department store, *Das Kaufhaus des Westens*, which still functions today. The Berliners called the church *Das Taufhaus des Westens* (the baptistery of the West).

13. P. O. Rave, "Die bildende Kunst" in H. Herzfeld, ed., *Berlin und die Provinz Brandenburg im 19. & 20. Jahrhundert* (Berlin, 1968), p. 593; Rave, *Berlin in der Geschichte seiner Bauten* (Berlin, 1966).

14. Architektenverein zu Berlin, ed., *Berlin und seine Bauten*, 2 vols. (Berlin, 1896).

15. Fritz Stahl, *Ludwig Hofmann* (Berlin, 1914), p. 14.

16. R. Hamann and Jost Hermand, *Gründerzeit* (Berlin, 1965), p. 23; Werner Hegemann, *Das Steinerne Berlin* (Berlin, 1963), passim.

17. The name was taken from a magazine published in Munich called *Die Jugend*.

18. Henry van de Velde, *Geschichte meines Lebens* (Munich, 1962), Kiaulehn, *op. cit.*, p. 367.

19. Harry Graf Kessler, *Gesichter und Zeiten* (Berlin, 1935).

20. Ebenezer Howard, *Garden Cities of Tomorrow* (London, 1902), reprinted, 1965 by the M. I. T. Press; Kiaulehn, *op. cit.*, p. 371.

21. Herrmann Muthesius, *Architektonische Teilbetrachtungen* (Berlin, 1900); Muthesius, *Das Englische Haus* (Berlin, 1904–1905).

22. Herrmann Muthesius, *Kleinhaus und Kleinsiedlung* (Munich, 1918), p. 6.

23. Quoted by Alfred Neumeyer, *Die Kunst in unsrer Zeit* (Stuttgart, 1961), p. 20. My translation.

24. Rave, "Die Bildende Kunst," p. 593; Walther Behrendt, *Alfred Messel* (Berlin, 1911); Alfred Messel, *Der Wertheimbau* (Berlin, 1899).

Notes

25. Neumeyer, *op. cit.*, p. 22.

26. Hegemann, *op. cit.*, pp. 232, 258, 272.

27. A. Schinz, *Berlin, Städtebau und Stadtschicksal* (Braunschweig, 1964), pp. 224, 226.

28. *Ibid.*, p. 242.

29. In the speech, quoted above, at the inauguration of the *Siegesallee*.

30. Kiaulehn, *op. cit.*, p. 378.

31. Karl Blechen, *Leben, Würdigungen, Werk*, ed. P. O. Rave (Berlin, 1940); Hans Mackowski, *Häuser und Menschen im alten Berlin* (Berlin, 1923).

32. Rave, "Die bildende Kunst," p. 577.

33. The literature on Menzel is extensive, though little of it is in English. Karl Scheffler, *Adolph Menzel* (Munich, 1955); Ludwig Justi, "A. Menzel," in *Deutsche Zeichenkunst im 19. Jahrhundert* (Berlin, 1919); Irmgard Wirth, *Mit Adolph Menzel in Berlin* (Munich, 1965); Emil Waldmann, *Der Maler Adolph Menzel* (Vienna, 1914); Mackowski, *op. cit.*

34. I have tried to show elsewhere why monumental paintings in the nineteenth century had become an anachronism. See *Prophets of Yesterday* (New York, 1961), p. 227.

35. Max Liebermann, *Gesammelte Schriften* (Berlin, 1921), p. 122.

36. Masur, *op. cit.*, p. 229; John Rewald, *The History of Impressionism* (New York, 1946); about Liebermann, see especially Karl Scheffler, *Max Liebermann* (Wiesbaden, 1953); and Liebermann's *Gesammelte Schriften* (Berlin, 1921), pp. 3–12.

37. Lovis Corinth, *Das Leben Walter Leistikows* (Berlin, 1910), p. 54. Corinth gives also a very illuminating description of the Munch exhibition of 1892. In 1908, the *Berliner Lokalanzeiger* asked a number of artists about the future of the arts in Berlin. Leistikow's very pessimistic answer is reprinted in *Jahrbuch des Vereins für die Geschichte Berlins*, 1953, p. 140.

38. E. Waldmann, *Die Kunst des Realismus und des Impressionismus im 19. Jahrhundert* (Berlin, 1930), p. 115.

39. Käte Kollwitz, *Ich will wirken in dieser Zeit*, ed. Hans Kollwitz (Frankfurt, n. d.).

40. Kiaulehn, *op. cit.*, p. 310.

41. Tilla Durieux, *Eine Tür steht offen, Erinnerungen* (Berlin, 1965); Werner Doede, *Berlin: Kunst und Künstler* (Recklinghausen, 1961).

42. See the article by Hugo von Hofmannsthal on van Gogh, *Ausgewählte Werke* (Frankfurt, 1957), 2: 494.

43. James Huneker, "Max Liebermann and some phases of German Art," in *Ivory Apes and Peacocks* (New York, 1917), p. 173. Huneker's article must have been written around 1912.

44. *Ibid.*, p. 188.

45. Hans Ostwald and Hans Zille eds., *Zilles Hausschatz* (Berlin, 1937).

46. Masur, *op. cit.*, p. 230.

47. The term *expressionism* was probably coined in France by Hervé for such artists as van Gogh and Matisse. It is a matter of controversy as to who introduced it in Germany. Some say the art historian Worringer; see W. H. Sokel, *Anthology of the German Expressionist Drama, A Prelude to the Absurd* (New York, 1963), p. ix. However, Fritz Redlich, "German Literary Expressionism and Its Publishers," *Harvard Library Bulletin*, 18, No. 2(1969): 143, gives a different version.

48. Fritz Stern, *The Politics of Cultural Despair* (New York, 1965), p. 177.

49. Peter Selz, *German Expressionist Painting* (Berkeley, 1957), pp. 10, 13.

50. *Ibid.*, p. 84.

51. *The Blue Rider* was a book published by Kandinski and Franz Marc in 1910; see Bernard Myers, *The German Expressionists* (New York, 1956).

52. Paul Fechter, *An der Wendezeit* (Gütersloh, 1950); Selz, *op. cit.*, p. 13.

53. Selz, *op. cit.*, p. 252; Lothar Günther Buchheim, *Die Künstlergemeinschaft Brücke* (Feldafing, 1956), p. 36. Herwart Walden's real name was Georg Levin; see Redlich, *op. cit.*, p. 147. The title *Der Sturm* was invented by Walden's first wife, Else Lasker-Schüler, a fine poet in her own right.

54. Neil Walden and Lothar Schreyer, *Der Sturm* (Baden–Baden, 1950), p. 26. "Kunst ist Gabe und nicht Wiedergabe . . . Der Maler malt, was er schaut mit seinen innersten Sinnen . . . jeder Eindruck von Aussen wird der Ausdruck von innen."

55. Selz, *op. cit.*, pp. 81–82, 88.

56. *Ibid.*, p. 69.

57. See E. L. Kirchner, "Art vs. Life," *New York Times*, April 6, 1969.

58. The German expression is "er hat seinen Mantel nach dem Wind gehängt," meaning: he is a weathervane. Of Justi it was said, "er hat seinen Mantel nach dem Sturm gehängt." See also Selz, *op. cit.*, p. 119.

59. Buchheim, *op. cit.*, p. 36.

60. Neumeyer, *op. cit.*, pp. 662–663.

61. Ernst Barlach, *Selbsterzähltes Leben* (Berlin, 1928); C. D. Carl, *Ernst Barlach* (Berlin, 1928).

62. Gottfried Benn, *Gedichte* (Wiesbaden, 1963), pp. 356, 372, 384; Kasimir Edschmid, "über den dichterischen Expressionismus," quoted in Walther Killy, *Deutsches Lesebuch*, 4 vols. (Frankfurt, 1958), 4: 151–153.

63. Georg Heym, *Dichtungen* (Munich, 1922), see especially the poem: "Der Krieg."

64. Curt Sachs, *Musikgeschichte der Stadt Berlin bis zum Jahre 1800* (Berlin, 1900); Adolf Weissmann, *Berlin als Musikstadt von 1740–1911* (Berlin, 1911); Werner Bollert, "Musikleben," in Hans Herzfeld, ed., *Berlin und die Provinz Brandenburg im 19. und 20. Jahrhundert* (Berlin, 1968), p. 605.

65. Georg Schünemann, *Die Singakademie zu Berlin*, 1791–1941, (Regensburg, 1941).

66. Bollert, *op. cit.*, p. 633; J. Kastan, *Berlin Wie Es War* (Berlin, 1919); Siegfried Ochs, *Gesehenes und Geschehenes* (Leipzig, 1922). S. Ochs was the conductor of the Singakademie–choir in the Wilhelminian period.

67. Bollert, *op. cit.*, p. 652.

68. Gerhart Hauptmann, *Das Abenteuer meiner Jugend*, quoted in Ruth Glatzer, *Berliner Leben* (East Berlin, 1963), p. 233.

69. Richard Strauss, *Betrachtungen und Erinnerungen* (Zürich–Freiburg, 1957), pp. 187, 224–238.

70. Glatzer, *op. cit.*, p. 240; see also Marie von Bülow, *Hans von Bülow, Ausgewählte Briefe* (Leipzig, 1919); Friedrich Herzfeld, ed. *Die Berliner Philharmoniker* (Berlin, 1960).

71. Bollert, *op. cit.*, p. 642.

72. Helene von Hülsen, *Unter Zwei Königen* (Berlin, 1889).

73. Bollert, *op. cit.*, p. 609.

74. *Ibid.*, p. 608.

75. Carl Fürstenberg, *Die Lebensgeschichte eines deutschen Bankiers* (Berlin, 1931).

76. Tuchmann, *op. cit.*, p. 301.

Notes

77. About the collaboration between Strauss and Hofmannsthal, see their *Briefwechsel* (Zürich, 1954). I have dealt with the artistic problems involved in an article on Hofmannsthal's *Arabella*, in *American German Review*, 22, No. 6(1954): 24ff.

78. Quoted in Tuchmann, *op. cit.*, p. 313.

79. *Ibid.*, p. 324.

80. See, Hofmannsthal's correspondence with Richard Strauss, *op. cit.*, pp. 95–135.

81. Ernst Krause, *Richard Strauss, Gestalt und Werk* (Leipzig, 1955), pp. 51–52.

82. See Strauss' letter to Ernst von Schuch, quoted in Krause, *op. cit.*, pp. 54–55. Hofmannsthal refused to yield to Hülsen's wishes.

83. Bollert, *op. cit.*, p. 621.

84. The best evaluation of the operetta and the lighter forms of entertainment is to be found in Kiaulehn, *op. cit.*, pp. 235ff. He quotes some of the popular songs which captured the imagination of the Berliners. They have, of course, a value as sociological documents of the period. See also Lange, *op. cit.*, pp. 538ff. A detailed study of the operetta and the *Posse* would be a rewarding subject.

85. Gerhard Wahnrau, *Berlin, Stadt der Theater, Der Chronik erster Teil* (Berlin, 1957); E. Catholy, "Berlin als Theaterstadt" in H. Rothfels ed., *Berlin in Vergangenheit und Gegenwart* (Tübingen, 1961); Hans Knudsen, *Deutsche Theatergeschichte* (Stuttgart, 1959); Knudsen, "Theater," in *Berlin und die Provinz Brandenburg im 19. and 20. Jahrhundert*, pp. 785ff.; Helene von Hülsen, *Unter zwei Königen, Botho von Hülsen* (Berlin, 1889). The critic, Paul Schlenther, published a pamphlet against Hülsen: *Botho von Hülsen und seine Leute* (Berlin, 1883).

86. Oscar Wilde, *The Soul of Man under Socialism* (London, 1904), p. 47.

87. Max Grube, *Geschichte der Meininger* (Berlin and Leipzig, 1926).

88. See R. Glatzer, *op. cit.*, pp. 107–109.

89. S. Jacobsohn, *Das Theater der Reichshauptstadt* (Munich, 1904), pp. 93–94.

90. Otto Brahm, *Kritische Schriften über Drama und Theater*, ed. Paul Schlenther (Berlin, 1913); Catholy, *op. cit.*, p. 53.

91. Paul Schlenther, *Wozu der Lärm, Genesis der Freien Bühne* (Berlin, 1889); A. Irene Miller, *The Independent Theater in Europe, 1887 to the Present* (New York, 1931), pp. 11–112.

92. Brahm, *op. cit.*, p. 30. These words were written for a new journal *Freie Bühne für modernes Leben*, in 1890.

93. There are many descriptions of this famous first night. See A. von Hanstein, *Das Jüngste Deutschland* (Leipzig, 1905), pp. 172–173; also F. Born, "Vorhang auf für eine Premiere," *Der Tagesspiegel*, February 6, 1966.

94. Eduard von Winterstein, *Mein Leben und meine Zeit*, 2 vols. (Berlin, 1947), 2: 33.

95. *Ibid.*, pp. 32–33.

96. Georg Lukàcs, *Beiträge zur Geschichte der Ästhetic* (Berlin, 1954), p. 5.

97. George Lichtheim, *Marxism* 2nd ed. (New York, 1965) pp. 395ff.

98. Gerhart A. Ritter, *Die Arbeiterbewegung im wilhelminischen Reich* (Berlin, 1959), pp. 223ff.

99. Heinz Selo, *Die Freie Volksbühne in Berlin* (doctoral dissertation) (Erlangen, 1930); S. Nestriepke, *Geschichte der Volksbühne, 1890–1914* (Berlin, 1930); Julius Bab, *Wesen und Weg der Berliner Volksbühnenbewegung* (Berlin, n. d.); Ritter, *op. cit.*, pp. 224–225.

100. Ritter, *op. cit.*, p. 224.

101. Selo, *op. cit.*, p. 9. Selo gives a moving quotation from the anarchist Gustav

Landauer, written in 1905, about the loss of enthusiasm among the leaders of the party for the people's stage movement.

102. Maxim Newark, *Otto Brahm, the Man and the Critic* (Kenosha, Wisconsin, 1937), p. 134.

103. H. H. Houber, *Verbotene Literatur*, 2 vols. (Dessau and Bremen, 1925–1928); Oscar Blumenthal, *Verbotene Stücke* (Berlin, n. d.), p. 7. The insolence of the remark of the chief of police is difficult to render in English, because he used Berlin argot.

104. Houber, *op. cit.*, 1: 352.

105. *Reden des Kaisers* (Munich, 1966), p. 78.

106. Winterstein, *op. cit.*, 2: 7. A very good impression of what Brahm and Reinhardt meant for actors outside of the empire can be found in Fritz Kortner, *Aller Tage Abend* (Munich, 1959), p. 73.

107. The literature about Max Reinhardt is copious but of uneven value. Only a small selection can be quoted here. G. Adler, *Max Reinhardt* (Salzburg, 1964); B. Fleischmann, *Max Reinhardt* (Wien, 1964); Franz Horch, *Die Spielpläne Max Reinhardts* (Munich, 1931); Max Reinhardt, *Ausgewählte Briefe, Reden und Schriften* (Wien, 1963); E. Stern and Heinz Herald, *Reinhardt und seine Bühne*, (Berlin, 1919); Oliver Sayler, *Max Reinhardt and his Theater* (New York, 1924); Huntly Crater, *The Theater of Max Reinhardt* (New York, 1914).

108. Sayler, *op. cit.*, pp. 346ff.

109. Hofmannsthal has written a number of essays on Max Reinhardt. See *Gesammelte Werke*, ed. H. Steiner (Frankfurt, 1959), pp. 316ff.

110. Reinhardt, *op. cit.*, p. 89.

111. Herbert Ihering, *Der Volksbühnenverrat* (Berlin, n. d.) p. 4.

112. Gustav Hillard, *Herren und Narren der Welt* (Munich, 1954), p. 247.

113. Kiaulehn, *op. cit.*, p. 446.

114. Hillard, *op. cit.*, p. 244. Hillard was a friend of the crown prince and joined the management of the Deutsche Theater after the end of the World War I.

[8] War and Revolution

1. Erwin Stein, ed., *Berlin* (Oldenburg, 1914); see especially the article "Das Finanz- und Steuerwesen," pp. 29–40. A good synopsis, based on statistical material, can be found in Dieter Petzina, "Materialien zum sozialen und wirtschaftlichen Wandel in Deutschland seit dem Ende des neunzehnten Jahrhunderts," *Vierteljahrsschrift f. Zeitgeschichte*, 3(1969): 528–538.

2. "Das höhere Schulwesen der Stadt Berlin," in Stein, *op. cit.*

3. *Ibid.*, p. 115.

4. "Die städtischen Krankenhäuser," *ibid.*, p. 58.

5. There were 5,598 paid municipal employees and about 25,000 honorary officials, not counting the teachers who numbered some 8,000, "Die Beamtenorganization," *ibid.*, p. 182.

6. See the statistics given by Peter Czada, *Die Berliner Elektroindustrie in der Weimarer Zeit* (Berlin, 1969), p. 55. He states that in 1918, 458,410 persons were employed in establishments of more than twenty-five people.

7. Werner Pölz, *Sozialistenfrage und Revolutionsfurcht* (Lübeck, 1960).

8. William Carr, *A History of Germany* (New York, 1969), p. 190; J. A. Nichols, *Germany after Bismarck* (Cambridge, Mass., 1958).

Notes

9. Michael Balfour, *The Kaiser and His Times* (London, 1964), p. 170.

10. Robert Zedlitz Trütchler, *Zwölf Jahre am deutschen Kaiserhofe* (Berlin and Leipzig, 1924), p. 201: "Die Verfassung habe ich nie gelesen und kenne sie nicht."

11. Carr, *op. cit.*, p. 199. About the *Zentralverein deutscher Industrieller*, see the recent study of Hartmut Kaelble, *Industrielle Interessenpolitik in der wilhelminischen Gesellschaft, Zentralverband deutscher Industrieller, 1895–1914* (Berlin, 1967); Hans–Jürgen Puhle, *Agrarische Interessenpolitik und preussischer Konservatismus im wilhelminischen Reich* (Hanover, 1966).

12. Klaus Epstein, *Matthias Erzberger und das Dilemma der deutschen Demokratie* (Berlin, 1962). I have used the German edition which was revised and enlarged by Epstein.

13. Balfour, *op. cit.*, pp. 333–334.

14. Eckhart Kehr, *Schlachtflottenbau und Parteipolitik* (Berlin, 1930); Kehr, *Der Primat der Innenpolitik*, ed. H. U. Wehner (Berlin, 1965).

15. Carr, *op. cit.*, p. 203; Walter Hubbatsch, *Der Admiralstab und die obersten Marinebehörden in Deutschland, 1884–1945* (Frankfurt, 1958).

16. Gerhard Ritter, *Staatskunst und Kriegshandwerk*, 3 vols. (Munich, 1959–1963); see especially, vol. 2, chapters 1–2.

17. I am aware that this is a controversial topic about which a large body of literature exists.

18. Carr, *op. cit.*, p. 221.

19. Balfour, *op. cit.*, p. 322.

20. Peter Gay, *The Dilemma of Democratic Socialism* (New York, 1952).

21. Eduard Bernstein, *Die Voraussetzungen des Sozialismus und die Aufgaben der Sozialdemokratie* (Stuttgart, 1899).

22. The best discussion of this problem is now to be found in J. P. Nettl, *Rosa Luxemburg*, 2 vols. (London, 1966), 1: 22.

23. Nettl, *op. cit.*, 2: 521.

24. Richard Müller, *Vom Kaiserreich zur Republik*, 2 vols. (Wien, 1924), 1: 24.

25. Carr, *op. cit.*, p. 212.

26. Two schools of thought have emerged from this controversy. Fritz Fischer, *Der Griff nach der Weltmacht*, 3d ed. (Düsseldorf, 1964), and, following him, his students attribute to the German government definite plans to obtain world power. Ritter, *op. cit.*, 3: 17, calls the policy of Bethmann–Hollweg "defensive." It would seem that the truth lies somewhere in between the two extreme positions. The German Foreign Office and even more the German General Staff were deeply concerned about the deterioration of Germany's international posture. They foresaw the day when Russia's might would surpass the combined German–Austrian forces at the eastern frontier. In addition, they were the prisoners of their own planning among which the famous Schlieffen-plan occupied first place. No other alternative was envisaged. In the light of these considerations, 1914 was thought to be propitious for the execution of their planning. As Bethmann–Hollweg expressed it, "If war must break out, better now than in one or two years time when the Entente will be stronger."

27. Egmont Zechlin, "Bethmann–Hollweg, Kriegsrisiko und S. P. D. 1914," *Der Monat*, No. 208 (January 1966), pp. 17ff; Zechlin, "Motive und Taktik der Reichsleitung 1914," *Der Monat*, No. 209 (February 1966), pp. 91ff.

28. Müller, *op. cit.*, 1: 27.

29. Already in 1909, a Dr. Renvers had diagnosed the mental conditions of the Kaiser as pseudologia phantastica. See Balfour, *op. cit.*, p. 297.

30. Even Bethmann-Hollweg, who should have known better, succumbed to the widespread psychosis, as his famous memorandum of September 9, 1914, reveals. See Ritter, *op. cit.*, 3: 41.

31. See the article by Hans Delbrück in the *Preussische Jahrbücher* of September, 1914, quoted by Müller, *op. cit.*, 1: 29.

32. Nettl, *op. cit.*, 2: 601.

33. Philip Scheidemann, *Der Zusammenbruch* (Berlin, 1921), p. 7.

34. A. J. Ryder, *The German Revolution* (Cambridge, 1967), p. 43.

35. There is a wealth of literature on this subject. I offer only a few titles. Carl Schorske, *German Social-Democracy 1905–1917* (Cambridge, Mass., 1955); Arthur Rosenberg, *The Birth of the German Republic* (London, 1931); Hermann Heidegger, *Die deutsche Sozialdemokratie und der nationale Staat* (Göttingen, 1956); from a strictly Marxian viewpoint, Jürgen Kuczynski, *Der Ausbruch des ersten Weltkriegs und die deutsche Sozialdemokratie* (Berlin, 1957); A. Lange, *Das wilhelminische Deutschland* (Berlin, 1967).

36. Georg Kotowski, Werner Pöls, Gerhard A. Ritter, eds., *Das wilhelminische Deutschland* (Frankfurt am Main, 1965), pp. 144–149.

37. Ernst von Wrisberg, *Wehr und Waffen, 1914–1918* (Leipzig, 1932); Gerald Feldmann, *Army, Industry and Labor in Germany, 1914–1918* (Princeton, 1966), p. 31. The deputy commanding general was charged with this duty, since the commanding general was with his corps at the battle front.

38. The speaker was Scheidemann, quoted by Ryder, *op. cit.*, p. 47.

39. Feldmann, *op. cit.*, p. 6.

40. Fritz Redlich, "German Planning for War and Peace," *Review of Politics*, 6 (July 1944): 319; see also Ernst Schulin, "Walther Rathenau," *Der Monat*, June 1968, p. 45. Schulin calls this Rathenau's "geschichtlich bedeutendste Tat."

41. The *Kriegsrohstoffamt* delegated the task of supplying the industry with raw material to several nonprofit companies whose duty it was to sequester existing raw material and to allocate it to the manufacturers engaged in war production. About the opposition to Rathenau, see Bernhard Guttmann, *Schattenriss einer Generation* (Stuttgart, 1950), p. 252, and Lange, *op. cit.*, p. 655.

42. Carr, *op. cit.*, p. 252.

43. Ritter, *op. cit.*, 3: 55, 59.

44. Otto Hamann, *Bilder aus der letzten Kaiserzeit* (Berlin, n. d.), p. 128. The quoted sentence was one of the marginal remarks which the Kaiser liked to write in imitation of Frederick the Great. In this instance it was a comment about an article in the *Frankfurter Allgemeine Zeitung*.

45. Georg Alexander von Müller, *Regierte der Kaiser?*, ed. Walter Görlitzer (Göttingen, 1959), p. 177.

46. Ritter, *op. cit.*, 3: 587.

47. *Ibid.*, p. 23.

48. R. Müller, *op. cit.*, 1: 167.

49. Nettl, *op. cit.*, 2: 167.

50. Fischer, *op. cit.*, pp. 105–131; H. Gatzke, *Germany's Drive to the West* (Baltimore, 1950).

51. Balfour, *op. cit.*, p. 366.

52. Quoted by Feldmann, *op. cit.*, p. 28.

53. *Ibid.*

54. R. Sichler and J. Tiburtius, *Die Arbeiterfrage, eine Kernfrage des Weltkrieges* (Berlin, 1925).

Notes

55. Feldmann, *op. cit.*, passim.
56. Feldmann, *op. cit.*, pp. 76–77.
57. Müller, *op. cit.*, 1: 56.
58. Lange, *op. cit.*, p. 656.
59. *Ibid.*, p. 659.
60. Clemens von Delbrück, *Die wirtschaftliche Mobilmachung in Deutschland 1914* (Munich, 1924), p. 94; Delbrück was vice-chancellor in the imperial cabinet in 1914.
61. August Skalweit und Hans Krüger, *Die Ernährungswirtschaft der grossen Städte im Weltkriege* (Berlin, 1917); August Skalweit, *Die deutsche Kriegsernährungswirtschaft* (Stuttgart, 1927), one of the few comprehensive studies of a very important but very elusive subject.
62. Skalweit, *op. cit.*, p. 200; Lange, *op. cit.*, p. 667; *Das Wilhelminische Deutschland*, p. 153.
63. Ryder, *op. cit.*, pp. 67–69; Albert Grzesinski, *Inside Germany* (New York, 1939), p. 40.
64. Ritter, *op. cit.*, 3: 253; see also Hans Herzfeld, *Der Erste Weltkrieg* (Munich, 1968), passim.
65. Feldmann, *op. cit.*, p. 118.
66. *Ibid.*
67. *Ibid.*, p. 119.
68. Müller, *op. cit.*, 1: 71.
69. Nettl, *op. cit.*, 2:639–641.
70. Feldmann, *op. cit.*, p. 162.
71. The author of this stilted phrase was Wichard von Moellendorff. See Feldmann, *op. cit.*, p. 171. For the functions of the newly created office, see Wilhelm Groener, *Lebenserinnerungen* (Göttingen, 1957).
72. R. H. Lutz, *The Fall of the German Empire*, 2 vols. (Stanford, 1932), 2: 99–103.
73. See the long debates in *Stenographische Berichte der Verhandlungen des . . . Reichstages* (Berlin, 1916), 308: 2156ff.
74. Feldmann, *op. cit.*, p. 306.
75. As does Lange, *op. cit.*, p. 670 for propaganda purposes.
76. Müller, *op. cit.*, 1: 76.
77. A case in point is the potato shortage. It has been estimated that of an average crop of twenty-three million tons, six million never reached the market. The farmers preferred to use them as fodder for the pigs, since meat commanded a higher price.
78. Skalweit, *op. cit.*, pp. 240–246.
79. Müller, *op. cit.*, 1: 78–79.
80. Feldmann, *op. cit.*, pp. 339–340.
81. Reinhard Göring, *Seeschlacht* (Berlin, 1917); Fritz von Unruh, *Das Geschlecht* (Munich, 1917); for an evaluation of both works see R. Samuel and R. H. Thomas, *Expressionism in German Life, Literature and the Theatre, 1910–1924* (Cambridge, Eng., 1939), pp. 48–53.
82. Th. von Bethmann-Hollweg, *Betrachtungen zum Weltkrieg*, 2 vols. (Berlin, 1919–1921), 2: 35.
83. E. Matthias and R. Morsey, *Der Interfraktionelle Ausschuss, 1917–18* (Düsseldorf, 1959), p. 20.
84. Ritter, *op. cit.*, 3: 545.
85. Matthias and Morsey, *op. cit.*, p. 18.

86. *Ibid.*, p. 21.

87. Epstein, *op. cit.*, pp. 206–228. The motives for Erzberger's change of attitude are rather complex and do not concern our study.

88. *Ibid.*, p. 207.

89. Matthias and Morsey, *op. cit.*, p. 11.

90. About the July crisis and the events which led to Bethmann's downfall, see Epstein, *op. cit.*, p. 215.

91. Ritter, *op. cit.*, 3: 551–584.

92. Feldmann, *op. cit.*, p. 456; Ernst Fränkel, *Deutschland und die westlichen Demokratien* (Stuttgart, Berlin, 1968), pp. 11–28.

93. The appeal was first published in *Preussische Jahrbücher*, vol. 196 (1917), and reprinted in Friedrich Meinecke, *Politische Schriften*, ed. G. Kotowski (Darmstadt, 1958), p. 194.

94. Fischer, *op. cit.*, pp. 437, 454.

95. J. M. Wheeler Bennett, *The Forgotten Peace, Brest Litovsk, March 1918* (New York, 1938); Richard von Kühlmann, *Erinnerungen* (Heidelberg, 1948), pp. 518–550.

96. Balfour, *op. cit.*, p. 390; Carr, *op. cit.*, p. 265.

97. Karl Kraus, *Die letzten Tage der Menschheit* (Munich, 1957), p. 9.

98. Hugo von Hofmannsthal and R. Borchardt, *Briefwechsel*, ed. H. Steiner (Frankfurt, 1954), p. 129; Borchardt occupied at that time a minor position in the German general staff.

99. Reprinted in Müller, *op. cit.*, 1: 194.

100. *Ibid.*, pp. 102, 202.

101. See the minutes of the meetings of the unions in *Beschlüsse d. Konferenz von Vertretern der Zentralsverbandsvorstände* (Berlin, 1919), pp. 82ff.

102. Ryder, *op. cit.*, p. 117.

103. Ernst Drahm and Susanne Leonhard, *Unterirdische Literatur im revolutionären Deutschland* (Berlin—Fichtenau, 1920).

104. Prince Max von Baden, *Memoirs*, 2 vols. (London, 1928), 1: 362ff.

105. Friedrich Ebert, *Schriften, Aufzeichnungen und Reden*, 2 vols. (Dresden, 1926), 2: 90–91.

106. Balfour, *op. cit.*, pp. 401–402.

107. Nettl, *op. cit.*, 2: 709.

108. *Ibid.*, p. 710.

109. Gustav Noske, *Von Kiel bis Kapp* (Berlin, 1920), pp. 17–27; Ryder, *op. cit.*, pp. 140ff.

110. Müller, *op. cit.*, 2: 51–58.

111. Ryder, *op. cit.*, p. 151.

112. Müller, *op. cit.*, 2: 16.

113. Nettl, *op cit.*, 2: 711; Ryder, *op cit.*, p. 160; Eduard Bernstein, *Die deutsche Revolution* (Berlin, 1921); Emil Barth, *Aus der Werkstatt der deutschen Revolution* (Berlin, n. d.).

114. Philip Scheidemann, *The Making of a New Germany*, 2 vols. (New York, 1929), 2: 261–262.

115. E. O. Volkmann, *Der Marxismus und das deutsche Heer im Weltkriege* (Berlin, 1925), p. 315; Ryder, *op. cit.*, p. 160.

116. E. O. Volkmann, *Revolution über Deutschland* (Oldenburg, 1930), p. 54.

117. Nettl. *op. cit.*, 2: 712.

118. *Ibid.*

Notes

119. Epstein, *op. cit.*, p. 316.
120. Nettl, *op. cit.*, 2: 756.
121. Richard Müller, one of the leaders of the revolutionary shop stewards, made the famous statement, "Nur über meine Leiche geht der Weg zur Nationalversammlung." Though he did not live up to his promise, he left us one of the most valuable accounts of these crucial months in Berlin.
122. Lange, *op. cit.*, p. 802.
123. Ryder, *op. cit.*, pp. 173–177.
124. Groener, *Lebenserinnerungen*, p. 475; Ryder, *op. cit.*, p. 186.
125. Ryder, *op. cit.*, p. 187.
126. Nettl, *op. cit.*, 2: 750.
127. *Ibid.*, p. 751.
128. It was the dismissal of Eichhorn, a member of the USPD, from his post as president of the police force and his replacement by a reliable member of the SPD which triggered the January riots.
129. Franz Schade, *Kurt Eisner und die Bayrische Sozialdemokratie* (Hanover, 1961); Müller, *op. cit.*, 2: 240–244.
130. G. A. Craig, *The Politics of the Prussian Army* (New York, 1955); F. L. Carsten, *The Reichwehr and Politics* (Oxford, 1967).
131. Meinecke, *Erlebtes*, p. 345.
132. Quoted by Ryder, *op. cit.*, p. 217.
133. About this famous meeting, see Feldmann, *op. cit.*, p. 533; for the far-reaching implications; see also K. Bracher, Wolfgang Sauer, and G. Schulz, *Die Nationalsozialistische Machtergreifung* (Köln–Opladen, 1962).
134. Wolfgang Sauer, "National Socialism: Totalitarianism or Fascism?" *American Historical Review*, 73, No. 1 (1967): 404–424.
135. This idea is strongly expressed in Eberhard Kolb, *Die Arbeiterräte in der deutschen Innenpolitik* (Düsseldorf, 1962); Ryder, *op. cit.*, seems to agree with Kolb. I have grave doubts about the feasibility of using the councils of soldiers and workers in any constructive way in the Germany of 1919. See also Frauke Bey Heard, *Hauptstadt und Staatsumwälzung, Berlin, 1919* (Stuttgart, 1969), p. 7.
136. Peter Gay, *Weimar Culture* (New York, 1968).
137. R. Samuel and R. H. Thomas, *op. cit.*, p. 1; see also Carl Zuckmayer's recent autobiography, *Als Wärs ein Stück von Mir* (Frankfurt, 1967), p. 311: "Diese Stadt [Berlin] frass Talente und Energien mit beispiellosem Heisshunger . . . Wer Berlin hatte, dem gehörte die Welt."
138. Hans Herzfeld, *Nationalsozialismus und deutsche Universität, in Universitätstage 1966* (Berlin, 1966).
139. See the *Memoirs* of Hitler's architect Albert Speer, which were serialized in *Die Welt* beginning August 23, 1969. They are now also available in book form.

BIBLIOGRAPHICAL NOTE

The historian of imperial Berlin who would like to offer his readers a bibliographical guide is faced with an embarrassment of riches. A complete list of all the titles bearing on his subject would make his volume top-heavy. Fortunately, students of Berlin can be referred to a comprehensive bibliography (1,012 pages) which includes all the material published prior to 1960: Bearbeitet von Hans Zopf u. Gerd Heinrich, *Berlin-Bibliographie (bis 1960)* (Berlin 1965).

The scholar who plans to explore special aspects of the capital's history should turn first to this imposing volume. My own list can, therefore, be asembled on a shorter and more selective basis. In the present table I do not include all the sources I have consulted, not even some of the material used in the notes. The notes and the bibliography must consequently be considered complementary and should be consulted with this in mind.

In order to avoid qualifying adjectives, I have starred those books which have been most useful to me in my work.

Achterberg, Erich. *Berliner Hochfinanz, Kaiser, Fürsten und Millionäre um 1900.* Frankfurt, 1966.
————. "Berliner Banken im Wandel der Zeiten." In *Festschrift zum 75 jährigen Bestehen des Bankhauses Hardy & Co.* Frankfurt, Berlin, 1954.
————. *Rudolf Virchow.* Stuttgart, 1957.
Adam, Lotte. *Geschichte der täglichen Rundschau.* Berlin, 1934.
Adlon, Hedda. *Hotel Adlon.* Munich, 1961.
Altmann, Wilhelm. *Chronik des Berliner Philharmonischen Orchesters, 1882–1901.* Berlin, 1902.
Apt, Max. *25 Jahre im Dienste der Berliner kaufmannschaft.* Berlin, 1927.
Archiv d. "Brandenburgia." *Gesellschaft f. Heimatkunde d. Provinz Brandenburg zu Berlin.* vols. 1–13. Berlin, 1894–1911.
Arendt, Max, ed. *Geschichte der Stadt Berlin.* Berlin, 1937.
Baedekers Berlin. Freiburg, 1964.
Balfour, Michael. *The Kaiser and His Times.* London, 1965.*

Bamberger, Georg. *Anno Tobak, Allerlei Ernstes und Heiteres aus dem alten Berlin.* Berlin, 1930.

Barkeley, R. *Die Kaiserin Friedrich.* Dortrecht, 1959.

Benjamin Walter. *Berliner Kindheit um Neunzehnhundert.* Frankfurt, 1950.

Bericht über die Verwaltung (1861–1911: *Gemeindeverwaltung) der Stadt Berlin.* Verein Berliner Kaufleute und Industrieller eds. *Berlins Aufstieg zur Weltstadt.* Berlin, 1929.

Bernhard, Georg. *Berliner Banken.* Berlin, 1905.

——. *Meister und Dilettanten am Kapitalismus im Reiche der Hohenzollern.* Amsterdam, 1936.

Bernhard, Ludwig. *Der Hugenberg Konzern.* Berlin, 1928.

Bernstein, Eduard. *Die Geschichte der Berliner Arbeiterbewegung.* 3 vols. Berlin, 1907–1910.*

Block, Paul. *Der verwandelte Bürger, Berlin vom Kriegsausbruch bis zur Revolution.* Zürich, 1919.

Blunck, Erich. *Die technische Hochschule zu Berlin.* Berlin, 1925.

Böckh, Richard. *Die Bewegung der Bevölkerung der Stadt Berlin in den Jahren 1869–1878.* Berlin, 1884.

Bode, Wilhelm. *Mein Leben.* 2 vols. Berlin, 1930.

Boehlich, Walter. *Der Berliner Antisemitismusstreit.* Frankfurt, 1965.

Boettcher, Helmuth Maximilian. *Walter Rathenau.* Bonn, 1958.

Bornhak, Conrad. *Geschichte des preussischen Verwaltungsrechtes.* 3 vols. Berlin, 1884–1886.

——. *Im Neuen Reich, Geschichte von 1871–1890.* Leipzig, 1924.

——. *Deutsche Geschichte unter Kaiser Wilhelm II.* Leipzig, 1922.

Brahm, Otto. *Kritische Schriften über Drama und Theater.* Edited by Paul Schlenther. Berlin, 1913.*

Buchholz, Arend. *Die Volksbibliotheken und Lesehallen der Stadt Berlin, 1850–1900.* Berlin, 1900.

——. *Die vossische Zeitung.* Berlin, 1904.

Bunsen, Marie von. *Die Welt, in der ich lebte.* Leipzig, 1929.*

——. *Zeitgenossen, die ich erlebte,* 1900–1930. Leipzig, 1932.

Clausewitz, Paul. *Die Städteordnung von 1808 und die Stadt Berlin.* Berlin, 1908.*

——. *Die Pläne von Berlin und die Entwicklung des Weichbildes.* Berlin, 1906.

Corinth, Lovis. *Das Leben Walter Leistikows, Ein Stück Berliner Kulturgeschichte.* Berlin, 1910.*

Craig, Gordon A. *The Politics of the Prussian Army, 1640–1945.* New York, 1956.

Czada, Peter. *Die Berliner Elektroindustrie in der Weimarer Zeit.* Berlin, 1969.

Dahms, Gustav. *Das literarische Leben, illustriertes Handbuch der Presse in der Reichshauptstadt.* Berlin, n. d.

Damaschke, Adolf. *Aus meinem Leben.* Leipzig, Zürich, 1924.

Damm-Etienne, Paul. *Das Hotelwesen.* Leipzig, 1910.

Demeter, Karl. *Das deutsche Offizierskorps.* Berlin, 1962.

Deutscher Maschinenbau 1837–1937 im Spiegel des Werkes Borsig. Berlin, 1937.

Dietrich, Richard, ed. *Berlin, neun Kapitel seiner Geschichte.* Berlin, 1960.*

Doogs, Kurt. *Die Berliner Maschinenindustrie und ihre Produktionsbedingungen seit ihrer Entstehung.* Berlin, 1928.

Dorpalen, Andreas. "Frederic III and the German Liberal Movement." *American Historical Review* 54, (1948): 1–31.

Einstein, Alfred. *50 Jahre Berliner Philharmonisches Orchester.* Berlin, 1932.

Bibliographical Note

Eloesser, Arthur. *Die Strasse meiner Jugend*. Berlin, 1919.

Epstein, Klaus. *Matthias Erzberger und das Dilemma der deutschen Demokratie*. Berlin-Frankfurt, 1962.*

Erman, Hans. *August Scherl*. Berlin, 1954.

Eulenburg, Franz. *Die Handelshochschule zu Berlin*. Berlin, 1930.

Eyck, Erich. *Das persönliche Regiment Wilhelms II*. Zürich, 1948.

Faden, Eberhard. "Berlin Hauptstadt—seit wann und wodurch?" *Jahrbuch f. brandenburgische Landesgeschichte*. 1(1950): 17–34.*

Faucher, Julius. *Vergleichende Kulturbilder aus vier europäischen Millionenstädten*. Hannover, 1877.

Fechner, Hanns. *Mein liebes altes Berlin*. Berlin, 1926.

Fechter, Paul. *Menschen und Zeiten*. Gütersloh, 1949.

Feldmann, Gerald. *Army Industry and Labor in Germany, 1914–1918*. Princeton, 1966.*

Fischer, Fritz. "Der deutsche Protestantismus und die Politik im 19. Jahrhundert." *Historische Zeitschrift* 171, (1951): 473–518.

————. *Griff nach der Weltmacht*. Düsseldorf, 1964.*

Fischer, Henry W. *The Private Life of Wilhelm II*. London, 1906.

Fontane, Theodor. *Briefe an Georg Friedländer*. Edited by Schreinert. Heidelberg, 1954.*

————. "Die Märker und das Berlinertum." In *Gesammelte Werke* 2, 9. Aus dem Nachlass. Berlin, 1908. Pp. 295–312.

————. *Wanderungen durch die Mark Brandenburg*. 4 vols. Berlin, 1872.

Forster, Erich. *Adalbert Falk*. Gotha, 1927.

Frank, Walter, *Hofprediger Adolf Stoecker und die christlich-soziale Bewegung*. Hamburg, 1935.

Fricke, Dieter. *Bismarcks Prätorianer*. East-Berlin, 1962.

Friese, Karl. *Geschichte der königlichen Universitätsbibliothek zu Berlin*. Berlin, 1910.

Fürstenberg, Hans. *Carl Fürstenberg, Die Lebensgeschichte eines deutschen Bankiers, 1870–1914*. Berlin, 1930.

Gedenkschrift der Freien Universität Berlin zur 150 Jahrfeier der Friedrich-Wilhelms Universität zu Berlin. 2 vols. Berlin, 1960.

Ginsberg, Ernst. *Abschied*. Zürich, 1965.

Glagau, Otto. *Der Börsen und Gründungsschwindel in Berlin*. Leipzig, 1876–1877.

Glatzer, Ruth. *Berliner Leben, 1870–1900*. East Berlin, 1963.

Götz, Harry. *Die Verwaltungsorganisation der Weltstädte, Paris, London, New York, Wien*. Berlin, 1931.

Greer, Sarah. *Outline of Government Organization within the Cities of London, Paris and Berlin*. New York, 1936.

Griebens Reisebibliothek. Berlin, 1891.

Guttman, Bernhard. *Schattenriss einer Generation, 1888–1919*. Stuttgart, 1950.

Gutzkow, Karl. *Berliner Erinnerungen und Erlebnisse*. Berlin, 1960.

Haacke, Wilmont. *Die politische Zeitschrift, 1665–1965*. Stuttgart, 1968.

————. *Julius Rodenberg und die deutsche Rundschau*. Heidelberg, 1950.

Haberland, Georg. *Aus meinem Leben*. Berlin, 1931.

————. *Grossberlin*. Berlin, 1917.

Hammann, Otto. *Unter dem Kaiser*. Berlin, 1919.

Harden, Maximilian. *Köpfe*. 4 vols. Berlin, 1910–1924.*

————. *Berlin als Theaterstadt*. Berlin, 1888.

Harnack, Adolf von. *Geschichte der königlich-preussischen Akademie der Wissen-*

schaften zu Berlin. 3 vols. Berlin, 1900.

Hartung, Fritz. *Deutsche Verfassungsgeschichte.* Stuttgart, 1964.*

———. *Deutsche Geschichte von 1871–1919.* Leipzig, 1939.

Das Hauptstadtproblem in der Geschichte. Tübingen, 1952.*

Heffter, Heinrich. *Die deutsche Selbstverwaltung im 19. Jahrhundert.* Stuttgart, 1950.

Hegemann, Werner. *Das steinerne Berlin.* Berlin, 1930.*

Heilborn, Adolf. *Käte Kollwitz.* Berlin, 1949.

Heimatchronik Berlin. Köln, 1962.

Helfferich, Karl. *Georg von Siemens.* 3 vols. Berlin, 1921.

———. *Deutschlands Volkswohlstand, 1888–1913.* Berlin, 1913.

Herzfeld, Friedrich, ed. *Berliner Philharmonisches Orchester, 1882–1942.* Berlin, 1942.

Herzfeld, Hans, ed. *Berlin und die Provinz Brandenburg im 19. und 20. Jahrhundert.* Berlin, 1968.*

———. *Der erste Weltkrieg.* Munich, 1968.

Heuss, Theodor. *Friedrich Naumann.* Stuttgart und Berlin, 1937.

Hinrichs, Karl. *Friedrich Wilhelm I.* Hamburg, 1943.

———. *Preussen als historisches Problem.* Berlin, 1964.*

Hintze, Otto. *Die Hohenzollern und ihr Werk.* Berlin, 1915.

Hoehn, Reinhard. *Die vaterlandslosen Gesellen.* Köln, Opladen, 1964.

Holborn, Hajo. *A History of Modern Germany.* 3 vols. New York, 1959–1970.

Holländer, Hans. *Geschichte der Schering Aktiengesellschaft.* Berlin, 1955.

Hollyday, Fredric B. M. *Bismarck's Rival, Albrecht von Stosch.* Durham, N. C., 1960.

Huard, Charles. *Berlin comme je l'ai vue.* Paris, 1907.*

Huber, Ernst. *Deutsche Verfassunggeschichte seit 1789.* 3 vols. Stuttgart, 1957–1963.*

Hübner, Oskar and Moegelin, Johannes, eds. *Im steinernen Meer.* Berlin, 1910.

Hülsen, Helene von. *Unter zwei Königen.* Berlin, 1889.

Huret, Julius. *Berlin.* Paris, 1909.*

Hürlimann, Martin. *Berlin.* Berlin, 1934.

Hutten Czapski, Bogdan Graf von. *60 Jahre Politik und Gesellschaft.* 2 vols. Berlin, 1936.*

Jachan, Elizabeth. *Bummelzug und Sechserbus.* East-Berlin, 1965.

Jahrbuch des Vereins f. d. Geschichte Berlins. Berlin, 1951.

Jahrbuch f. brandenburgische Landesgeschichte. Berlin, 1950.

Jahrbuch f. die Geschichte Mittel- und Ostdeutschlands. Tübingen-Berlin, 1952.

Kaeber, Ernst. "Die Oberbürgermeister Berlins." *Jahrbuch d. Vereins f. d. Geschichte Berlins.* (1952), pp. 53–114.*

———. *Beiträger zur Berliner Geschichte.* Berlin, 1964.*

Kaelble, Hartmut. *Industrielle Interessenpolitik in der Wilhelminischen Gesellschaft.* Berlin, 1967.

Kapp, Julius, ed. *Richard Strauss und die Berliner Oper.* Berlin, 1934.

Kastan, Isidor. *Berlin wie es war.* Berlin, 1919.

Kehr, Eckhart. *Schlachtflottenbau und Parteipolitik.* Berlin, 1930.

———. *Der Primat der Innenpolitik.* Edited by H. U. Wehner. Berlin, 1965.

Keller, Mathilde Gräfin von. *40 Jahre im Dienste der Kaiserin.* Berlin, 1935.

Kerr, Alfred. *Die Welt im Drama.* 5 vols. Berlin, 1917.

Kessler, Harry Graf. *Walter Rathenau, sein Leben und sein Werk.* Berlin-Grunewald, 1928.

———. *Gesichter und Zeiten.* Berlin, 1935.

Kiaulehn, Walter. *Berlin Schicksal einer Welstadt.* Munich, Berlin, 1958.*

Bibliographical Note

Kladderadatsch, Facsimile Querschnitt durch. Munich, 1965.

Kladderadatsch, Das Bismarckalbum. Berlin, 1895.

Kolb, Eberhard. *Die Arbeiterräte in der deutschen Innenpolitik.* Düsseldorf, 1962.

Die Korporation der Kaufmannschaft von Berlin. Berlin, 1920.

Kotowski, Georg et al. *Das wilhelminische Deutschland.* Frankfurt, 1965.

Krammer, Mario. *Berlin im Wandel der Jahrhunderte.* Berlin, 1956.*

———. *Berlin und das Reich.* Berlin, 1935.

Kühlmann, Richard von. *Erinnerungen.* Heidelberg, 1948.

Kupisch, Karl. *Quellen z. Geschichte d. deutschen Protestantismus, 1871–1945.* Göttingen, 1945.

———. *Zwischen Idealismus und Massendemokratie.* Berlin, 1955.

Laforgue, Jules. *La Cour et La Ville.* Paris, 1922.*

Landé, Dora. *Arbeits- und Lohnverhältnisse der Berliner Maschinenindustrie zu Beginn des 20. Jahrhunderts.* Leipzig, 1910.

Lange, Annemarie. *Berlin zur Zeit Bebels und Bismarcks.* East-Berlin, 1959.

———. *Das wilhelminische Berlin.* East-Berlin, 1968.*

Lange, Helene. *Lebenserinnerungen.* Berlin, 1930.

Lederer, Franz. *Schönes altes Berlin.* Berlin, 1930.

Leixner, Otto von. *Soziale Briefe aus Berlin.* Berlin, 1894.*

Lenz, Max. *Geschichte der Königlichen Friedrich Wilhelms Universität zu Berlin.* 4 vols. Halle, 1910–1918.*

Lepsius, Bernhard. *Das Haus Lepsius.* Berlin, 1933.

Leyden, Friedrich. *Berlin, Geographie einer Weltstadt.* Berlin, n.d.

Lidtke, Vernon L. *The Outlawed Party: Social-Democracy in Germany 1871–1890.* Princeton, 1966.*

Lindenberg, Paul. *Am Kaiserhofe zu Berlin.* Berlin, 1894.

———. *Berlin als Kleinstadt.* Berlin, 1893.

———. *Berliner Polizei und Verbrechertum.* Berlin, 1892.

Löbe, Paul. *Der Weg war lang.* Berlin, 1954.

Ludwig, Hans. *Erlebnis Berlin.* East-Berlin, 1965.

Luft, Friedrich, ed. *Facsimile Querschnitt durch die Berliner Illustrierte Zeitung.* Munich, 1965.

Mackowski, Hans. *Alt- Berlin und Potsdam.* Berlin, 1929.

———. *Häuser und Menschen im alten Berlin.* Berlin, 1923.*

Marcks, Erich. *Wilhelm I.* Munich, 1918.*

Matschoss, Conrad. *Die Berliner Industrie einst und jetzt.* Berlin, 1906.

———. *Preussens Gewerbeförderung und ihre Männer, 1821–1921.* Berlin, 1921.

Matthias, E. and Morsey, R. *Der Interfraktionelle Ausschuss, 1917–1919.* Düsseldorf, 1959.

Meinecke, Friedrich. *Erlebtes, 1862–1901.* Leipzig, 1941.*

———. *Strassburg, Freiburg, Berlin, 1901–1919, Erinnerungen.* Stuttgart, 1949.*

———. *1848, Eine Säkularbetrachtung.* Berlin, 1948.

Mendelssohn, Peter de. *Zeitungsstadt Berlin.* Berlin, 1959.*

Meyer, Hans Georg. *Der richtige Berliner in Wörtern und Redensarten.* Munich, 1966.

Mieck, Ilja. *Preussische Gewerbepolitik in Berlin, 1806–1844.* Berlin, 1965.

Mirbach, Ernest Freiherr von. *Die Kaiser-Wilhelm Gedächtniskirche.* Berlin, 1897.

Modrow, Hans Otto, ed. *Berlin 1900.* Berlin, 1936.

Müller-Jabusch, Maximilian. *So waren die Gründerjahre.* Düsseldorf, 1957.

———. *Die Aussprüche des Bankiers Carl Fürstenberg.* Berlin, 1941.

Müller, Richard. *Vom Kaiserreich zur Republik.* 2 vols. Vienna, 1924.*
Muncy, Lysbth. *The Junker in the Prussian Administration under William II, 1890–1914.* Providence, R. I., 1944.
Nadler, Josepf. *Literaturgeschichte des deutschen Volkes.* 4 vols. Berlin, 1938.
Nalli-Ruthenberg, Agathe. *Mein liebes altes Berlin.* Berlin, 1912.*
Nelson, Walter Henry. *The Berliners.* New York, 1968.
Nestriepke, Siegfried. *Geschichte der Volksbühne Berlin.* vol. 1. Berlin, 1930.*
Nettl, J. P. *Rosa Luxemburg.* 2 vols. London, 1966.*
Nipperdey, Thomas. *Die Organisation der deutschen Parteien vor 1918.* Düsseldorf, 1961.
Nordegg, L. von. *Die Berliner Gesellschaft.* Berlin, 1907.*
Nostitz, Helen von. *Berlin, Erinnerungen und Gegenwart.* Leipzig, 1938.*
Ochs, Siegfried. *Geschehenes, Gesehenes.* Leipzig, Zürich, 1922.
Osborn, Max. *Berlin.* Leipzig, 1926.
———. *Berlins Aufstieg zur Weltstadt.* Berlin, 1929.
Oschilewski, Walter Georg. *Berlin.* Berlin, 1951.
———. *Grosse Sozialisten in Berlin.* Berlin, 1956.
Ostwald, Hans, ed. *Zilles Hausschatz.* Berlin, 1937.
Ostwald, Hans. *Kultur- und Sittengeschichte Berlins.* Berlin, n. d.
Parthey, Gustav. *Jugenderinnerungen.* 2 vols. Berlin, 1907.
Paulsen, Friedrich. *Geschichte des gelehrten Unterichts auf den deutschen Schulen und Universitäten.* 2 vols. Leipzig, 1896–1897.
Pflanze, Otto. *Bismarck and the Development of Germany.* Princeton, 1963.*
Philippi, Felix. *Alt-Berlin.* Berlin, 1913–1915.
Philippson, Martin. *Max von Forckenbeck.* Dresden, 1898.
Pinson, Koppel S. *Modern Germany.* New York, 1966.*
Planck, Max, ed. *25 Jahre Kaiser Wilhelm Gesellschaft.* Berlin, 1936.
Poschinger, Heinrich von. *Fürst Bismarck und die Parlamentarier.* 3 vols. Breslau, 1894–1896.
Preradovich, Nikolaus von. *Die Führungeschichten in Österreich und Preussen, 1805–1918.* Wiesbaden, 1955.*
Preuss, Hugo. *Die Entwicklung des deutschen Städtewesens.* vol. 1. Leipzig, 1906.
Pulzer, P. G. *The Rise of Political Antisemitism in Germany and Austria.* New York, 1964.*
Rachel, Hugo et al. *Berliner Grosskaufleute und Kapitalisten.* Berlin, 1934.
Radziwill, Marie Fürstin. *Briefe vom deutschen Kaiserhof, 1889–1915.* Berlin, 1936.*
Ranke, Leopold von. *Tagebücher.* Munich, 1964.
Rathenau, Walther. "Die schönste Stadt der Welt." In *Nachgelassene Schriften.* Berlin, 1928, 2: 259–280.
Rave, Paul Ortwin. *Berlin.* Leipzig, 1941.
———. *Berlin in der Geschichte seiner Bauten.* Munich-Berlin, 1960.
Redslob, Edwin. *Berliner Frauen.* Berlin, 1957.
Reicke, Georg. *Ein Bürger zwischen Welt und Stadt.* Berlin, 1923.
Reidemeister, L. and Otto, Karl, eds. *Berlin, Ort der Freiheit.* Berlin, n. d.
Rich, Norman and Fischer, M. H., eds. *The Holstein Papers.* 4 vols. Cambridge, 1955–1963.*
Richter, Werner. *Kaiser Friedrich III.* Zürich, 1938.
Ritter, Gerhard. *Staatskunst und Kriegshandwerk.* 4 vols. Munich, 1954–1968.*
Ritter, Gerhard A. *Die Arbeiterbewegung im wilhelminischen Reich.* Berlin, 1959.*
Rodenberg, Julius. *Bilder aus dem Berliner Leben.* 3 vols. Berlin, 1891.

Bibliographical Note

Rogge, Helmuth. *Holstein und Harden*. Munich, 1959.*
Rosenberg, Hans. *Grosse Depression und Bismarckzeit*. Berlin, 1967.*
Rothfels, Hans, ed. *Berlin in Vergangenheit und Gegenwart*. Tübingen, 1961.*
Ryder, A. J. *The German Revolution of 1918*. Cambridge, 1967.*
Sachse, Arnold. *Friedrich Althoff und sein Werk*. Berlin, 1928.
Scheffler, Karl. *Berlin*. Berlin, 1931.
———. *Max Liebermann*. Wiesbaden, 1953.
———. *Adolph Menzel, der Mensch und das Werk*. Munich, 1955.
Schiffer, Eugen. *Rudolf von Gneist*. Berlin, 1929.
Schinz, Alfred. *Berlin, Stadtschicksal und Städtebau*. Braunschweig, 1964.
Schleich, Karl Ludwig. *Besonnte Vergangenheit. Lebenserinnerungen*. Reinbeck, 1960.
Schmidt, Erich, ed. *Jahrhundertfeier der Königlichen Friedrich Wilhelms-Universität zu Berlin*. Berlin, 1911.
Schorske, Carl. *German Social Democracy, 1905–1917. The Development of the Great Schism*. Cambridge, Mass., 1954.*
Schrenck, Oswald. *Berlin und die Musik*. Berlin, 1940.
Schriften des Vereins für die Geschichte Berlins, 1865–1940.
Schroeder, Rudolf Alexander. *Berlin einst und jetzt*. Berlin, 1954.
Schünemann, Georg. *Carl Friedrich Zelter*. Berlin, 1932.
———. *Die Singakademie zu Berlin, 1791–1941*. Ratisbon, 1941.
Selz, Peter. *German Expressionist Painting*. Berkeley-Los Angeles, 1957.*
Sethe, Paul. *Berlin-Wien*. Frankfurt, 1936.
Siemens, Georg. *Geschichte des Hauses Siemens*. 3 vols. Munich, 1947–1952.
Siemens, Werner von. *Lebenserinnerungen*. Berlin, 1892.
Simmel, Georg. "Die Grossstädte und das Geistesleben." In *Jahrbuch der Gehestiftung zu Dresden*, vol. 9 (1903).
Skalweit, August and Krüger, Hans. *Die Nahrungsmittelwirtschaft der grossen Städte im Kriege*. Berlin, 1917.
Skalweit, August. *Deutsche Kriegsernährungswirtschaft*. Stuttgart-Berlin, 1927.*
Sombart, Werner. *Die deutsche Volkswirtschaft im 19. Jahrhundert*. Berlin, 1913.
———. *Die Juden und das Wirtschaftsleben*. Leipzig, 1911.
Spiero, Heinz. *Berlin in Geschichte und Kunst*. Munich, 1928.*
Spranger, Eduard. *Berliner Geist*. Tübingen, 1966.*
———. *Volk, Staat, Erziehung*. Leipzig, 1932.
———. *Wilhelm von Humboldt und die Reform des Erziehungswesens*. Berlin, 1910.
Statistisches Jahrbuch der Stadt Berlin. Berlin, 1874–1920.
Steffen, Karl Friedrich. *Das Berliner Verfassungsrecht*. Berlin, 1936.
Stein, Erwin, ed. *Berlin*. Oldenburg, 1914.*
Stenographische Berichte . . . der Stadtverordnetenversammlung . . . Berlin. Berlin, 1874.
Stenographische Berichte . . . des preussischen Landtages. Berlin, 1872.
Stenographische Berichte über die Verhandlungen des Reichstages. Berlin, 1871.
Stolper, Gustav. *Deutsche Wirtschaft seit 1876*. Tübingen, 1964.
Strauss, Richard and Hofmannsthal, Hugo. *Briefwechsel*. Zürich, 1954.
Strousberg, Bethel Henry. *Dr. Strousberg und sein Wirken*. Berlin, 1876.
Syrup, Friedrich and Neulow, Otto. *100 Jahre staatliche Sozialpolitik*. Stuttgart, 1957.
Tuchmann, Barbara. *Proud Tower*. New York, 1965.
Ullstein, Heinz. *Spielplatz meines Lebens*. Munich, 1961.
Ullstein, 50 Jahre, 1877–1927. Berlin, 1927.
Ungewitter, C. *Chemisch-Industrielle Wirtschaftspolitik*, 1877–1927. Berlin, 1927.

Vassili, Paul Graf. *Hof und Gesellschaft zu Berlin.* Budapest, 1884.*

Vierhaus, Rudolf, ed. *Das Tagebuch der Baronin Spitzemberg Aufzeichnungen aus der Hofgesellschaft des Hohenzollernreiches.* Göttingen, 1960.*

Vizetelly, Henry. *Berlin under the New Empire.* London, 1879.

Wahl, Adalbert. *Deutsche Geschichte von d. Reichsgründung bis zum Ausbruch des Weltkrieges.* 4 vols, Stuttgart, 1926–1936.

Weber, Marianne. *Max Weber, Ein Lebensbild.* Heidelberg, 1950.

Wehner, H. U., ed. *Moderne deutsche Sozialgeschichte.* Köln, 1966.

Weigelin, Paul. *Berlin im Glanz.* Berlin-Vienna, Zurich, n. d.

Weingartner, Felix. *Erlebnisse eines "Königlichen Kapellmeisters" in Berlin.* Berlin, 1912.

Weischedel, Wilhelm, ed. *Idee und Wirklichkeit einer Universität.* 2 vols. Berlin, 1960.*

Weissbach, Werner. *Und Alles ist zerstoben, Erinnerungen aus der Jahrhundertwende.* Vienna, Leipzig, Zürich, 1937.

Weissmann, Adolf. *Berlin als Musikstadt.* Berlin, Leipzig, 1911.

Wendland, Walter. *Siebenhundert Jahre Kirchengeschichte Berlins.* Berlin, Leipzig, 1930.

Wenzel, Steffi. *Jüdische Bürger und kommunale Selbstverwaltung in preussischen Städten 1808–1848.* Berlin, 1967.

Wermuth, Adolf. *Ein Beamtenleben, Erinnerungen.* Berlin, 1922.

Wickert, Lothar. *Theodor Mommsen.* Frankfurt, 1959.

Wiedfeld, Otto. *Statistische Studien zur Entwicklungsgeschichte der Berliner Industrie von 1729–1890.* Leipzig, 1898.

Wilamowitz-Moellendorff, Ulrich von. *Erinnerungen 1848–1914.* Leipzig, 1928.

Young, Harry F. *Maximilian Harden, Censor Germaniae.* The Hague, 1959.

Zahn-Harnack, Agnes. *Adolf von Harnack.* Berlin, 1951.

Zedlitz-Trütschler, Robert Graf. *Zwölf Jahre am deutschen Kaiserhof.* Stuttgart, Berlin, 1923.

Ziekursch, Johannes. *Politische Geschichte des neuen deutschen Kaiserreichs.* 3 vols. Frankfurt, 1925–1930.

Zobeltitz, Fedor von. *Berliner Pflaster.* Berlin, 1891.

———. *Chronik der Gesellschaft unter dem letzten Kaiserreich 1894–1914.* Hamburg, 1922.

INDEX

Aachen, 8
academic freedom, 99
academies, 143, 189
Academy of Fine Arts, 159, 223, 224
Academy of Music, 234
Academy of Science, 19, 35, 190, 214
Adenauer, Konrad, 141
Addresses to the German Nation, 35
Adlon Hotel, 137–138
administrative functions, increase in, 139–140, 257
adult education, 108
advertising, 70, 71; Littfass column, 49
AEG, 128–129, 272
AGFA, 130
Agrarian League, 259
Aktion, Die, 229
alcoholism, 107
Alexanderplatz, 68, 69
Algeciras, conference of, 262
Alldeutsche Blätter, 178
Allgemeine Elektrizitätgesellschaft, 218
Althoff, Friedrich, 189–191
ammunition industry, 77, 268, 271, 276
Anglo-Russian treaty (1907), 262
Anna Karenina, 167
annexationists, 278, 280
Anti-Semitic League, 114
anti-Semitism, 36, 65, 88, 96, 99, 109–119, 196, 237–238; liberalism and, 75
Antoine, André, 251
apartment houses, 73–74, 133, 215
apartments, basement, 68–69
arbitration courts, 259
architecture, 15, 17, 19, 21–22, 27–28, 38–39, 80–81, 213–219, 293; decadence of, 74
Arco, Count, 291

Arhold, Eduard, 94
aristocracy, court, 28, 85–88, 120; funded, 95; Junker, 18, 36, 40, 47, 49, 61, 87, 95, 119; landed, 46–47, 95
aristocratic privileges, 61
armament race, 261
Arme Teufel, Der, 186
army, 18, 19, 22, 259; reform of, 33, 51–53
Arndt, Ernest Moritz, 37
Arnim, Achim von, 36, 42, 153, 161
Arnold, Eduard, 209, 245
art, 19, 26–28, 205–213, 220–232, 293; expressionist, 228–232; impressionist, 221–228. *See also* architecture
art collectors, 95, 209–210
artisans (*see* craftsmen)
Aschinger Bierstuben, 135
Association of Berlin Architects, 219
Association of Berlin Artists, 224
Association of the Friends of the Kaiser Friedrich-Museum, 208
atomistic ideology, 36
Auerstädt, battle of, 31
August Wilhelm, 253
Augusta, empress, 86
Augusta Victoria, empress, 213
Aus dem Leben eines Taugenichts, 161
Austen, Jane, 161
Austerlitz, battle of, 31
Austria, 8, 20, 31, 38, 44, 46, 48, 53, 54, 111, 262, 281
Austro-Prussian dualism 25, 53
authoritarianism, 52, 61, 146, 223–224
auxiliary service law, 276–277

Bach, Johann Sebastian, 234, 236
bacteriology, 198–199

Index

bakeries, mechanized, 134
Bakunin, Mikhail Aleksandrovich, 47
Balance of the Century, The, 122
Ballin, Albert, 93, 115–116, 269, 272
Baltic provinces, 281
Baltic Sea, 17, 18
Baluschek, Hans, 227
Balzac, Honoré de, 161, 172, 246
Bamberger, Ludwig, 110
bankruptcy petitions, 46
banks, 22, 50, 64, 77–79, 117
Barlach, Ernst, 232
Basel, peace of, 31
basement apartments, 68–69
Baum, Vicki, 137
Bavaria, 53, 96, 291
Bebel, August, 102, 105, 112, 116, 120, 145, 146, 246
Becker, Carl, 200, 294
Beethoven, Ludwig van, 26, 122, 234–236, 246
Before Dawn, 171, 172, 245
Begas, Reinhold, 122, 231
Behrens, Peter, 218, 219
Belgium, 41
Bellevue Park, 3
Benn, Gottfried, 232
Bennett, Arnold, 137
Berenson, Bernard, 207
Bergmann Corporation, 129
Berlin-Bagdad Railway, 281
Berlin-Coelln, 13–15
Berlin University (*see* University of Berlin)
Berliner Abendblätter, Die, 36
Berliner Handelsgesellschaft, 128, 131
Berliner Illustrierte Zeitung, 71–72, 122
Berliner Lokalanzeiger, 70–72
Berliner Morgenpost, 71, 72
Berliner Tageblatt, 70, 173, 174, 244
"Berliner Unwille," 15
Berliner Zeitung, 70, 72
Berliner Zeitung am Mittag, 71
Berlioz, Louis Hector, 236
Bernhard, Georg, 174, 181
Bernstein, Eduard, 72, 105, 247, 263–264, 286
Bethmann-Hollweg, Theobald von, 260, 265, 270, 275, 278, 279
Beuth, Christian Peter Wilhelm, 41
Biedermeier, 38, 43, 74, 98, 220, 236
Bierstuben, 135
Bildung, 233
bill of rights, 61
Bilse, Benjamin, 235
Bismarck, Otto von, 15, 16, 52–55, 59–62, 65–67, 72, 73, 75, 76, 78, 79, 88–91, 103–106, 114, 120, 122, 169, 177, 179, 182, 184, 185, 194, 206, 258–262, 266
black cabinet, 40
Black Eagle, order of the, 221
black marketeering, 272, 273, 277
Blankenfelde, Katharina, 16
Blech, Leo, 240
Blechen, Karl, 220
Bleichröder, Gerson von, 65, 78, 88, 110
Bleichröder, house of, 77–78
Blue Rider, The, 239
Böcklin, Arnold, 224
Bode, Wilhelm, 207–211
Boer war, 182
Bolshevism, 286, 288
book-burnings, 226, 294
Borchardt, Rudolf, 281
Born, Max, 200
Börne, Ludwig, 44, 154
Borsig, August, 42
Borsig Works, 42, 73, 127
Bosch, Karl, 268
Bourgeois Gentilhomme, 96
bourgeoisie, 93–102, 119; educated, 97–100, 118, 280, 292; feudalization of, 94–96; petty, 100–102, 112, 146, 292; propertied, 97, 99, 100, 118; upper, 93–95
Boxer rebellion, 91
Boyen, Hermann von, 32, 40
Brahm, Otto, 175, 177, 178, 244–245, 248–250, 253
Brahms, Johannes, 122, 155, 235
Brandenburg, 13–17, 131, 156
Brandenburg, Count, 47
Brandenburg, house of, 16–17
Brandenburg Gate, 27, 32, 37, 94, 220, 267
Brandenburg-Prussia, 18, 213
Brandes, Georg, 177, 180
Braun, Lilli, 144
Brecht, Bertolt, 248
Bremen, 253–254, 261, 291
Brentano, Bettina, 42–43
Brentano, Clemens, 36, 153
Breslau, University of, 43–44
Brest-Litovsk, peace of, 281
Breysig, Gustav, 197
breweries, 94, 135
Briefadel, 86
Brücke, Die, 229, 232
Brunswick, 291
Buber, Martin, 180

Index

budget (1912), 257
building industry, 133; speculation and, 64–67
building ordinances, 49–50
Bülow, Bernhard von, 90–92, 94, 183, 260
Bülow, Hans von, 235
Bund, 48
Bund der Landwrite, 99, 259
Bundesrat, 59
Bundesstaat, 46
Bundestag, 59
Burckhardt, Jakob, 63–64, 98, 115, 154–155, 194
Bürgertum, 93
Burggraf of Nuremberg, 14
Burgtheater (Vienna), 243–244
Busoni, Ferruccio, 235–236
Byzantianism, 93

cabarets, 139, 250
Calvinists, 16–17, 23
camarilla, 47, 183
canals, 43, 127
capitalism, 112, 263–264, 275
capitalistic exploitation, 69, 108, 133
Caprivi, Leo von, 90, 259
Carlsbad Decrees, 40
Carsten, J. A. W., 66–67
Caruso, Enrico, 240
Cassirer, Ernst, 193
Cassirer, Paul, 226
caste prejudices, 61
Catholic Center party, 260, 290
Catholic party, 70, 112
Catholics, 23, 75, 91, 109, 279
cemeteries, 81
censorship, 43–44, 47–48, 73
Center party, 261, 278
Central Association of German Industrialists, 80, 270
Central Purchasing Agency, 272
chain stores, food, 134
Chamber of Industry and Commerce, 50
Chamberlain, Joseph, 141
Chamisso, Adelbert von, 153
charitable organizations, 143–144
Charlemagne, 7
Charles I (king of England), 52
Charlottenburg, 3, 27, 66, 68, 74, 126, 132–133, 138, 214, 240
Checkpoint Charlie, 139
Chekov, Anton Pavlovich, 170, 251
chemical industry, 50, 77, 130, 131, 272
child-labor legislation, 42
choral singing, 233–234

Christian Germanic Association, 35–37, 109
Christian-Germanic ideology, 43
Christian-socialist movement, 113
Christian Socialist Workers party, 109
Christian Wahnschaffe, 170–171
Christianity, 24, 96, 109, 112, 179, 193, 197
church, working class and, 108–109
churches, 15, 16, 21, 67, 213
citizenship rights, 49, 113, 140
city council, 140, 145
city planning, 66–68, 219
"civic truce," 265, 267, 270–271, 278
civil law, 61
civil service, 99, 101
civilian mobilization, 275–277
civilianism, militarism and, 96–97, 262
Clairvaux, Bernhard de, 13
Coblenz, 38
coffee houses, 44, 186
collective protectionism, 77, 79, 258
Cologne, 6, 13, 38, 50, 141
commercial expansion, 40–43. *See also* economic upswing; industrialization
commode, 21
communism, 46, 47, 287
Communist party of Germany, 289
Comte, Auguste, 192
concentration, policy of, 259–260
Confederation of 1815, 60
Congress of Vienna, 38, 44
conservative press, 173
conservatives, 47, 54, 75, 97, 112, 259, 260, 267, 275, 278
Constantinople, fall of, 6
consular representation, 61
continental blockade, 32
Conze, Alexander, 208
Corinth, Lovis, 225, 227
corporation law, reform of, 65
Council of the People's Commissars, 286–289
Council of Soldiers and Workers, 290
court aristocracy, 28, 85–88, 120
courts, 7–9, 33; arbitration, 259
"cow-trading," 260
craft guilds, 15
craftsmen, 100–101; home-based, 41
crash of 1873, 74–75, 78, 106, 111, 113, 258
crime, 42, 69
Croatians, 46
Croce, Benedetto, 200
cultural sciences, 191–198
currency, standardization of, 50–51, 61

Index

Curtius, Ernst, 98
Czechs, 46
Czernin von und zu Chudenitz, 281

Dahlem, 133, 189–190
Daily Telegraph affair, 92, 185
dairy farming, 66
D'Albert, Eugen, 235–236
Damaschke, Adolf, 101
dance halls, 139
Danube basin, 8
Danube River, 13, 155
Danzig, 6
Darmstaedter Bank, 78, 79
Darwin, Charles, 122
Das Kapital, 40
David, E., 275
decentralization, original forces of, 7
Declaration of Notables, 114
Dehmel, Richard, 172
Delbrück, Hans, 177
Democratic party, 290
department stores, 94, 117, 134, 217–218
depression of 1873, 74–75, 78, 106, 111, 113, 258
"Der Berliner," 4, 23
Dessauer Bauhaus, 216
Deutsche Bank, 63
Deutsche Bund, 38
Deutsche Rundschau, 98, 177, 178
Deutsche Theater, 245, 250, 252, 253
Deutsche Zeitung, 173
Deutscher Zentralbauverein, 67
Dickens, Charles, 161, 162
Dilthey, Wilhelm, 177, 192–193, 197, 198
Disconto Gesellschaft, 77
Diskonto Bank, 50
distilleries, 94
Döblin, Alfred, 69
domestic system, 41
Dörpfeld, Wilhelm, 208
Dostoevski, Fëdor, 161, 170–171
Dresden, 21, 206, 220, 221, 225, 228, 229, 239, 252–254, 293
Dresdener Bank, 78
Dreyfus case, 118
Droysen, Johann Gustav, 194, 195
Du Bois-Reymond, Emil, 98–99, 191, 199
Durieux, Tilla, 226
Duveen, Joseph, 207
dye trust, 77, 130
dyes, synthetic, 130–132, 199
dynastic ambition, 15, 18, 61

East Elbia, 13, 68, 132
Ebert, Friedrich, 185, 279, 283, 285, 286, 288–291
economic integration, 41
economic liberalism, 63, 68, 75–76
economic nationalism, 80
economic unification, 55
economic upswing, 41–43, 48–51; French reparations and, 62–63; speculation and, 63–75. See also industrialization
Eden Hotel, 138–139
Edict of Potsdam, 17
Edison, Thomas A., 128
educated bourgeoisie, 97–100, 118, 280, 292
education, 9, 32, 108, 143, 187–201, 294
educational reform, 33–35
Edward VII, 72, 89
Effi Briest, 155, 166–168
Ehrlich, Paul, 180, 198–199
Eichendorf, Joseph von, 161
Einstein, Albert, 4–5, 199, 294
Eisner, Kurt, 72, 284, 291
electoral districts, 144
electoral law, revision of, 47
electoral system, 47, 60–61, 100, 140, 145, 267, 278, 280
electors, 8, 15
electric trains, 77, 127–128
electro-industry, 50, 127–130, 272
elevated railway, 68, 142
emergency public-works program, 46
emperor, choosing of, 8, 15; title of, 60
Engels, Friedrich, 44, 46, 72, 103, 104, 146, 154, 246, 263
England, 31, 41, 64, 111, 118, 141, 182, 187, 191, 261–263
enlightened bureaucracy, 33, 35, 39, 40
Enlightenment, the, 23–25, 36, 108, 153
entrepreneurs, emergence of, 42
Ersatz, 268, 273
Erzberger, Matthias, 260, 278, 279
Eschenbach, Wolfram von, 160
Esplanade, 138
Essence of Christianity, 193
Eulenberg affair, 181–185
expressionism, 228–232

Fabians, 263
factory system, 41
Fagus factory, 219
Falkenhayn, Erich von, 267
Fallersleben, Hoffman von, 43–44
Farben, I. G., 77, 130
Farmers' League, 270
fascism, 27

Index

Federation of Agrarians, 80
Federation of Farmers, 80
Federation of Industrialists, 270
Feininger, Lyonel, 229
feudalism, 7; neo-, 61, 94, 96; rental, 50
feuilleton, 71, 174, 175
Fichte, Johann Gottlieb, 26, 32, 34, 35, 81, 153
Figaro, 73
films, 299–300
finances and buildings, director of, 140
fire department, 49
Fischer, Karl, 121
Fischer, Samuel, 178, 244
Fischl, Oskar, 210
Flaubert, Gustave, 161, 162
Flesch, Karl, 234–235
Flying Dutchman, The, 92, 237
Foch, Ferdinand, 282
Fontane, Theodor, 23, 85, 90, 91, 95, 97, 115, 133, 139, 147, 155–170, 172, 175, 222
food chain stores, 134
food rationing, 272–273, 277
food shortage, 272–274, 278, 280, 286, 293
Forckenbeck, Max von, 141
foreign labor, importation of, 22–23, 68
Forum Fredericianum, 21, 52, 80
France, 7, 31, 32, 41, 55, 62–64, 78, 111, 118, 182, 187, 188, 191, 262, 263, 276–277
Franco-Prussian War, 55, 62, 63, 136, 158, 206, 223
Frank, James, 200
Frankfurt, 6, 50, 53, 253–254
Frankfurt am Main, 8, 38, 44–45, 64, 81, 154
Frankfurt an der Oder, 43
Frankfurt constitution (1849), 60
Frantz, Konstantin, 75
Franzosenzeit, die, 32
Frau Jenny Treibel, 97, 165–166
Frederick the Great, 15, 16, 20–26, 28, 31, 156, 194, 200, 220–222, 233
Frederick I (Brandenburg-Prussia), 18–19
Frederick II (house of Hohenstaufen), 7–8
Frederick III, 52, 86, 88–89, 206–207
Frederick William (the Great Elector), 17, 18, 206
Frederick William, crown prince (*see* Frederick III)
Frederick William I, 17, 19–20
Frederick William II, 26

Frederick William III, 26, 206
Frederick William IV, 43–45, 51, 89, 206, 237, 242
free conservatives, 259
"Free Hand" policy, 262
Free Stage movement, 171–172, 175, 179, 244–249
free trade unions (*see* trade-union movement)
freedom of the press, 38, 69–70. *See also* newspapers
Freikorps, 290–292
French Revolution, 36, 86, 112, 113, 194
Freytag, Gustav, 87, 89, 161
Friedländer, Max, 209, 210
Friedländer-Fuld, Herr von, 94, 116
Friedrich, Caspar David, 220
Friedrichstrasse, 20, 73, 137, 245
furniture industry, 100–101
Fürstenberg, Karl, 78, 110, 115–116, 128, 148, 181

garment industry, 73, 106, 131–132
Gärtner, Eduard, 221
gaslight, introduction of, 42, 66
Generalbebauungsplan, 50
Georg II, duke, 243
Georg, Stefan, 121, 171, 172
Gerhard, Adele, 170
Gerlach, Leopold von, 47
Gerlach, Ludwig von, 47
German Customs Union, 55
German History (Treitschke), 194, 195
German National Theatre, 26
German Workers' Congress, 46
Germania, 112
Gesamtkunstwerk, 27
Geschlecht, Das, 277
Gesellenhäuser, 136
Ghosts, 172, 245
Giampietro, Josef, 241
Gilbert, Jean, 240
Gilbert, William S., 233, 240
Gilly, David, 27
Gilly, Friedrich, 27
Gluck, Christoph Willibald, 26, 235
Gneisenau, August Niethardt von, 32
Gneist, Rudolf, 98
Goebbels, Joseph Paul, 118, 137, 226, 238
Goering, Reinhard, 277
Goethe, Johann Wolfgang von, 9, 22, 26, 27, 34, 37, 97, 122, 153, 154, 160–161, 164, 233, 234, 242, 246, 251
Gogol, Nikolai Vasilievich, 161, 251
Golden Bull, 8

Index

Gorki, Maksim, 245, 247, 251
Götterdämmerung, 146, 154
gradualism, 263
graphic art, 206, 210
Grau Kloster, 16, 37
gray international, 75
Gregor, Hans, 240
Grillparzer, Franz, 154, 155, 241
Grimm, Hermann, 177
Grimmelshausen, Hans Jakob von, 160
Groener, Wilhelm, 276, 286, 288–289
Gropius, Walter, 218, 219, 293
Grosse Schauspielhaus, 219
Grosstaat, 194–195
Grosstadt, 125
Gründerjahre, 63, 64, 73, 74, 81, 111, 159
Grüne Heinrich, 161
Grunewald, 66, 67, 73, 94, 181, 217
guilds, craft, 15; merchant, 42; supervision of, 20
Gutzkow, Karl, 154, 161
gymnasia, 143, 187–188

Haase, Hugo, 286
Habel restaurant, 135
Haber, Fritz, 191, 268
Habsburg dynasty, 8, 14
Hahn, Otto, 191
Hainauer, Oskar, 209
"halcyon days," 38–39
Halske, Johann Georg, 127
Hamburg, 14, 22, 66, 81, 241, 253–254, 261, 284, 288
Hammer und Amboss, 161
Händel, Georg Friedrich, 234
Hanover, 19, 53
Hanover, house of, 18
Hanseatic League, 14, 15
Hanseman, David, 50
Harden, Maximilian, 120, 179–186, 244, 249
Hardenberg, Karl August von, 32
Harnack, Adolf von, 93, 190, 193, 280
Hart, Heinrich, 172, 244
Hart, Julius, 172, 244
Hauptmann, Gerhart, 138, 171–172, 175, 177, 225, 235, 245, 247, 249–250, 252–253
Havel River, 13, 139, 157
Haydn, Franz Joseph, 234, 235
Haym, Rudolf, 176
Hebbel, Friedrich, 154, 155, 251
Heckel, Erich, 229
Hegel, Georg Wilhelm Friedrich, 26, 39, 81, 153–154, 197

Hegelianism, 39–40, 154
Heidelberg, 153, 171, 293
Heidelberg University, 197, 198
Heine, Heinrich, 5, 44, 154
Helfferich, Karl, 79
Helmholtz, Hermann von, 199, 234
Henry, prince, 21, 34
Herder, Johann Gottfried von, 10, 26
Hermann, Georg, 170
Herrenhaus, 47, 188
Hertling, Georg von, 279
Hertz, Gustav, 200
Hertzog, Rudolf, 94
Herwegh, Georg, 44, 154
Herz, Henrietta, 28
Herzfeld, Hans, 294
Herzl, Theodor, 186
Heuss, Theodor, 178
Heym, Georg, 232
High Imperial Chamber, 8–9
Hilfe, Die, 178
Hilferding, Rudolf, 286
Hindenburg, Paul von, 274–275, 277, 280
Hinkeldey, Carl Ludwig von, 49
Hintze, Otto, 197
historians, 193–198
Historical Political Essays, 194
Historicism and Its Problems, 198
Historische Zeitschrift, Die, 195
Hitler, Adolf, 3, 15, 71, 114, 117, 118, 137, 149, 226, 241, 292–295
Hobrecht, Arthur, 141
Hofmann, E. T. A., 153
Hofmann, Ludwig von, 214, 225
Hofmannsthal, Hugo von, 138, 147, 171, 238, 239, 249, 251
Hohenlohe, Chlodwig Karl, 90, 183, 260
Hohenstaufen dynasty, 7–8
Hohenzollern dynasty, 10, 14–17, 22, 60, 85–86, 119, 138, 181, 184, 189–190
Hölderlin, Friedrich, 27
Holland, 17, 41, 111, 118, 119, 136, 191
Holstein, Friedrich von, 90, 181, 183
Holy Roman Empire, 8–9, 38, 86
Holy See, 34
Holz, Arno, 170, 172
homosexuality, 120, 183–185
horseback riding, 94–95
horse-drawn streetcars, 66, 68, 142
hospitals, 142–143, 257
Hospize, 136
hotel industry, 135–139
House of Lords, 47
housing, 42–43, 68–69, 73–74, 106, 133–134, 139, 215–217

344

Index

Huguenots, 17–18
Hulschinsky's gallery, 209
Hülsen, Botho von, 242
humanism, 27, 97; neo-, 34, 187
humanities, 191–198
Humboldt, Alexander von, 26, 45, 122
Humboldt, Wilhelm von, 26, 32, 34, 40, 154, 187, 189
humor, 148–149
Huneker, James, 226–227, 238
hunting parties, 94–95

Ibsen, Henrik, 162, 171, 172, 245, 249, 251
illegitimacy, 68–69
Im Schlaraffenland, 170
Imperial Court Royal, 8–9
imperialism, 201, 262, 264, 265, 275
impressionism, 221–228
incest, 68–69
indemnity law, 54
independents, 284, 286, 289, 290
industrialization, 20, 22, 40–43, 48–51, 77, 126–134; speculation and, 64; war production, 271–272. *See also specific industries*
inflation, 209, 292
Innere Mission, 109
intermarriage, 95
international postal association, organization of, 77
interparty committee, 278–280
Iron Cross, 47, 269
Iron Curtain, 158
Irrungen, Wirrungen, 163
Isherwood, Christopher, 74, 294
Italy, 6–8, 16, 51, 111, 262, 268, 274

Jacobsen, Jens Peter, 177
Jacobsohn, Siegfried, 178
Jaeger, Werner, 294
Jahn, Friedrich Ludwig, 37
Jansen, Hermann, 219
Januschau, Oldenberg, 260
Jaurès, Jean Léon, 266
Jena, battle of, 26, 31
Jena, University of, 26
Jerusalem declaration, 91–92
Jew-baiters, 65
Jewish liberals, 65, 113
Jewish parliamentarians, 110
Jewish population, increase in, 110
Jewish press, 75
Jews, 21, 25, 28; citizenship rights, 140; civic equality for, 38; economic emancipation of, 110; immigration into

Berlin, 110. *See also* anti-Semitism
Joachim, Joseph, 234
joint stock companies, 50, 63, 67, 110, 128–129
journalism, 69–73, 173–187
Judaism, 24, 114
Jülich-Cleve, 16–17
Junker-bourgeois coalition, 80, 120, 169
Junker-bourgeois conspiracy, 76
Junkers, 18, 36, 40, 47, 49, 61, 87, 95, 119, 259
Justi, Ludwig, 230

Kabale und Liebe, 164
Kaiser Friedrich-Museum, 207–210, 214
Kaiser Wilhelm Gesellschaft, 190–191
Kaiser Wilhelm Memorial Church, 67, 213
Kaiser Wilhelm Real Gymnasium, 3
Kaiserhof, Der, 137
Kandinski, Vasili, 229
Kant, Immanuel, 24, 122
Karl Franz Joseph, 281
Kautsky, Karl, 72, 105, 286
Keller, Gottfried, 154, 161, 177, 244
Kempinski restaurant, 134–135
Kennedy, John F., 4
Kerenski, Aleksander, 280
Kerr, Alfred, 175
Kessler, Harry, 216
Kirchner, Ernst Ludwig, 229, 230, 232
Kirschner, Martin, 141
kitsch, 223, 253
Klee, Paul, 229, 293
Kleine Journal, 70
Kleist, Heinrich von, 36, 153, 244, 251
Knights Templars, 13–14
Knobelsdorff, Georg von, 21
Koch, Robert, 180, 198
Kokoschka, Oskar, 230
Kolbe, George, 232
Kollo, Walter, 240
Kollwitz, Käte, 225, 227
Komische Oper, 240
Königgrätz, battle of, 53, 54
Königsplatz, 79, 212, 280
Köpenick, 96–97
Kraus, Karl, 186, 281
Kretzer, Max, 170
Kreuzzeitung, 69, 157, 173
Krüger, Franz, 220
Kruger telegram, 91
Kugler, Franz, 221
Kulturkampf, 258
Kulturnation, 35
Kurfürstendamm, 67, 74, 213, 225

Index

labor strikes, 146, 271, 272, 277, 282, 285
Lagarde, Paul de, 75, 113
La Motte-Fouqué, Friedrich, 153
Lamprecht, Karl, 180
Landwehrcanal, 43
Langbehn, Julius, 228
Lange, Helene, 144
Langhans, Carl Gotthard, 27
L'Arronge, Adolf, 245
Lasker, Eduard, 65, 110
Lassalle, Ferdinand, 102, 104
Laue, Max, 199
Le Corbusier, 218, 219
Legien, Carl, 271, 292
Léhar, Franz, 240
Lehmbruck, Wilhelm, 232
Leibl, Wilhelm, 226
Leibniz, Gottfried Wilhelm von, 19, 190, 197
Leinsdorf, Erich, 238
Leipzig, 132, 156, 241, 277
Leipzig, battle of, 37
Leipzigerstrasse, 68, 73, 134, 217–218
Leistikow, Walter, 225, 226
Lenin, Nikolai, 136, 146, 280, 281, 286, 287
Lenz, Max, 195
Lerchenau, Ochs von, 239
Lessing, Gotthold Ephraim, 24, 25, 242, 251
Levin, Rachel, 28
liaison officer, 80
liberal press, 72–73, 75–76, 173–174
liberalism, 52, 61, 113; anti-Semitism and, 75; as conspiracy, 75; economic, 63, 68, 75–76
liberals, 43, 51–54, 61, 97, 112, 113, 119–120, 141; Jewish, 65, 113; radical, 264
liberation, of serfs, 33; war of, 37–40
libraries, 80, 136, 143, 214
Lichtenberg, 132–133
Lichterfelde, 66, 133
Liebermann, Max, 148–149, 181, 212, 223–225, 227
Liebknecht, Karl, 102, 120, 144–146, 270, 271, 275, 283–285, 287, 288, 290
Liebknecht, Wilhelm, 59, 72, 102, 105, 108, 144, 246
Lincke, Paul, 240
Lister, Samuel Cunliffe, 122
literature, 26, 27, 31, 34, 36, 48, 153–173, 293; expressionist, 232
Littfass column, 49

lobbies, 80
lobbying, 99–100
Loewe, Ludwig, 77, 209
London, 6, 9, 40, 77, 102, 125, 135, 137, 147, 157
London Times, 73, 186
Loos, Adolf, 217
Louis XIV, 17
Louise, queen of Prussia, 26, 122
Lübeck, 6, 170
Lucca, Pauline, 237
Ludendorff, Erich Friedrich, 274, 275, 278, 279, 281, 282, 286
Lukács, Georg, 246
lumenproletariat, 103, 107
Luther, Martin, 16, 194
Lutheran state church, 108, 109
Lutheranism, 16
Lutherans, 17, 23
Luxemburg, Rosa, 102, 120, 146, 264, 266, 271, 272, 275, 287–290

Maassen, Karl, 40–41
MacDonald, James Ramsay, 266
machine industries, development of, 50
Macke, August, 229
Madame Bovary, 155, 167
Magic Mountain, The, 161
Magyars, 46
Mahler, Gustav, 236, 238
Main River, 8, 31, 53–54
Mainz, 6, 13
Man with the Golden Helmet, 208
Mann, Heinrich, 170, 237
Mann, Thomas, 161–163, 170
Manteuffel, Otto Theodor von, 51
Marc, Franz, 229
Marcks, Gerhard, 232
Mark Brandenburg, 13–16, 23, 157–158, 214
Marne, battle of the, 268
Marr, Wilhelm, 114
Marshalk, Max, 175
Marx, Erich, 195
Marx, Karl, 39–40, 42, 44, 46, 48–49, 76, 100, 102, 103, 136, 146, 154, 242, 246, 247, 258, 263, 264
Marx, Paul, 174
Marxism, 105, 106, 145, 174, 178, 246, 247, 263
Marxists, 72, 145, 258
Massary, Fritzi, 241
materialism, 98, 113, 247, 258
Mautner, Fritz, 170
Max, prince of Baden, 283, 284
Max Planck Institutes, 191

Index

mayors, 141
measures and weights, standardization of, 50–51, 61
Mebes, Paul, 218–219
mechanized bakeries, 134
medicine, 198–199
medical care, 142–143, 257
medieval emperors, enterprises of, 7–8
Mehring, Franz, 72
Meier-Gräfe, Julius, 175
Meinecke, Friedrich, 4–5, 35, 90, 100, 119–120, 175, 178, 195, 280, 292, 294
Meitner, Lise, 191
Mendelssohn, Moses, 25
Mendelssohn-Bartholdy, Felix, 234, 235
Menzel, Adolf, 55, 88, 122, 221–223, 226, 234
merchant guilds, 42
Messel, Alfred, 217–219
messianic nationalism, 35
Metternich, Klemens Wenzel von, 38, 40
Meyer, Eduard, 196
Meyer, Konrad Ferdinand, 154, 177
Meyer, Rudolf, 75
Meyerbeer, Giacomo, 236–237
Michaelis, Georg, 279
militarism, 52, 61, 95, 98, 120, 146, 264, 279–280; civilianism and, 96–97, 262; postwar, 291–292
military caste, 88, 96
millionaires, 93–94, 117; peasant, 67
Millöcker, Karl, 240
Minna von Barnhelm, 24
Mississippi Bubble, 64
Mitteleuropa, 281
Mittelstand, 93
mixed marriages, 28, 116
"modern Germany," 89
Moellendorff, Wichard von, 267
Moeller van den Bruck, 21
Molière, 96, 251
Moltke, Helmuth von, 54, 59, 61, 86, 122, 146, 183, 184, 234, 264
Mommsen, Theodor, 98, 177, 195, 196
monasteries, 16
monastic orders, 13–14
Moroccan crisis, 182, 184, 262
Morris, William, 216
Moscow, 6, 9, 37, 40
Mosse, Rudolf, 70, 71, 94, 110, 209
Mosse family, 173, 174
most favored nations, principle of, 259
motion pictures, 299–300
Motz, Friedrich von, 40–41

Mozart, Wolfgang Amadeus, 26, 234, 235
Müller, Adam, 36
Müller, Richard, 277
Multhesius, Hermann, 216–217
Munch, Edvard, 224–225
Munich, 21, 147, 153, 170, 171, 186, 206, 221, 225, 228, 229, 241, 252–254, 284, 291, 293
municipal reforms, 33–34
museums, 3, 15, 27, 95, 126, 139, 143, 205–210, 214, 224
Museums Insel, 208
Musham, Erich, 186
music, 26, 48, 139, 233–241

Nachsommer, 161
Napoleon I, 28, 31–33, 36–37, 122, 264
Napoleon III, 53–54, 158
Nathan the Wise, 24
national assembly, 286, 288, 290
National Gallery, 205–206, 211, 224, 226–227, 230
National-Liberty party, 54, 113, 259, 260, 278
national-socialist party, 118, 178–179
nationalism, 52, 59, 61, 98; economic, 80; messianic, 35; radical, 36; romantic, 36–37; Slavic, 262
natural sciences, 191–192, 198–200
naturalism, 171, 177, 247–249
naturalistic drama, 171, 172
Naumann, Friedrich, 105, 119–120, 127, 173, 178–179, 281
navy, 259, 261–263, 270, 284
Nazi revolution, 146
Nazis, 135, 253
neofeudalism, 61, 94, 96
neohumanism, 34, 187
neomercantilism, 76–77
Nerfititi, 95, 208
Nernst, Walther, 199
Neue Preussische Kreuz-Zeitung, Die, 47
Neue Rundschau, 178
Neue Wache, Die, 27
"New Course," 260–261
New People's Stage movement, 248
New York Times, The, 73, 186
newspapers, 69–73, 173–187; freedom of the press and, 38, 60–70. *See also* names of papers
Nicolai, Christoph Friedrich, 25
Niebuhr, Barthold Georg, 40, 154
Nietzsche, Friedrich Wilhelm, 63–64,

Index

Nietzsche, Friedrich Wilhelm (*cont'd*)
111–112, 118–119, 122, 136, 155, 162, 172, 228, 235
Nikisch, Arthur, 235–236
nobility, 86, 87, 93, 96
Nolde, Emil, 228–230
Norden, Eduard, 196
Noske, Gustav, 284, 289–291
North German Federation, 54
Novalis, 161
novels (*see* literature)
November revolution, 283–291
Nuremberg, 5, 8, 215; Burggraf of, 14

Oberburgermeister, 33
Oberrealschulen, 143, 188, 257
Occasional Remarks about Universities in a German Sense, 34
Of Things to Come, 129
Offenbach, Jacques, 233, 240, 251
Office for War Material, 268
old-age pensions, 76, 106
Old Museum, 27
Old West, 74, 80, 98
Oliven, Oskar, 209
Olmütz, Treaty of, 48
opera, 26, 139, 233, 236–240
Opera House, 21, 34, 233, 234, 239
operettas, 240–241, 251
optical-instruments industry, 130
Orange, house of, 14, 17
orchestras, 235–236, 241
organic theory of the state, 36

paintings (*see* art)
Pan-Germanic League, 178, 261
Paris, 6, 7, 9, 28, 67, 68, 70, 125, 126, 137, 141, 147, 172, 186, 244
Paris Commune, 102–103
parks, 3, 21, 27, 66, 67, 77, 257
parliament, 51, 52, 54, 55, 59–61, 79, 89, 259, 260, 279
Parsifal, 160
patrician upper class, 14, 15
"Peace and Bread," 281
peasant millionaires, 67
Peasants' League, 270
Pechstein, Max, 229
People's Naval Division, 287, 289, 290
People's Stage, 246–249, 252
petty bourgeoisie, 100–102, 112, 292; Nazi revolution of, 146
Pfemfert, Franz, 229
Pflanze, Otto, 61
pharmaceutical industry, 50, 130
Philharmonic Orchestra, 235–236, 241

philosophy, 19, 23–25, 31, 39, 48, 108, 153–154, 192–193, 197, 198
photographic industry, 130
physical fitness, instruction in, 37
physicists, 199–200
Pintsch enterprises, 127
Piscator, Erwin, 248
Planck, Max, 4–5, 199, 294
Platen, August von, 154
Poelzig, Hans, 218–219
poetry (*see* literature)
Poggenpuhls, Die, 165
Poland, 17, 18, 111, 274, 281
police, president of, 140, 141
police force, 33–34, 104, 105; reorganization of, 49
police headquarters, 69
political structure, transformation of, 33–34
political surveillance, 47–48
polytechnic institutes, 188–189
Polytechnic University, 217, 219
population expansion, 22, 42, 49, 62–63, 132–133, 257; Jewish, 110
porcelain, 22
Posse, 240, 244
Potsdam, 20–21, 43, 66, 87–88
Potsdam, Edict of, 17
power brakes, 127
precision-tools industry, 130
press, freedom of the, 38, 69–70. *See also* newspapers
pressure groups, 80, 100, 259, 261, 270
Preussische Jahrbücher, 98, 113, 176–177, 194
Primacy of Foreign Policy, 194
Prince of Homburg, The, 36
Pringsheim, Peter, 200
printing industry, 132
progressives, 54, 113, 114, 278
prostitution, 42, 69
protective tariffs, 75–76, 106, 258
Protestant church, 108, 109
Protestantism, 39
Protestants, 75, 279
provisional government, 286
Prussian Ministry of Commerce, 41
Prussian Reform, 32
Prussian State Bank, 78
Prussian State Library, 80
"Prussian style," 21, 27, 62
public baths, 37
"public safety," maintenance of, 278
public-works program, emergency, 46
pubs, 107
Pulitzer, Joseph, 186

Index

Putbus, Prince, 65

racial purity and strength, glorification of, 37, 114
radical liberals, 264
radical nationalism, 36
Radio Berlin, 241
railroads, building of, 43, 50; nationalization of, 127
Ranke, Leopold von, 81, 88, 98, 154–155, 193–196
Ranke Renaissance, The, 195
Rathenau, Emil, 128, 218
Rathenau, Walther, 74, 79, 115–116, 129, 132, 180, 181, 185, 267–268
Rats, The, 172
Rauch, Christian Daniel, 220
real estate, speculation and, 64–67, 216
Realgymnasium, 187–188
realism, 48, 162, 221, 222, 243
realpolitik, 48
Realschulen, 188, 257
"red Berlin," 144
red international, 75
Redern family, 137–138
Reformation, 8, 15–16, 206
Reger, Max, 236
regionalism, 7, 8
Reichsbank, 78
Reichstag, 8, 54–55, 59, 60, 76, 79, 80, 89, 92, 95, 102–105, 110, 114, 141, 144–146, 183, 259–262, 264, 266, 267, 269, 270, 274–276, 278, 294
Reichswehr, 291, 292
Reinhardt, Edmund, 252
Reinhardt, Max, 5, 179, 219, 250–253
religious conflicts, 17
religious life, 108, 299
religious toleration, 17–18, 23, 24, 38
Renaissance, 15–16, 91, 193, 231
rental barracks, 49–50, 106, 172
research institutes, 189–191
restaurants, 126, 134–135
Reuter, Gabriele, 170
revenue, principal sources of, 142
revolution of 1848, 43–48
Rheinische Zeitung, 44
Rhine River, 8, 13, 16, 18, 155
Riemenschneider, Tilman, 232
Rilke, Rainer Maria, 171, 172, 180
Ringbahn, 68
Ritter vom Geiste, 161
robber barons, 14
Rodenberg, Julius, 177
Rolandsplatz, 212
Rolland, Romain, 239

Roman conquests, 7
Roman History (Mommsen), 196
Roman law, 7
Romanovs, 14
romantic nationalism, 36–37
romanticists, 153–154, 220
Rome, 5, 6, 125, 137, 147
Röntgen, Wilhelm, 130–131
Roon Albrecht Theodor von, 51, 54, 61, 66, 86, 212
Rossini, Gioacchino, 237
Rote Fahn, Die, 287
Rothschilds, 78, 96
Royal Berlin porcelain, 22
Royal Library, 136, 214
Royal Opera, 5, 233, 236, 240, 241
Royal Orchestra, 236
Royal Theatre, 241–244
Ruge, Arnold, 44, 154
Ruhr, 261
Rumania, 64, 268, 274
Runge, Philipp, 220
Ruskin, John, 216
Russell, Bertrand, 266
Russia, 3, 6, 14, 17, 31, 37, 48, 102, 111, 182, 262, 265, 271, 274, 280–282, 288
Russian revolution, 274, 278, 281

Saar, 261
Savigny, Friedrich Karl von, 35
Saxe-Meininger, 243
Saxe-Weimar, 86
Saxony, 22, 38, 53
Schadow, Wilhelm, 27, 220
Scharnhorst, Gerhard Johann von, 32, 81
Scheffler, Karl, 175, 229
Scheidemann, Philipp, 267, 285, 286
Schelling, Friedrich Wilhelm von, 26, 34
Scherer, Wilhelm, 177
Schering, Ernst, 130
Scherl, August, 70–71, 94, 173
Scheunenviertel, 42
Schiller, Johann von, 9–10, 26, 27, 34, 164, 233, 242–244, 251, 252
Schilling, Max von, 240
Schinkel, Karl Friedrich, 27–28, 137–138, 206, 220
Schlaf, Johannes, 172
Schlafburschen, 60
Schlegel, August Wilhelm von, 26, 153
Schlegel, Friedrich von, 26, 153
Schleicher, Kurt von, 288
Schleiermacher, Friedrich Ernst, 34, 35, 153

Index

Schlenther, Paul, 175
Schleswig-Holstein war, 53
Schlüter, Andreas, 19, 21, 220
Schmidt-Rottluff, Karl, 229, 230
Schmoller, Gustav, 99, 177, 197
Schnabel, Artur, 234–235
Schnitzler, Arthur, 245, 251
Schöneberg, 66, 67, 74, 214
Schopenhauer, Arthur, 48, 122, 154
Schubert, Franz Peter, 235
Schuch, Ernst von, 239
Schulenberg, Friedrich Wilhelm, 31–32
Schwarze Ferkel, 135
Schwertadel, 86
science(s), 19, 48, 268; cultural, 191–198; natural, 191–192, 198–200
"scissor crisis," 274
sculpture, 19, 27, 220, 231–232. See also art
Second International Congress, 264
secretaries of state, 59–60
sectionalism, 7
Sedan, battle of, 55
Seeckt, Hans von, 291
Seeschlacht, 277
self-government, 20, 33, 34, 140–142
serfs, liberation of, 33
Seven Years' War, 31
Seven Weeks' War, 53
sewer system, 68
sexual permissiveness, 294
Sezession movement, 224–227, 229
Shakespeare, William, 251, 252
Shaw, George Bernard, 170, 251
shop stewards, 272, 277, 282, 287, 290
sickness insurance, 142
Siegesallee, 211–213, 231
Siemens, Karl von, 292
Siemens, Werner von, 127
Siemens and Halske, 73, 77, 127–129, 272
Siemens family, 63
Siemensstadt, 73
Simmel, Georg, 193
Simon, Eduard, 94, 209
Simon, James, 94, 95, 245
Simplicius Simplicissimus, 160
Simson, Eduard von, 110
Singer, Paul, 112, 144, 145
Skarbina, Franz, 225
Slavic nationalism, 262
Slavic tribes, 13
sleep-ins, 69
sleeping car, first, 77
Slevogt, Max, 225, 227
Snow, C. P., 191

Social Democratic Labor party, 102
social-democratic party, 72, 76, 99, 101, 103–107, 109, 112, 119, 120, 144–146, 162, 246, 247, 259, 263–267, 270, 271, 275, 278, 279, 281–289
social-democratic press, 72
social legislation, 75–76, 106, 258–259
social security, 106, 145–146
Social Teachings of the Christian Churches, 197
social-welfare program, 48–49
socialism, 102–105, 108, 112, 178, 259, 263, 286
Socialist Law, 72, 73, 76, 103–105, 144, 258–259
socialist press, 72, 174, 178
socialists, 75, 97–98, 113, 264, 266
society, 28, 85–122. See also aristocracy; bourgeoisie; working class
Sociology of Religion, 197
soldiering, 19–20
Soll und Haben, 161
Sombart, Werner, 197
Sommerfrische, 139
South Sea Bubble, 64
Soviet system, 291
Spandau, 132–133, 214
Spanish Succession, War of the, 18
Spartakus movement, 275, 276, 282–285, 287–290
SPD (see social-democratic party)
speculation, 63–75, 216
Spielhagen, Friedrich, 161
Spitzenberg, Baroness von, 91
Spontini, Gasparo, 236, 237
sports, 299
Spree River, 13, 104, 139, 205
Staatenbund, 46
Staatsnation, 35
Städteordnung, 33
Staël, Madame de, 28, 153
Stahl, Friedrich Julius, 48
Stalin, Joseph, 146
stamp tax, 70
Standards for Judging Matters Historical, 197–198
Stanislavski, 251
steam engines, introduction of, 41–42, 127
Stechlin, Der, 85, 133, 168
"steel and rye," 259, 260
Steglitz, 121, 214
Stendhal, 161
Stephan, Heinrich, 77
Stephenson, George, 122
Stettin, 43, 261

Index

Stifter, Adalbert, 154, 155, 161
Stinnes, Hugo, 292
stock exchange, 64, 75, 78, 129, 130
Stoecker, Adolf, 108–109, 113, 114, 173
Storm, Theodor, 154–156, 172, 177
Strassman, Wolfgang, 110
Strassmann, Fritz, 191
Strauss, Johann, 233, 240
Strauss, Richard, 5, 176, 235, 236, 238–240
street lighting, electric, 77, 127
streetcars, 66, 68, 142
streets, 17, 20, 50, 73. *See also names of streets*
Streseman, Gustav, 80, 278, 279
Strindberg, August, 135, 245
Strousberg, Henry Bethel, 64–65, 70, 110
Stuarts, 14
Stumm, Baron von, 95–96
Sturm, Der, 229, 230
Stuttgart, 147, 284
submarine warfare, 270, 277
subsidies, 17–18, 43, 139, 173
subway, 142
Sudermann, Hermann, 172
Sullivan, Arthur Seymour, 233, 240
Sullivan, Louis Henri, 214, 217
Suppé, Franz von, 240
Supreme War Office, 276
Sybel, Heinrich von, 177, 194–196
synthetic dyes, 130–132, 199

Tag, Der, 71, 173–174
Tagebuch, Das, 294
Tagliche Rundschau, Die, 70, 173
tariffs, 41, 55; protective, 75–76, 106, 258
Taubert, Wilhelm, 235
Taut, Bruno, 218–219
tax boycott, 53
tax collectors, 20
tax evasion, 65
tax exemptions, 17–18, 43
taxation, 140, 141; armament race and, 261; stamp tax, 70
telegraphy, 70, 127, 128
telephone, 70, 77
television, 299
Tempelhof, 74
Tempelhof Aerdrome, 14
Teutonic Knights, 16
textile industry, 17, 19–20, 22, 131
Thackeray, William Makepeace, 161, 162
theatre(s), 3, 26, 36, 117, 126, 139, 241–254, 293–294

Third Reich, 70, 114, 177, 241, 294
Thirty Years' War, 8, 16, 18, 19, 160, 243
This Book Belongs to the King, 42–43
three-class electoral system, 47, 100, 140, 145, 267
Tieck, Ludwig, 153
Tiergarten, 3, 21, 27, 33, 67, 73, 94, 95, 98, 138, 212
Tirpitz, Alfred von, 261, 270
To My People, 37
Toller, Ernst, 248
Tolstoi, Lev Nikolaevich, 161, 162, 167, 245, 251
Tönnies, Ferdinand, 60
tourism, 135–139
trade, 5, 55, 131
trade-fair (1896), 125–127, 130, 136
trade-union movement, 271, 275, 277, 292
Trakl, Georg, 232
transportation, 43, 50, 66, 68, 77, 127–128, 142
Treitschke, Heinrich von, 10, 50, 62, 81, 98, 99, 113–114, 176–177, 194–196
Treptow, 74, 126
tribal duchies, 7
Triple Entente, 262, 264, 281
Troeltsch, Ernst, 197–198, 280, 294
Trollope, Anthony, 161
Trotsky, Leon, 146, 274, 281
Trübner, Wilhelm, 226
Tschudi, Hugo, 211
Tunnel, The, 156
Turgenev, Ivan Sergeevich, 161, 162
Turnverein, 37

U-bahn, 142
UEG, 129
Uhde, Max von, 224
Ukraine, 281
Ulbricht, Walter, 15
Ullstein, Leopold, 70–72, 94, 110
Ullstein family, 173, 174
unemployment, 46, 49, 106
United States, 118, 127, 131, 136, 188, 268, 274, 277–278, 280–281
universal conscription, 271
universal manhood suffrage, 54, 59
universities, 9, 32, 34–35, 188, 189, 191, 198; liberal spirit in, 37, 40
University of Berlin, 3, 21, 34–35, 39, 98–99, 113, 114, 130, 154–155, 177, 187–201
Unruh, Fritz von, 277
Unter den Linden, 3, 17, 21, 27, 33, 37,

Index

Unter den Linden (*cont'd*)
 55, 73, 78, 80, 134, 135, 137, 214,
 220, 222, 236, 241
urban planning, 66–68, 219
urbanization, 9, 49, 132
Uri, Lesser, 225
Urvolk, 35
USPD, 284, 286, 289, 290

Valois, house of, 14
Vasa dynasty, 14
Vaterlandspartei, 270
vaudeville, 117, 127, 241–242, 250
Velde, Henry van de, 216, 217
venereal disease, 68–69
Verdun, 274
Versailles, Royal Palace in, 59
Versailles Treaty, 291
Victoria, daughter of Queen Victoria, 52,
 88
Vienna, 8–9, 21, 25, 26, 38, 116, 118,
 125, 137, 141, 147, 153, 186, 200,
 225, 238, 243
Vienna, Congress of, 38, 44
villas, 66, 73, 133
Virchow, Rudolf, 45, 98, 191
Vitzliputzli, 95
Voight, Wilhelm, 96–97
Voissische Zeitung, 71, 173–175
"völkische" ideology, 37
Volkskultur, 9
Volkszeitung, 69
Vorwärts, Der, 72, 281–282, 290

Wagner, Adolf, 99
Wagner, Richard, 27, 48, 122, 155, 177,
 237–238
Walden, Herwart, 229
Waldoff, Claire, 241
Wallot, Paul, 79
Walter, Bruno, 240
Wanderings, 158
war of liberation, 37–40
War of the Spanish Succession, 18
war loans, 63, 64
war production, 271–272
Warburg, Otto, 191
Wassermann, Jacob, 69, 170–171
water supply, potable, setting-up of, 42
waterways, 43, 127
Weavers, The, 249
Weber, Karl Maria von, 236–237
Weber, Marianne, 144
Weber, Max, 61, 89, 99, 119–120, 144,
 178, 197, 277
Wedding, 74, 218

weights and measures, standardization of,
 50–51, 61
Weimar, 26, 153, 216, 290
Weimar Republic, 129, 176, 178, 185,
 208, 219, 240, 248, 252, 254, 290–
 295, 299–300
Weingartner, Felix, 236
Weinstube restaurant, 135
Weissbach, Werner, 210
Wels, Otto, 289
Weltbühne, Die, 284
Weltpolitik, 115
Weltstadt, 125
Werkbund, 217
Wermuth, Adolf, 141
Werner, Anton von, 223–224
Wertheim's department store, 217–218
Werther, 164
Westend, 66–68, 133
Westphalen, Ferdinand von, 47–48
Westphalia, 291
wheeler-dealership, 260
white-collar workers, 101–102
Wieland, Christoph Martin, 26
Wilamowitz-Moellendorff, Ulrich, 4–5,
 196
Wilde, Oscar, 238, 239, 242, 251
Wildenbruch, Ernst von, 170
Wilhelmstrasse, 20, 33, 64, 73, 94, 262
Wille, Bruno, 247
William I, 51–52, 55, 86, 88, 122, 137,
 206, 212, 222
William II, 3, 60, 67, 72, 80, 89–96, 99,
 105, 114–115, 119–121, 125–126,
 134–135, 138, 141, 169, 170, 175,
 179–185, 188–190, 205, 208–212,
 216, 219, 221, 223–227, 231, 238,
 239, 241, 246, 247, 250, 253, 258–
 261, 265–267, 269, 270, 273, 278–
 280, 283, 284
Wilmersdorf, 66, 67, 132–133, 138
Wilson, Woodrow, 185, 277–278
Witkowski, Arnold, 179
Wittenberg, 16
Woche, Die, 71
Woelfflin, Heinrich, 193, 210
Wolff, Theodor, 174, 181, 244
working class, 102–108; church and,
 108–109; levels of, 107; living conditions of, 42–43, 68–69, 106, 133–134;
 and revolution of 1848, 43–48
world trade, 50, 55, 131
World War I, 3, 100, 129–130, 133,
 136, 178, 185, 197, 201, 208, 219,
 253, 257–258, 264–283
World War II, 4, 130, 158, 206

Index

Worms, 8
Wright, Frank Lloyd, 214, 217
Wumba, 275–276
Würtemberg, 53

Yiddish, 23
Young Germany, 44, 154
youth movement, 121–122

Zehlendorf, 133
Zeit, Die, 173
Zeitgeist, 187

Zeitungsviertel, 71
Zelter, Karl Friedrich, 234
Zentralverband deutscher Industrieller, Der, 77
Zeughaus, 19
Zille, Heinrich, 227
Zionism, 118, 186
Zola, Émile, 162, 170, 171, 177
Zollverein, 40–41, 49
zoning laws, 73–74
Zukunft, Die, 180–181, 183–186

353